Parties In Crisis
Party Politics In America

Ruth K. Scott
Pepperdine University, Formerly University of Utah

Ronald J. Hrebenar
University of Utah

John Wiley and Sons
New York   Chichester   Brisbane   Toronto

Library of Congress Cataloging in Publication Data:

Scott, Ruth K 1945—
    Parties in crisis.

    Includes index.
    1. Political parties—United States. I. Hrebenar,
Ronald J., 1945—joint author. II. Title.

JK2261.S38   329'.02   78—14362
ISBN 0-471-01796-5

To our parents

PREFACE

As teachers of political party courses at the university level, the authors have felt the need to deal with certain issues that are not commonly discussed in contemporary political party textbooks. Consequently, if we are asked "what is the use of one more political party textbook at this time?" we offer the following justification. Essentially most party texts are written in a neutral manner and seek to avoid controversy. However, we have discovered that political party classes are seldom taught this way. Frequently, such classes have a set of themes that the professor utilizes to structure the details of party behavior. We offer such a set of themes in this book; although we know that many users of this book will disagree with some of these themes, we present them as a starting point for discussion and further thinking about political parties in America.

In attempting to provide a framework for party analysis, we have tried to be as comprehensive as possible, describing the various forces and institutions that affect political parties. However, we have not dealt with interest groups or the broader questions of public opinion because we believe that the specific subject—political parties— is significant and broad enough to justify the focus of a basic textbook.

The first chapter, "The 'New' Politics and the 'Old' Parties," introduces the main themes that the reader will encounter throughout the following ten chapters. Our central theme is that American political parties are declining, especially in their normal electoral functions of nominating, campaigning, and guiding the electorate, because of fundamental changes in our nation's electoral environment. We are not claiming that our parties are dead or dying. Quite the opposite; we argue strongly that they appear certain to play an important, but reduced, political role in the foreseeable future.

The second chapter attempts to place contemporary political institutions within the broader framework of American political history. Such a historical perspective, we believe, is essential so that students can adequately comprehend the present plight of the party system. In the third chapter, we analyze the interrelationship among the parties, electoral laws, and institutions. Although this subject is usually dealt with in a perfunctory way in most textbooks, we believe that it is important in order to be able to understand the institutional supports behind the two party system in the United States. In the fourth chapter, we examine the vitality of party organizations, especially as found in three major states—California, Illinois, and Texas—which illustrate three major models of party organzation and behavior. Chapter 5 traces the changes that have occurred in recent years among the electorate, including the phenomena of antipartyism and the declining loyalty of millions of Americans to party organizations.

The revolutionary changes that have taken place in the art of political campaigning are dicussed in Chapter 6, including the various developments that have shifted the primary responsibility for campaigning from the party organization to the non-party professionals. Of all political party activities, political finance has changed more fundamentally than any other activity since the early 1970s. Chapter 7 describes and evaluates the 1974 and 1976 federal election campaign finance laws with respect to their impact on the party system. Another area of great change since the mid-1960s has been the rules, both formal and informal, for selecting the American president. Lessons learned from the 1976 primaries, conventions, and the general election are presented as evidence in Chapter 8 that a new era of presidential politics has emerged.

In Chapter 9 we examine the role of the party as an organizer of government on both the federal and state-local levels—in the executive, legislative, and judicial branches. The continuation of an influential party role in organizing government helps to sustain the party structure and guarantee its survival. The future and, more precisely, the prospects for survival of the parties are discussed in the tenth chapter. Specific threats and party responses are summarized, and probable future party roles are discussed.

Chapter 11, the final chapter—"Tools for Analyzing Parties"—is an analysis and synthesis of various theoretical approaches to the study of political parties. We placed this chapter at the end so that readers could examine the theoretical frameworks regarding parties after they had familiarized themselves with the prerequisite facts. We offer this theoretical analysis not as the *final* step in understanding political parties, but as the *first* step toward a broader comprehension of the role of parties in a democratic society.

We thank all the people who facilitated the writing of this book. Special thanks must go to L. Kent Kimball, chairman of the Political Science Department at the University of Utah, who in many ways encouraged this project and to Donald M. Freeman, who read the first several drafts of the manuscript and offered many constructive suggestions. Terrie Buhler typed the various drafts and coped with copy arriving at all hours of the day and night. We are grateful to Paul Warr who assisted in the writing of Chapter 11 and the index. Many people at Wiley contributed to the final version of this book, especially Wayne Anderson, who had the initial faith in the idea and encouraged us throughout the project. We extend our special appreciation to Eugene Patti and Charlotte Allstrom for their copy editing. Finally, although we can never adequately compensate our families for the three years we spent on this manuscript, we want to thank our spouses for their support and understanding.

Parties in Crisis really has no senior author. It was a joint effort in all respects from the writing of the prospectus to the checking of the page proof. Ideas and data were frequently exchanged on the various chapters, but the primary responsibility for writing chapters was divided as follows: Chapters 2,3,4,7, and 8 were written by Ronald Hrebenar; Chapters 1,5,6,9, and 11 were the responsibility of Ruth Scott. Chapter 10 was the joint responsibility of both authors.

Ruth K. Scott, Los Angeles
Ronald Hrebenar, Salt Lake City

CONTENTS

1
The "New" Politics and the "Old" Parties: Parties In Crisis

In the latter half of the 1970s the two major American political parties were in serious trouble. The parties had suffered a substantial loss of public support. In September 1975 a Gallup poll indicated that Republican affiliation had declined to its lowest point in 35 years and the number of independents was at a record high. While the number of independents rose steadily, the number of voters who chose to split their tickets also grew. In the election of 1936, 5 of the 48 states elected Republican senators while at the same time electing a Democratic president. In the 1972 presidential election, however, 16 of the 49 states elected a Democrat for the Senate while choosing a Republican for president. Again, in 1976, there was substantial ticket splitting of this type in 15 of the 50 states.

Parties have increasingly seen their major campaign services slip away one by one as historical eras and the nation's needs have changed. Party services have also been severely curtailed because of modern technology. Candidates are relying increasingly upon the mass media, public opinion polls, and public relations experts rather than upon the parties. The parties are thus being challenged by non-party political actors for the delivery of campaign services.

Experiences in the 1960s and 1970s confirm a belief that has been growing steadily —that the parties are losing their clout with the American electorate and their monopoly on candidate recruitment. These events raise the question: "Are the American political parties moving toward functional obsolescence?" In other words, "Will the political parties cease to exist as a dominant part of the political landscape because they no longer have a job?" This chapter begins with an explanation of the meaning of "party function." Then it examines the various functions attributed to parties, the extent to which these functions are currently being performed by the parties, and the changes that have occurred in the 1960s and 1970s (called the "new politics"), which have led some political scientists to start planning the parties' wakes.

FUNCTIONS ATTRIBUTED TO PARTIES
Advanced students of political parties claim that in order to understand the basic nature of parties one must first assess their role in the governing process. Political

Table 1.1 Functions Attributed to American Political Parties

1. Establishment and maintenance of national authority and legitimacy.
2. Moderation of social conflict and promotion of political consensus.
3. Aggregation and articulation of interests within society.
4. Provision of structure for citizen participation.
5. Vehicles for social change (initiate and support public policies).
6. Mechanisms for popular representation (party structures).
7. Leadership recruiting and training.
8. Selection device for administrative personnel.
9. Offering of alternative government (concept of opposition).
10. Information and cue provider to the electoral public.
11. Provision of campaign support for political candidates.

parties can be viewed as organizations that perform certain functions. "Function," as used here, refers to the activities of and the contributions made by parties that either directly or indirectly aid the operation of the political system. Most writers use the term "function" to denote the party activities that lead to services being performed for the political system. The term is used interchangeably in the literature to describe the roles played by, the contributions made by, and the activities indulged in by the parties.

Our problem is to unravel the list of activities attributed to parties, while asking the following questions:

- To what extent are parties performing these functions?

- What agents or circumstances are challenging the parties' monopoly of these functions?

- Will the political parties be destroyed by these challenges or will they adopt new functions?

- If the parties' functions are completely absorbed by other political actors, what will be the consequences for American politics?

Traditionally, the parties have been celebrated for their role in "democratizing" American politics as independent agencies in the political system. Building on the assumption that "modern democracy is unthinkable save in terms of the party," students of politics have attributed to parties a vast range of political functions without carefully examining what parties actually do. Most writers on parties note what they believe to be the functions of parties, but they fail to ask whether parties actually perform these functions. Further, students of parties cannot seem to agree on a specific set of party functions. Lists of party functions can be found in almost every book on either political parties or American government. However, a careful review of these "lists" indicates that the differences are often largely semantical; while one author will encompass the basic party activities in four points, another will list the same activities in 15-points.

The numerous and wide-ranging functions attributed to parties are presented in Table 1.1. Although not a comprehensive listing, this table synthesizes the views of many authors.

This list can be condensed by reducing the party functions to six: (1) educating the public, (2) mobilizing and structuring the vote; (3) aggregating and articulating interests; (4) formulating policy, (5) organizing the government; and (6) recruiting leadership and providing campaign support for candidates. While these functions may be difficult to measure, they are not so difficult to describe.

Educating the Public
This is often categorized as a "latent" function or one of the "unplanned consequences of party activity." Many people believe that parties enhance the stability and legitimacy of the political system by transmitting information to large numbers of present and future voters. In their scurry for electoral support, parties preach the value of political loyalty and participation, and provide voters with information about the chaotic political system.

Mobilizing and Structuring the Vote
It is believed that parties generate support for the political system by stimulating interest in public affairs, drawing attention to issues, and simplifying the voters' choices. Parties encourage support when they extol democracy and the American form of government, publicize the political process, and give the voters a sense of participating in it. The value attributed to the party as a mobilizer and simplifier is often lofty. Some claim that the party prevents the voter from being confronted with a long, confusing ballot of candidates representing a great number of interests. Although the parties may simplify our choices, they limit our capacity to make decisions. As Schattschneider pointed out, "The parties frame the question and define the issue. . . . In doing this they go a long way in determining what the answer will be."[1]

Aggregating and Articulating Interests
Articulation simply means that the parties channel the views and demands of individuals and groups to public officials. The parties are said to reflect the concerns and policy preferences of the electorate. Since neither party can feel assured of winning national elections, it must be attentive to the voters' preferences. Parties are credited with aggregating, or gathering together, the interests and demands that have been articulated by the electorate. They also serve as modifiers of social conflict and vehicles of social change because they have a vested interest in minimizing highly controversial issues and in unifying the electorate. Some people view parties as essential components of democracy because they promote compromise among conflicting interests and encourage political consensus.

Formulating Policy
Parties are usually credited with the role of translating demands into specific policy.

The "out" party—the one that has lost the last election—examines and criticizes the majority party programs and suggests alternatives. Here, the party is performing the vital service of "countercheck" or "loyal opposition." To fulfill their function, out parties must "oppose the proposals of the majority, develop alternative proposals for the electorate to consider at the next election, and keep a close watch on those who are executing the laws under the direction of the majority party."[2] Increasingly during the last three decades, critics of our party system have demanded that the parties take a greater role in formulating and implementing public policy.

Organizing the Government

The party that wins the election fills the offices of government: "To the victors belong the White House limousines." It is reported that when the Nixon Administration succeeded the Johnson Administration, Washington real estate agents were happy; it meant that "Democrats would be selling their houses and Republicans would be buying them."[3] Described as the "grasp" of political parties, the organization and management of government is usually listed as one of the major functions of parties. Nearly all the state legislatures and Congress are organized along party lines. Party, as an important basis for organizing decision-makers, extends its influence not only into the legislative but also into the executive and judicial branches of government through the appointment process.

Recruiting Leadership and Providing Campaign Support for Candidates

It has been held that recruiting leadership and conducting campaigns are the parties' most vital reasons for existence. Inherent in the recruitment process is a commitment to provide campaign support to political candidates; having nominated them, the parties must exert some effort to see that their candidates are elected. The parties, therefore, provide candidates with a reservoir of resources, skills, and manpower, which are essential for election victory. Seeking to elect government officeholders under a given label, parties set up and operate the machinery that places citizens in public office.

These are the traditional functions of political parties. However, a review of party activities since the late 1920s indicates that parties are no longer adequately performing most of them. The parties are losing their dominance of the political process.

CHANGES AND CHALLENGES: THE "NEW" POLITICS

A number of changes in the parties' environment have helped to bring about their decline. These changes have occurred since the period of World War I and may be summarized as follows:

1. Changes in the party-clientele relationship: The replacement of patronage systems with merit appointment programs.
2. Changes in the electorate: The increasing education and political sophistication of the voter.

3. Development of the "new" politics: The replacement of the candidate's old-style campaign techniques with the political management firm's use of public opinion polls, advertising techniques, and mass media.
4. Changes in the government-electorate relationship: The increasing role of government in dispensing social and economic aid to its clientele.
5. Changes in the relationship of parties to other political organizations: The proliferation and growth of alternative political and interest groups.
6. Changes in finance: The new legislation limits parties in their acquisition and expenditures of campaign funds.

Changes in the Party-Clientele Relationships

With the widespread adoption of the merit system, parties declined as dispensers of spoils—the distribution of government jobs to those who were active party members or supporters of a party candidate. The Pendleton Act of 1883 provided for the recruitment of persons to fill positions in government by competitive examination. It also created the Federal Civil Service Commission to act as a central agency for recruiting, examining, and appointing government workers. Political neutrality was extended further by the Hatch Act of 1939, which prevented federal employees from taking part in the political management of campaigns, though they could still express their opinions on all political subjects and candidates. The decline of the American political party began with the events of 1883. At present, more than 75 percent of all federal jobs are appointed under the Civil Service Commission's merit system. A number of states have followed the federal example by adopting similar statutes.

Changes in the Electorate

Although there is little evidence suggesting that voters are either more or less concerned with issues today than they were 20, 30, or 50 years age,[4] the decline in party support by the voter has coincided with a rise in the educational level and the size of the middle class. However, there is no direct cause and effect between these events.

One answer to the question, "What has happened in America since the 1950s?" is that most people have become self-identified members of the middle class. The number of persons attending college has remained at a high level throughout the 1960s and 1970s, with a greater percentage of the total American population having completed four or more years of college than at any earlier time in our history. Together with increasing affluence and schooling has come a rise in the number of independents, third party interest at both ends of the political spectrum, and a widespread boredom with conventional politics. This anti-major party attitude is particularly evident from an analysis of the independent voter. Studies of independent voters in the 1950s found these people to be less informed and less likely to vote than party adherents. However, DeVries and Tarrance found the new independent voter of the 1970s to be as concerned about public issues and as likely to vote as professed Republicans and Democrats.[5]

Development of the "New" Politics

The political environment of the 1960s and 1970s has been labeled the "era of the new politics." This term has two distinct meanings: first, a particular campaign style; and second, the applicaton of marketing technology to politics. "New politics" denotes a campaign style first associated with Eugene McCarthy and Robert Kennedy, then later with George McGovern. This style of campaigning includes an issue-oriented candidate, young political activists who infiltrate into and attempt to capture the party nomination process, and an effort to organize voters at the grass-roots level. In 1968 college students converged on New Hampshire to work for Senator Eugene McCarthy, a liberal Democrat who was strongly opposed to the war in Vietnam. In 1972 George McGovern presented himself as a new type of candidate who was "above the petty compromises of politics."[6] His youthful supporters, outsiders to the traditional Democratic presidential nomination processes, displaced many of the seasoned party faithful.

"New politics" also denotes the candidates' increased reliance on the mass media, public opinion polls, and public relations experts. There are two important elements here: first, the candidates' appeals are made directly to the voter through the mass media; and second, the techniques used to make these appeals, such as polls, computers, and television, are "scientific" and sophisticated. Labeled "new" incorrectly, the use of marketing technology in political campaigns has been growing over time. The "new" politics is systematic campaigning, using advanced technology under the guidance of a professional campaign manager. Traditionally, parties and candidates depended upon door-to-door voter mobilization and direct personal appeal to the electorate. Now, campaigning through the media substitutes for personal contact via the party organization. Since the 1950s, political candidates have increasingly used newspaper, radio, television, billlboards, and direct mailings. These technological tools are used both to sell the candidate to the public and to take the political pulse of the voters. Political pollsters can assess a candidate's chances of winning and identify for him the issues that are important to the public. The use of television and radio to bring the candidate into the living room and the use of polls to identify relevant issues have led to a description of the new politics as "nothing more than good communications between candidates and voters."[7]

The professional campaign manager must be included in this list of new technological tools. Whether one calls the paid political consultant a "technocrat" or a "propagandist," candidates are increasingly turning to professionals for help. As larger numbers of candidates bypass the traditional party structure and as party organization declines, professional campaign management is becoming a very big business. Ronald Reagan has stated that he "would never run for office. . . without the help of professional managers like Spencer and Roberts."[8] The campaign manager has one objective: to see that his candidate wins. Toward this end the manager assumes the technical and administrative responsibility for the entire campaign. An experienced manager commands as much as $25,000 for running a campaign, or about $2000 a week, plus expenses. The emerging professional campaign manager is one who has both party experience and technical know-how. More candidates sought professional help in 1974 than in any previous election campaign. One estimate is that 75 percent of all candidates for the Senate and 30 to 40 percent of those who ran for the House used paid experts. Heavy reliance on professional assistance continued in 1976, with the incumbent presidential candidate Jerry Ford turning to the campaign management team of Stuart Spencer and William Roberts after a very poor campaign start. Clearly, the paid consultant has become an established part of American politics.

Application of the new marketing technology to politics has raised complaints of "dirty politics." Do the techniques increase communication between candidate and voter, or do they give the politician greater ability to manipulate the electorate? A succinct reply was offered by James Perry, political reporter and columnist for the *National Observer:* "Political campaigns in America are not sponsored by the Ethical Society—not now, not ever."[9]

Changes in the Government-Electorate Relationship

Poverty in America has been substantially reduced since the 1950s. By 1973 the percentage of Americans living in poverty had been reduced to 11.1 percent.[10] This reduction reflects the increasing role of the government as a dispenser of welfare. Beginning with the New Deal, and continuing through later administrations, governments has replaced the party as a "provider." No longer does the citizen look to the parties for jobs, loans, or coal. Now he applies for social security benefits, unemployment insurance, and Aid of Families with Dependent Children. By the early 1970s approximately 14 million Americans were receiving benefits from the public welfare system—an increase of more than 70 percent in a 5-year period. Governmental programs have replaced party leaders as the "somebody that any bloke can come to—no matter what he's done—and get help. Help, none of your law and justice, but help."[11]

Changes in the Relationship of Parties to Other Political Organizations

As American politics becomes less of a contest between the Democrats and Republicans and more of a free-for-all among candidates and their personal followings, candidates are depending less on party resources. Increasingly, political groups are finding that they no longer have to channel aid to a candidate through the party. The Watergate affair revealed that vast amounts of cash were given directly to the Committee to Reelect the President (CREEP) rather than to the Republican Party in 1972. Contributions by interest groups to congressional campaigns reached a record of $22.6 million in 1976, an increase of $10 million over contributions in 1974. The leading recipient of campaign contributions in the congressional races was Senator Vance Hartke (D-Indiana), who, in his losing bid for reelection in 1976, received $245,000 from various interest groups. On the House side, Minority Leader John J. Rhodes (R-Arizona) received $99,000 from business and other professional groups. Interest groups (business, industry, and labor) provided nearly two-thirds of the money spent by 15 major House committee chairmen to win reelection in November 1976.

Table 1.2   Interest Group Contributions to Congressional Candidates: 1974, 1976

	1974	1976
Business/professionals/agricultural	$4,804,473	$11,562,012
Business	2,506,946	7,091,374
Health	1,936,487	2,694,910
Lawyers	—	241,280
Agricultural	361,040	1,534,447
Labor	6,315,488	8,206,578

Source. Common Cause, *Frontline,* April-May 1977, p. 7.

Parties are caught in a vicious circle. As the relationships weaken between the parties and the electorate, the electorate gives the party fewer dollars, skills, and personnel. Thus, the parties have fewer resources to give the candidates, and so the candidates turn to other political organizations or specific interest groups. The parties, therefore, face increasing competition with outside organizations for financial support and expertise, candidate support, and ultimately candidate allegiance.

The new politics is expensive. Common Cause has reported that interest groups, such as labor unions and business organizations, are contributing much larger sums than they used to. The magnitude of expenditures by some of these interest groups is indicated in Table 1.2.

Changes in Political Finance

In one of the many "how to get elected" guides, the author sums up how to finance a campaign with the admonition: "Money—get it early, get as much as you can."[12] This is exactly what the 1976 presidential hopefuls did. The top contenders, including 13 Democrats, 2 Republicans, and 1 independent, had gathered $19.1 million from 1973 to the end of 1975, long before the nominating conventions. One candidate, George Wallace, had raised almost $6 million, while Senator Henry Jackson (D-Washington) had gathered $3.4 million. And by 3 months before the conventions—a period of heavy campaigning— the 2 Republican and 13 Democratic candidates had spent a total of $52.6 million and received a total of $18.8 million in federal campaign funds.[13]

Expenditures have long been a part of the election process, but large-scale finance is related in part to increased party competition, reliance on the (expensive) tools of the new politics, and the wish to reach larger numbers of independents and indifferent party adherents. A review of the campaign expenditures of the major party presidential candidates since 1948 reveals the high cost of politics (Table 1.3).

While one might have assumed that the Watergate investigation and the tales of exceptionally large campaign contributions would have put an end to extravagant financing, campaign expenditures have continued to soar. In addition to a candidate's incumbency in office, money has usually been an important ingredient for success in politics. The winners in the 1974 Senate races raised more than twice as much as the losers. In 32 of the 34 Senate races, the biggest spenders won. A similar pattern was seen in the House races.

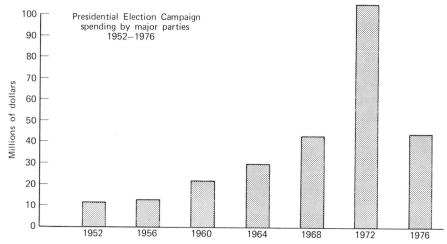

Source: Congressional Quarterly Service, *Politics in America*, 1945-1968, 3rd edition, May 1969, P 114; 1972: Herbert E. Alexander, Financing The 1972 Election (Princeton, N.J.: Citizen Research Foundation), 1976, pp 85.

Of course, money alone does not buy election victory. Many of the biggest campaign spenders lost where the "pocketbook advantage" did not pay off. Out of five incumbent Senate candidates who spent more than $1 million in the 1976 election, four lost. Although economic resources alone do not ensure election victory, the high cost of campaigning sets limitations as to who can afford to run. It is disturbing to think of the favors a candidate may owe his supporters once he has been elected. The largescale contributor perceives the election campaign as an investment, and, as with any other investment, he expects a net return. And the investor is often rewarded; in 1972, for example, the Department of Agriculture overcame its early reluctance and approved government price supports for milk after top midwestern milk cooperative leaders met personally with President Nixon. Shortly thereafter, the cooperatives contributed more than $400,000 to the Nixon reelection campaign. Because of such financial influence, legislation has been enacted to curb fund-raising and spending. There have been three basic strategies to try to prevent abuse: limitations on the giving, receiving, and spending of political money; disclosure of the sources and uses of money; and governmental subsidies of campaigns. Congress has passed three different measures intended to control federal election campaigns. The Revenue Act of 1971 provided for a tax checkoff, which allowed taxpayers to designate $1 of his/her tax obligation to subsidize presidential campaigns. The object was to raise money that had no strings attached. The Federal Election Campaign Act of 1971 emphasized disclosure of all receipts, expenditures, and debts. The Watergate disclosures led to a near-panic effort to reform campaign financing even more. Out of Watergate and other election scandals of 1972 emerged the 1974 Federal Campaign Reform Act. Effective as of January 1975, this legislation was acclaimed by the *New York Times* and Gerald Ford as "the most sweeping set of political reforms in the nation's history."[14] Designed to remove the influence of big money from federal elections and reduce skyrocketing campaign costs, this act has four major components: (1) strict disclosure requirements on the sources and uses of campaign cash, and the establishment of a new enforcement agency; (2) limits on individual and organizational contributions to federal campaigns; (3) limits on over-all spending for presidential primaries and general elections; and (4) provision for public funds to be used for major-party presidential candidates. The history and development of federal action to control campaign abuses will be discussed in Chapter 8.

PARTIES NOW: FUNCTIONAL OBSOLESCENCE?

An assessment of the current functions of parties indicates that parties may be moving toward functional obsolescence. Of the six major functions described earlier, none belongs exclusively to the parties now. At present the parties are struggling to retain three functions: recruitment of leadership, campaigning, and organizing the elected decision-makers. an evaluation of party services indicates that parties may have to adopt new functions in order to survive.

Vanishing Party Functions

Contemporary parties have lost their historical role in socializing Americans into the political system. During the nineteenth century millions of Americans were introduced to "politics" through the party machines of the urban East Coast. Many new immigrants were literally met at the dock and enrolled in "the party." In the past, the party machinery provided direct assistance by helping the poor and unacculturated deal with the bureaucratic demands of urban government. In Thomas Dye's view, "the [party] machine personalized government! With keen social intuition, the machine recognized the voter as a man generally living in a neighborhood, who had specific personal problems."[15] Since the New Deal, however, government has assumed the responsibility for providing for the minimal needs of the poor. The growth of the welfare state has robbed the parties of opportunities to serve as dispensers of charity. The replacement of the patronage system with the merit system has further reduced the parties' opportunities to function as socializers. People no longer rely on parties for their initiation into politics, for ombudsman services, or for large numbers of patronage jobs. The once broad river of immigration has now become a relatively minor stream, but there are still hundreds of thousands of Asians, Latins, and Europeans who immigrate to the United States during one given year. Are any of today's immigrants introduced to American politics and political traditions through the medium of the Republican or Democratic parties?

Parties are also in danger of losing their function of aggregation and articulation to proliferating interest groups. Today one usually does not turn to the Republicans or the Democrats to articulate ecological or energy concerns; instead, one might seek out the Sierra Club or the American Petroleum Institute. Special-interest organizations, tend to focus the government's attention on such issues as energy, inflation, ecology, Vietnam, or campaign spending. Ralph Nader and his consumerism movement and Common Cause with its fervent call for limits on campaign contributions and expenditures exemplify the groups that are competing with parties as articulators and mobilizers of public concern.

Some claim that parties serve as vehicles of social change and moderators of social conflict. Others disagree; according to Everett Carll Ladd, American political parties have never been vehicles of social change.[16] Usually they have lagged far behind the policy waves that have periodically swept our nation. Historically, the parties have not figured prominently in the episodes of change. Those who have initiated change, such as Martin Luther King, Caesar Chavez, and Ralph Nader, have operated outside the party system. It is not clear whether parties served in the past as moderators of social conflict, in any event, they have not performed this function well since the 1950s. For example, neither party was able to channel urban conflict or the Vietnamese conflict into normal paths of expression.

Although "the minimum function of a political party in a modern democracy'. is to structure the vote, the political party is no longer the primary determinant of voting behavior.[17] Rejecting (or lacking) party cues on how they should feel, vote, and think about a given issue, voters have turned to other sources. Although party identification is still the most important influence on voting behavior, it is now being challenged by candidate appeal and issues. This decline in party influence can be seen by comparing the voters' responses in 1970 with those of the 1940s and 1950s to the question: "As you make up your mind about political matters, what are the most important things that come to mind?" Table 1.4 shows the voters' answers in descending order of importance.

Walter DeVries, of the political consulting firm of DeVries and Associates, summarizes the change in the parties' exalted position as "cue providers" for voting behavior:

> Today when you ask people how they make up their minds about candidates, [they answer]. . .the candidate's ability to handle the job, personality, his stand on issues, party affiliation and so on. This rank order was not true 20 or 30 years ago, and, indeed, some of my colleagues still believe that people make up their minds on the basis of party first, then group affiliations, candidates and issues. This [information] emphasizes the continued decrease of party influence and the increase of importance in the candidate's ability to handle the job and his stand on issues.[18]

This change is further underscored by the increase in ticket-splitting; growing political independence is evident. Until World War II more than 80 percent of the electorate voted the straight party ticket. Now more than 50 percent of the voters indicate divided preferences. This is due in part to blocs of voters who have cut loose from their past allegiances. The South is becoming more Republican, New England more Demo-

Table 1.4   How Voters Make Up Their Minds about Candidates

In 1970	During the 1940s and 1950s
1. *Candidates* Ability to handle the job Personality	1. Party
2. *Issues* Candidates' stands Candidates' and party's ability to handle problems	2. Group Affiliations
3. *Party* Identification Membership	3. Candidates
4. *Group Affiliations* Religious Ethnic Occupational	4. Issues

Source. This information is from Walter DeVries, "Taking the Voter's Pulse," *The Political Image Merchants: Strategies in the New Politics,* edited by Ray Hiebert, Robert Jones, John Lorenz, and Ernest Lotito (Washington: Acropolis Books, 1971), p. 67. Copyright by the University of Maryland College of Journalism.

cratic, and minorities are shifting their vote to achieve their own specific goals. The extent of ticket-splitting can be appreciated by examining the division of party control of the executive and legislative branches of government. Between 1945 and 1978, control of the U.S. government has been divided for 16 years (see Table 1.5).

Aside from the role parties play in the selection of leadership, they have had three opportunities to influence policy: through the content of political thought and discussion, through the adoption of specific policies or programs that party leaders feel obliged to implement, or through exerting pressure on the government to adopt particular programs. Winning elections, however, is the overriding concern of American political parties; they are often described as "constituent" rather than "responsible" parties. The responsible party formulates policies or programs; it outlines issue positions, carries them to the electorate, and implements programs if its candidates are elected. The constituent party is concerned, not with the output of the political process, but with organizing and operating the machinery of government. Thus, American parties cannot be evaluated according to a European party model. According to Lowi, "Parties in the European democracies tend to be bi-functional or 'responsible'; parties in the United States tend to be uni-functional or 'constituent,' "[19] The failure to make this distinction has led to a barrage of "suggested party reform" literature which assumes that parties ought to formulate policy. American parties, however, seem to avoid taking positions on most issues.

At the beginning of the 1970s environmental problems emerged as major issues on the nation's public agenda. In January 1970, President Nixon signed the National Environmental Policy Act, which required all federal agencies to try to assess the

Table 1.5 Divided Government in Washington Since World War II

	Party in Power at White House		Party in Control of Congress
1945-46	Democrats	Franklin Roosevelt, Harry Truman	Democrats
1947-48	Democrats	Truman	Republicans
1949-50	Democrats	Truman	Democrats
1951-52	Democrats	Truman	Democrats
1953-54	Republicans	Dwight Eisenhower	Republicans
1955-56	Republicans	Eisenhower	Democrats
1957-58	Republicans	Eisenhower	Democrats
1959-60	Republicans	Eisenhower	Democrats
1961-62	Democrats	John Kennedy	Democrats
1963-64	Democrats	Kennedy, Lyndon Johnson	Democrats
1965-66	Democrats	Johnson	Democrats
1967-68	Democrats	Johnson	Democrats
1969-70	Republicans	Richard Nixon	Democrats
1971-72	Republicans	Nixon	Democrats
1973-74	Republicans	Nixon, Gerald Ford	Democrats
1975-76	Republicans	Ford	Democrats
1977-78	Democrats	Jimmy Carter	Democrats

environmental impact of all actions proposed by the national government. The impetus for this legislation did not come from either the Democratic or Republican parties, but from a coalition of interest groups, including the Sierra Club, Friends of the Earth, and the Wilderness Society.

Continuing Party Functions

Organization of Government. Government is organized along party lines; however, parties do not govern. It is one thing to recruit leadership and administrative personnel; it is quite another to motivate those officeholders to support the party's position. Both the proponents of more responsible parties and pragmatic party observers agree that the parties' control of government is quite limited. Party is the basic unit of organization in Congress. There, both parties in both houses caucus at the beginning of each congressional session to:

- Select the party leadership—a party leader, a whip, assistant whips, and a party policy committee;
- Select candidates for congressional leadership positions—Speaker of the House and President pro tempore of the Senate.

After the initial organization, the parties' influence begins to wane. A review of party unity roll calls—those on which a majority of voting Democrats opposed a majority of voting Republicans—indicates that parties have difficulty mobilizing their members to support party programs. Table 1.6 reveals the proportion of party unity roll calls from 1971 to 1977.

Table 1.6   Party Unity Scoreboard

	Total Recorded Votes	Party Unity Recorded Votes[a]	Percent of Total
1977			
Both Chambers	1341	567	42
Senate	635	269	42
House	706	298	42
1976			
Both Chambers	1349	493	37
Senate	688	256	37
House	661	237	36
1975			
Both Chambers	1214	584	48
Senate	602	288	48
House	612	296	48
1974			
Both Chambers	1081	399	37
Senate	544	241	44
House	537	158	29
1973			
Both Chambers	1135	463	41
Senate	594	237	40
House	541	226	42
1972			
Both Chambers	861	293	33
Senate	532	194	36
House	329	89	27
1971			
Both Chambers	743	297	40
Senate	423	176	42
House	320	121	38

[a]Those votes in which a majority of voting Democrats opposed a majority of voting Republicans.

Source: Congressional Quarterly Almanac, 1976, 1977.

Although V.O. Key is correct in stating that "party affiliation is the most persistent factor associated with the action of Senators and Representatives,"[20] an analysis of roll call votes demonstrates that unanimity is rare; fewer than half the votes taken in Congress reflects partisan divisions. The parties also extend their reach into the executive and judicial branches, where their influence is largely indirect. Party influence here depends mainly upon whether the decision-makers' values coincide with party positions on key programs.

Operating as executive-centered coalitions, American political parties grant the president four party leadership roles. The chief executive can simultaneously be a symbol of the party, an electoral leader, an organization leader, and a policy leader.

It is the president who symbolizes the party, its programs, and its performance to the nation. Unlike congressmen, his constituency is the nation. His electoral success or failure affects the fate of other party candidates. Because he appoints the party's national chairperson, the president maintains power over the party organization. As executive power has grown, the president has increasingly become a policy leader and initiator of legislation. To pursue his policy programs, the president turns for support to legislators who identify with his party. As explained by Woodrow Wilson: "He [the president] is expected by the nation to be the leader of his party as well as the chief executive officer of the government and the country will take no excuses from him."[21] Although party unity is generally low, congressmen tend to support or oppose presidential programs on the basis of party affiliation. Table 1.7 illustrates the level of party support for presidential policies in Congress from 1972 to 1977, according to the percentages of support for or opposition to those issues on which the president took a stand.

During these years of Republican control of the White House, substantial Democratic support for the president's programs indicated that party cohesiveness was weak; thus, the "out" party seldom constituted a viable opposition. The president must rely primarily on his power of persuasion; he cannot simply command compliance. In domestic affairs the legislators have an independent electoral base, a narrower constituency. A president who faces a Congress controlled by the other party often finds it difficult to secure even the support of his own party.

There are also substantial ties between the parties and the judiciary; in fact, party cohesion can be found in the judiciary. Studies made in the 1960s have found that Democratic and Republican judges decide cases differently. Nagel determined that Democratic judges are more likely to decide for the defendant in criminal cases, and in favor of the claimants in workmen's compensation, unemployment compensation, and auto collision cases.[22] This is due to the values represented by the parties. People with similar values joined the same party before occupying the bench. Furthermore, party affiliation is an important factor in making judicial appointments.

Table 1.7 Presidential Support Scores[a]

	1973		1974—Nixon		1974—Ford		1975		1976		1977	
	Dem.	Rep.	Dem.	Rep.	Dem.	Rep.	Dem.	Rep.	Dem.	Rep.	Dem.	Rep.
Support												
Senate	44	66	39	57	39	55	47	68	39	62	70	52
House	47	64	46	65	41	51	38	63	32	63	63	42
Opposition												
Senate	41	20	50	31	47	27	41	22	44	23	21	38
House	37	22	42	27	45	35	51	31	23	27	28	50

[a]These scores are based on party identification. The *Congressional Quarterly* analyzes all presidential messages, press conferences, and other public statements to determine what president personally, as distinct from other administration spokesmen, does or does not want in the way of legislative action. *Source:* CQ Almanac, 1977, 1976. 1974, 1973.

Although political parties can be found "everywhere in American legislatures and executives and even in American judiciaries,"[23] they are unable to govern because of the following reasons: there is a separation of power between the branches of government, the electorate tends to divide control of Congress and the presidency between the parties, and political candidates tend to build personal campaigns rather than party organizational campaigns.

Recruitment of Leadership and Campaign Support

Parties have gradually lost their control over the selection of candidates that will run for office under their label; and, just as seriously, they have been quietly and firmly pushed aside during the campaign by non-party, private enterprise organizations. Before the first decade of this century, candidates for public office were selected by the party organization, meeting either in caucus or convention. The earliest presidential candidates were selected in the caucus, a closed meeting of party leaders. Eventually, the early smoke-filled rooms were replaced with conventions, which were made up of delegates usually chosen directly by party members. In both, the party elders could manipulate their resources and confer the party's blessings on whomever they chose. However, with all of the states now using the direct primary, candidates usually owe nothing to the party leaders or the party organization for getting on the general election ballot. The direct primary system makes it possible for the party's nomination to be captured by a maverick group or a colorful individual with no previous party responsibility. Frequently, as happened in Utah and New York in 1974, the party leaders were rejected by the voters in the primaries, and so the anti-mainstream candidates became the party nominees. In the 1974 U.S. Senate race in Utah, the Democratic party head, Governor Calvin Rampton, opposed the nomination of Representative Wayne Owens; the latter was nominated, but lost in the general elections. All of the major New York State Democratic party-endorsed candidates lost in the state primary election. Even in the last major party organization stronghold—Cook County, Illinois—the party choice is sometimes defeated in the primary election.

Even the major plum of party politics—the presidential nomination—is slipping away from one-time certain party control. In 1976 more than 75 percent of the national party convention delegates were chosen by primary elections in 30 states. Four years earlier only 23 states had used primaries to select convention delegates.[24] Non-party groups are now able to capture party nominations on a regular basis. Non-party candidates who have enough resources and skills to run a media-oriented, private campaign focus their efforts on primary elections. Robert Casey, a Democratic candidate for governor of Pennsylvania, was beaten in the party primary by the millionaire, big-business maverick Milton Shapp. Casey summed up the party's waning grip on the candidate selection process: "You have to do what he [Shapp] did. You have to use the new sophisticated techniques, the polling, the television, the heavy staffing and the direct mail. You can't rely any more on political organizations. They don't work anymore."[25] Casey speaks from experience: Never before in Pennsylvania party history had a Democratic candidate for governor, strongly favored by the party leadership, been beaten in a primary. This primary battle was a striking example of the new technology pitted against the old style political organization.

This brings us to a second concern—the declining role played by parties in modern campaigning. It is clear that, first of all, the parties no longer have many politically significant services to offer candidates; and second, even if the parties had such services, they can do little since they must remain neutral before the primary election.

Candidates for every level of government office are frustrated with party organizations that have little to offer. Most urban government positions are filled in a formally non-partisan election, where the parties play a very small role. However, even in partisan elections for state offices, where the parties would normally be expected to provide significant campaign support, they usually do not. In a typical state, the candidates are expected not only to staff and finance their won campaigns, but to provide funds for the support of others' campaigns for higher office. James MacGregor Burns, an academician who got his feet wet in real politics, voiced the candidate's frustration with the party:

> When I ran for Congress some years ago I was about to ask a local party chairperson for a contribution; before I could open my mouth he said, with only mild embarrassment, "Jim, could you contribute to the local committee? We're broke." This happened several times. The party organization was so feeble that I formed my own personal organization throughout the district.[26]

There is seldom much party support for any statewide or federal races. Almost all statewide races are now run by independent candidate organizations, which employ professional campaign management firms.[27]

There is a circular debate about whether the party's organizational failure leads candidates to seek help elsewhere, or whether the development of the new politics has pushed parties aside during the campaign. And regardless of which point of view one takes, it is a fact that there is now a new breed of professional politicians. Candidates are turning more and more to the "retail" campaign, that is, they are bypassing the party organization in order to reach the voters directly. Voter mobilization has become a major responsibility of the new professional groups employed by the candidates rather than a responsibility of the traditional party organizations. Today's campaigns focus on the candidate's personality, and many campaign organizations are financed largely by the candidate himself or by non-party sources. Wealthy businessman Robert Munks, running against incumbent Edmund Muskie (D—Maine) in the 1976 senatorial election provided $530,000 of his $600,000 campaign budget. H. John Heinz III (R—Pennsylvania) spent $2.5 million from his own personal fortune in his successful bid for a U.S. Senate seat. Increasingly, the politics of personality is filling the vacuum left by flabby parties.

Parties cannot provide campaign support for numerous reasons. They are now competing with interest groups for funds and volunteers. Party workers seldom have the necessary expertise and skills of the new politics, and the parties are plagued with an almost constant turnover of personnel. According to Agranoff, modern campaign specialists include advance men, market researchers, television coaches, graphic designers, and computer printing specialists.[28] By contrast, those who work for state, or even national, party organizations seldom ever have these talents. Gordon Wade, a former member of the Republican National Committee, has compared the parties' problems with those of big business; the parties' sales forces "are unclear about the clients...or the products they are selling; do not know how much they are expected to sell; do not know the best way to sell them; have the right to choose their own boss; and can walk off the job at any time ..."[29]

Campaigns are a seasonal activity. The cost of the expertise needed to run them is such that parties cannot afford to employ such persons on a full-time basis. Also, with so many campaigns to run simultaneously, a large number of experts may be needed at crucial times. Another problem stems from the primary nomination procedure. Since candidates are usually chosen by means of primary elections, parties traditionally do not offer assistance to any of the candidates in contested primaries. Consequently, candidates win primary victories without the assistance of the party. Once a candidate has pieced together a winning team, chosen his themes, established contacts, and made most of his own major decisions during the primary campaign, it is not likely that he would want a party-organized campaign for the general election even if the party could help.

CONCLUSION: PARTY OBSOLESCENCE OR NEW FUNCTIONS?

Observers of the political scene will be watching to see parties continue to stagnate organizationally in the coming years or whether they will be transformed and take on new functions. If the parties fail to adapt rapidly enough to the demands of newly emerging social groups, and to the needs of the "old" clients, there will be even more discontent and a feeling that the parties are inflexible and unresponsive. Modern communications and computer technology have had a significant impact on the practice of politics. There has also been a widespread erosion of faith in the political process, which has further discredited the parties. In addition, it is clear that the political parties have relinquished many significant functions that they used to perform. Aware of these difficulties, both party leaders and party observers have been busily outlining plans for revitalizing the parties. From an assessment of party functions, it appears that there will be either a gradual withdrawal of political parties as an important factor in politics or a reassertion of their former functions and roles.

Some functions (such as political socialization) have apparently become too eroded, while others (such as campaigning and public policy determination) could possibly be revived somewhat. One thing seems clear, however: there are no new major functions on the horizon that could reverse the pattern of party decline during the twentieth century. The American political environment—including both political institutions and voter behavior—will probably not change in such a way as to reinvigorate the parties. Perhaps the only asset the parties have in their battle for survival is the general agreement that American politics will continue to be channeled into two parties; thus, their function as "gatekeepers" to the ballot will guarantee their continued survival.

FOOTNOTES

1. E.E. Schattschneider, quoted in Theodore Lowi, "Toward Functionalism in Political Science: The Case of Innovation in Party Systems," *American Political Science Review LVII* (1963), pp. 570-583.

2. E.E. Schattschneider, *Party Government* (New York: Rinehart, 1942), p. 51.

3. Milton C. Cummings, Jr., and David Wise, *Democracy under Pressure* (New York: Harcourt Brace Jovanovich, 1974), p. 204.

4. Although trust in government has declined since the mid-1960s, survey research does not indicate that voters are more issue-oriented. See Arthur Miller, "Political Issues and Trust Government: 1964-70," and Jack Citrin, "Comment: The Political Relevance of Trust in Government." Both articles in *American Political Science Review* LXVIII (September 1974), pp. 951-972 and pp. 973-988, respectively.

5. Walter DeVries and V. Lance Tarrance, *The Ticket Splitter: A New Force in American Politics* (Grand Rapids, Mich.: William Ferdmans, 1972).

6. For a brief discussion of the new politics as a campaign style, see Penn Kemble and Josh Muravchik, "The New Politics and The Democrats," *Commentary* (December 1972).

7. Walter DeVries, "Taking the Voter's pulse," in *The Political Image Merchants: Strategies in the New Politics*, edited by Roy Hiebert, et al. pp. 42-61.

8. Ronald Reagan, quoted in James M. Perry, *The New Politics* (New York: Clarkson N. Potter, 1968), p. 16.

9. Jerry M. Perry, "Loaded Guns and Other Weapons," in *The Political Image Merchants: Strategies in the New Politics*, op cit., p. 210. (Washington, D.C.: Acropolis Books, 1971).

10. Data prepared by U.S. Bureau of Census. Reported in Ben Wattenberg, *The Real America*, (Garden City, N.Y.: Doubleday, 1974), p. 60.

11. Clinton Rossiter, *Parties and Politics in America*, (Ithaca, N.Y.: Cornell University Press, 1960), p. 52.

12. Chestor Atkins, Barry Holly, and Robert Martin, *Getting Elected* (Boston: Houghton, Mifflin, 1973).

13. Bruce F. Freed, "Federal Funds Prop Up Debt Ladden Candidates," *Congressional Quarterly*, February 14, 1976, p. 318; "Electing a President to Cost Less in 1976," *U.S. News and World Report*, June 28, 1976, p. 13.

14. Quoted in Shana Alexander, "The Panic to Reform," *Newsweek*, January 6, 1975, p. 84.

15. Thomas Dye, *Politics in States and Communities* (Englewood Cliffs, N.J.: Prentice-Hall, 1969), p. 257.

16. Everett C. Ladd, Jr., *American Political Parties: Social Change and Political Response* (New York: Norton, 1970), p. 307. Ladd describes parties as dependent variables. He notes; "Social

change the United States has had aplenty, but the parties have neither been initiators nor custodians of it." P. 307.

17. Leon D. Epstein, *Political Parties in Western Democracies* (New York: Praeger, 1968), p. 77.

18. Walter DeVries, "Taking the Voter's Pulse," in *The Political Image Merchants: Strategies in the New Politics*, op. cit., p. 66.

19. Theodore I. Lowi, "Party, Policy, and Consitution in America," in William N. Chambers and Walter Dean Burnham, *The American Party Systems* (New York: Oxford University Press, 1967), p. 264.

20. V.O. Key, *Politics, Parties and Pressure Groups* (New York: Thomas Y. Crowell, 1964), p. 678.

21. Woodrow Wilson, *Congressional Government* (New York: World Meridian Books, 1956), p. 82.

22 Stuart Nagel, "Political Party Affiliation and Judges' Decisions," *American Political Science Review LV* (1961), pp. 843-850.

23. Frank Sorauf, *Political Parties in America*, (Boston: Little, Brown, 1976), p. 381.

24 Associated Press, April 27, 1975, "Presidential Primaries Now Dated in 30 States: Will They Soon Take the Place of the Convention?" All of the ten largest states in the nation held presidential primaries in 1976.

25. Robert Casey, quoted in Jerry M. Perry, *The New Politics*, op. cit., p. 48.

26. James MacGregor Burns, "Coming to the Aid of the Parties," *Newsweek*, December 2, 1974, p. 15.

27. Darly Babitz, executive director of the American Association of Political Consultants, says it appears that more candidates sought professional help in 1974 than in any previous election campaign. It is estimated that 75 percent of all candidates for the Senate and 30 to 40 percent of those running for the House used paid experts. A review of how Democrats and Republicans are using the new technology is provided by Jerry M. Perry, "It's a Rich Yield of Eager Democrats," *National Observer*, November 23, 1974.

28. Robert Agranoff, *The New Style in Election Campaigns* (Boston: Holbrook Press, 1972), p. 17.

29. Gordon Wade, quoted in Jerry M. Perry, *The New Politics*, op. cit., p. 61.

2
From a Pre-Party Era Toward an Un-Party System: American Parties In Historical Perspective

During the two full centuries since the Revolutionary War, America has had five discernible national party systems,* six major party formations, and a dozen or so significant third parties. In this chapter we will examine these various parties and their relationship to the broader patterns of American politics. We will also look at the so-called critical realignments of 1860, 1896, and 1932 as well as at realignment in general in order to discover how much political force is required to destroy an existing party system and create a new party alignment. Later, the post-1964 period will be examined to determine whether the 1932 Roosevelt party system has been destroyed and whether a sixth party system was created in the 1960s. Finally, six scenarios will be presented of possible party systems that could emerge in the 1980s, one of which is the end of traditional party politics—an un-party system.

COLONIAL POLITICS

When the Federalist and Jeffersonian Republican parties came into existence in the late 1790s, they constituted the first political parties not only in America but in the world.[1] They predated the emergence of parties in Great Britain and elsewhere.[2] Ironically, the British tradition of representative institutions was partly responsible for the development of party politics in America. All of the original thirteen colonies established legislative assemblies which became the training ground for many of the

---

*William N. Chambers defines a competitive party system as "a pattern of interaction in which two or more political parties compete for office or power in government and for the support of the electorate. . . . This pattern is marked by durability and thus by relative predictability of consequences on both institutions and behavior." William N. Chambers and Walter Dean Burnham, *The American Party System*, (New York: Oxford, 1967, p. 6).

post-Revolutionary leaders at both the state and national levels. In the Virginia House of Burgesses and its counterpart in the other colonies, politicians met periodically to help determine policy and pass laws for their respective colonies. The assemblies became centers of opposition to the Royal Governors and the perceived "heavy handed" rule from London. Colonialists had recourse to relatively disciplined caucus groups, sometimes called "juntos," which made life difficult for the governors.[3] The pre-party legislative groupings dealt with the interests of the ruling colonial families; they were extremely ephemeral and self-serving and they helped to create a deep-seated distrust of men who gathered together for political purposes.[4]

After 1776 when the state assemblies lost their common focus, that is, opposition to the crown, the legislators formed factional groups. Factional differences taught the Americans to argue, polemicize, legislate, and—on occasion—make compromises. The modern political party can be traced back to the political experience that was gained during this factional era.[5] Not all of the colonies developed a uniform pattern of factional politics during the period of the revolution or the confederation (1776-1789). Pennsylvania had two rather permanent factional alignments that were based on cleavages other than family or personal ties to leading politicians; thus, its arrangement was quite similar to the modern party system. Five other states also had two major factions, five others had three or four major factions, and Delaware had a number of cliques. In the first years after the war the thirteen original states had more than 30 discernible groups operating in their legislatures.[6]

THE RISE OF POLITICAL PARTIES

One issue that began to divide men into separate political camps was the debate over the proposed new constitution. The great Federalist/Anti-Federalist debates dealt with more than simply the merit of changing governmental structures; there was the issue of who would benefit from such a change and what the role of government should be. The ratification debate groupings did not immediately coalesce into either legislative or election oriented parties. Cleavages began to occur among the political élite over several significant issues during 10 years following ratification of the Constitution: Hamilton's economic programs of 1790-1793, war with either England or France in 1793, ratification of the Jay Treaty, and the Adams Administration's attempt to gain crisis powers in 1798-1799.[7] The newly formed Republican Party, like the Federalist Party, was made up of both former opponents and former supporters of the Constitution; Anti-Federalism was never a dominating principle.[8] The Jay Treaty controversy of 1795 led to the holding of many mass meetings from Georgia to New Hampshire to protest the Treaty.[9] Here for the first time were the outlines of popular parties on a national level. The Federalists denounced those who attended the meetings as the scum of society; after President Adams had signed the Treaty, the real contest over it began, for the Republicans tried to prevent its implementation.

> *The immediate political results of the Jay Treaty may be seen in the*
> *changes of party affiliation which it brought about and in the way in which*

approval or disapproval of it became an issue in the elections of 1796. It altered party alignments and caused each group to close ranks. . . . Probably more important in the eventual Federalist defeat than the open defection of such leaders as (Charles Pinckney and John Dickenson) was the Federalist loss at this time of many less prominent men who had nevertheless been the backbone of the party.[10]

Clearly, the first two American parties began on a national and not on state or local levels. Congress was the real birthplace of the new parties, and even as late as 1798-1799 there were still no constituency organizations, party tickets, or regular use of party symbols. The new Republican Party first endorsed candidates for Congress and the presidency and later on for state legislative and other state races.[11] Development of parties in the 1790s varied from state to state. The more diverse a state was, the more advanced was its party development. In his historical analysis of the first party system, Paul Goodman noted: "In some states a strong two-party system developed and persisted; in others it did not survive much beyond the election of 1800, and one party dominated thereafter. . . . Some social structures nourished competitive politics while others discouraged it . . . social differentiation and social change . . . weakened habits of deference and generated rivalry which promoted party development."[12] Parties languished in the deference-oriented South and were never established in the states that joined the original thirteen.

Why did modern political parties appear in the United States around the beginning of the nineteenth century? The distinguished party historian William N. Chambers has identified four major reasons:

1. *Diversity of society.* The development of social or socioeconomic structures that featured substantial variety, differentiation, or complexity in the society and economy.
2. *The decline of deference politics.* The emergence of democratic or mass styles of conducting politics, or the promise of a democratic mode of political life.
3. *Common political arena.* The establishment of governmental institutions and structures conducive to party politics.
4. *An élite's need for a political vehicle.* The desire for structures so that the élite could conduct political business in a reasonably predictable manner.[13]

Those who founded the parties were not consciously seeking to do so. Since they did want public support for their policies, they sought to win it by trying to influence voters, win elections, and satisfy diverse group interests; consequently, parties were invented.[14]

THE DECLINE OF THE FIRST PARTY SYSTEM

It turned out that the first party system had an unusually short life span. If one dates its inception at the time of the election of 1796, one can reasonably claim that it ended at the time of the election of 1800. After Thomas Jefferson's so-called Revolution of 1800, the Federalists never regained their pre-1800 electoral strength and they soon disappeared from the national political arena. Perhaps the final blow to the party's hopes for a comeback happened when the party called the Hartford Convention during the War of 1812 to discuss the future of New England. The convention recommended that New England secede gradually from the United States, and the adverse public reaction to this proposal virtually destroyed the remnants of the Federalist party.

As noted earlier, there was a great deal of anti-party sentiment in the 1790s. George Washington, the first president and essentially a nonpartisan national leader, issued a strong warning against the evils of partisan politics. After having watched Hamilton and Jefferson gradually develop their opposing groups, Washington said in his oft-quoted Farewell Address of September 1796:

> It [the spirit of party] serves always to distract the Public Councils and en-
> feeble the Public administration. It agitates the Community with ill-founded
> jealousies and false alarms, kindles the animosity of one part against another,
> foments occasional riot and insurrection. It opens the door to foreign influ-
> ence and corruption, which find a facilitated access to the government itself
> through the channels of party passions.... A fire not to be quenched; it
> demands a uniform vigilance to prevent its bursting into a flame, lest instead
> of warming it should consume.[15]

James Madison, the real founder of the Jeffersonian Republican Party, had intense anti-party feelings during the constitutional ratification debate a decade earlier. However, the need to extend political participation to the general public under the rules of the new Constitution soon made parties essential to the aspirations of the ruling elite.

After 1800 the Federalists were unable to compete effectively with the Republican Party. Whereas they had been the dominant party in 1796, they became a regional New England party in 1800 and completely disappeared on the national level after 1816.[16] The last Federalist to run for the presidency, though not formally nominated, was Rufus King of New York, and he won only three states in 1816. After this, the Federalists competed on a statewide basis only in Massachusetts and Delaware. All power and decision-making proceeded to flow to the Republicans. "Party organizations decayed, ideological and programatic differences were blurred and many Federalists in search of office jointed their erstwhile enemies."[17]

President James Monroe, the last of the Revolutionary War figures and of the Virginia dynasty to rise to the presidency served from 1816 to 1824 in a one-party environment. The Republicans had no opposition in Congress, and this body, like many Southern legislatures in recent years, developed factions within the one-party framework. The period from 1816 to 1828 was dubbed the "Era of Good Feelings" in partial acknowledgment of the decline of partisan strife.

Other explanations for the demise of the Federalists include the ending of the Republican-French and Federalist-English cleavage with the conclusion of the War of

1812, and the decline of foreign policy as a dividing factor in American society.[18] Party loyalties were quite fragile even at the height of the first system. No one had been born a Federalist, and when the Republicans demonstrated some governmental talent, it was easy to shift to the ranks of the winners. Finally, the various party leaders had no well-defined self-concept of their role as party leaders. Most of them tended to view politics as a duty rather than as a profession; thus, there was little commitment or dedication to building their organizations. The first experiment with structures that attempted to link political leadership to a limited but, at that time, huge portion of society ended in late 1810s. However, when there emerged an environment that was conducive to electoral competition in the third decade of the nineteenth century, there was a model for future leaders to copy.

THE RISE OF THE SECOND PARTY SYSTEM

James Monroe was reelected in 1820 without opposition. However, American political life and its leaders were too diverse and too ambitious to continue the "Era of Good Feelings." For, despite the fact that the Missouri Compromise of 1820 had temporarily removed slavery as a divisive issue, other issues soon destroyed the political harmony of the 1820s. These new issues (protective tariffs, internal improvements, and the need to find a successor to the presidency once the Virginia dynasty had run its course) established the conditions for a new party system.

While the first party system originated in the cleavages in the new United States Congress, the second party system can be traced to the revitalized competition for the presidency. During the presidential election of 1824, the National Republicans failed to choose among the candidates who were seeking the Republican nomination. There were five major contenders to succeed Monroe: William H. Crawford, the Secretary of the Treasury and the choice of the old-line party leaders; Henry Clay, Speaker of the House and the voice of the West; John Quincy Adams, of the State Department and powerful in the Northeast; Secretary of War John C. Calhoun of the South; and Old Hickory, Andrew Jackson of Tennessee. By 1822 the presidency seemed to be Crawford's, but he suffered a paralyzing stroke in September 1823; this, together with the poor tactics used by his supporters made the 1824 election a free-for-all among the Republicans.[19] Up to and including this election, the normal method of nominating presidential candidates was by congressional caucus of the Republican Party members. Since only 66 out of 212 Republican members attended the caucus in 1824, Crawford was nominated. Clay, Jackson, Adams, and Calhoun were nominated later, either by state legislatures or popular conventions. When the electoral votes were counted (132 electoral votes were needed for election), Crawford had 41, Adams 84, Jackson 99, and Clay 37; as in 1800, the House of Representatives chose the new president.[20] With the assistance of Clay, Adams was elected with 13 out of the 24 states. Later, President Adams repaid Clay for his assistance by naming him to the post of Secretary of State.

Immediately following the election, a Jacksonian coalition began to form; the individual and group followers had almost nothing in common except their hope for a

Jackson victory in 1828. Martin Van Buren led the remnants of the Crawford forces into Jackson's camp, and there joined Calhoun and other politicians who sensed that theirs would be a victorious coalition. By the 1828 election there was still only one party—the Republicans—but two very clear factions had emerged since 1824: the National Republicans and the Democratic Republicans. Jackson was nominated by state legislatures, local mass meetings, legislative caucuses, and state conventions, since there were no central nominating procedures. The subsequent Jackson victory over the incumbent President Adams was a coalitional victory under such diverse labels as Democratic Republicans, National Republicans, "Republican Friends of General Jackson," or "Jackson Men." More significantly, the 1828 campaign was a popular one in the sense that it was the first really public-oriented presidential campaign with parades, buttons, and speeches at mass meetings. "A new democracy, ignorant, impulsive, irrational, but rooted in the American soil, had its way in 1828."[21] Jackson gained 56 percent of the popular vote and 178 electoral votes (versus 83 electoral votes for John Q. Adams).

As president, Jackson helped to clarify the differences between his new Democratic Party and the remnants of the National Republicans by establishing patronage politics or, as Jackson called it, "rotation in office," and the concept that one's political loyalties must be to one's party. Soon, the coalition was reformed with Van Buren named as heir apparent and the Calhounites breaking away from the Jacksonians over the tariff question.

In 1832, the old Adams/Clay faction, keeping the name National Republicans, nominated Henry Clay by convention—the same method used by the Democrats to nominate their vice president in Baltimore. A third party, the Anti-Masonic, held its first convention that year and nominated candidates for the presidency. Following Jackson's 1832 victory, it was not clear whether his coalition could survive his retirement in 1836 and the probable nomination of Martin Van Buren, a man who was opposed by many members of the Democratic Party. The struggle over Andrew Jackson's successor proved to be the final catalyst in the formation of the second party system. Anti-Jackson groups began to form in order to oppose the nomination of the vice president, Martin Van Buren, to the presidency.

> Under a broad umbrella, National Republicans, Anti-Masons, bank Democrats, and states' rights men, mostly Southerners, drew together in a conservative alliance against this tribune of the people (Jackson) who was too radical on currency and other economic matters and too high handed in using the powers of his office. They adopted the name Whig because it had been used in the American Revolution by the opposition to royal tyranny.[22]

This opposition coalition decided it would be inexpedient to hold a national nominating convention in 1836, and so it ran three regional candidates against Van Buren. However, New England's Daniel Webster, the West's General William Henry Harrison, and the South's Senator Hugh L. White failed to prevent Van Buren's election. The

Whigs were encouraged, though, because they polled 739,795 votes to 765,483 for Van Buren.

Emerging during the one-party era of 1824, the second party system reached complete realization in 1840 with the intense campaign of the two Whig candidates, folk hero William Henry Harrison and John Tyler of Virginia under the slogan "Tippecanoe and Tyler too." The 1840 campaign was undoubtedly the "greatest" in American history up to that time in terms of citizen participation.

> *Conventions and mass meetings, parades and processions with banners and floats, long speeches on the log-cabin theme, log-cabin songbooks and log-cabin newspapers, Harrison pictures, Tippecanoe handkerchiefs and badges, log-cabin headquarters at every crossroads, with the latchstring out and hard cider always on tap—all these devices and more were used to arouse enthusiasm that soon surpassed anything the nation had ever experienced. Crowds of unheard-of proportions turned out for Whig rallies. Ten acres of people (numbers would not suffice) were reported present at a Dayton, Ohio, jamboree. The Democrats also held meetings and parades but, with an unaccountable display of moral rectitude, rejected hard cider and posed as the party of virtue.*[23]

Harrison eked out a narrow victory over Van Buren but died after only a month in office. Despite the narrowness of the presidential victory, the new party won control of both houses of Congress. President Tyler and Henry Clay (the leader of the congressional Whigs) were soon at odds, and the Whig president tried to win the Democratic nomination for president in 1844 after it became apparent he had lost control of the Whig Party.

By the early 1840s slavery had reemerged as a central issue; in less than two decades it would completely destroy the Whigs, rip the Democratic Party apart, and create a new majority party—the Republicans. The Whigs were ultimately doomed because they, unlike the Democrats, could not retain both Southern and Northern votes in order to be a national party and control the federal government. Significant strains were experienced by the Whigs during the 1840s, but the party began to disintegrate quickly during the 1850s. As a partial result of the Compromise of 1850, the Northern Whigs abandoned the Southern sector of the party in order to join the abolitionists in the North whose views were reflected by a growing third party—the Free Soil Party.* By 1852, the abolitionists had gained control of the Whigs and soon thereafter the bonds between the Northern and Southern Whigs were dissolved.

---

* The Compromise of 1850 was a legislative attempt to lessen the tensions of the extension of slavery into the territories. It consisted of several separate bills supported by U.S. Senators Douglas and Clay and dealt with admission of California as a free state, the organization of New Mexico and Utah as territories, and a more stringent fugitive slave law. These and other parts of the compromise passed in 1850 and reduced political tensions for several years.

Southerners continued to campaign under the Whig label, but they were divorced from the national party and ran on local issues.[24]

There were a number of significant differences between the first and second party systems. The former originated in Congress while the latter emerged from the presidency. The second system required more than 16 years to mature while the first took only 4 or 5 years. Nominations for high public office in the first system were by caucus of party officeholders, and in the second by convention. The participation rates of white adult voters increased greatly under the second system, rising from 40 to 80 percent of the eligible voters. And finally, the second system was national in scope, encompassing all of the states (except possibly South Carolina), while the first system was regional with the Federalists in New England and the Jeffersonian Republicans in the South and West.[25]

THE DECLINE OF THE SECOND PARTY SYSTEM

The second party system's collapse during the 1850s began with the disintegration of the Whigs on the national level and continued with the rise of the Republican Party in 1854 and the split in the Democratic Party in 1860. The Whigs were caught in a serious dilemma. If the Whigs wanted to survive as a national party, they would have to keep their Southern supporters happy; but if they compromised with the South over slavery, they would be doomed in the North. Sundquist's thesis that centrist or middle-ground parties are invariably destroyed in a realignment crisis appears to be true in the case of the Whigs.[26]

As abolitionist sentiment swept the North, the voters wanted a new party that would reflect these feelings. Since the Democratic Party continued its historical Northern businessmen-Southern planters alliance, it did not appeal to the rising tide of dissatisfied Northern voters. Many meetings were held in the North during 1854; one such meeting in Ripon, Wisconsin, called for a new fusion party of Whigs, Free Soilers, Know Nothings, and Democrats to be called the Republican Party. In their first congressional campaign in 1854, the Republicans elected enough congressmen to capture the speakership.[27] John Fremont, the explorer, carried the Republican presidential banner in 1856 but lost in a relatively close race against the Democrat James Buchanan. Meanwhile, the Northern Democrats suffered heavy defeats in the congressional campaign of 1858 and lost the House of Representatives to the Republicans.

The election of 1860 was a critical turning point in American history, for it confirmed the Republicans as the new dominant party in the North and led to the disintegration of the primary opposition party, the Democrats. That election was really a four-way contest: Lincoln running under the Republican label; Senator Steven A. Douglas, Lincoln's old nemesis in the 1858 Illinois senatorial race, as the candidate of the Northern Democrats; the Southern Democrats nominated Vice President John Breckinridge of Kentucky; and finally, the moderate conservatives formed the Constitutional Union Party and nominated Senator John Bell of Tennessee. Yet in most states it was a two-party fight: Lincoln and Douglas in the North, and Bell and Breckinridge in the South.[28] Lincoln carried all of the free states except several of New Jersey's electors; Bell won Kentucky, Virginia, and Tennessee; Douglas carried Missouri; and Breckinridge won the rest. In electoral votes, Lincoln had 180, Breckinridge 72, Bell 39, and Douglas 12. Thus, in 1860 the demise of the Whig Party was complete, the Republicans were triumphant, and the Democrats were hopelessly divided on a North-South cleavage.

A year later the South left the Union and the Civil War began. In the North, many Democrats "rallied to the flag" and took the name "War Democrats;" other Democrats (the "Copperheads") were against the war and provided a real opposition to the Lincoln Administration. Some students of the Civil War era believe that much of the Northern victory was due to the beneficial effects of the functioning two-party system in the North. Strong political opposition forced the Lincoln government to seek a winning leadership team and strategy. The South, on the other hand, without a party system, had no organized political pressure on the Confederate government. "The Confederacy may have suffered real and direct damage from the fact that the political organization lacked a two party system."[29] However, the greatest source of opposition to Lincoln's war efforts came from within his own party—the so-called Radical Republicans—who wanted more congressional guidance of the war effort, the emancipation of the slaves, and radical political reconstruction of the South after its surrender. In an attempt to reduce the influence of his Radical Republican opponents, Lincoln resorted to coalitional politics and broadened the Republican Party to include the War Democrats. First in Ohio and later in other states the new Republican Party became the Union Party. Although the Radical Republicans would have preferred another candidate for president in 1864, the Union Party nominated Lincoln, who then defeated General George B. McClellan, the War Democrats' standard-bearer, whom Lincoln had earlier removed from command of the Union Army. For a while, it seemed as if Lincoln would lose to McClellan, but Union military victories at Atlanta and Mobile Bay brought the radicals to his support.

THE THIRD PARTY SYSTEM

Following Appomattox and the assassination of Lincoln, a War Democrat, Vice President Andrew Johnson attempted to carry out Lincoln's policies, but he was impeached and nearly convicted by the vindictive Radical Republicans. The South reentered the Union and the Democrats assumed the role of the main opposition party. However, the next 40 years were to be a period of frustration and minority status for the Democrats. By the mid-1870s a "tideless era" began in which the Republicans usually barely won the White House with a less than majority popular vote and the Democrats normally dominated Congress.

Two characteristics primarily distinguish the third party system from its predecessors. First, the era was one of militant political groups that organized to such a degree that the normal floating or independent vote almost completely disappeared. Militant

politics and parties reached their height in the political machines that came to dominate so many American cities in the late nineteenth and early twentieth centuries.
Second, both parties eventually became tools and willing servants of industrial capitalism, which dominated nearly every section of America from 1870 to 1900.

> *The Business class wanted an industrial America under its custodianship.
> It wanted the entire social system bent to its needs of industrialization,
> wanted governmental power committed to policies and programs on behalf
> of the ascendent industrial order: the protective tariff, a national banking
> structure, aid to Pacific railway, a program of sound money, a docile labor
> force, high profits able to mount at the expense of labor.*[30]

The Republicans emerged as big business's favorite party, and psychologically they
were better able to preserve, protect, and expand the industrialists' interests than was
the Southern- and rural-oriented Democratic Party.

Party loyalty of a military fervor and discipline helped boost the voting rates to between 80 and 90 percent in 1876, 1888, and 1896. As millions of people emigrated
to the cities, some from rural areas but most from abroad, they were quickly enrolled
in the voting armies of the two parties. The first and longest lasting machine was
Tammany Hall, which was established in New York City in 1789. At the outset, it was
a benevolent Masonic society, but then it entered politics to promote Thomas Jeffer--
son for president. Thus, the honor of being the first "machine boss" in America went
to Aaron Burr, vice president of the United States under Thomas Jefferson. Later,
William M. Tweed and the Tweed Ring were "charged" with stealing more than
$20 million in New York City funds, although present-day research has found that
this figure was grossly exaggerated by Tweed's political enemies. His successor, George
Plunkett, resorted only to "honest graft" after Boss Tweed's fall from power.

> *There's honest graft, and I'm an example of how it works. I might sum up
> the whole thing by saying: "I seen my opportunities and I took 'em." Sup-
> pose it's a new bridge they're goin' to build. I get tipped off and buy as much
> property as I can that has to be taken for approaches. I sell at my price later
> and drop some more money in the bank. . . . It's honest graft, and I'm lookin'
> for it every day in the year.*[31]

Philadelphia's notorious Republican Gas Ring did an equally effective job for decades. In San Francisco, Abe "Curly" Ruef was the Republican boss who did favors
for business in exchange for large bribes. Political corruption and election frauds
undermined democracy in many cities to the point that it became meaningless. If
necessary, the machines stuffed ballot boxes, voted repeaters, and terrorized opponents in order to win "a mandate" and receive their share of the city's resources.

Surprisingly, it was not revulsion against the corrupt bosses and their machines
that destroyed the equilibrium of the third system. Rather, it was the abandonment
of the average American by both major parties and their nearly total support of

industrial capitalism in the Northeast. By the early 1870s midwestern farmers realized that the game was being played in such a way that they were almost always the major losers. Since neither party was responsive to the farmers' interests, they moved to take political power into their own hands. Between 1870 and 1896 many anti-major party organizations emerged, enjoyed varying degrees of political success, and then disappeared from the national scene. In 1873 the Granger Movement had 7325 local Granges, but had come to an end politically by 1876; the Greenback Party rose and declined in the 1870s and 1880s; and the more politically oriented Farmers' Alliance enjoyed several successes during this time as well. However, it was the People's Party— better known as the Populists—that threatened the very existence of the two-party system.

America had fundamentally changed during the 1880s. It shifted from being an agricultural to being an industrialized nation, and Americans were convinced they and their communities no longer controlled their own fate. Local farmers were dependent upon world market fluctuations; absentee corporations and Eastern bankers' speculations affected local labor conditions; and the two parties increasingly represented these business élites and not the debtors of society.[32] This situation bred frustration and tension, and when the first major industrial depression hit, the party system could no longer function as it had in quieter, pre-industrial days.

THE FOURTH PARTY SYSTEM

Ironically for the Democrats, they were cruelly taunted by unprecedented prosperity (during the 1860-1896 period) before the disaster. The "bloody shirt waving" of the post-Civil War era was fading away in many voters' minds and they were turning toward the Democrats.[33] In the elections of 1890 and 1892, the Democrats won control of the House of Representatives[34] and captured the White House with Grover Cleveland. Two years later, the Democratic Party was shattered by the huge Republican congressional landslide—the largest transfer of seats from one party to another in American history. The Republicans gained a majority of 132 seats; in 24 states not a single Democrat was elected; and in six others only one Democrat was returned in each.[35] Two years later, in 1896, McKinley defeated William Jennings Bryan for the presidency, and for 16 years the Republicans controlled the White House, "leaving the Democrats to wander in the political wilderness for a generation."[36] The congressional Democratic defeat in 1896 was so crushing that outside the South, there were only a dozen Democratic Congressmen left—half of whom were from New York City.[37]

What forces were strong enough to crush a party at the peak of its glory and doom it to 36 years of minority-party status? The defeat of the Democratic Party was due to many problems; one of the most significant was the Depression of 1893, which led to an unemployment rate of 20 percent while the Democrats controlled Congress and the presidency.[38] This earthshaking economic disaster was especially hard for the cities and the growing urban working class. President Cleveland, a fiscal conservative somewhat like the later Republican president, Herbert Hoover, could not seem to deal with that type of problem. To compound the difficulties of the party of Jackson, it was captured in 1896 by its Western faction, which represented the farmers and the soft money, pro-silver forces. Under the leadership of the "Boy Orator from Nebraska," William Jennings Bryan, the Democratic Party embarked on a crusade on behalf of the debtor class. By virtually ignoring the cities, Bryan managed to convince a new generation of urban working class voters that their future was with the Republican rather than with the Democratic Party. "Free silver was at best uninteresting to the urban population and, at worst, anathema to them."[39] The cities swarmed to the Republican Party—only 12 of the largest 82 cities went to Bryan, and 9 of these were in the South or silver regions. After 1896 the Republican Party emerged as the party of respectability, wealth, and the Union, as well as the party of progress, prosperity, and national authority. While the Republicans had branded the Democrats as the party of "Rum, Romanism, and Rebellion," a fourth "R"—Radicalism—was added during the 1890s. An additional handicap for the Democrats was the great difference between McKinley's campaign organization and that of Bryan. McKinley's manager, Marcus A. Hanna, ran the first modern high-powered campaign. Efficient, honest, media-oriented, and well-financed by assessments made on Big Business, the Republicans easily overwhelmed Bryan's simple evangelical crusade.

In the first decade of the twentieth century, a new wave of reform demands organized as the Progressive Movement, swept the nation. The Republicans were able to adapt to these demands more quickly than their divided opponents, and the Republican Theodore Roosevelt became one of the Progressive leaders. The Progressives espoused many reforms that eventually had a great impact on the party system; these included the referendum, direct primary, recall, initiative, non-partisan elections, more sophisticated civil service regulations, and a general anti-party bias. When William Howard Taft succeeded Theodore Roosevelt as president, many Progressives felt betrayed by Taft's conservative policies; after being denied the 1912 Republican nomination, Roosevelt bolted from the Republican Party and formed his own third party—the Progressive or Bull Moose Party.[40] Split into two large camps, the regular Republicans and the Progressives, the usual Republican majority lost the presidency to Woodrow Wilson, the minority Democratic party candidate, in both 1912 and 1916. The Progressive-Bull Moose ticket polled enough votes in 1912 so that the regular Republican Party declined to third place. However, the Progressives could not survive as a separate political force, and most of them rejoined the Republican Party by 1916. The two major parties were able to avoid realignment from 1900 to 1920 period primarily because the Republican Party and then the Wilsonian Democratic Party adopted the Progressive ideas. In short, the reformers did not have to go outside the two-party system to implement most of their program.

The nation returned to normalcy and Republican domination during the 1920s. The fourth party system was extremely sectionalized: the South was a solid Democratic stronghold; the Northeast and Midwest were also one-party areas, but Republican. Urban Northern voters and rural Republicans continued to cast huge Republican majorities for Harding, Coolidge, and Hoover during the 1920s. In fact, by 1928, the Republican presidential victories and congressional majorities were of the same magnitude as during the late 1890s. Like the Cleveland victory before the 1893 Depression, Hoover's victory in 1928 left the Republicans as unprepared for the following two decades of powerlessness as the Democrats had been some 30 years earlier.

When the cities rallied to the Republican side in 1896, it helped to assure almost solid Republican victories until 1932. Actually the loyalties of the urban areas were in flux during the 1920s, but there was a shift toward the Democratic Party during the 1928 candidacy of Catholic, urban, ethnic-oriented Al Smith. Smith became a spokesman for the largely ignored urban immigrants and their families and thus attracted a new class of voters to the Democratic Party. As seen in Table 2.1, the Republican Party began to lose its urban base early in the 1920s; it reached rock bottom in 1936 with Roosevelt's second term landslide.[41]

THE FIFTH PARTY SYSTEM

Two major factors contributed to the shift of power to Roosevelt in 1932. First, the economic crisis of unprecedented magnitude—the 1929 Depression—had resulted in such high levels of unemployment and economic dislocation that the Hoover Administration was completely discredited. Second, millions of young people, mostly from nonpolitical immigrant families, reached voting age between 1924 and 1932. To most, the trauma of the 1929 Depression established their preference for the Democratic Party which lasted until the late 1960s.

In Congress, the Democratic Party won huge majorities. In 1932 they held a 193-seat majority; in 1934 their majority increased to 216 seats in the House of Representatives, the first time a presidential party had gained rather than lost seats during an off-year congressional election. However, Democratic strength in Congress and in the presidential elections declined throughout the latter part of the 1930s and the 1940s. Despite the fact that Pearl Harbor undermined a central part of the Republi-

Table 2.1 Party Preferences in Nation's 12 Largest Cities

Presidential Election	Net Party Plurality
1920	1.5 M Rep.
1924	1.3 M Rep.
1928	.2 M Dem.
1932	1.8 M Dem.
1936	3.5 M Dem.
1940	2.1 M Dem.
1944	2.2 M Dem.
1948	1.5 M Dem.

Source: Lubell, *The Future of American Politics* (New York: Harper & Row, 1965), p. 49.

can platform, the minority party provided responsible opposition during World War II with such issues as unnecessary censorship, discrimination against Negroes, war profiteering, and inflation. There were more Republican successes during the war years than during the Depression.[42] In 1942, for example, they won half of the nation's governorships, including New York and California. The Republicans were looking forward to defeating President Harry Truman in the 1948 election after four straight defeats at the hands of Franklin Roosevelt. Truman, a product of the Pendergast machine in Kansas City, was quite unprepared for becoming president after Roosevelt died in 1945. Despite Truman's quick adaptation to the presidency, the postwar problems were so great that by 1948 a movement had begun to substitute General Eisenhower as the Democratic candidate for president. The issue was settled when the general refused to run for president in 1948 under either party label. Anti-Truman Southerners bolted and set up a Dixiecrat ticket with Governor Strom Thurmond as their presidential candidate. Their goal was simple—to thwart the liberal civil rights advocate, Harry Truman, by throwing the contest into the House of Representatives, where they hoped to bargain with the two parties on civil rights questions. There was also a fourth ticket in this 1948 election: "a hybrid of radicals and non-party liberals of all hues and shades united behind former Vice President Henry Wallace and the title of Progressive Party."[43] As the election drew near, it appeared that the Republican nominee, Governor Thomas Dewey of New York, would be the inevitable victor. Truman's campaign was underfinanced, poorly staffed, and generally not supported by the party organization. All it had was one of the most unusual campaigners in American history who embarked on a 30,000-mile railroad tour to take his message to the people. Apparently the message was received, for when the votes were counted, Truman was elected for his own 4-year term.[44]

After 1950, national politics entered a "tideless era," in which Democrats dominated Congress and the two parties alternated in the White House. Two terms with Eisenhower, 8 years with Kennedy and Johnson, and the same period with Nixon and Ford.[45] As has happened so often in our history, the out-of-power party in near desperation turned to a non-party, hero-type candidate—General Dwight David Eisenhower—in the hope of capturing the presidency in 1952 and 1956. Looking back, President Eisenhower seemed well-suited for an era of "normalcy" after the chaos of the 1940s and the coming turmoil of the 1960s. Twice he had little difficulty in defeating Adlai E. Stevenson.

Kennedy went on to secure the 1960 nomination after a spirited series of encounters in the primaries against Hubert Humphrey, Lyndon Johnson, and others. The Democrats regained the White House in one of the closest contests in our political history. The final tally showed Kennedy with a 114,000-vote edge over Richard Nixon, out of a total of almost 69,000,000 votes. Despite his image, which captured the attention of the nation, Kennedy's failures in domestic policy made him vulnerable as the 1964 election approached. By the fall of 1963, the conservative wing of the Republican Party had already prepared the way to capture of the party organization from the

THE FIFTH PARTY SYSTEM

Eastern Republican leaders. In an attempt to strengthen his support in the South, John Kennedy made a fateful trip to Dallas, Texas, and was assassinated in November 1963. The new president, Lyndon Johnson, went on to secure a tremendous landslide in the 1964 election over Senator Barry Goldwater, the conservative Republican candidate. Johnson won 61.1 percent of the vote and the Democratic Party increased its majority in the House to 140 seats.

From their triumph in 1964 until the Carter victory in 1976, the Democrats were relegated to the political wilderness as Humphrey and McGovern tried to lead a divided party. Meanwhile the Republicans' euphoria over the Nixon victories of 1968 and 1972 vanished with the Watergate scandal and the resignation of both Agnew and Nixon. In the late 1970s party politics had largely stabilized as both the Democrats and the Republicans attempted to reconstruct their organizations after the unsettling events of the preceding decade.

In this chapter so far we have examined the five party systems that have helped to shape much of American political history in the last two centuries. Although two centuries of history cannot really be condensed in a few pages, we hope that the reader will have a better grasp of some of the broad patterns that still influence American politics today.

Each party system made significant contributions to the political development of our nation. The first (1795-1816) helped to legitimize the new national government and to shape governmental policies while mobilizing segments of the electorate behind alternative policies.[46] In the 1790s and again in the 1820s several parties were invented by American politicians. The second system (1830-1860) saw the maturation of parties into institutions we could easily recognize today as parties. They also accommodated themselves to increased demands by the public—although white, adult, and male—for a greater voice in politics. People viewed the parties and politics as entertainment; the 1840 election, with 80 percent of the electorate voting, indicates people's interest and excitement in the politics in the era. The second system was also characterized by a shift away from élitist caucuses to popular conventions. It was also the only national party system we have experienced, for both Whigs and Democrats competed fairly equally in all sections of the nation. Chambers has called the post-1865 party systems "derivative," that is, they were characterized by adjustment rather than creativeness.[47] The changes made were incremental, not radical, and most of them came during the first two decades of the twentieth century as a result of the Progressive Movement. Yet even the third and fourth (1860-1896 and 1896-1930) systems were noteworthy. Millions of immigrants and their offspring were socialized into the American political system by the urban machines. Furthermore, both parties, but especially the Republicans, nurtured conditions favorable to tremendous economic growth. The fourth system is perhaps best remembered for the reformers and their advocacy of the direct primaries and all the other measures that have contributed to the decline of party organizations. The last system has seen the rise of the managerial state under the leadership of the Roosevelt-Democratic party coalition. Under the managerial state the national government has a much more significant role as a regulator, protector of the disadvantaged, intervener into previously privately controlled areas, and guarantor of continued economic prosperity.[48] The fifth system has also seen the continued decline of parties because political campaigns have changed fundamentally. The entire communications industry has been undermining the electoral functions of the parties (Table 2.2).

It should be clear that party politics appears to operate on a cyclical pattern with one party dominant, then both competitive, and then a swing toward one party leading to another period of dominance. We have had at least five major party systems as well as a number of discernible subperiods reflecting a specific pattern of politics that differed from what preceded or followed it.

THE THEORY OF PARTY REALIGNMENTS

Periodically, throughout American political history, established political parties have been destroyed, new parties constituted, and old parties affected by great shifts of voter allegiance and support. Such great transformations occurred in the elections of 1860, 1896, and 1932. The following discussion will deal with these important elections and the shift of millions of voters from one political party to another and the reasons behind these shifts. The present political system will also be analyzed to determine if we are in another period of realignment.

V. O. Key, one of the great modern political scientists, first analyzed these party system transformations and constructed a *theory of critical elections*. A *critical election* is one in which the depth and intensity of participation by the electorate is high and sharp and there is a durable electoral realignment between the parties.[49] Expanding upon this concept, Walter Dean Burnham defined critical elections as:

1. Involving profound disruptions of traditional party voting patterns.
2. Characterized by abnormal intensity and conflict over nominations and platforms. There is also ideological polarization, first in one party, then between the parties.
3. Occurring periodically, rather than at random.
4. Associated with great policy direction changes.[50]

Both Burnham and Kevin Phillips (in his book *The Emerging Republican Majority* [1968]) postulate a "generational theory" of party realignment. This means that every 25 or 30 years, the reasons that had led millions of people to support one or another party become less relevant and so the parties become reconstituted.[51] Burnham argues that since parties do not deal adequately with unusual demands, there are increasing "strains" upon the system over time. Such unresolved problems as slavery, agricultural-populist disenchantment, and the breakdown of the economic system in 1929 ultimately brought about political crises for the parties.[52]

The concept of critical elections was expanded by Gerald Pomper into a typology of key presidential elections. Using a two-dimensional classification, the two important variables are the outcomes of the election and the degree of continuity or change in electoral cleavage.[53]

Table 2.2 Summary of American Political Party Systems

Party System	Political Era	Dominant Party (Presidency)	Dominant Party (Congress)	Principal Opposition Party	Significant Third Parties (Peak Dates, Percent Total Vote for President)	Political Style of Era	Party System's Characteristics	President
Pre-Party I —1788	Colonial	None	In Legislatures pro-crown	In legislatures anti-crown	None	Limited electorate, factional in legislatures, cliques, deferential voting patterns, whisky campaigning	None	None
Pre-Party II 1789-1795	Early years under Constitution of 1787	Administration	Opposition	None	None	Continued deferential voting patterns, divisions in Congress beginning to be firm over policies of new government	Parties developing in few states, not at all in most. Campaigning still individually based. No formal parties as such.	Washington
First party system 1796-1815	The rise of parties	Democratic-Republican	Democratic-Republican	Federalists	None	Beginnings of partisan self-identification. Belief in party's fate and success tied to nation's concept of loyal opposition began.	Nominations by caucus of party officeholders. Slightly expanded electorate. Newspaper campaigning.	Adams Jefferson Madison

Table 2.2 Summary of American Political Party Systems (continued)

| One party government 1815-1832 | The "Era of Good Feelings" | Democratic-Republican | Democratic-Republican | None | Anti-Masons (1832 8%) | General public withdraws from national level politics. No major issues to divide public. | A one-party system after Federalists disappeared as an effective party. All major decisions occurred in D.R. Congressional caucus. Return to faction as basis of congressional division. Parties began to develop around candidates for the presidency. | Monroe J. Q. Adams |
| Second party system 1832-1860 | Pre-Civil War politics | Democratic Party | Democratic Party | Whigs | Freesoil (1848, 10.1%); American (1856, 21.4%); Breckinridge Democratic (1860, 18.2%); Constitutional Union (1860, 12.6%) | Presidential election opened to public participation after Jackson, weak presidents. One-term presidents. Rising crisis of slavery causing great tension in the two national parties. | Whigs solidify by 1840 as principal opposition party to Democrats. Whig "hero" candidates win presidency periodically. Extremely well-balanced and competitive in all parts of the nation. The only such balanced system in U.S. history. | Jackson Van Buren Harrison Tyler Polk Taylor Filmore Pierce Buchanan |

Table 2.2 Summary of American Political Party Systems (continued)

Party System	Political Era	Dominant Party (Presidency)	Dominant Party (Congress)	Principal Opposition Party	Significant Third Parties (Peak Dates, Percent Total Vote for President)	Political Style of Era	Party System's Characteristics	President
Third party system 1860-1894	Civil War Period 1860-1865	Republican and Union Party (1864)	Republican	War Democrats, "Copperhead Democrats"	None	Strong opposition in North to Republicans; No parties in South. War issues. Stirrings of rural discontent. Shift of nation to industrialism. Business enters politics to secure favorable climate for development.	Northern opposition to Lincoln from War Democrats, Copperhead Democrats, and Radical Republicans. Republican edge in North; Republican dominance in South based on Reconstruction carpetbagger governments.	Lincoln
	Reconstruction Period 1865-1876	Republican	Republican	Democratic				Johnson Grant
	First "Tideless Era" 1876-1894	Republican	Dem-H of R Rep-Senate	Democratic	Greenback Populists (1892, 8.5%)	Both parties serve needs of industrial capitalism. Extremely close races for president. Growing prairie discontent. Weak presidents, great power in U.S. Senate.	Machine politics rise in big cities. Almost no independent votes. Democrats recapture and build a "Solid South." Boring politics with few real issues.	Hayes Arthur Cleveland Harrison Cleveland

Table 2.2 Summary of American Political Party Systems (continued)

Fourth party system 1895-1932	Era of industrial capitalism	Republican	Republican	Republican	Democratic	Roosevelt Progressive (1912, 27.4%); Socialists (1912, 6.0%); LaFollette Progressives (1924, 16.6%)	Evangelical under Bryan, triumph of the reformers and Progressives change the rules to include anti-party devices.	Great shift of labor and urban voters to Republicans. Years of great Republican victories except 1912 and 1916, when T. Roosevelt bolted allowing Wilson to win Presidency.	McKinley T. Roosevelt Taft Wilson Harding Coolidge Hoover
Fifth party system 1932-?	The Roosevelt coalition 1932-1950	Democratic	Democratic	Democratic	Republican	Bolting Dixiecrats and remnants of socialist parties in 1930s and 1940s Union Party (1936)	Government becomes an active intervener in political and economic process. Beginning of Southern Democratic and Republican congressional alliance.	Constant opposition role for Republicans throughout era. Alliance of South, Labor, urban, poor, minorities under F.D.R. leadership.	F. Roosevelt Truman
	Second "Tideless Era"	Mixed	Democratic	Republican	Republican	American (1968, 13.5%)	Rapid decomposition of voter party ties and of services provided by parties. Rise of media politics. Watergate scandal.	Alternation in presidency between parties in 8-year blocs. Strong Democratic hold on Congress. State races very competitive. South leaves Democratic presidency coalition. Crisis politics.	Eisenhower Kennedy Johnson Nixon Ford Carter

Majority Party

Electoral Cleavage		Won	Lost
	Continuity	Maintaining	Deviating
	Change	Converting	Realigning

A *maintaining election* is one in which the hitherto dominant party continues its dominance with only limited or marginal changes. Needless to say, most presidential elections in our history have been maintaining elections. A *deviating election* is one in which the existing party loyalties are not seriously altered, but in which short-term forces have combined to allow the minority party candidate to win. Another term for this phenomenon is "surge" and well describes those election anomalies such as Eisenhower's two victories in 1952 and 1956 and Woodrow Wilson's 1912 and 1916 triumphs.[54] On the other hand, a *converting election* is one in which the dominant party wins the election, but in which significant changes have taken place in its coalitional support and in that of its main opponent. The latest converting elections were in 1928 and possibly 1964. Lastly, a *realigning election*, the most significant of all four types because of its over-all effect on society and politics, is characterized by:

1. Massive and enduring shifts of coalitional elements at the mass base.
2. Visible effects on the presidential level as well as in congressional and state electoral patterns.
3. Unusual intensity over the issues, with sharp polarizations among the electorate, and the heavy turnout of hitherto non-voting groups.
4. Significant consequences for the later development of public policy.[55]

There have been five great realigning elections in our history: Jefferson's Revolution of 1800, Jackson's revitalization of the party system in 1828, Lincoln's shattering 1860 victory, Bryan's disastrous defeat of 1896, and Hoover's landslide defeat by the Roosevelt coalition in 1932.[56]

THIRD PARTIES—A HARBINGER OF REALIGNMENT?

It is interesting and instructive to note that in at least the last three party realignments, third parties played a major role in signaling the change. The 1860 realignment was preceded by the emergence of the Abolitionist Party in 1840 and 1844; the Free Soil Party in 1848 and 1852; and the American or Know Nothing Party in 1856. Populist discontent found an outlet in the 1876-1888 Greenback Party and the Populist Party in 1892 before gaining control of the Democratic National Convention in 1896. Just a few years after Bryan's defeat, the Socialist Party gained strength in the Midwest and North, securing nearly 1 million votes in 1912 and 1920. Until the emergence of George Wallace's American Independent Party in 1968, the fifth party system had experienced only "bolting" third-party efforts, that is, splinter groups leaving one or another major party for one election but returning during the next election. George Wallace's movement secured the largest third-party vote (in total *number* of votes) in American history. The highest *percentage* of total votes went to the American (Know Nothing) Party in 1856 and Theodore Roosevelt's Progressive Party in 1912 (see Table 2.3).

Third parties have often served as temporary havens for dissatisfied groups who broke away from one major party on the way to the other or perhaps a new major party.[58] None of the third parties has long survived as a significant party; each one was either absorbed into one of the major parties, replaced one of the major parties, or dwindled as an insignificant group (such as the Prohibitionists or Socialists).

In 1976 the third party presidential vote was as follows:

Independent	(McCarthy)	745,042
Libertarian	(MacBride)	183,187
American Independent	(Maddox)	170,673
American	(Anderson)	153,009
Socialist Workers	(Camejo)	90,109
Communist	(Hall)	58,689
People's	(Wright)	48,891
U.S. Labor	(La Rouche)	40,008

Source: *New York Times*, 13 December 1976.

Kevin Phillips noted that since 1860 each cyclical upheaval in American presidential politics has coincided with a rise in splinter party activity.[59] Could the 1968 American Independent Party and its 1972 successor (the American Party) be the harbingers of a sixth party system?

IS THE UNITED STATES CURRENTLY UNDERGOING A REALIGNMENT?

Before discussing the details of electoral changes since the 1950s, let us consider what forces could bring about a realignment. James L. Sundquist of the Brookings Institute has constructed an analytical framework for studying these phenomena.[60] He suggests that five variables influence the timing, form, and magnitude of political realignments:

1. The breadth and depth of an underlying grievance, or what Scammon and Wattenberg called a "Voting Issue"—a controversial matter of such importance that it breaks voter ties to one party or another.
2. The capacity of a proposed remedy to provoke resistance among an important sector of society. For if an idea sweeps all before it, there is no reason to alter contemporary social institutions.
3. The motivation and capacity of the party leadership when matched against the

Table 2.3 Significant Third Parties in Presidential Elections[57]

Year	Party	Percentage of Total Votes Cast
1832	Anti-Mason	8.0
1848	Free Soil	10.1
1856	American (Know Nothing)	21.4
1860	Breckinridge Democrats	18.2
	Constitutional Union	12.6
1892	Populist (People's)	8.5
1912	Theodore Roosevelt Progressive	27.4
	Socialist	6.0
1924	La Follette Progressive	16.6
1968	American Independent	13.5

strength and momentum of the issue. "The historical realignments of the American party system occurred when the leaders either did not try to mediate and compromise the issue or tried and failed."[61]

4. The division of viewpoints between the parties will either accelerate the solution to the problem or delay the ultimate decision. If one party is composed of voters who strongly favor an issue, that party will probably embrace it. However, if the issue's supporters are in both parties, then a delay in resolving the issue may encourage the creation of a third party.

5. The strength of the ties that bind voters to the existing parties.[62]

There are only a limited number of realignment possibilities within the framework of a two-party system. One is that a *major realignment would be averted*; although there might be some minor realignment over the new issue, it would soon lose its potency and the voters would return to their usual parties. A second possibility is that there might be a *major realignment of both major parties* with massive voter shifts from one party to another for a long-term commitment. A third possibility is that a *third party might capture or be captured by one of the two major parties*, thus realigning the system. Fourth, a *third party might completely replace one of the existing major parties.* And finally, *both existing major parties might be completely replaced by two new major parties*—an event that has not happened in United States history, but is theoretically possible.

FUTURE PARTY SCENARIOS

Predicting the future may seem to be a rather fruitless venture, especially in the field of politics. In 1962 who could have predicted the Johnson landslide of 1964, the tragic assassinations, the triumph and tragedy of Richard Nixon, and the Carter presidency? However, there have been some general patterns in the recent past, and we have selected eight scenarios to illustrate some of the plausible paths of the future.

Minor Realignment: A Tideless Era

The least radical of the scenarios sees the post-1960 period as one of minor realignment within the existing party structure and sees an increasingly competitive party
system on the national level. The Republicans will continue to attract voters in the
South and border states, while the Democrats will gain strength in the traditional
Republican bastions of the Midwest and mountain states. No party will dominate
the presidential elections during this period, and a series of "surge" candidates will
represent both parties. People will vote for president according to personality and
issues; and short-term factors will be reflected in vast fluctuations in the party support
level, with very close contests followed by landslides. Since 1960 we have had precisely this pattern in presidential elections; out of a total vote of 357 million in these
five elections, the Republicans led by less than 1 million (Table 2.4).

The "tideless era" of 1876-1896 differed in several significant ways. While the Republicans won three elections (Hayes, Garfield, and Harrison) and the Democrats
twice with Cleveland, the pluralities of the winners were extremely small.[63] By contrast, the post-1960 "tideless era" alternated between huge landslides and squeekers.
Secondly, in the post-Civil War era the parties split control of Congress, with the
Democrats usually winning the House and the Republicans the Senate. With the
single exception of 1953-1954 in the more recent period, the Democrats have controlled both houses of Congress, while the Republicans have been reduced to almost
a permanent minority (Table 2.5).

At present, we may have entered a period of 8-to-12-year presidential cycles instead
of the earlier 32 or 36-year cycles.

> *Under this circumstance, the GOP cycle that began in 1968 could peter
> out in 1976 or 1980. Local politics would mirror some of these national-level
> shifts, but there would be no clear parallel. . . . Since 1952 The United States
> has had eight years of one party, then eight years of the other. The phenome-
> non of incumbency is also involved: Presidents win re-election (none have
> lost), and then the opposition takes over, beginning a new eight year regime.
> Prior to 1952, there are no such examples of eight year alternations, and
> party regimes were longer lasting. [Emphasis added.]*[64]

Table 2.4   Post-1960 Presidential Election Total Vote

	Dem.	Rep.
1960	34,226,731 (Kennedy)	34,108,157 (Nixon)
1964	43,129,566 (Johnson)	27,178,188 (Goldwater)
1968	31,275,166 (Humphrey)	31,785,480 (Nixon)
1972	29,170,383 (McGovern)	47,169,911 (Nixon)
1976	40,830,763 (Carter)	39,147,793 (Ford)
Totals	178,632,609	179,389,529

Source: America votes 12 (Washington D.C.: Congressional Quarterly, 1977).

Table 2.5 Comparison of "Tideless Era" Congressional Parties' Strength

| House of Representatives | | | | | |
Election Year	D	R	Election Year	D	R
1874	181	107	1956	234	201
1876	156	137	1958	283	154
1878	150	128	1960	263	174
1880	130	152[a]	1962	258	176
1882	200	119	1964	295	140
1884	182	140	1966	248	187
1886	170	151	1968	243	192
1888	156	173[a]	1970	255	180
1890	231	88	1972	244	191
1892	220	126	1974	290	144
			1976	292	143

| U.S. Senate | | | | | |
Election Year	D	R	Election Year	D	R
1874	29	46[a]	1956	49	47
1876	36	39[a]	1958	66	34
1878	43	33	1960	64	36
1880	37	37	1962	68	32
1882	36	40[a]	1964	67	33
1884	34	41[a]	1966	64	36
1886	37	39[a]	1968	58	42
1888	37	47[a]	1970	55	45
1890	39	47[a]	1972	57	43[b]
1892	44	38	1974	61	39[b]
			1976	61	39

[a]Republican control of chamber.

[b]Totals include 1 Independent-Democrat (Virginia) and 1 Conservative Republican (New York).

Figure 2.1 depicts this "tideless" or "short-term" presidential party era. It shows a minor realignment of certain blocs of voters between the parties and the fairly common shifting of groups due to short-term factors, issues, events, and personalities. Jimmy Carter's Democratic victory in 1976 appears to have kept intact this "tideless" pattern of 8-year periods.

The Rise of the Republican Hegemony

In his influential book, *The Emerging Republican Majority*, Kevin Phillips proclaimed the death of the Roosevelt coalition (the fifth party system) and the creation of a sixth party system with a dominant Republican presidential party. In 1969 the new majority was conservative and Republican. Phillips concluded that the 1972 election results seemed to indicate that the Republican coalition of Southern, midwestern, mountain, and southwestern states was becoming a reality in presidential elections. Figure 2.2 depicts the shifts that would be reflected in such an enduring Republican-

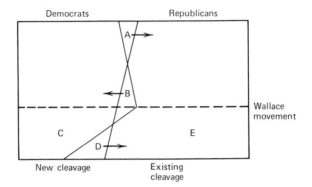

Figure 2.1 Minor realignment within existing
party framework: tideless.

A Ex-Democratic presidential Northern ethnic
voters to presidential Republican coalition
B Silk stocking, university type Republicans
to Democratic presidential coalition
C Some former Southern national level Democrats return to national Democratic Party
D Other former Southern Democrats find semi-
permanent home in Republican National
presidential coalition
E Some conservative Republicans who supported Wallace in 1968 and 1972 return
home

dominated coalition. However, the Watergate scandal, Nixon's resignation, and the
subsequent conviction of many of his associates have severely undermined the prospects of this coalition. Perhaps even more significant is the abandonment of the Republican Party by some of the archconservatives who sought unsuccessfully to establish a new conservative party in 1976.[65] These events, together with the Ford defeat
in 1976, seem to have ended the dream of a long-term Republican hegemony (Figure
2.2).

The Revitalization of the Democratic Party

Perhaps not even the eternal optimist, the late Hubert Horatio Humphrey, would have
wanted to predict a complete revival of the old Roosevelt coalition of labor, blacks,
other minorities, ethnic groups, and the South. The Roosevelt coalition at the presidential level is dying. It suffered a serious blow with the withdrawal of the Southern
contingent in 1948 and subsequent elections. Democratic strategists like Ben Wattenberg and Richard Scammon have argued that most of the rest of the coalition could
be saved and that it could still win the presidency except in Republican "surge"
years. The pattern of voting that emerged from the 1976 presidential election tends to
support the Wattenberg and Scammon argument of at least a partial revival of the old

Democrats   Republicans

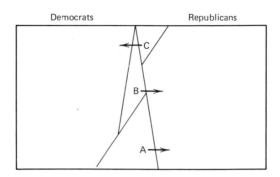

Figure 2.2 Realignment with Republican Party dom-
           inant.

A Southern Wallacites (former Southern Democrats
   on presidential level) to national Republican Party
B Part of Northern Democratic vote (ethnics and
   Wallace supporters) to national Republican Party
C A few liberal Republicans to Democratic coalition

Roosevelt coalition. Carter managed to reunite labor, minorities, the Northeast, liberals, and the South—the major elements in the Roosevelt coalition. However, Ladd
and Hadley persuasively argued that, although similar in some broad aspects, the
1976 Carter coalition was not a genuine revival of the Roosevelt coalition of the
1930s. They noted that Carter failed to win a majority of the Southern white vote
and that he showed weakness among the white, working class voters who formed
the foundation of the New Deal Democratic Party.[66]

   Phillips as well as Scammon and Wattenberg have based their electoral strategies on
estimates of which parts of the old Roosevelt coalition have defected permanently
and which parts could be lured back. The Carter election seems to indicate that no
groups within the old Democratic Party coalition have completely defected to the
Republican Party and that possibly a winning formula could be reestablished under
a new generation (Figure 2.3).

   Can Big Labor, the white ethnics, and the minorities live together, work together,
and win together? At first glance, probably not. Certainly, the Republican strategists
would make this argument. However, Michael Novak, author of the *Rise of the Unmeltable Ethnics* and spokesman for the "PIGS" (Poles, Italians, Greeks, and Slavs)
lists many reasons why blacks and ethnics can and should work together to achieve
urban political power. These two huge groups have not cooperated in the past because of differences in political style, culture, motivations, life style, and values.
Novak believes that such a coalition would be more stable than one composed of
intellectuals and blacks, since both blacks and ethnics have essentially the same interests—homes, neighborhood services, schools, jobs, job advancement and status.
He feels that a black-ethnic coalition is inevitable. It does not have to be built on a
foundation of love; mutual respect or even mutual need will suffice.[67]

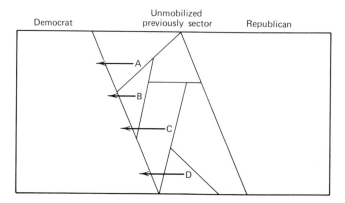

Figure 2.3 The Revitalization of the Democratic Coalition. Labor,
Blacks, Ethnics, Intellectuals and Youth?

A   Blacks, Chicanos, and Puerto Rican voters registered and voted
    increasingly for Democratic presidential nominees
B   Mobilization of some of the youth vote (college) for Democratic
    candidates
C   Big Labor voted for moderate Democratic candidates
D   Return of the big city white ethnic vote to the Democratic
    column

If, and it is a big "if," the Democratic leadership can patch up the ethnic-black differences, then the party can hope to rebuild the coalition by means of organization and mobilization of previously unregistered and inactive voters. In July 1975, Congress began the debate on postcard voter registration for federal elections. Democratic presidential majority coalition: A Northeast Plus California political base pecially among the young, the poor, and the more highly mobile—those who tend to vote Democratic. Mark Siegal, executive director of the Democratic National Committee, noted: "It would bring a minimum of 10 million new voters—and perhaps a maximum of 17 million. They are poor; they are black; they are Spanish-speaking; and they are not Republicans."[68]

Many Democratic leaders are looking in this direction for a revival of the Democratic presidential majority coalition: A Northeast Plus California political base (Quadcali, see FN 66), the black-ethnic alliance, the South, and increased mobilization of previous nonparticipants. While "Quadcali" seems to be a reasonable strategy, the black-ethnic coalition has yet to appear, but the mobilization effort has begun.

AN END TO THE TWO-PARTY SYSTEM: THREE, FOUR, MORE?

Third-Party Alternatives
Third parties have frequently played a significant role in presidential elections; however, seldom have they persisted over time and never have we had a three-party system last for several consecutive elections. The right wing of the political spectrum often talks

about forming an ideologically pure party to represent their values. In February 1975, the Conservative Political Action Conference, attended by nearly every major conservative spokesman except Senator Barry Goldwater (R-Arizona) and columnist William F. Buckley, Jr., actively discussed leaving the Republican Party and forming a Conservative Party.[69] A special committee was set up to study whether to establish a third political party or to try to remake the Republican Party from within.

> *Simply put, it is time to take up the cudgels against a liberal Establishment that has abetted Southeast Asian defeat, weakened national defense, massively promoted inflationary social welfare spending, imposed cruel and foolish guidelines from busing to racial quotas and otherwise eviscerated national strength ... Such a new [conservative] party may take shape all across America by 1976, ready to field a bipartisan fusion Presidential slate if the two existing party establishments prove unresponsive. Gerald Ford is a decent man, but Whiggism has become intolerable. It took Teddy Roosevelt to give the United States a Square Deal, Franklin Roosevelt to shape a New Deal, and Harry Truman a Fair Deal. Could it be that a fusion of Ronald Reagan and George Wallace is necessary to finally give America the Right Deal?*[70]

This statement by former arch-Republican strategist Kevin Phillips is faintly reminiscent of the original Republican orators who, in 1853, called for a new party and the abandonment of the intolerable Whigs and Democrats.

George Gallup and Louis Harris, national pollsters, reported in May 1975 that Americans were increasingly receptive to the idea of a third presidential party. Gallup in his poll of April 20, 1975 discovered that more than one-fourth of the electorate was willing to support a conservative third party, and Harris confirmed this finding a month later.[71]

The remnant of George Wallace's 1968 campaign, the American Party, was viewed as a possible platform for a revitalized conservative third party. However, by the late 1970s the American Party had splintered itself almost out of existence. Thus, there seems to be two alternatives for those who want to establish a major conservative party: create a new one or take over the already existing Republican Party and reconstruct it accordingly. The conservatives had apparently decided on the latter course, at least for the moment. The difficulties inherent in establishing a new party are so enormous as to make such a course highly improbable. Too many people have a vested interest in the continued existence of the Republican Party. Given the supportive nature of state electoral laws, it is extremely difficult to replace a major political party with a new one.

Still another possibility would be a third ticket, but not a third party in the usual sense of the word (Figure 2.4). Perhaps this ticket (a candidate running for the presidency and relying on his own personal organization and the media rather than on party organization) would be an independent one that would appeal to the 40 percent

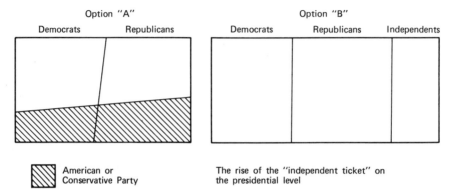

Figure 2.4   Establishment of a three party system.

of the electorate who view themselves as independents. Eugene McCarthy's 1976 independent presidential campaign proved how difficult this is to accomplish.

Four or More?

Between 1824 and 1968 approximately 1050 party names have appeared on our nation's ballots.[72] It is at least possible that a conservative party or ticket might emerge in the early 1980s; the radical to moderate left is also talking about establishing a new presidential party. Former Democratic presidential aspirant Eugene McCarthy carried the banner of the Left in the 1976 presidential election, and the Right was represented by weaker candidates from the American Party and several of its splinter groups. If these movements become a permanent part of our political landscape, we may have a four-party system that looks something like the diagram shown in Figure 2.5.

Destruction of the Republican Party?

So far we have looked at six scenarios that assume the continuation of the present two-party system, but with changed coalitions or added actors. The hypothetical prospects could be far more drastic for the Republicans and Democrats: one or both of our historic parties could be eliminated. Since the industrialization of America after the Civil War, we have had the same two major parties. Only twice in our history has an existing major party disappeared—in the 1810s (the Federalists) and 1850s (the Whigs).

However, certain conditions exist at present that could bring about the destruction of the Republican Party. For example, if a new conservative party came into existence that was made up of a significant group of disaffected Republicans, Southern Democrats, and some dissatisfied Northerners, such a party could reduce the Republicans to functional impotence (Figure 2.6).

But for reasons previously noted, it is quite unlikely for the Republican Party to be replaced by a new conservative party. The conservatives have simply concluded that

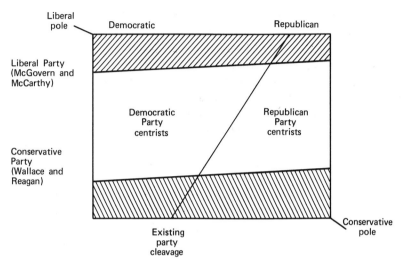

Figure 2.5　The Development of a multiparty system in the United States.

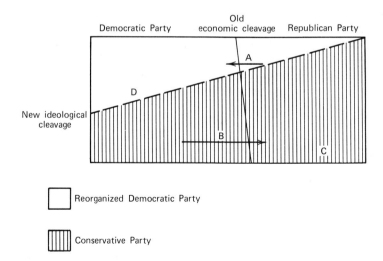

Figure 2.6　The destruction of the Republican Party and its replacement by the Conservative Party.

A　Former Ripon Society Liberal Republicans to Democratic Party
B　Former Conservative Democrats to Conservative Party
C　Former Conservative Republicans form base of the Conservative Party
D　Liberal and Moderate Democrats still foundation of Democratic Party

it has become too difficult to displace an established national political party short of a national catastrophe.

Although it is possible that the convulsions that occurred during the 1968 and 1972 presidential conventions will become worse in the future and rip the Democratic Party apart, leading to an organization of the new left or liberal party, this doesn't seem to be a likely scenario. A weakened, fragmented Democratic Party, yes; a re-organized Democratic Party, possibly; but an alternative to this party, improbable. Since the Left has a voice in the Democratic Party, its incentive to leave and build a new party is weak.

A Whole New Game

The most radical of possible changes would be the complete replacement of the existing parties with two or more new major parties. Figure 2.7 illustrates such a revolution. The destruction of only one party requires such extraordinary circumstances that this has not happened for more than 125 years.

In simple terms, dual party replacement would require a crosscutting issue of incredible magnitude that would destroy the remaining bonds between the voters and the established parties and the creation of new parties oriented around the new issue. Since 1932, four great issues have challenged the fifth party system. Three of those four no longer have force required to realign the parties: communism, Vietnam, and the social issue.[73] Only the issue of race and several related subissues could possibly realign our parties or even destroy the existing parties. However, a racial realignment appears extremely unlikely since there is little black political power on the national level.

Another, but less racially polarized prospect, is David Apter's suggestion of a division based upon different adjustments to post-industrial social demands;[74] he singled out three main groupings:

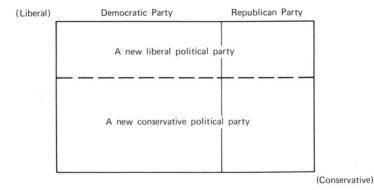

Figure 2.7 The replacement of both the Republican and Democratic parties by at least two new parties.

1. *The Technologically Competent:* This group is made up of many of the older upper class and many contemporary academics—particularly in the natural and social sciences—as well as a large number of their students, journalists, and those employed in the electronic media.
2. *The Technologically Superfluous:* This group is composed of those without marketable skills in the post-industrial society. There is a disproportionately large number of unskilled blacks and other racial (and otherwise handicapped) groups.
3. *The Technologically Obsolete:* This group is made up of substantial parts of "Middle America"—from both the working class and white collar strata.

This pattern identifies the top and the bottom of society as distinct from the middle: the Competent and the Superfluous against the Obsolete. This combination appeared in the 1972 presidential campaign: McGovern's coalition of intellectuals, liberals, and minorities faced Nixon's "silent majority." If McGovern's coalition continued to represent the Democratic Party, it would probably be doomed to a permanent minority status. However, Jimmy Carter's victory of party moderates in 1976 has altered this coalition.

The Burnham Model: An Un-Party System
This last model of the future has been so closely identified with its main proponent, Walter Dean Burnham, that we will call it the Burnham Model. It begins with the fact that parties in the mid-twentieth century lost some of their earlier functions, a phenomenon Burnham calls the "decomposition of American political parties." Parties, simply, are not as important as they once were, and Burnham believes that they will never be significant again except in the limited capacity as ballot gatekeepers, that is, restricting the final voter choice to several nominees. Furthermore, the late 1960s saw a realignment, but not like any previous one in our history.[75] Instead of shifting power among various party organizations, the realignment shifted voters away from the existing parties. In addition to a detectable conservative shift of the electorate, there has been a long-term dissolution of party-related voting, which is best seen in the increase of independent or ticket-splitting voters. From these phenomena, Burnham concludes that:

1. American electoral politics appears to have been decisively restructured along office-specific lines, with significantly different coalitions appearing at the presidential, gubernatorial, senatorial, and congressional levels,[76] as well as in each succeeding election.[77]
    "The Presidency has become the vortex for all the combined passions, intensities, and multiple cleavages over values, relative social status and relative deprivation that now are at work in the electorate."[78] This imporant office is now separated from other, lesser offices and has its own level of commitment; it does not significantly influence congressional and local elections. The Senate and House have now institutionalized and separated themselves from the presidential

    race so that the coattail effect seldom appears.
2. "The critical realignment of the 1970s works against rather than through the
    traditional mechanism of two party competition. It involves the dealignment of
    of the American electorate."
3. The present-day dealignment is due to the inability of the traditional two-party
    system to handle successfully the number, strength, and diversity of the contem-
    porary political polarizations.
4. "The emergence of office-specific electoral coalitions greatly reinforces the cen-
    trifugal, fragmenting policy effects of the American Constitutional structure."
5. "An American equivalent to a multiparty system is being created on the ruins of
    the older major parties. . . . Today we have a 'four party system' at the grass roots,
    i.e., separate Congressional and presidential coalitions in the electorate."[79]
6. In the short run, today's realignment represents a victory for the political Right.
    Although there is no stable presidential voting coalition, the over-all pattern is pre-
    dominately conservative, though hardly Republican.[80]
7. With this "Triumph of the Right":
    a. "If the 'great middle' becomes revolutionized politically under the over-
        whelming pressure of sharp blows, the result could be the emergence of even
        stronger extreme right, racist and perhaps militarist movements. . . . Our next,
        and perhaps last critical realignment would almost certainly follow."[81]
    b. Or, if there is no adequate nationwide stimulus (economic disruption, intense
        racial conflict), probably the executive will have unchecked power in policy-
        making.

Of those who disagree with the Burnham model, one critic has written:

> *Burnham's various scenarios are grim. Either the system falls into the hands
> of an unfettered executive and a right wing mass and change is blocked by a
> no-party system, or else the sixth party system emerges with either option
> characterized by an intensive class and status polarization of civil war propor-
> tions. However, in my view, these dramatic scenarios seem excessively tied to
> the political climate of 1964-1968.*[82]

CONCLUSIONS ON REALIGNMENT

Will any of these scenarios come to pass? The authors believe that there may be a
combination of several of the scenarios presented here. A possible short term prospect
is a three or four-party system, with the remote possibility of a conservative party
either gaining control of or destroying the Republican Party. Any realignment, thus,
will not occur as it has in the past, that is, as the result of a crisis and manifested in
a critical election. A new type of realignment could occur because the existing parties
do not seem to be able to resolve the growing desire of the conservatives for a "pure
party" and because the parties can no longer cope with countless social pressures and
the declining interest in existing parties.

We agree with certain aspects of Burnham's analysis and see a gradual, long-term reduction in the electoral function of American parties. Although the two existing parties will undoubtedly continue for the foreseeable future, they will increasingly become simply "labels." However, electoral functions and services that they once offered will be handled more and more by others. One reason for the continuation of the two parties is that the electoral laws of the Untied States, written by friends of parties, serve to shield them from outside competition. These laws and their cumulative effects on the party system will be discussed in the next chapter.

FOOTNOTES

1. There are many excellent books on American political party history. The following have been relied on quite heavily by the authors in this chapter: William N. Chambers and Walter D. Burnham, eds., *The American Party Systems*, 2nd ed. (New York: Oxford University Press, 1975); the Capricorn Series on *Political Parties in American History, Vol. I, 1789-1829*, edited by W.E. Bernard; *Vol. II, 1828-1890*, edited by F. E. Bonadio; *Vol. III, 1890-Present*, edited by Paul L. Murphy (New York: Capricorn, 1974). See also H. James Henderson, *Party Politics in the Continental Congress* (New York: McGraw-Hill, 1974), and Steven E. Petterson, *Political Parties in Revolutionary Massachusetts* (Madison, Wis.: University of Wisconsin Press, 1974). in addition, Arthur M. Schlesinger's edited four-volume collection of documents and essays, *History of U.S. Political Parties* (New York: Chelsea House, 1973). Others will be noted as encountered in the remainder of the chapter.

2. Richard Hofstadter's classic study of the first 60 years of American parties, *The Idea of a Party System: The Rise of Legitimate Opposition in the United States, 1780-1840* (Berkeley: University of California Press, 1969), argues that English politics during the American Revolution had not yet developed the Cabinet system, nor enlarged the electorate to a base for non-elite style politics, and Parliament was still factionally organized. By the 1820s, Richard Pares talks of an English "tendency" toward a two-party style of politics, but it was not until 1868 that a prime minister took an unfavorable election result as a mandate from the people and resigned without testing a vote in Parliament, pp. 40-41.

3. Hofstadter, *The Idea of a Party System*, op. cit., pp. 41-43.

4. See also Arthur M. Schlesinger, ed., *History of U.S. Political Parties*, Vol. I-IV (New York: Chelsea House, 1973).

5. Hofstadter, *The Idea of a Party System*, op. cit., p. 43.

6. Forest McDonald, *We the People: The Economic Origins of the Constitution* (Chicago: University of Chicago Press, 1958). See especially Chapter 2.

7. Joseph Charles, *The Origins of the American Party System* (New York: Harper, 1956), p. 12.

8. Ibid., p. 98.

9. Ibid., p. 83.

10. Ibid., pp. 116-117.

11. Everett C. Ladd, Jr., *American Political Parties* (New York: Norton, 1970), p. 81.

12. Paul Goodman, "The First American Party System," in Chambers and Burnham, op. cit., p. 65.

13. William N. Chambers, "Party Development and American Mainstream," in Chambers and Burnham, op. cit., p. 10.

14. Charles, op. cit., p. 92; also Chambers, ibid., p. 10.

15. Quoted in Ladd, op. cit., p. 79.

16. Ibid., p. 83.

17. Goodman, op. cit., p. 85.

18. Actually the first party system was the only system in our history to be built around a major foreign policy cleavage in the electorate.

19. Eugene H. Roseboom, *A Short History of Presidential Elections* (New York: Collier, 1967), pp. 31-33.

20. Party endeavors reached their culmination in the elections of 1800. Adams sought a second term and once again Jefferson was his obvious rival. A caucus of Republican members of Congress met at Marache's boarding house in Philadelphia to nominate Burr formally for the vice-presidency in the first national nominating caucus. Intense propaganda efforts followed in state after state, with Jefferson, the *Aurora*, and other party spokesmen or organs issuing manifestoes which, in effect, stood as early party platforms. In several states formal "Republican Tickets" or presidential electors were distributed to voters, and Burr coordinated the strenuous efforts to mobilize the mass electorate of New York City. The result was a triumph in which the Republicans won the presidency, the Senate, and the House—and yet it was close. The electoral vote for Jefferson and Burr was 73 to 65 for the Federalist ticket; their national majority depended upon New York's 12 electoral votes. The Republican majority in the New York legislature, which chose the electors, depended in turn upon the Republican members from Manhattan, and their average margin of victory was a bare 490 votes. Moreover, Jefferson and Burr were tied under the original electoral system, which gave each elector two votes without distinction as to presidential or vice-presidential candidates; thus, the election was thrown into the House of Representatives. After a perilous stalemate that continued through 35 ballots in the House in 1801, Jefferson was finally named president and Burr vice president. W. N. Chambers, *The Democrats 1789-1964* (Princeton: Van Nostrand, 1964), pp. 19-20.

21. Roseboom, op. cit., p. 39.

22. Ibid., p. 48.

23. Ibid., p. 53.

24. James Sundquist, *Dynamics of the Party System* (Washington, D.C.: Brookings, 1973), p.61.

25. Richard P. McCormick, "Party Development and the Second Party System," in Chambers and Burnham, op. cit., pp. 90-116.

26. Sundquist, op. cit., see Chapter 13, "The Realignment Process."

27. Franklin L. Burdette, *The Republican Party: A Short History* (New York: Van Nostrand, 1972), p. 16.

28. Roseboom, op. cit., p. 78.

29. See Eric L. McKitrick, "Party Politics and the Union and Confederate War Efforts," in Bonadio, op. cit., pp. 669-704.

30. Ladd, op. cit., p. 115.

31. Alfred Steinberg, *The Bosses* (New York: Mentor, 1972), p. 3. Generally listed as W. Marcy Tweed, but Professor Leo Herschkowitz, in his analysis of Tweed's role in New York City, *Tweed's New York* (New York: Anchor, 1977), argues that the middle initial "M" was never spelled out by Tweed, but probably stood for Magear, his mother's maiden name, p. 5.

32. Between 1887 and 1893, more than 11,000 farms were foreclosed in Kansas alone, and in 15 of its counties more than three-fourths of the land was owned by mortgage companies.

33. "Bloody shirt waving" was a favorite Republican campaign tactic in this 1865-1895 era, when they posed as the party that had saved the Union; they pictured the Democrats as pro-South and asked the voters to vote as they shot.

34. "'The election is a landslide.'' 'The Republican Party is permanently disabled' and 'fallen to pieces' proclaimed the press in November, 1892 as Grover Cleveland swept back into the White House on a swell of popular votes.... For the first time since the presidency of Buchanan (1856-1860), Democrats would control both houses of Congress and the White House simultaneously." J. Rogers Hollingsworth, *The Whirligig of Politics: The Democracy of Cleveland and Bryan* (Chicago: University of Chicago Press, 1963), p. 1.

35. Carl Degler, "American Political Parties and the Rise of the City," in Murphy, op. cit., p. 950.

36. Degler, ibid., p. 950.

37. Sundquist, op. cit., p. 135.

38. By 1893 more than 500 banks and 16,000 businesses had gone under. To this disaster President Cleveland replied that the depression was a business problem that businessmen should resolve. A year later, in 1894, 2½ million workers were unemployed, which represented about 20 percent of the work force. Hollingsworth, op. cit., pp. 918, 926.

39. Degler, op. cit., p. 955.

40. Among the tales that explain why the 1912 Progressive Party was called the "Bull Moose Party" is that Theodore Roosevelt, in responding to a newsman's question about his health, reportedly said, "I feel like a bull moose."

41. Samuel Lubell, *The Future of American Politics* (New York: Harper and Row, 1965), p. 49.

42. See Donald R. McCoy's fascinating essay on the Republicans during World War II, "Republican Opposition during Wartime, 1941-1945," *Mid-America XLIX* (July 1967), pp. 174-189.

43. Roseboom, op. cit., p. 220.

44. The popular vote in 1948 showed an interesting pattern with third parties doing very well: Truman, 24,179,345; Dewey, 21,991,291; Thurmond, 1,176,125; Wallace, 1,157,326; Thomas (Socialist Party), 139,572; Watson (Prohibition), 103,900; Teichert (Socialist Labor), 29,241; and Dobbs (Socialist Worker), 13,614.

45. Walter Dean Burnham, "Party Systems," op. cit., p. 303.

46. Chambers, op. cit., p. 7.

47. Ibid., see Chambers for a very good discussion of party contributions to the development of the United States.

48. Ladd, op. cit., p. 181.

49. V. O. Key, "A Theory of Critical Elections," *Journal of Politics XVII* (February 1, 1955), pp. 3-18.

50. Walter Dean Burnham, *Critical Elections and the Mainspring of American Politics* (New York: Norton, 1970). Also by the same author are "The End of American Party Politics," *Transaction VII* (December 1969); "The Changing Shape of the American Political Universe," *American Political Science Review LIX* (March 1965), pp. 7-29; "Party Systems and the Political Process," in Chambers and Burnham, *op. cit.*, pp. 277-307; "The United States," in Richard Rose, *Electoral Behavior* (New York: Free Press, 1974), pp. 653-726.

51. Kevin Phillips, *The Emerging Republican Majority* (New York: Doubleday, 1969). And better articulated in Phillips's later book *Mediacracy* (New York: Doubleday, 1975).

52. Burnham, *Critical Elections*, op. cit., especially, but also found in varying degrees in his other publications.

53. Gerald M. Pomper, *Elections in America* (New York: Dodd, Mead, 1968), p. 104.

54. Charles Sellers, "The Equilibrium Cycle in Two Party Politics," in *Electoral Change and Stability in American Political History* edited by J. Clubb and H. Allen (New York: Free Press, 1971), p. 153.

55. Burnham, *Electoral Behavior*, op. cit., p. 665.

56. Ibid., p. 666.

57. Daniel A. Mazmanian, *Third Parties in Presidential Elections* (Washington, D.C.: Brookings, 1974), p. 5.

58. Phillips, *Mediacracy*, op. cit., p. 138.

59. Ibid., p. 143.

60. Sundquist, op. cit., especially Chapters 1, 2, 3, and 13.

61. Ibid., p. 31.

62. Ibid., pp. 28-36.

63. President Hayes (R) won in 1876 with 256,000 fewer votes than Democrat Tilden; Garfield (R) won in 1880 with fewer than 10,000 votes over Hancock (D); Cleveland (D) won by 23,000 over Blaine (R); and Harrison (R) won the electoral vote over Cleveland, while trailing by more than 100,000 in the popular vote in 1888.

64. Phillips, *Mediacracy*, op. cit., p. 146.

65. Ibid., especially in the first and last chapters.

66. Everett C. Ladd, Jr., and Charles D. Hadley, (Transformations of the American Party System (New York: W. W. Norton, 1978), pp. 275-291. It should be noted that in 1971 Richard M. Scammon and Ben J. Wattenberg outlined presidential election campaign strategy. They called it "QUADCALI" and it called for the Democratic candidate to capture the quadrangle from Massachusetts to Washington, D.C., to Illinois, to Wisconsin and then add in California. With 266 electoral votes needed to win the White House, "Quadcali" encompasses 270 of them. "Carry Quadcali—win the election." Richard M. Scammon and Ben J. Wattenberg, *The Real Majority* (New York: Coward, McCann and Geoghegon, 1971), p. 69.

67. M. Novak, *The Rise of the Unmeltable Ethnics* (New York: MacMillan, 1971).

68. Associated Press, July 20, 1975, "Postcard Signup a Hot Issue."

69. Associated Press, February 15, 1975, "Conservative Split: Third Party Looms."

70. Kevin Phillips, "A Reagan-Wallace Ticket," *Newsweek*, May 19, 1975.

71. Gallup Poll April 20, 1975.

72. Burnham, *Electoral Behavior*, op. cit., p. 663.

73. Sundquist, op. cit., pp. 308-331.

74. David Apter, *Ideology and Discontent* (London: Free Press, 1964), see Chapter 1.

75. Burnham, "American Politics in the 1970s," in Chambers and Burnham, op. cit., p. 308.

76. Burnham, "American Politics," op. cit., p. 338.

77. Burnham, *Electoral Behavior*, op. cit., p. 722.

78. Burnham, "American Politics in the 1970s," op. cit., p. 344.

79. Ibid., p. 337.

80. Ibid., p. 350.

81. Burnham, *Critical Elections*, op. cit., p. 193.

82. James F. Ward, "Toward a Sixth Party System? Partisanship and Political Development," *Western Political Quarterly XXVI* (September 1973), pp. 385-413. The quote is from page 412, but the entire article is a scathing attack on the Burnham model.

3
To Preserve and Protect:
The Rules of the Electoral Game*

Political parties have to function within an environment composed of various forces over which the parties exercise different degrees of control. Some of these forces are sociological and will be discussed at length in Chapter V. Other forces are more institutional in nature and can be controlled by the party organizations. These institutional forces are largely the federal and state laws that affect the parties not only directly, but indirectly through the political arenas in which they function.

The most basic force affecting the nature of American parties is the United States Constitution. This document, adopted in 1789, established federalism and the separation of powers as fundamental principles of the new American government. In his book *Party Government* E.E. Schattschneider described political parties as the river of American politics and the Constitution as the river bed whose contour shapes the stream. He noted that although the river is the captive of the bed within which it flows, occasionally the river (parties) can transform the landscape (the Constitution).[1]

Federalism and the ultimate creation of 50 major political subdivisions (states), together with the other centrifugal forces, made the fragmentation of major political parties almost inevitable. Today we have more than 100 major parties—a Republican and Democratic Party in each state—which normally exist as totally independent organizations. Periodically, these parties may join together in trying to elect a person affiliated with one of the state party organizations to the presidency; but in the mid-twentieth century, significant portions of the "national coalition" of a party have declined to participate in these campaigns. In the Goldwater campaign of 1964, the Humphrey campaign of 1968, and the McGovern campaign of 1972, large sections of their respective parties decided to ignore the presidential campaign and to concentrate on state and local party races. Furthermore, the separation of powers among the three branches of government has led to additional fragmentation as different electorates select legislators and executives. While these general constitutional provisions

---

*The title of this chapter is taken from the U.S. Constitution, Article I, section 2; it is also the title of Allen Drury's novel, *Preserve and Protect*.

have had a tremendous impact on the broad pattern of American political party development, there are many specific party statutes and election laws that affect the parties.

THE RULES OF THE ELECTORAL GAME

Every game has a set of rules that determines who or how many can play and how they are to do so. Just as a player in Monopoly cannot build a hotel on his property until he has met certain requirements, a political party must act according to a set of rules (or laws). Unfortunately, the complete rules of the party game are not written down in a convenient form; they are scattered across the country in the statute books of the federal government, the 50 states, and their thousands of political subdivisions. Not only do the basic rules governing parties and elections differ from state to state, but they often differ in adjoining counties or cities within the same state. While the laws regulating the organization and structure of the parties will be discussed in Chapter IV, this chapter will deal with the laws affecting suffrage and elections.

Since the development of political parties was not foreseen by the framers of the Constitution, they made no mention of parties in the original document. The Constitution leaves most of the responsibility for electoral decision-making to the states. Therefore, the state statute books contain the rules for regulating the parties, the voters, and the systems that are used for electing candidates to more than one-half million offices in this nation.[2]

The Legalization of a Political Party and Gaining Access to the Ballot

In the early days of our Republic it was fairly easy to form a political party and set up an election. A group merely printed up a number of "tickets" with its nominees listed thereon and offered them to prospective voters who would cast the "tickets" by placing them in the ballot box on election day. Slowly, but surely, the rules became more formal as the states assumed the responsibility for printing ballots and restricting access to the ballot. The states were given the power to control elections (and implicitly, political parties) in Article I, section 2, of the Constitution:

> *The House of Representatives shall be composed of Members chosen every second Year by the People of the several States, and the Electors in each State shall have the qualifications requisite for Electors of the most numerous Branch of the State Legislature.*

Judicial interpretation has held this to mean that the states have complete control, subject to specific constitutional provisions, to define the qualifications of voters and to regulate the electors' qualifications. Also, the states can conduct the elections, establish the official ballot, and decide how candidates will be nominated.[3] An early legal definition as to what constituted a political party is as follows:

> *An Unincorporated Association of persons which sponsors certain ideas of government or maintains certain political principles or beliefs on the public*

policies of government and which is formed for the purpose of urging the adoption and execution of such principles in governmental offices through officers of like beliefs.[4]

Almost without exception, the states have tended to define political parties quantitatively according to their success in attracting votes. Illinois, for example, defines a political party as a political organization that polls 5 percent of the statewide vote in the last gubernatorial general election. The right of a state to regulate parties by requiring them to secure a minimum percentage of the vote in a general election has been repeatedly upheld by the courts.[5] Other states have developed categories of parties and have electoral laws providing different routes to the ballot access for each category. In Ohio, a *major* party is one that has more than 20 percent of the total vote for governor in the last election; an *intermediate* party 10-20 percent of the vote; and a *minor* party between 5 and 10 percent of the vote. Ohio also stipulates that when any political party fails to receive 5 percent of the total vote for governor or president, it ceases to be a political party.[6] Oregon also defines major parties as those with more than 20 percent of the vote and minor parties as those with more than 5 percent of the vote.[7] Several states recognize political parties on less than a statewide level. For example, Washington accords major party status to any party that can gain 10 percent of the total vote in the last general election in whatever political arena it chooses to operate.[8] See Table 3.1.

The original justification for many of the state laws regulating elections and parties was the professed desire to eliminate election corruption and to reduce each voter's choices to a reasonable number.[9] Some students of American politics began to suspect that these laws were also intended to protect the two major parties from new competition and to assure their survival.[10] The early state requirements were quite reasonable in allowing a third party to appear on the ballot. "The required number of (petition) signatures varied from 50 in Mississippi to 10 percent of the total votes cast in the previous general election in Nevada. As a rule the requirement was around 1 or 2 percent of the vote."[11] The states also attempted to ensure that elections were more efficient and better organized by initiating filing dates.

> *Connecticut, for instance, required the parties to nominate candidates three weeks prior to the day of election; in some states the deadline fell even closer to the election. Generally, filing dates left officials enough time to print the ballot, while allowing new parties or factions dissatisfied with the nominees selected at the state or national conventions of the major parties to enter candidates.*[12]

During the 1920s, there were several challengers to the two major parties and the state legislatures, which were dominated by these parties, moved to protect them. In 1924 the Progressive Party found the state laws "almost insurmountable obstacles to a new party."[13] During the 1930s, the fear of foreign controlled parties led to

Table 3.1   Access to the Ballot in the 50 States

State	Political Party Defined— Ballot Access Guaranteed	Methods by Which New or Minor Parties Gain Ballot	Independent Candidates
Alabama	20% (entire statewide vote)[a]	(N.M.)[b]	(N.M.)
Alaska	10% (Gov.)	Petition: 3% (Pres.)[c]	Petition: (1000)
Arizona	5%	Petition: 2% (Gov.) in at least 5 counties	(N.M.)
Arkansas	7% (Gov. or Pres.)	Petition: 7% (Gov. or Pres. total vote)	Petition: 15% (total Gov. vote)
Calif.	2% (any statewide office) or register 1% of entire statewide vote. If registration drops to 1/15 of 1% of total state registration, it ceases to be a political party.	Petition: 10% (statewide vote)	Petition: 5% (statewide total)
Colorado	10%	Independent process	Petition: (300)
Conn.	20% (Gov.)	Minor political parties 1-10% of vote; use convention 5 weeks before election.	(N.M.)
Delaware	10%	(N.M.)	(N.M.)
Florida	5% (total registered voters)	Petition: 3% (total registered voters)	Petition: 5% (total registered voters)
Georgia	Register with Sec. of State; Fee; Party organization	Same as in Col. 1	Petition: 5% (total vote for office sought)
Hawaii	No requirements	Petition: (25)	Petition: (25)
Idaho	3 or more candidates for statewide office in last G.E. or 1 candidate for any statewide office gaining 3% of Gov. total vote.	Petition: (1500)	Petition: (1000); 50 maximum in any 1 county
Illinois	5% (Gov.)	Petition: (25,000) with a maximum of 13,000 from the same county.	Same as minor party requirements.
Indiana	10% (Sec. of State)	Minor—1/2 of 1% of Sec. of State total vote. Petition: 1/2 of 1% (Sec. of State total vote)	Petition: 1/2 of 1% (Sec. of State total vote)

Table. 3.1   Access to the Ballot in the 50 States (continued)

State	Political Party Defined— Ballot Access Guaranteed	Methods by Which New or Minor Parties Gain Ballot	Independent Candidates
Iowa	2% (Gov.)	Petition: (50) non-party political organization—1 signature from at least 1/2 of the state's counties.	Petition: (1000)
Kansas	5% (Sec. of State)	Minor 1-5% vote (S of State); convention nomination.	Petition: (2500)
Kentucky	20% (Pres.)	Minor 2% (Pres.); choice of convention or primary.	Petition: (1000)
Louisiana	5% (Gov. or Pres.)	Petition: (1000)	Petition: (1000) non-political party registered voters
Maine	5% (Gov.)	5% (Gov.)	Petition: 5% (Gov.)
Maryland	10% (Pres.)	Partisan organization 3% of vote; use primary meeting to nominate.	Petition: 3% (registered voters)
Mass.	3% (Gov.)	1/10th of 1% (Gov.) plus petition 3% (Gov.)	Petition:3% (Gov.)
Michigan	5% (Sec. of State)	1% (Sec. of State vote by principal candidates in statewide contest). Petition: 1% (Sec. of State vote; 100 in at least 9 congressional districts).	(N.M.)
Minn.	5%	(N.M.)	Petition: 1% (statewide total vote) or 2000 signatures, whichever is less.
Miss.	(N.M.)	(N.M.)	Petition: (1000)
Missouri	2% (Gov.)	Petition: 1% (Gov. vote in each Cong. district) or 2% (in 1/2 Cong. districts if 2% of total Gov. vote)	Petition: 1% (in all Cong. districts) 2% (in half of C.D. if 2% of Gov. total vote)

Table 3.1   Access to the Ballot in the 50 States (continued)

State	Political Party Defined—Ballot Access Guaranteed	Methods by Which New or Minor Parties Gain Ballot	Independent Candidates
Montana	3% (Cong. state-wide total)	If under 3% total, use convention.	(N.M.)
Nebraska	(N.M.)	Convention (750 delegates)	Petition: (1000)
Nevada	5% (Cong. total)	Petition: 5% (total vote in last G.E.)	Petition: 5% (of total votes in last G.E.)
N.H.	3% (Gov.)	Same as major party	Petition: (1000)
N.J.	10% (Gen. Assem. total)	Petition: 2% (total G.A. vote)	Petition: 2% (total G.A. vote)
N.M.	Fulfill state organization requirements	Petition: 3% (Gov.)	(N.M.)
New York	50,000 votes for Gov.	5% of enrolled voters of that pol. party or Petition: (20,000), whichever is less.	Petition: (20,000) 100 in each of 1/2 of states Cong. districts.
N.C.	10% (Gov.) or 10,000 registered voters in party.	Petition: (10,000) by July 1	Petition: 10% (Gov.) by first Sat. in May.[d]
N.D.	5% (Pres.)	(N.M.)	Petition: (300)
Ohio	5% (Gov. or Pres.)	Petition: 1% (Gov.)	Petition: (5000)
Oklahoma	5% (Gov. or Pres.) or 10% of this vote gained in at least 3 other states in last G.E.	Petition[e]	Petition
Oregon	20% (Pres.)	Petition: 5% (total Cong. vote)	Petition: 5% (total Cong. vote)
Penn.	2% (largest vote for any statewide office in 10 counties) and 2% (total statewide vote)	Petition: 1/2 of 1% (any statewide candidate in last G.E.)	Same as minor or new party.
R.I.	5% (Gov.)	(N.M.)	Petition: (500) for Pres. Primary: (1000)
S.C.	Meet state requirements	(N.M.)	Petition: (10,000)[f]

Table 3.1   Access to the Ballot in the 50 States (continued)

State	Political Party Defined— Ballot Access Guaranteed	Methods by Which New or Minor Parties Gain Ballot	Independent Candidates
S.D.	10% (Gov.)	Petition: 10% (Gov.)	Petition: 2% (Gov.)
Tenn.	5% (Gov.) or registration of 2.5% of total Gov. vote	Petition: 5% (Pres.)	25 signatures[g]
Texas	Major party (200,000 votes for Gov.)	Minor parties by convention and petition 1% (Gov.)	Petition: 1% (Gov.)
Utah	2% (Cong. total)	Petition: (500) 10 in each of at least 10 counties	Same as minor party requirements.
Vermont	5% (Gov.)	1-5% of vote—nomination by convention	Petition: 1% (Gov.)
Virginia	10% (statewide)	Petition: 1/2 of 1% (total registered voters)	Same as minor party requirements.
Wash.	10% (any statewide race total)	Convention or primary day with 100 registered voters in attendance.	(N.M.)
W.V.	10% (Gov.)	Petition: 1% (total statewide vote)	Same as minor party requirements.
Wisc.	10% (any statewide office)	Petition: 1/6 of vote for Gov. in at least 10 counties	Petition: (3000)
Wyoming	10% (Cong.)	(N.M.)	Petition: 5% (Cong. total vote)

Source: Data obtained from the statute books of the 50 states.

Notes:

[a]   The information in parentheses explains the vote upon which the percentage requirement is based. For example, Alabama requires a party to poll 20% of the entire statewide vote; Alaska, 10% of the entire vote for governor, etc.

[b]   N.M. = not mentioned in the state's statewide statutes or electoral code.

[c]   For president and vice president only. If a party fails to receive 10% of the total presidential vote, it ceases to be a party.

[d]   This was reduced from 25% in 1973.

[e]   The number of signatures required on the petition is not specified.

[f]   A candidate cannot gain access to the general election ballot by means of an independent petition if he has lost a primary election for that office.

[g]   This was repealed. Apparently the Tennessee statutes do not provide for independent petitions.

additional restrictions to deny "un-American" parties a place on the ballot. Illinois has a clause to ban subversive parties:

> No political organization or group shall be qualified as a political party. . .
> or given a place on the ballot, which organization is associated, directly
> or indirectly with Communist, Fascist, Nazi or any other Un-American
> principle and engage in activities or propaganda designed to teach subser-
> vience to political principles and ideals of foreign nations or the overthrow
> by violence of the established constitutional form of government of the
> United States and the state of Illinois.[14]

Despite the "era of good relations" during World War II, those parties that were associated with Communist philosophies were banned, together with those that leaned toward fascism. Phrases like "or any other Un-American principle" and "to teach subservience to political principles and ideals of foreign nations" make one wonder whether minority representation and such foreign electoral devices as proportional representation would be banned in Illinois. In 1968, 60 percent of the states still barred Communist or "Un-American" parties.[15]

Most states provide for minor or new party access to the ballot by petition. The states often require so many signatures that the major parties do not have to worry about minor parties on the ballot. Illinois, long divided geographically into major party factions, used to have one of the toughest laws for minor or new parties. Such a party had to gather 25,000 signatures from qualified voters, including a minimum of 200 signatures in each of at least 50 of the state's counties. If you can imagine a left-wing party collecting signatures in some of the rural, arch-Republican downstate counties, you can understand how this law worked against minor or third parties. Complaints by the Wallace supporters and other minor parties, as well as a successful court challenge prompted the legislature to change the law in 1974 to require the same number of signatures but a maximum of 13,000 from a single county. Although the law has been liberalized it still presents a formidable obstacle to third parties.[16] After a long existence, the Socialist Party in 1970 was still trying to secure a place on various state ballots. It challenged New York's electoral law, which specified that the Socialist Labor Party was *not* a political party because it had not secured at least 50,000 votes in the preceding gubernatorial election.[17] Thus, it had to settle for designation as an "independent body," forcing it to qualify for a place on the ballot by the petition process. In this case the New York District Court decided for the Socialist Labor Party and struck down the law.

However, the state of Georgia has a far more restrictive statute which was upheld in 1970 (*Georgia* v. *Fortson*): "Any political organization in Georgia which receives less than 20% of the vote in the preceding gubernatorial or presidential election is a 'political body' rather than 'political party.' " In order for a group to nominate a candidate, it must file a nomination petition with 5 percent of the total number of electors' signatures who were eligible to vote in the last election.[18]

An Ohio electoral law proved to be extremely difficult for the 1924 Progressives; it was also the toughest obstacle in 1968 for George Wallace's American Independent Party. As Richard Claude has noted, in 1968 both the AIP and the persistent Socialist Labor Party were barred from the ballot in Ohio:

> *The state had effectively foreclosed its presidential ballot to all but Nixon Republicans and Humphrey Democrats. It did so by prohibiting write-in votes, by eliminating all Independent Candidates through a rule that nominees must enjoy the endorsement of a political party, and by defining "political party" in such a way to exclude all but the two major parties.*[19]

The Supreme Court allowed the American Independent Party to be placed on the ballot, but the Socialist Labor Party was barred because of the lateness of its request.[20]

Some states have traditionally made it relatively easy for new or minor parties. Washington state only requires that a party petition contain 100 valid voter signatures and that a party nominating convention be held on primary election day. However, this is quite unusual.[21] The North Carolina requirement for new and minor parties (10 percent of the last gubernatorial total vote or 10,000 valid voter signatures before July 1 of the election year) is more common. Up until 1973 North Carolina required independent candidates to collect voter signatures equal to 25 percent of the previous gubernatorial total vote. However, the reduced percentage will still probably exclude almost all candidates except those of the major parties.[22] In 1968, 37 states required all minor parties to file nominating petitions, and some had established such early filing dates that splinters or disgruntled party groups could not run separate slates of candidates.[23]

At the present time, legally speaking, a political party is pretty much whatever a state legislature defines it to be. Most state legislatures have made it very difficult for any party (except the Republican and Democratic parties) to get on the ballot. However, in the 1972 general election, ten minor parties were on the ballot in at least one state, with the American Independent Party the most prominent. During the 1974 general election in California, three minor parties, the AIP, the Peace and Freedom, and La Raza Unida, obtained enough votes to retain their status as political parties under California law and continue on the ballot in 1976.[24]

States are tending to liberalize their laws with respect to access to the ballot. As recent judicial opinions have implied, a state's desire to limit the ballot choices to a reasonable number and to have an effective election administration cannot be used to exclude third parties. Probably the liberalization will not threaten the position of the Republican and Democratic parties. As Burnham and others have persuasively argued, perhaps we have progressed beyond the traditional political realignment and perhaps there is no longer enough political energy to transform the system significantly, so that the Republican and Democratic parties may be safe simply by virtue of inertia. One of the major results of Eugene McCarthy's 1976 independent presidential campaign was its challenge to many of the restrictions that have protected the major parties from competition. It remains to be seen how the party system will be affected in the long range, but the parties acting through the state legislatures will probably institute new methods for protecting themselves (such as giving special subsidies to presidential candidates) while imposing almost prohibitive restrictions on independent and third party candidates.

AMERICAN ELECTORAL SYSTEMS

The states, although called laboratories for political experimentation, have proved, with only a handful of exceptions, to be almost totally unimaginative and conservative in designing and utilizing electoral systems. Among the many variations in governmental form, no state has chosen a parliamentary form of government similar to those found in Canada. It is either a sad commentary on American imagination and creativeness or a great tribute to the framers of our Constitution, that Nebraska's unicameral legislature is the prime anomaly of American state government. The standard American electoral system is the single-member, single-vote system, which has been copied from our English friends. Our simple plurality arrangement awards elective office to the candidate who wins the most votes; normally there is no requirement for an absolute majority. Thus, in the following hypothetical contest:

Party	Candidates	Vote	Percentage
Republican	Brown	17,874	40.59%
Democrat	Green	17,653	40.09%
AIP	White	8,517	19.32%
		44,044	100.00%

the Republican candidate would be declared the winner although a majority of the electorate voted for their other candidates. This system obviously has a major party bias, which can be clearly demonstrated by examining the results of a partisan city election. The voters of Cincinnati elected as aldermen 31 Republicans and 1 Democrat. From these results it might appear that Cincinnati was a stronghold of Republican strength. Quite the contrary! The party breakdown in that election was Republican, 68,000 votes (53%); Democrat, 61,000 votes (47%). However, the nature of the electoral system gave all but one alderman's seats to the Republicans.[25]

In election after election, in state after state, and city after city the skew of the simple majority or plurality electoral system can be seen whenever the dominant party wins far more than its proportionate share of the seats. In 1976 four southern states elected legislators with the following party affiliations.[26]

State	House		Senate	
	Dem.	Rep.	Dem.	Rep.
Louisiana	101	4	38	1
Mississippi	119	13	50	2
Alabama	105	0	35	0
Arkansas	96	4	34	1

Could there possibly be so few Republicans in Louisiana and Alabama? In most U.S. Senate races in these states, the Republicans poll 20 to 35 percent ot the vote, and elects 30 percent of the congressmen in Alabama. In many of the state legislative districts, the Republicans do not even bother to put up a candidate. Apparently many candidacies are unopposed simply because of the opposition's feeling of futility of doing so under the plurality electoral system. The positive consequences of the plurality system include a quick winner (there is no delay due to double or triple counting or runoff elections), the discouragement of minority parties and candidates that would prevent legislative or electoral majorities (a coalition is not necessary to govern), and the ease with which most voters can understand the system.

A one exception to this standard state pattern is that of Illinois. In 1870 Illinois adopted a unique system of cumulative voting to ensure minority (but not minor) party representation in each legislative district. Following the Civil War, the state was deeply divided with strong sectional bastions for each major party. It was arranged that in the elections for Illinois's lower house, each district would have three representatives and each voter could cast three votes. All three votes could be given to one candidate, 1 1/2 votes to each of two candidates, two to one candidate and one to another, or one vote to each of three candidates. In a typical election there will be two Democrats and one Republican elected in Democratic districts and the reverse in Republican districts. It should be noted that this system awards seats accurately on a proportionate basis when viewed against the statewide vote, *and* it eliminates all minor-party candidates. Illinois's system of cumulative voting thus gives representation to the supporters of the weaker major party, helps to smooth over sectional differences, and produces narrow majorities in the Illinois legislature. The disadvantages of the system are also significant, for this arrangement squeezes minor parties out of existence, tends to overrepresent the weaker party in a district, leads to party slating of nominations (including the tendency of both parties to nominate a total of only three candidates for three positions), and finally tends to preserve the status quo and thus is an obstacle to reforming the Illinois legislature. When cumulative voting was first adopted, many reformers thought it was the way of the future, but, like Nebraska's unicameral legislature, it remains unique among American political structures. Apparently cumulative voting is well accepted in Illinois, for when the state rewrote its constitution in 1970 cumulative voting was retained.[27]

The degree to which proportional and preferential voting has been adopted throughout the world makes it the most popularly used electoral system. Almost every Latin American nation uses some form of proportional representation, and only one-party Mexico has seen fit to adopt the simple majority system for both legislative houses.[28] All of Western Europe (except Great Britain and France) uses proportional representation.[29]

What characterizes this system that has so much appeal elsewhere in the world? Proportional representation or "PR" has many variations, but all share the common goal of proportioning the seats in a legislatures according to the proportion of the total vote received by each party. There are two basic types of PR: the party list and the single transferable vote systems. The party list system, which has never been used in the United States, means that each party puts up a list of candidates for office equal to the number of seats to be filled. Then a voter casts his or her ballot for a candidate or a party in some variation, and the parties are awarded seats proportionately to their percentage of the total vote. If a *closed list* is used, the candidates are elected as they are ranked by the party organization; if there is an *open list*, the voters indicate their preferences among each party's list of proposed candidates.[30]

The most proportionate and simplest type of PR system is called the *"largest remainder system."* First, a quota is computed as the initial price for each seat. The quota equals the total vote for all candidates divided by the number of seats to be awarded. For example, if there were a total of 100,000 votes cast and ten seats at stake, the quota would be 100,000 ÷ 10 = 10,000 votes. Thus, a party would need 10,000 votes for every seat. In the first round of distributing seats, each party that won 10,000 or more votes is awarded the number of seats to which it is entitled. Then, the appropriate number of votes (10,000 for one seat, 20,000 for two, etc.) is subtracted from that party's vote total. In the second round, the remaining seats, if any, are distributed in the following manner: the party with the largest remainder gets one seat, the party with the second largest remainder gets the second, and so forth, until all the seats have been distributed. If all the seats are awarded on the first round, then the seat distribution process ends. This largest remainder system is now used in Israel, Italy, and Denmark (Table 3.2).[31]

The second type of PR system is the *"single transferable ballot"*; it has been tried in the United States, but almost completely abandoned. Here, the voter rank-orders the candidates from the various parties on the ballot, marking his first choice, second

Table 3.2 Example of Largest Remainder System of Proportional Representation

Party List total vote	First round seats	Remainders	Second round seats	Total Seats
Party A 6,000	0 seats	6,000	1	1
Party B 33,000	3	3,000	0	3
Party C 39,000	3	9,000	1	4
Party D 12,000	1	2,000	0	1
Party E 10,000	1	0	0	1
Total ———	–		–	–
vote 100,000	8		2	10

No. of seats 10 Quota 10,000 Party	Percentage of Seats Won	Percentage of votes won	Proportionates
A	10	6	+ 4
B	30	33	- 3
C	40	39	+ 1
D	10	12	- 2
E	10	10	0
	100%	100%	0

choice, third choice, and so forth. All of the ballots are counted and the first choices for each candidate are separated. Then all of the valid first-choice ballots for each candidate are laid out on a table and stamped with a serial number for possible later tracing, if necessary. The total valid vote of the election is determined and the "quota" (the number of votes needed to elect a candidate) established. The quota is figured out by dividing the total number of votes by the number of seats to be filled plus one, and then adding one to that total. In Cincinnati, which used this system from 1925 to 1951, the total valid vote in the 1953 election was 143,188 and 9 seats were to be filled on the city council:

$$\frac{143,188}{9+1} = \frac{143,188}{10} = 14,318 + 1 = 14,319$$

Therefore, a candidate needed at least 14,319 votes to be elected to the council. If a candidate's total votes exceeded the quota in the original count, he was declared elected. To ensure that no votes were wasted, any votes received over the quota were given to the second choices marked on the ballots. From this point on, the candidate with the lowest total was dropped and his votes transferred to the second choices on his ballots; this process would be repeated until nine candidates reached the quota.[32]

Critics of this PR system have argued that it is too complicated and confusing. Some opponents have even charged that 95 percent of the voters did not understand how their votes were counted. Are American voters less sophisticated than voters of other democratic nations? Other critics have charged that the necessary delay of 6 to 7 days led to confusion and a decline in voters' interest. This last criticism appears to have some validity, especially today when there is instant media analysis of voting returns and announcements of victory within minutes of the polls closing. However, wouldn't it be possible to use modern ballot systems that would allow computers to count the votes and produce a set of winners within a very short time? Couldn't technology, one of the strengths of this nation, overcome this objection?

A total of 25 American cities have tried proportional representation, but all except Cambridge, Massachusetts (the home of Harvard University) had abandoned it by 1963. How did the PR experiment affect the party system? In New York City, which used PR from 1937 to 1945, it gave new electoral life to the patronage-oriented, pathetically weak Republican Party and allowed minor parties a chance to win seats on the city council. In 1935, the last regular simple majority election before the adoption of PR, the Democratic Party won 95.3 percent of the council seats with 66.5 percent of the vote—the party division being 62 Democrats and 3 Republicans. After adoption of the single transferable ballot type of PR, the Democrats won only 13 of the 26 seats on the smaller council; the Republicans won 3 seats, and a variety of minor parties captured 9 seats.[33] The Democrats naturally opposed the change, but surprisingly they were joined by the Republicans in attempting to eliminate PR. Why would the Republicans want to change a system that allowed them to increase their strength? It must have been because of the successes of the minor parties which threatened their own monopoly on nominations and patronage. By emphasizing the presence on the council of the left-wing American Labor Party representative and two Communist Party councilmen elected in 1943 and reelected in 1945, the Democrats and Republicans successfully urged a return to the single-member, simple-majority system. Following the readoption of the simple majority system, the Democrats reestablished their old supremacy and won 24 out of the 25 seats in the 1949 election. The Republicans apparently were willing to sacrifice their seats in order to save the two-party system. If the minor parties can win under PR and threaten the two major parties' positions, one needs only to change the rules in order to exclude them.

In 1969 the New York State Legislature provided for PR to be used in New York City school board elections "to ensure adequate representation for minority groups— ethnic, ideological, racial and religious."[34] In this case PR has fulfilled its supporters' goals by increasing minority group membership on the board proportionate to their composition within the city's population. In 1973, 38 percent of the board members were black, Chinese, or Puerto Rican, and these groups made up approximately 36 percent of the total population. It appears that PR is quite satisfactory in this situation because of the factionalized community; there is no serious agitation for its replacement by a different electoral system.[35]

In his study *The Political Consequences of Electoral Laws*, Douglas Rae noted that a statesman has a choice:

> *On one hand he may opt for highly proportional election outcomes, in which case he is likely to encourage the fractionalization of party systems over time. Or, on the other hand, he may opt to encourage the development and maintenance of two parties ... with the price being less proportionate outcomes.*[36]

As pointed out earlier, American electoral law, written by representatives of the two major parties, is clearly designed to protect those parties from possible challenge. The record of about 125 years without a successful third party replacing an existing major party stands as testimony to its effectiveness.

GERRYMANDERING, MALAPPORTIONMENT, UNIT VOTING, AND OTHER PARTY TRADITIONS

One favorite method by which the parties have sought to make their environment more stable and predictable is to draw the election district boundaries in such a way as to guarantee a certain allocation of seats between the two major parties. Traditionally, most states have left district-drawing to their state legislatures, and often there is a "map room" in some obscure vault in the state capitol's basement. Here, the legislative party leaders (frequently just from the majority party) juggle the various voting districts into dozens of possible combinations in order to gain political advantages for their party. The result is often strange-shaped election districts with no logical reason for existence except the political advantages or disadvantages they offer one or another party. Several methods of "gerrymandering" have been and continue to be used by party leaders.

> *The gerrymander. . .consists of one party's drawing district lines in such a way as to use its own popular vote most efficiently while forcing the other party to use its vote inefficiently. That goal can be achieved in one of two ways: either by dividing and diluting pockets of the other party's strength to prevent it from winning offices, or (if the other party's strength is too great for dilution) by bunching its strength into a few districts and forcing it to win elections by large, wasteful majorities.* [37]

On occasion, both the majority and minority parties will join together to gerry-mander a state's legislative districts for their own individual purposes. The minority party will agree to its continued minority position if the majority party will cooperate by eliminating some of their more troublesome incumbents. Several methods can be used to eliminate such mavericks or undesirable party members: his supporters can be redistributed into several new districts, two independents can be placed in the same district, or his district can be abolished and added to another powerful incumbent's district thus ensuring the troublesome candidate's defeat. [38] Gerrymandering is very difficult to oppose unless it is done in a clumsy way, such as having districts composed of non-contiguous territory or districts of substantially unequal numbers of people as compared with other districts which is now unconstitutional. [39] In fact, the practical *de facto* anticipation that each party would redistrict to its own advantage has received *de jure* recognition by the courts as being legal so long as other court-established criteria are also met. [40]

The battle over reapportioning the various state legislatures usually consisted of the underrepresented urban voters trying to compel the overrepresented rural legislators to redistrict the state legislature so that it more accurately reflected population changes. During the first half of this century there was a significant population shift from the rural to the urban areas in most states. In 1900 less than 40 percent of the nation's population was urban; by 1950, 64 percent was urban. However, some states have not redistricted their legislatures during this entire half-century. In 1962 Tennessee had a situation in which a voter in Moore County (in the rural southcentral area, pop. 2340) had a vote that equalled 23 times the value of a vote in Shelby County, Tennessee (pop. 312,345). Table 3.3 indicates what percentage of voters could elect a majority to the state legislatures before and after court ordered reapportionment. Not only did the state legislatures maintain their rural bias, but many states appor-tioned their senates by counties, and many counties with only a handful of voters had the same number of senators as most populous counties. In Nevada, in 1962, for ex-ample, 8 percent of the state's population could elect a majority in the state senate. In neighboring California, the 6,038,771 people in Los Angeles County and the 14,294 people in a rural mountain county were represented by one state senator each.

Table 3.3 Minimum Percentage of Population That Could Elect a Majority

	State Senate		State House	
	1962	1968	1962	1968
Alabama	25	48	26	48
Alaska	35	51	49	48
Arizona	13	52	NA	51
Arkansas	44	49	33	48
California	11	49	45	49
Colorado	30	50	32	54
Connecticut	33	48	12	44
Delaware	22	53	19	49
Florida	12	51	12	50
Georgia	23	48	22	43
Hawaii	23	50	48	43
Idaho	17	47	33	47
Illinois	29	50	40	49
Indiana	40	49	35	49
Iowa	35	45	27	45
Kansas	27	49	19	49
Kentucky	42	47	34	45
Louisiana	33	48	34	47
Maine	47	51	40	43
Maryland	14	47	25	48
Massachusetts	45	50	45	46
Michigan	29	53	44	51
Minnesota	40	48	35	47
Mississippi	35	49	29	48
Missouri	48	52	20	49
Montana	16	47	37	48
Nebraska	37	49	--	--
Nevada	8	50	35	48
New Hampshire	45	52	44	46
New Jersey	19	50	47	50
New Mexico	14	46	27	46
New York	41	49	33	49
North Carolina	37	49	27	48
North Dakota	32	47	40	47
Ohio	41	50	30	47
Oklahoma	25	49	30	49
Oregon	48	47	48	48
Pennsylvania	33	50	38	47
Rhode Island	18	50	47	49
South Carolina	23	48	46	46
South Dakota	38	47	39	47
Tennessee	27	49	29	47
Texas	30	49	39	47
Utah	21	48	33	48
Vermont	47	49	12	49
Virginia	38	48	37	47
Washington	34	48	35	47
West Virginia	47	47	40	46
Wisconsin	45	48	40	45
Wyoming	27	47	36	46

Source: Book of the States, 1968-69 (Lexington, Kentucky: Council of State Governments, 1968), pp. 66-67.

Actually, the political repercussions of malapportionment extended far beyond the rural-urban conflict. Often, the malapportioned legislature also reflected a permanent party division which was protected by the legislature's refusal to reapportion. In the North, the rural-oriented Republican Party tended to be overrepresented and it often dominated the state senates which tended to be based on geographical representation. Southern malapportionment protected the rural-based Democratic Party at the expense of the urban-based Republican Party. For example:

> Georgia had one of the most egregious malapportionments in the country. The smallest senate district in 1961 had 13,050 people, the largest 556,326. House districts ranged from 1,876 to 185,422 in population, and the rural grip on both houses was absolute. But after reapportionment, the heavily urbanized areas went from 6 to 57 seats in the house and from 1 to 21 seats in the senate. The average age dropped from 51 to 35 years; in the house the number of college educated members rose from 69 to 85. Blacks went from 1 seat to 11, Republicans from 2 to 23.

Until 1960, the only source of relief for urban voters and minority parties in gaining legislative representation was through the courts, which consistently refused to act on this issue. In the strongest statement of this hands-off attitude, the United States Supreme Court in 1946 refused to order reapportionment in Illinois, where the population difference between its largest and smallest congressional district was more than 800,000. In *Colegrove* v. *Green*, the court dismissed the suit by a 4-3 vote. Speaking for the majority, Justice Frankfurter said that the court lacked jurisdiction in this area, which should be handled by the state legislatures, and that it was inadvisable for the court to decide "party contests."[42] In short, the court told the petitioners to go back to their legislature and ask it to do something it had previously refused to do.

The Warren Court did a dramatic turnabout in *Baker* v. *Carr* (1962) by returning the case to a lower federal court, which subsequently ordered reapportionment.[43] Later cases, such as *Reynolds* v. *Sims* (1964), applied the "one man-one vote" principle to the upper houses of state legislatures and ruled that the federal analogy did not apply to subdivisions that were subordinate to the state government and thus counties were not entitled to equal representation in a state senate.[44] As Chief Justice Earl Warren argued so effectively: "Legislators represent people, not trees or acres."[45] The courts also ruled that large population differences among subdivisions could not be permitted without compelling reasons.[46]

The rural and party interests tried to get judicial support for their position. Their allies, including the melodious, late U.S. senator from Illinois, Everett McKinley Dirksen, led an attempt to amend the U.S. Constitution to permit states to apportion one of their legislative chambers by criteria other than population. But their failure to get enough support for this amendment, together with various court defeats, doomed the old malapportioned system so that today "one man-one vote" is the standard for all legislative chambers.

The third way in which the dominant party used districts to control challenges to its position was through unit voting. Several states adopted systems resembling the federal Electoral College so that the winner took all of a certain number of predetermined unit votes. Georgia enacted the county unit system in 1917 for its primaries for all statewide elected offices and Congress. Each county's total votes reflected the number of seats it had in the state house of representatives. The candidate who won a plurality of votes cast in a certain county would win all of that county's unit votes; the candidate who won a majority of the unit votes in the state received the nomination (which, for the Democratic candidate, was tantamount to being elected). In 1960, Fulton County (Atlanta) with a population of more than half a million had the same number of unit votes as three small rural counties with a combined population of less than 7000. Unit voting was also used in Maryland and was proposed in Tennessee in an attempt to check Boss Crump's control of the state Democratic Party from Nashville. Unit voting in state elections was one of the casualties of the Warren Court reapportionment decisions.[47]

Reapportionment has had a significant impact on the parties and legislatures. The party division has changed drastically in many state legislatures, and women, minorities, and other previously unrepresented and underrepresented groups began to be elected to these bodies. However, those who expected revolutionary changes in policy, giving greater advantages to the cities, have been disappointed, partly because city legislators have not been able to unite on various issues, whereas suburban and rural lawnmakers often think alike, especially when it comes to opposing central cities.

REFEREEING ELECTORAL CONTESTS

State electoral law is quite detailed and complicated. Each state's statutes regulating elections and parties are bound in a volume or volumes that may run to more than 500 pages in length. Some of these laws were intended to curb party excesses during the first two decades of this century. Some were written by the two major parties in an attempt to control their environment, specifically to eliminate potential competitors. A state's electoral code may confer electoral advantages on one party or the other, but almost never on third or minor parties or independent candidates.

Corruption has always been a troublesome part of American elections.[48] In New York City's mayoralty contest in 1824, the victorious Whigs were paying $22 a vote to noncommitted voters.[49] The great political machines of Frank Hague, James Curley, Ed Crump, Huey Long, and Tom Pendergast won not only because of their intensely loyal followers, but occasionally because of the timely stuffing of ballot boxes. "It ain't how the ballots go into the box that counts. Its how they come out."[50] Frank Hague's Jersey City machine intimidated, assaulted, arrested, and literally counted out its opposition in either party. "Hague voted dead people and repeaters. In one district, the number of voters was larger than the number registered to vote; and in a polling place where some Republicans were known to vote, the Democrats were recorded with 100 percent of the votes."[51] Voters in Chicago and a few other parts of the country today might appreciate the fortuitous "counting errors" the people in Jersey

City suffered for more than three decades. It should not be inferred that the well-known Democratic machines of Chicago, Memphis, and other cities have been stealing their electoral victories. Usually they had more than enough legal votes to retain power, but the pressure on political workers to produce large majorities sometimes resulted in voting irregularities. However, the increased utilization of voting machines, the use of impartial officials, and improved electoral procedures have eliminated many of the earlier election irregularities.[52]

Elections during the colonial period used oral voting. Needless to say, this form of voting did not lend itself to the most honest counting and was appropriate only in the smallest communities. In the early days of the Republic, each candidate printed his own distinctly colored ballot, and the voter often had to sign it before casting. Neither did the "ticket" ballot offer any anonymity to the person who wanted to keep his vote secret. Thus, a machine could purchase a vote and verify whether the seller had voted "correctly."

After 1890, the Australian ballot, which provided for secret elections, swept the United States. It has the following advantages: it is printed by the government; it contains the names of all authorized candidates for an office on the same sheet; and it is secret.[53] However, since a ballot box is "stuffable," voting machines have been gaining widespread acceptance across the nation since 1945. They were first introduced in the New York state elections of 1892, and by the mid-1960s more than one-half of all American voters were using voting machines. One of the machine's advantages is that a vote cannot be registered until the curtain has been closed and the selections made, and then the lever must be pulled to register the vote and open the curtain. The advantages of such voting are significant: there is less fraud; fewer officials are needed; and the totals can be tallied quickly. The main disadvantages are the cost of the machines, storing them between elections, and transporting them to and from the polls at election time.

Two new voting methods, punch card devices and optical scanning systems, promise to modernize voting even further.

> *Punch card voting devices employ ballots in the form of an IBM card or a booklet. These are fitted over a template or over locating pins, according to the device used. In one system, the voter uses a stylus to punch a hole in the space numbered to correspond with the number of the candidate. In another system, he moves a knob that will cause a hole to be punched mechanically next to the candidate's name on the ballot. The ballot is then removed from the voting position and is dropped in a ballot box. At the closing of the polls, the boxes are transported to a central counting station for computer tabulation.*[54]

This punch card device is quite inexpensive and easy to store; the disadvantages include its complexity, the small print used, multiple cards, transportation risks, and the need for professionally trained "counters." The optical scanning system of voting uses light sensitive scanners. One type uses a special fluorescent ink that is read under ultraviolet light. Oregon's Multnomah County (Portland) has such a system in which the voter uses a stamp containing a special ink to mark each voting decision. In the 1972 election, 5 of the 100 largest metropolitan areas used optical scanning systems, 16 employed punch card systems, 8 relied on paper ballots, and 71 continued with lever-type machines.[55]

BALLOTS AND VOTER INFORMATION SYSTEMS

On November 5, 1974, the voters of San Francisco confronted a ballot that could only be described as formidable in the number of decisions it asked the voter to make. Besides choosing among the candidates for a governor and other major state executive judicial, and legislative offices, each voter was asked to decide on 14 city and 17 state initiatives and referenda.

Ballot length is regulated exclusively by the state government, and it has reflected either of two basic philosophies of state government. The *long ballot* exemplifies the concept of the *responsible representative*; the idea is that all of the major state (and local) officials should be directly responsible to the electorate and thus directly elected. A state such as Washington regularly elects many statewide officials (including the Superintendent of Public Education, Public Lands Commissioner, and Insurance Commissioner). Ohio voters who participated in the state's Democratic primary had to select among 285 candidates those to be delegates or alternates to the party's national convention.[56] Supporters of short ballot argue that the federal ballot should serve as a model for state elections and that only the most important state officials should be elected by ballot. All other offices would be appointed by the governor. Four states (Alaska, Hawaii, Michigan, and New Jersey) use the short ballot; it exemplifies the executive leadership philosophy of state government. One consequence of the long ballot for the parties is that there is a noticeable falloff in voting going from the top of a ballot down.[57] Also, when a voter is faced with unfamiliar candidates for an obscure office, he tends to resort to familiar guideposts (for example, party label, presumed ethnic religious background, or even position on the ballot).[58]

Also, whether a state groups together on the ballot the candidates for an office by party or by office will affect the degree of straight party voting. Sixteen states use the office block ballot, which usually has no provision for straight party voting. Since party leaders do not like this type of ballot, they devised the party-column ballot in 1888 to facilitate party voting. This ballot, used by 34 states, groups the candidates of each party together under the name and symbol of their party. The parties have not been too successful in urging the adoption of the advantageous party straight ticket voting option, for 23 states still require separate votes for each candidate.[59]

A third type of ballot—the nonpartisan—theoretically operates against parties in general since it prohibits the use of party labels with candidates' names. Although it is used in only one state—Nebraska—on the state level, it is relatively common on the local level.

Another idea that emerged from the reform movement—nonpartisan elections—has become quite popular; at present, 61 percent of all cities whose population exceeds 5000 have banned party labels in local elections.[60] Without doubt, nonpartisan ballots represented an attempt to rid urban politics of the evil influence of political parties, and some cities succeeded beyond the reformers' wildest dreams. Some cities, though formally nonpartisan, are as party-dominated as ever (Chicago); in others, the parties share electoral functions with ad hoc citizen groups (Cincinnati, Albuquerque, and Wichita); some cities have substituted citizen groups for the parties, but they perform the same functions (Kansas City, Dallas, Fort Worth, Nashville); and some cities hold true nonpartisan elections.[61]

What effects do nonpartisan ballots have on the major parties? The weight of available data and the most recent and comprehensive studies indicate that a bias toward Republican candidates is built into the system. From a logical point of view, it seems that when all party labels disappear in a city, politics is likely to be dominated by organizationally talented businessmen and professionals who can be elected (even in a heavily Democratic city) if their political affiliation is hidden behind a cloak of nonpartisanship. In a 1973 study, Willis D. Hawley concluded: "In large cities the Republican bias of nonpartisanship is quite clear and that bias tends to increase as the population of the city and the proportion of low social-economic-status citizens increases."[62]

Absentee ballots are available to those who cannot vote in their districts on election day. This service began during the Civil War for the Union soldiers and was expanded during World War II and by the 1970 Voting Rights Act. The rules differ greatly from state to state as to who can apply and what conditions must be fulfilled in order to cast an absentee vote. Yet, one aspect of absentee voting seems quite clear—it usually favors Republican candidates. The complexity of the process, the need for farsighted planning, and the tendency of businessmen and travelers (often Republicans) to cast absentee votes leads to a majority of absentee votes being cast for Republican party candidates.

Write-in votes are usually intended as protest votes, or they are cast for such minor positions as precinct committeemen or local party offices. Only a couple of times have write-in votes been significant at the national level. Henry Cabot Lodge's huge write-in vote in the 1964 New Hampshire presidential primary helped propel him into that year's presidential race, and Strom Thurmond was elected to the U.S. Senate in 1954 with a write-in vote of more than 143,000.[63]

Several states try to help their voters understand the prevailing election system, the candidates and their viewpoints, the ballot propositions, and even how to cast a vote. California, Washington, and Oregon publish a special voters' pamphlet for each state election giving arguments for and against each ballot proposition, biographies and statements by each candidate (including the minor party candidates!), and information on the voting system or ballots being used. This service to the voters appears to be well worth the cost. These states as well as several others also print sample ballots and voter guides/pamphlets in various languages, particularly Spanish.[64]

Election Disputes

Although the state and federal constitutions specify that each legislative body shall be the final judge as to who shall be seated in election disputes, most of these conflicts are settled by the state election commission or the courts. Bipartisan election boards often have the final say in cases of disputed ballots in close elections. As usual, minor or third parties have no representation on these crucial boards.

Urban political machines tried to ensure their electoral strength in the early part of this century by controlling the election board. A more contemporary example has been the Chicago machine, which has had close ties with the Chicago Election Board.

> It has never happened, but if an independent somehow managed to build an organization big and enthusiastic enough to find seventy thousand independent voters who will sign his petition, he would probably need an extra thirty thousand signatures to be sure of getting it past the Chicago Election Board, which runs the city's elections and rules on the validity of nominating petitions. Names can be ruled invalid for anything short of failing to dot an "i." An illiterate's "X" might be acceptable on a Machine candidate's petition, but the Election Board is meticulous about those of anybody else. The Board used to be run by a frank old rogue, Sidney Holzman, who summed up its attitude toward the aspirations of independents, Republicans, and other foreigners: "We throw their petitions up to the ceiling and those that stick are good."[65]

Of course, not all election boards are this partisan, but interesting coincidences do occur. In the 1974 New Hampshire race for U.S. Senator, the Republican Louis Wyman was declared the winner on election night; the Democrat, John Durkin, led after the recount by 10 votes; the Republican-dominated state Ballot Law Commission then reviewed 400 contested ballots and found that Wyman had won by 2 votes. Since the U.S. Senate was unable to decide which claims were valid, New Hampshire rushed a special provision through its legislature for a new election, which was won by the Democrat, John Durkin.[66] Other recent elections on the federal and state levels have ultimately been decided by the courts, which ordered, for example, a new election in Louisiana's 1976 congressional race.[67]

State governments are under increased pressure to provide for the responsible administration of elections. Most states vest legal responsibility in the office of the secretary of state or the lieutenant governor, but, in effect, most election problems are handled by local officials. The most pressing need is to find how politicians can make impartial decisions on electoral disputes, which carry such significance for the state's major parties. Perhaps the courts offer the best chance for honest, impartial decision-making.

We have examined these details of the American electoral system because they significantly affect the operations and fortunes of our political parties. The rules of the party game are manipulated by the various players to gain electoral advantage, for they have a vested interest in the outcome of the game. The electoral laws that define parties, apportion legislative districts, and draw district boundaries are used by the two major parties to preserve and protect their advantages.

> *In the state of Ohio the ballot has been changed six times during the twentieth century, and in each case the Republican majority tried to gain an advantage for itself by tampering with the election machinery. In 1940 Governor Bricker tried to avoid the influence of F.D.R.'s coattails by calling a special session of the legislature which approved a separation of the ballot carrying national races from the one on which state and local races appeared.* [68]

Delaware followed Ohio's example in 1941 for the same reason, and in 1949 Ohio changed its ballot from party column to office group in order to help Senator Robert A. Taft build his vote count. [69]

It should be noted that American parties manipulate the details of the election law rather than the main structures (such as the U.S. Constitution). Other countries, however, sometimes abandon their whole system of government simply in order to gain political advantage. Perhaps the current trend toward federal financing of presidential campaigns will rank with the adoption of primary elections as one of the most significant reforms of American electoral laws. Hugh Bone has written that many laws were intended for no other purpose than to ensure the advantage of the current majority party and they appear to be working well in terms of achieving this objective. [70]

SUFFRAGE: THE 200-YEAR-OLD BATTLE TO BE ALLOWED TO PLAY THE GAME

Ratification of the Twenty-sixth Amendment to the United States Constitution in 1971 culminated a 200-year debate over who should comprise the American electorate. [71] By the 1972 general election, America had almost universal suffrage for the first time. Prior to 1972 there had been persistant (and often ingenious) attempts to restrict the number and types of people who could participate in the great political game.

Many of the American colonies restricted suffrage in ways that might seem unbelievable to us today. [72] Some colonies imposed religious tests: New York barred Jews and Catholics from voting until 1777. Although most religious tests were abandoned at the end of the Revolution, Rhode Island did not end electoral discrimination against Jews until 1842. [73] Most of the early voting restrictions were based on income or property qualifications. Normally, voters were required to own estate in land, often with stipulations as to the size or income yield. This practice effectively excluded all who rented or leased property in the colonies, with the exception of New York and Virginia, which allowed those with lifetime leases to vote. [74] Connecticut, for example, required a prospective voter to have land that produced an income equivalent to at least 40 shillings a year. After independence, most states continued the colonial requirement of land ownership or minimum income for voting. Four of the original 13 states had landowning requirements, but they specified certain levels of income: New Jersey—50 pounds clear estate; Georgia—ownership of 10 pounds of taxable property or engagement in any "mechanic trade;"[75] and Pennsylavnia and New Hampshire established poll or other public tax payments.[76] The only state to enact universal manhood suffrage before the adoption of the U.S. Constitution was Vermont in 1777.

Because of the various suffrage restrictions, only 120,000 people were eligible to vote out of a total free population of more than 2 million immediately after the Revolutionary War.[77] However, since most of the laws were only loosely enforced due to a general attitude of indifference, it is claimed that more than half of the free men in the new nation could have voted if they wanted to. Apparently, most of them didn't care to vote in the presidential election of 1804: only 23,320 of Pennsylvania's 600,000 total state population voted—less than 3.9 percent of the total adult male population. Even as late as 1828, only 9 percent of the adult male population voted for president. Gradually the property requirements were eased during the first quarter of the nineteenth century. By 1812 both property and tax qualifications had been eliminated in Vermont, Maryland, South Carolina, Georgia, and New Hampshire. Until 1826 New York continued to have dual voting requirements: an income of 20 pounds for assembly voting, and an income of 100 pounds to vote for state senator and governor. Basically, the property and wealth requirements did not accord with the growing preference in America for nonclass access to the ballot. As Peirce has noted, four factors contributed toward the broadening of the franchise in the 1820s and 1830s:

1. The emerging political parties were hungry for new supporters and sought to make many previously disfranchised citizens eligible.
2. Western states that needed labor offered the vote as an inducement to workers to go west.
3. The propertyless exerted pressure for access to the ballot.
4. The new states that entered the Union from 1800 to 1823 tended not to require property qualifications in order to vote, thereby establishing a precedent.[78]

By 1850 the United States had achieved universal white manhood suffrage, and the adoption of the Fifteenth Amendment (1870) extended suffrage to former Negro slaves and prohibited voter discrimination on the basis of race.[79] The states retained the right to establish voter qualifications so long as they did not discriminate against blacks. With the end of Reconstruction in the South, the white-controlled Southern governments sought to rescind the voting rights of blacks. Various legal methods of disfranchisement were instituted, including the white primary. In these post-Reconstruction years the Democratic Party became dominant in the South, so that winning the Democratic monination was tantamount to victory. The whites moved to exclude blacks from the meaningful election—the Democratic primary—allowing them to vote in the nearly meaningless general election. Southern state legislatures declared the Democratic Party a private club and provided that only whites could participate in its primary election.[80] Thus, blacks could not vote in any meaningful sense of the word until 1944, when the Supreme Court declared (in *Smith* v. *Allwright*) that the white primary violated the Fifteenth Amendment.[81]

Other devices that served to restrict black voting (primarily in the South) included the use of lengthy, complicated registration forms; the rejection of many black applications due to minor "errors;" the use of poll taxes; the delay of up to 2 weeks in publishing the names of new voters in the local newspapers; and the use of literacy tests which often prevented college-educated blacks from registering when they failed to interpret complex legal documents "properly."[82] The combined effect of these devices was to disfranchise many thousands of American citizens from the most significant access point in Southern politics—the Democratic Party primary—and to preserve white control of Southern political systems through the Democratic Party.

Following the outlawing of the white primary in 1944, Southern blacks steadily increased their voting registration as follows: 5 percent in the 1940s, 20 percent in 1952, 25 percent in 1956, 28 percent in 1960, and 39 percent in 1964.[83] These registration increases were mainly of urban blacks. In the mid-1960s a series of federal civil rights acts effectively eliminated many of the registration and voting obstacles in the South. The Civil Rights Act of 1964 made it unlawful for registrars to apply unequal standards in registration procedures or to reject applications because of minor errors. The Twenty-fourth Amendment, ratified in 1964, outlawed the poll tax for national elections, and in 1965 the Supreme Court barred it from state and local elections as well. Despite these reforms, Southern registrars still used long lunch hours, delays, and shortages of registraton forms to minimize black registration. The Voting Rights Act of 1965, which provided for federal registrars in the South, facilitated the black registration; by 1970 65 percent of the eligible Southern blacks were registered, as compared with 70 percent of the eligible Southern whites. Increased black registration in the South enabled blacks to win election victories, and by 1974 there were 85 black state house members and 10 black state senators.[85]

Women were generally prohibited from voting in Colonial America with the two exceptions of Massachusetts (1691-1780) and New Jersey (1776-1807). Usually they were denied suffrage because they legally could not own property and they could not meet a legal requirement to vote. In 1848, the women's suffrage movement was launched and gained great publicity under the leadership of Susan B. Anthony and Virginia L. Minor in the 1870s. After losing a United States Supreme Court case in 1875, women shifted their cause to the state level and Wyoming and Utah territories granted the vote to women in 1869-1870. Opposition to extending suffrage to women came from the party machines, corporations, and liquor interests. Additional states granted suffrage to women in the 1910s, and in 1920, the Nineteenth Amendment of the U.S. Constitution was ratified—in time for women to participate in the presidential election of that year.

Since the mid-1960s the main voting rights issues have been extending the vote to 18-to-20-year-olds and correcting the more restrictive residency rules. Before 1970 only three states (Georgia, Kentucky, and Alaska) allowed 18-to-20-year-olds to vote.[84] The pressures of the Vietnam war and the fact that 18-year-old men were subject to the draft reduced the resistance of those who opposed a voting age of 18. In another example of how the federal government can coerce the states into adopting policies that they have rejected many times, the Voting Rights Act of 1970 extended suffrage to 18-to-20-year-olds in federal elections regardless of state law, abolished residency requirements of more than 30 days for federal elections, and suspended all literacy tests. The Twenty-sixth Amendment formalized the 18-year-old vote, and because of the impracticality of maintaining separate registration books for federal and state elections, most states quickly adopted the amendments.

VOTER REGISTRATION REQUIREMENTS IN THE 1970s
Of all Western democratic nations, the United States consistently has the lowest voter turnout for national elections. Since the end of World War II France and Great Britain have had average voter turnouts of more than 80 percent. Canada (76 percent), Austria (95 percent), West Germany (86 percent), and Australia (98 percent) have almost phenomenal voter turnouts. Australia's high figure reflects its compulsory voting law, which provides for easy voting procedures and imposes a penalty for unexcused non-voting. Voting turnouts in the United States for the five recent presidential elections have been as follows:

Year	Percent
1960	63
1964	62
1968	61
1972	56
1976	54

Why does the United States (in comparison with other Western democracies) have such low voter turnouts? Could it be due to growing apathy among American voters? Could there be some factor that is unique in the American electoral system? Phillips and Bluckman have argued that the low American voter turnout is mostly a result of political and socioeconomic/cultural factors found within the American political system. The lack of ideological, and class tnesions, the heterogeneity of our society, the specific mixture of ethnic groups in the United States, many of which have a history of low participation votes in politics, and the general American apathy toward politics all contribute toward the reduction in American voting percentages. Many political observers and American electoral officials have pointed to difficulties and obstacles in the American system of voter registration, and the passivity of the American government.[85]

Responsibility rests almost entirely with the individual citizen to register to vote in the United States. A citizen who wishes to vote must seek out a registrar, establish his eligibility, and over a period of years maintain his eligibility. He may lose his eligibility merely by changing his address within the same voting district. Also, in many states, a citizen loses the right to vote if he fails to vote during a certain period of time or number of elections (see Table 3.4). South Carolina requires re-registration every 10 years no matter how many times the citizen has voted. Millions have been deprived of their right to vote because they failed to vote in two consecutive general elections.[86] California registrars removed 3.5 million names, a total of 36 percent of the total state electorate, from the registered voter rolls because they did not vote in the 1974 general election. Although the Voting Rights Act of 1970 helped to ease the long residency requirements in a state, county, or district (now 30 days are normal), more than 47 million people in 1976 were eligible to vote but were not registered. While America leaves nearly all of the responsibility to the individual voter, the Canadian government arranges for house-to-house canvassing and reports that 98 percent of those eligible to vote are registered.[87]

Of course, with our federal system, there is no attempt to ensure uniform state voter registration laws. South Dakota is the only state that has no voter registration system—the voters simply establish their eligibility at the polls. Election statistics from South Dakota indicate that its voting records are slightly better than the national average. Parts of Ohio and Wisconsin do not require registration. Some states have tried to make it easier for citizens to register; Oregon has a system of deputy registrars, and Texas, New Jersey, and Minnesota have mail registration programs.[88] In spite of everything, there seems to be a limit to what individual initiative will accomplish. A University of California study reported that the presidential election turnout would increase by more than 10 percent (or 15 million new voters) if there were easier registration practices. The largest increases would be among minority groups, Southerners, and those with low levels of education.[89] The study concluded that registration is no longer handicapped by the crude methods of the not-so-distant past, but by the registrars' irregular hours, periodic purges of the voter lists, and above all, the early cutoff dates. Arizona and Georgia, for example, permit no registration within 50 days of an election—exactly the time when interest in elections in beginning to pick up. Many other states cut off registration 30 days before the election.

Governmental canvassing before general elections might solve most of the above-mentioned problems. The most significant reason why it has not been undertaken here is the tremendous cost. It has been estimated that such canvassing in a presidential election year might cost $50 million, or 50 cents per voter.[90] This cost is difficult to evaluate because we do not know how much the present piecemeal systems of registration cost.

CONCLUSIONS

American political parties operate within the constraints of state electoral law. These laws do not affect all political actors impartially, but confer advantages upon certain established participants and disadvantages upon newer political organizations. The rules of the game have tended to preserve and protect the political privileges long

Table 3.4 Voter Registration Cancellation for Failure to Vote

State	Failure to Vote	Voter Notified
Alaska	4 years	yes
Arizona	last general election	yes
Arkansas	4 years	yes
California	last general election	yes
Colorado	last general election	yes
Delaware	2 consecutive general elections	yes
Georgia	3 years	yes
Hawaii	general election	no
Idaho	4 years	no
Illinois	4 years	yes
Indiana	2 years	yes
Iowa	4 years	yes
Kentucky	last general election	yes
Louisiana	4 years	yes
Maryland	5 years	yes
Michigan	6 years	yes
Minnesota	4 years	yes
Montana	last presidential election	yes
Nevada	last general election	no
New Jersey	4 years	some cases
New Mexico	2 general elections	yes
New York	2 years	yes
North Carolina	4 years	yes
Ohio	4 years	yes
Oklahoma	2 years	yes
Oregon	if voter pamphlet undelivered	yes
Pennsylvania	2 years	yes
Rhode Island	5 years	yes
South Carolina	2 years	yes
South Dakota	4 years	yes
Tennessee	4 years	yes
Texas	3 years	yes
Virginia	4 years	no
Washington	30 months	yes
West Virginia	2 general elections	yes
Wisconsin	2 years	yes
Wyoming	last general election	yes
District of Columbia	4 years	yes

Source: League of Women Voters, *Registration and Absentee Voting Procedures by State 1974* (Washington, D.C.: 1978).

enjoyed by the organizations. The most significant protected advantage is the parties' near-monopoly of access to the state's ballot. Increasingly, the American political parties' chief raisons d'être are the label they offer a candidate, the candidate's subsequent ease of getting on a ballot, and the narrowing of a voter's choices to a reasonable number.

Even the small details of state election laws carry political impact. Statutes that regulate the type of ballot, election district size and boundaries, and availability of absentee ballots usually benefit one or both major parties. The dominant political party often manipulates election details in order to gain further political advantages.

Another aspect of the rules of the electoral game regulates the number and the nature of the players—the voters. While America presently has nearly universal adult suffrage, registration requirements still exclude millions of potential voters from their right to vote.

FOOTNOTES

1. E.E. Schattschneider, *Party Government* (New York: Farrar and Rinehart, 1942), p. 124.

2. In 1970 there were 508,720 elected local officials and 13,038 elected state officials in the United States. These included 74,199 county; 143,927 municipal, 129,603 township, 107,663 school, and 56,943 special district officials. Chester G. Atkins, *Getting Elected* (Boston: Houghton, Mifflin, 1973), p. xii.

3. *American Jurisprudence* (San Francisco: Brancroft Whitney, 1966), p. 697.

4. Ibid., p. 800.

5. See *Cunningham* v. *Cokely*, 79 WV60, 90SE 546.

6. Ohio Revised Code, Sections 3501.01, 3517.00.

7. Oregon Revised Statutes 280.010.

8. Revised Code of Washington, 29.01.090.

9. Daniel A. Mazmanian, *Third Parties in Presidential Elections* (Washington, D.C.: Brookings, 1974), p. 88.

10. Ibid., p. 89.

11. Ibid., p. 91.

12. Ibid.

13. Kennth C. MacKay, The Progressive Movement of 1924 (New York: Octogon, 1966), pp. 179-183.

14. From *Illinois Annotated Statutes*, Chapter 46. "Elections," Section 386, enacted May 11, 1943. The California "subversive party" clause is also worded to include any type of subversive activities: No party shall be recognized or qualified to participate in any primary election which either directly or indirectly carries on, advocates, teaches, justifies, aids, or abets the overthrow of the U.S. or state government by unlawful means; or which directly or indirectly carries on, advocates, teaches, justifies, aids, or abets a program of sabotage, force or violence, sedition or treason against the U.S. or state government. *California Annotated Codes*, Section 6431.

15. Mazmanian, op. cit., p. 96.

16. Illinois Annotated Statutes 10-1, Revised 1974.

17. New York Election Law 1-422.

18. *Pennsylvania Law Journal*, Vol. 2, 1971, p. 433.

19. Richard Claude, *The Supreme Court and the Electoral Process* (Baltimore: John Hopkins Press, 1970), p. 240. For a new party in Ohio to gain access to the ballot, it had to: (1) collect signatures on a petition equaling more than 15 percent of the total vote in the previous gubernatorial election; (2) elect a state central committee with two members for each congressional district and establish a county central committee for each county in the state;

(3) elect delegates and alternates at the primary election to a national convention, and these persons must not have voted as a member of a different party during the preceding *4 years*; and (4) make sure that the nominating petitions were signed by "qualified electors" not linked with an established party (that is, those who had never voted before!).

20. *Williams* v. *Rhodes* 393 U.S. 23 (1968). In 1972 Ohio reduced the requirement for signatures on a nominating petition from 15 percent of those voting in the previous gubernatorial election to 7 percent and moved the filing date up to 90 days before the election day. New York State also changed its rules for petition signatures from 12,000 with at least 50 from each county to 20,000 with at least 100 in each of half the number of congressional districts. Mazmanian, op. cit., p. 99.

21. With these liberal ballot-access laws, Washington state in the 1972 general election had, in addition to the Republican and Democratic parties, presidential and vice-presidential candidates running under the labels of the Independent, Socialist Labor, Communist, Peoples, Socialist Workers, and Libertarian parties.

22. General Statutes of North Carolina, Section 163-122.

23. Mazmanian, op. cit., p. 95.

24. The California Election Code (Section 6430) states that if a party's candidate for any statewide office gets 2 percent of the entire vote; or if 1 percent of the entire statewide vote register as members of that party; or if that party collects petitions totaling 10 percent of the last statewide vote, that party can remain on the ballot for the next general election. In 1974, the Peace and Freedom Party candidate for lieutenant governor won 2.5 percent of the total vote; the AIP candidate for secretary of state received 3.4 percent, the treasurer received 4.6 percent, and the controller 3.7 percent. Furthermore, if a party's percentage of the state registered voters drops below 1/15 of 1 percent, it loses its place on the ballot and is deemed to have been abandoned by the voters.

25. Ernest Patterson, *Black City Politics* (New York: Dodd, Mead, 1974), pp. 76-77.

26. For excellent thumbnail descriptions of each state's pattern of politics, elected officials, and recent election results, see M. Barone, G. Ujifusa, and P. Matthews, *The Almanac of American Politics—1978* (Boston: Gambit, 1977).

27. For a more detailed discussion on the Illinois system of cumulative vote, see Charles W. Dunn, "Cumulative Voting in Illinois Legislative Elections," *Harvard Journal on Legislation 9*, No. 4 (May 1972), p. 627ff. See also George S. Blair, *Cumulative Voting* (Urbana: University of Illinois Press, 1960); J. Sawyer and Duncan MacRae, Jr., "Game Theory and Cumulative Voting in Illinois: 1902-1954," *American Political Science Review LVI* (1962), pp. 936-946; James Kuklinski, "Cumulative and Plurality Voting: An Analysis of Illinois' Unique Election System," *Western Political Quarterly XXVI*, No. 4 (1973), pp. 726-746.

28. Ronald H. McDonald, "Electoral Systems, Party Representation, and Political Change in Latin America," *Western Political Quarterly XX*, No. 3 (1967), pp. 694-708.

29. Gordon Smith, "Party Systems," *Politics in Western Europe* (New York: Holmes and Meier, 1972), pp. 80-91.

30. For the best summary of each of several types of electoral systems used around the world, see Douglas W. Rae, *The Political Consequences of Electoral Law* (New Haven: Yale University Press, 1971). See also Enid Lakeman, *Nine Democracies: Electoral Systems of the Countries of the European Community* (London: Arthur McDougall Fund, 1973).

31. Ibid., pp. 42-44.

32. Patterson, op. cit., p. 75.

33. This section draws heavily on the best article on New York City's experience with proportional representation, Hugh Bone and Belle Zeller, "The Repeal of P.R. in New York City—Ten Years in Retrospect," *American Political Science Review XLII*, No. 4 (1948), pp. 1127-1148.

34. Joseph F. Zimmerman, "A Proportional Representation System and New York City School Boards," *National Civic Review LXIII*, No. 9 (1974), p. 472.

35. Ibid., p. 493.

36. Rae, op. cit., p. 145.

37. The term "gerrymander" comes from a salamander-shaped congressional district constructed in Massachusetts while Elbridge Gerry was governor. A racial gerrymander was overturned by the Supreme Court in *Gomillion* v. *Lightfoot*, 364 U.S. 399 (1960). In Tuskegee, Alabama, a 28-sided piece of territory had been detached from the city specifically to weaken the political power of Tuskegee Institute and certain black voters by placing them outside the city limits and to assure white control of the city. The court forbade this action on the ground that the right to vote in city elections had been denied on account of race.

38. Walter Karp, *Indispensable Enemies* (Baltimore: Penguin, 1974), p. 32

39. *Noun* v. *Turner*, 196 N.W., 2nd 209 (1972).

40. *Ferrell* v. *Oklahoma*, 339 F., Suppl. 73 (1971). The problem of multimember districts has been examined within the framework of equal votes and gerrymandering. In the 1972 election, 27 states used multimember districts for their lower legislative chamber and 15 used them for their senates. Of those previously using multimember districts, 9 states and 5 state houses returned to single member districts in 1972. In Mississippi and Texas, large multimember districts (12-18 seats each) were struck down by the court, which ordered them to be redrawn. Such districts had practically reached their ultimate limit in Cleveland in 1958, when 116 candidates entered the Democratic Party primary in one legislative district, Council of State Governments, *Reapportionment in the Seventies* (Lexington, KY.: Council of State Governments, 1973).

41. Neal R. Peirce, *Government and Politics in the American South* (New York: Norton, 1972), p. 326. This is but one volume in Peirce's series of studies of each major region of the nation; it is extremely valuable for pointing out the historical political patterns in each state.

42. *Colegrove* v. *Green*, 328 U.S. 549 (1946).

43. *Baker* v. *Carr*, 369 U.S. 186 (1962).

44. *Reynolds* v. *Sims*, 377 U.S. 533 (1964).

45. Ibid.

46. *Whitecomb* v. *Chavis*, 403 U.S. 124 (1971).

47. Peirce, op. cit., p. 314, In 1946 Eugene Talmadge won the Democratic nomination for governor in Georgia although he was second in the popular vote. *Gray* v. *Saunders*, 372 U.S. 368 (1963).

48. Among the favorite illegal practices favored by the machine were padding registration books, substituting election officials, failing to initial the ballots of hostile voters, short-pencilling, double marking, making errors in transposing totals, substituting ballots, stuffing ballot boxes, following irregular voting and recount procedures, and initiating violence. John Landesco, "The Gangster and the Politician," in *Organized Crime in Chicago* (Chicago: University of Chicago Press, 1968), pp. 183-189.

49. George Thayer, *Who Shakes the Money Tree?* (New York: Simon and Schuster, 1973), p. 29.

50. Alfred Steinberg, *The Bosses* (New York: Macmillan, 1973), p. 40.

51. Ibid., p. 37.

52. Hugh Bone, *American Politics and the Party System* (New York: McGraw Hill, 1971), p. 459.

53. Council of State Governments, *Modernizing Election Systems* (Lexington, Ky.: Council of State Governments, 1973), p. 30.

54. *Modernizing Election Systems*, op. cit., pp. 30-31.

55. *Modernizing Election Systems*, op. cit., p. 31.

56. Office of Federal Elections, *A Study of Election Difficulties in Representative American Jurisdictions: Final Report* (Washington: U.S. General Accounting Office, 1973), pp. v-12.

57. In Washington State the falloff from the number of votes cast for president to the that for Superintendent of Public Instruction was more than 27 percent during the 1908-1956 era. Yet in South Dakota it was only 16.6 percent. Bone, *American Politics and the Party System*, op. cit., p. 469.

58. Smart politicians have used ballot positions to gain extra votes because Americans tend to vote for the first name that appears on the candidates' list for a particular office. To counter this tendency, about half of the states include a provision in their election code for rotating the various candidates' names on the ballots. The other half have more arbitrary means for deciding which name to list first. The Council of State Governments recommends ending the rotation system because it is complicated and expensive. *Modernizing Election Systems*, op. cit., p. 25.

59. Bone, *American Politics*, op. cit., p. 465.

60. Willis P. Hawley, *Non-Partisan Elections and the Case for Party Politics* (New York: Wiley, 1973), p. 16.

61. Charles R. Adrain, "A Typology for Non-Partisan Elections," *Western Political Quarterly XII*, No. 2 (1959), pp. 449-458. See also Heinz Eulau, Betty Zisk, and K. Prewitt, "Latent Partisanship in Non-Partisan Elections," in *The Electoral Process* edited by M. Kent Jennings and L.H. Ziegler (Englewood Cliffs, N.J.: Prentice-Hall, 1966), pp. 208-237; A.C. Hagensick, "Influences of Partisanship and Incumbency in a Nonpartisan Election System," *Western Political Quarterly XVII*, No. 1 (1964), pp. 117-124; and Chester B. Rogers and H.D. Arman, "Non Partisanship and Election to City Office," *Social Science Quarterly LI*, No. 1 (1971), pp. 941-945.

62. Hawley, op. cit., p. 98.

63. Bone, *American Politics*, op. cit., p. 463.

64. *State Government News*, December 1974. Spanish-language voting aids or pamphlets were found in Washington, California, Arizona, Pennsylvania, Connecticut, New Mexico, New York City, New Jersey, and Kansas.

65. Mike Royko, *Boss* (New York: New American Library, 1971), pp. 76-77.

66. Associated Press release, January 15, 1975, "Seat Dispute Flares in Senate."

67. Associated Press release, January 8, 1977, "GOP Claims Victory in Louisiana."

68. Jack Walker, "Ballot Forms and Voter Fatigue: An Analysis of Office Block and Party Column Ballots," *Midwest Journal of Political Science X* (1966), pp. 448-449.

69. V. O. Key, *Politics, Parties, and Pressure Groups* (New York: Crowell, 1952), p. 654.

70. Bone, *American Politics*, op. cit., p. 470.

71. The Twenty-sixth Amendment simply reads: "The right of citizens of the United States, who are 18 years of age or older, to vote shall not be denied or abridged by the United States or by any state on account of age." (Its ratification was completed June 30, 1971).

72. This section draws heavily on Neal R. Peirce's excellent study on the Electoral College and suffrage, *The People's President* (New York: Clarion, 1968), especially Chapter 7, "The Right to Vote in America," pp. 205-252.

73. Dudley O. McGovney, *The American Suffrage Medley* (Chicago: University of Chicago Press, 1949), pp. 13-16.

74. Chilton Williamson, *American Suffrage from Property to Democracy* (Princeton, N.J.: Princeton University Press, 1960), p. 12.

75. This liberal law was repealed in 1789.

76. Peirce, *The People's President*, op. cit., p. 207.

77. William Miller, *A New History of the United States* (1958) quoted in Peirce, *The People's President*, op. cit., pp. 208-209.

78. Peirce, Ibid., pp. 210-211.

79. Thomas Dye, *Politics in States and Communities*, 2nd ed. (Englewood Cliffs, N.J.: (Prentice-Hall, 1973), p. 75.

80. "In most of these states, preservation of the primary's racial 'purity' was left to the party itself. Texas, however, sought to guarantee this system, and in 1923 passed a statute that prohibited blacks from voting in any Democratic Party primary. An early challenge was dismissed, *Chandler* v. *Neff*, 298 F. 515 (W.D. Tex. 1924), when the judge ruled primary elections not elections within the meaning of the 15th Amendment and the question was a political not a legal question. The Supreme Court invalidated this law in 1927 in *Nixon* v. *Herndon*, 273 U.S. 536 (1927)." Source: "The Application of Constitutional Provisions to Political Parties," *Tennessee Law Review XL*, No. 2 (1973), pp. 217-234.

81. *Smith* v. *Allwright*, 131 F 2nd 593 (5th Cir, 1942). The many white primary court cases settled the issue once and for all that persons cannot be excluded from the elective process at any stage where a final decision is actually made.

82. Dye, op. cit., p. 76.

83. Ibid., p. 75.

84. Georgia in 1944 was the first to allow 18-year-olds to vote.

85. K. Phillips and P. Blackman, *Electoral Reform and Voter Participation*, (Washington, D.C.: American Enterprise Institute, 1975), Chapter 4. For an excellent discussion of the major weakness of American registration and voting law, see *Modernizing Election Systems*, op. cit., pp. 25-26; and Peirce, *The People's President*, op. cit., pp. 231-232.

86. The right of the state to purge its voters' registration list for failure to vote has been upheld by the courts as within a state's proper administrative role. See Citizen Committee for Recall of *Joseph Willar* v. *Marston*, 109 ARI 18V 507.

87. *Modernizing Election Systems*, op. cit., p. 11.

88. Minnesota and New Jersey used their mail registration system for the first time in the 1974 general elections, and both experienced a sharp increase in registration with virtually no evidence of fraud. Minnesota allowed a very flexible system of registration at the polls on election day if the prospective voter had lived in the state for at least 20 days. What evidence was acceptable? A driver's license or other valid state document, or an affidavit from another

voter in the same precinct that the prospective voter was a resident of that precinct. Salt Lake City *Desert News*, January 1, 1975, "Registration by Mail."

89. Tom Wicker, *New York Times*, October 17, 1976.

90. The President's Commission on Registration and Voting Participation, *Report on Registration and Voting Participation* (Washington, D.C.: U.S. Government Printing Office, 1963).

Most conservatives would probably agree with Kevin Phillips that the 7 or 8 million new voters who would be able to and would vote are not worth the cost and the dangers posed by federal intervention in this area of state rights—voter registration. Furthermore, almost all of the new voters would be liberal or radical in their voting patterns. See Kevin Phillips and Paul H. Blackman, *Electoral Reform and Voter Participation*.

4
The Decline of the Party Organization: Structure, Machines, Competition, and Nomination Procedures

On paper American political parties appear to be formidable organizations, hierarchically organized with many levels of interlocking committees and culminating in a national committee with a national party chairman. In reality, however, the party organizations more accurately resemble a Hollywood movie set with the public side of party politics appearing quite healthy and stable, while the unseen side is held up by slender and decaying supports. The 1976 Republican Party national convention is a case in point. Vigorous, exciting, well organized, but the dry rot that infests the party could not be seen because of the temporary sets. Others remember the power of the old urban machine and conjure up contemporary images of powerful local party organizations, but nothing could be further from the truth today.

In this chapter, the weak underpinnings of our party organizations will be examined, together with those factors that helped to produce such conditions. Weak organizations can continue to flourish when there is no vigorous competition between the major parties as in the one-party states or even in the so-called two-party states. In some states, such as California, weak party organizations have been the inevitable result of a systematic and largely successful attack on the parties, beginning with the Progressive Movement in the early part of this century. The vitality of party organizations is also related to whether the organizations having meaningful tasks to accomplish. Increasingly, the parties are losing their two essential functions (nominating and campaigning) to a host of competitors, and the net result is a further deterioration of the parties' organizational strength.

Party Structure: From Grassroots to National Committees
Grassroots political organization in the United States means precinct politics. In our approximately 178,000 precincts, or voting districts, representatives of the two major parties serve as precinct captains, committeemen, or chairmen. Precinct party leaders are usually chosen either by election in the primaries or by precinct caucuses. If the

caucus system is used, the post of precinct chairman often means being a delegate to county and state conventions. In Utah, for example, state law requires that each voting district elect a chairman, vice chairman, secretary, treasurer, and several other committeemen. Frequently, there are not enough people at a caucus to fill all of these posts, but everyone realizes that it really doesn't matter because as soon as the meeting is over, all of the elected party officials will quickly forget that they were ever legal party functionaries. In those states that elect their precinct leaders in primaries, it is common knowledge that an individual with a handful of friends can put together a machine to secure the position with a 5 to 4 or 8 to 6 majority. Many, if not most, of the nation's positions for precinct party chairmen go unfilled, and thousands of such positions have names filled in on some organization chart in a county party office, but the party has great difficulty finding grassroots leaders when the nitty-gritty work of politics must be done.[1] So, the party's grassroots are usually more grass than roots and reflect the fundamental weaknesses that haunt our parties right up to the top.

If there is a level where the parties have shown some organizational strength, it would have to be at the county level.[2] Rural American political machines were often based on county courthouse patronage. The most effective urban machines were usually countywide organizations that controlled county patronage based on the pluralities accumulated by the central city strongholds. As reforms commonly made city elections nonpartisan, the county became the lowest level of partisan politics. Thus, while city mayors and councilmen are elected on a nonpartisan ballot, county executives and such other officials as clerks, attorneys, and sheriffs are elected on Republican or Democratic tickets. However, it should be noted that for every relatively effective county party organization, there are dozens that have almost no organization at all. The party county central committee is often an unwieldy body whose responsibility is to provide leadership in county politics. But since these county central committees are usually composed of all the precinct chairmen in the county, these committees may have hundreds of members.[3]

State party organizations are closely regulated by state law. All states have some type of state committee which varies greatly in terms of composition, selection processes, and numbers. Some state committees have only a few dozen members, while others may approach California's 1500-member state Republican committee. The effectiveness of a state party committee depends upon whether the party can be competitive in at least some regions of the state, if not on a statewide basis. Seldom can one talk about a statewide party, for usually even in the most competitive states, parties are made up of a few effective county organizations that dominate the state committee and elect the state party chairman. Large, competitive states tend to have full-time, professional party leadership and staff at the state level, while smaller, competitive and noncompetitive states have nonprofessional, part-time leadership and sometimes little or no staff.[4] Little has changed since James MacGregor Burns gave his evaluation of the effectiveness of state party organizations (1963):

> *At no level, except in a handful of industrial states, do state parties have the attributes of organization. . . . Most of the state parties are at best mere jousting grounds for embattled politicians; at worst they simply do not exist, as in the case of the Republicans in the rural South or Democrats in the rural Midwest.* [5]

The very top of our party structures also tends to be weak and disorganized. The Democrats have had a national committee and chairman since 1848, and Republicans have had them since 1856. Until 1972, the national committees have usually been composed of a man and woman from each state. But demands for greater representation have compelled the Democrats, in particular, to expand the size and nature of the representation on their national committee. At the present time the DNC membership was made up of the following:

104 Opposite-sex pairs from the 50 states, the District of Columbia, and Puerto Rico.
200 Apportioned on the basis of delegate allocations to the national convention. Thus, states that elect Democrats to major offices are rewarded.
 31 Awarded to significant party groups, that is, the Democratic Governors Conference, Young Democrats, Democratic Mayors Conference.
 <u>**25**</u> Chosen at large by the above 335 DNC members. [6]
360 members

DNC members are elected for 4-year terms that span the period from one national nominating convention to the next. National committeemen and women are usually quite powerless, and the post is usually given to a party member in recognition for past services or large financial contributions. [7] The national committees have almost no significant functions; they plan the national conventions and do public relations work between conventions.

It is the national chairmen of the Republican and Democratic parties who run the day-to-day activities of the national parties (Table 4.1). Since the national committees meet so infrequently, the chairmen and their staffs have responsibility for the administrative leadership of their parties. In theory, the national committees select the national chairmen, but actually they are chosen by the presidential nominees. Therefore, the party chairmen prosper or fade into obscurity depending upon the success of the presidential candidate. If he wins, the party chairman usually receives a high appointive position in the new administration. If the candidate is defeated, then both he and his appointed party chairman quickly lose influence. Sometimes, a party chairman selected by the losing presidential candidate is quickly replaced; this happened to Jean Westwood, George McGovern's personal choice in 1972. However, even chairmen of the victorious parties have soon learned how frustrating it is to administer a hollow shell. Between presidential elections, the chairman's main task appears to be to prevent the national organization from disappearing completely; for if the party wins the White House, all power shifts to that office, and if the party loses, there is

Table 4.1 Democratic and Republican National Committee Chairmen 1968-1978

DNC Chairmen		RNC Chairmen	
1968-1969	Lawrence O'Brien	1965-69	Ray Bliss
1969-1970	Fred Harris	1969-71	Rogers Morton
1970-1972	Lawrence O'Brien	1971-73	Robert Dole
1972-1972	Jean Westwood	1973-74	George Bush
1972-1976	Robert Strauss	1974-77	Mary L. Smith
1976-1977	Kenneth Curtis	1977-	William Brock
1977-	John C. White		

little interest in its national structure. Therefore, it should be clear that there is very little continuity in the post of national chairman. Presidential campaigns are reputed to be the national committees' prime function with other assignments such as research, candidate recruitment, propaganda, and program development decidedly secondary or tertiary functions.[8] Yet, a close look at the presidential campaigns of Nixon, Goldwater, McGovern, Ford, and Carter suggests that the respective national committees did little to assist their candidates. In 1976 Jimmy Carter's victorious effort almost completely ignored the DNC in planning, organizing, and carrying out the campaign. Richard Nixon's 1972 reelection campaign almost exclusively the product of the Committee to Re-elect the President (CREEP). One editorial columnist commented on the nonrelevance of the RNC in the Ford's 1976 campaign:

> No one in his right mind ever expects the Republican National Committee to do anything. Every Republican presidential candidate knows that and sets up his own campaign organization independent of the RNC. The function of the RNC, as anyone who has covered politics in Washington knows, is to provide jobs for the party faithful and for bright young things just out of school. If it refrains from doing active harm to Republican candidates and their party, what more can be asked?. . . And whatever the outcome of the November election, neither credit nor blame will be laid at the door of the Republican National Committee.[9]

In their 1972 study of party structures and performance, John S. Soloma and Frederick H. Sontag pointed out that the national committees were "shadow committees" and that party influentials called them "deadwood, anachronisms, or a gigantic political fraud."[10] Despite the opportunities offered by impressive technical communications equipment for campaign leadership, the DNC and RNC neither plan nor communicate. Since 1960, the national committees have also been stripped of their traditional patronage functions at the presidential level.[11] It is little wonder that a major study of national committees and their impact on American politics has been entitled *Politics without Power.*[12]

Other Party Organizations

Both parties have established a variety of auxiliary organizations in an attempt to promote party interests. Women and students in particular have been given special representation through their own party organizations; these provide formal access routes into politics for youth and women, two groups that historically have been underrepresented in politics. There are also various party committees in Congress that do research, discuss ideological issues, or raise campaign funds. These will be discussed in greater detail in Chapter 9.

The Rise and Fall of Party Machines

In years past many of our nation's largest cities had powerful party organizations called "machines." The machines were so named because of their ruthless efficiency in converting raw resources into pure political power. Their objective was surprisingly simple—to assure their survival by controlling their political environment. In dozens of major cities the machines flourished in the late nineteenth and early twentieth centuries.

Most books and articles dealing with the machine era are quite negative. They dwell on the graft and corruption, the patronage and preferments, the vote-stealing and judge-buying. However, as the machines faded away in city after city, students of parties and urban government began to appreciate the significant contributions the machines had made to the variety of clients they served so well. First, they acted as unofficial welfare organizations during a period in our history when almost all social services were provided by churches or private organizations. From the end of the Civil War to the 1930s, the demands for social services increased as dramatically as did the urban population. Many of the 38 million immigrants who came to America between 1830 and 1930 lived in big cities and worked in dreary factories. Although many of the early immigrants came from England or Ireland and could obtain employment relatively easily, the later immigrants from Eastern and Southern Europe had difficulty coping with an alien environment. The machines gave these newcomers assistance in the form of jobs, food, housing, legal advice, translation, and hundreds of other essential services. In exchange for these services, the machines asked for only two things: the newcomers' votes and loyalty. Both of these things seemed cheap to the immigrants, who didn't particularly value their vote and were quite willing to give their loyalty to those who had supported them.

Business constituted the second group of clients. The business community needed certain services that it could obtain only from local government: transportation networks, utilities, contracts, legal assistance in its battles against organized labor, and the need to shortcut the frustrations of fragmented local government. The machines provided these services in return for an essential element of successful political organization—money (usually in the form of kickbacks on governmental contracts). Another set of clients also had an important stake in the machine's survival. The machine leaders were among the first professional politicians in urban America. The honor of being the first "political boss" in America goes to Aaron Burr, who created the organization that later became the Tammany Hall, New York City's Democratic

Party organization. Besides Burr, a listing of the machine bosses since 1850 includes many politicians who certainly must rank among the most powerful men in our history: Mayor Frank Hague of Jersey City ("I am the law"), Ed Crump of Memphis ("We don't need politics in Memphis"), Huey Long of Louisiana ("I'm the Constitution around here"), "Big Bill" Thompson of Chicago, Enoch "Nucky" Johnson of Atlantic City, the O'Connell brothers of Albany, Abe "Curly" Ruef of San Francisco, Dr. Albert Ames of Minneapolis, George Cox of Cincinnati, "Colonel" Edward Butler of St. Louis, and last—but not least—Tammany's William Tweed.[13]

The machine did not take root and prosper in all cities, for it needed special soil to sustain itself. Large numbers of new, unassimilated residents provided the electoral clout; an obsolete governmental structure and philosophy enabled the machine to establish a symbiotic relationship with business; and control of public office enabled it to satisfy both of the aforementioned groups. And last, but not least, a machine needed a political culture that valued ends more than means. Thus, machines never developed in Seattle or Los Angeles because of the moralistic nature of their respective political cultures; by contrast, the people of Chicago often viewed the antics of local politicians as part of the metropolis's entertainment package.[14]

Patronage was the key to the machine's continuity of power. Armies of patronage workers who were loyal to the machine would go to the polls on election day to ensure the organization's victory. Tammany could claim 12,600 jobs in the 1860s, Boss Croker later tripled that number, and it is estimated that the late Mayor Richard Daley's Chicago-Cook County machine controlled 35,000 public jobs as well as about 10,000 jobs in the private sector. Multiply each patronage job by a factor of seven (wives, in-laws, children, friends, parents, and so forth), and it becomes clear why the base vote of the Chicago machine was about 350,000.[15]

Patronage was one of the prime targets of reformers in their attempts to do away with machines. For if a machine's financial and voting base could be eliminated or at least significantly reduced, the machine would be in serious difficulty. Reform laws provided for jobs in local government to be covered by merit or civil service requirements. After taking office in the early 1970s, Mayor Coleman Young of Detroit commented that he could make only about 100 appointments, and that most of these required special training or education. Other reform attacks were aimed at the party aspect of the machine. City elections were made nonpartisan and ward subdivisions were abolished, while at-large elections weakened the ties between the politicians and the neighborhoods. Also, new governmental structures (such as the commission and city manager) were adopted to reduce the power of mayors.

However, the hardest blow to the vitality of the machine was delivered in the 1930s as the federal government responded to the needs brought about by the Depression. It readily became apparent that state and local governments could or would not satisfactorily alleviate the economic problems of both urban and rural America. Franklin Roosevelt's New Deal provided for unemployment compensation, workmen's disability, welfare payments, and many other training and public assistance programs in the years that followed. These programs offered a far more efficient alternative than the sporadic benefits of the machine. Furthermore, with the return of prosperity in the 1940s, millions of immigrant families that had relied so heavily on the machine in earlier years now became middle class. Material benefits no longer seemed so attractive to these people, for, together with their new economic status, they achieved a middle class preference for voting on issues and a new appreciation of the value of their votes.

In a 1967 article, Theodore J. Lowi concluded, "The machine is nearly dead."[16] We suspect that the classical form of the machine has now passed into history, but that machines in new and different forms will continue to exist and perhaps proliferate in the future. One of the classic machines—that of the late Mayor Richard Daley in Chicago and Cook County—has managed to adapt to modern urban life. It is without a doubt the most powerful party organization in the United States. Its dominance has been built on powerful ward organizations such as the West Side's Twenty-fourth Ward, which in the 1959 mayoral election turned out 20,300 machine votes to 800 for the Republicans. In the 1977 Chicago mayoral election (held to select a replacement for the late Mayor Daley) and the 1978 Illinois Democratic Party primary election, the machine demonstrated that it was still in relatively good condition. However, the 1976 general election indicated that the electoral power of the machine beyond the city of Chicago is rapidly declining, for it failed to carry the state for Carter; lost the governorship to an old enemy, Jim Thompson; and even failed to win the post of Cook County State's Attorney.

Other cities have remnants of the once-overpowering machines which survive in relative obscurity. Metropolitan submachines or weakened machines continue to function in Buffalo, Pittsburgh, Philadelphia, Baltimore, Gary, New York City (in the Bronx, Brooklyn, and Queens), Albany, and Philadelphia.[17] Less formidable fragmented organizations can still be found in Kansas City, St. Louis, Cleveland, Cincinnati, Boston, and Jersey City.[18]

Although most attention is usually given to urban machines, there have been some very powerful rural machines. Two of them are found in the Deep South—in Plaquemines Parish, Louisiana, and Duval County, Texas. In the 1976 Democratic primary to select a successor to Louisiana's retiring congressman, F. Edward Hébert, machine candidate James A. Moreau received 5509 votes to 597 for his opponent, Richard A. Tonry, in Plaquemines Parish. Texas machines tend to be rural and based on the Mexican-American vote, which is tightly controlled by large landowning families. Lopsided majorities can be delivered by these "jefes" or bosses. The most famous of the Texas rural machines is found in Duval County under the leadership of various members of the Parr family. The Parrs were directly responsible for the early successes of Lyndon Johnson. When Johnson won his U.S. Senate seat in a special election in 1947 by a margin of 87 votes, Duval County gave Johnson 4622 votes to 40 for his opponent. In almost every Duval County election between 1924 and 1948 that was studied by V. O. Key, the leading candidate received more than 90 percent of the county's votes. Another significant indication of a rural machine is a pattern of sudden shifts of support from one candidate to another in successive elections. For example, Duval County supported a candidate in his campaign for the governorship in 1934 with 97 percent of the county's vote; however, when the same candidate ran for the same office in 1936, he received only 1.3 percent of the county's vote.[19]

At present, the political machine may be in a dormant phase before it reemerges as a newly constituted, rebuilt political organization. Evidence to support this possibility can be found in the changing social and economic makeup of our nation's largest cities. Since the early 1950s, the middle class (with its distinctive voting patterns) has been leaving the big cities; the vacuum is being filled by a rising tide of new immigrants: blacks, Chicanos, Orientals, and other minority groups. Chicago is a good illustration of this phenomenon. The 1940 census found 227,000 blacks in Chicago; it is estimated that by 1980 blacks will number 1,540,000 out of a total city population of 3,774,000, or 41 percent of the city's residents. More than 1 million blacks have emigrated from the South to the Windy City, and there have arrived between 350,000 and 500,000 Spanish-speaking persons. It seems inevitable that power in Chicago will pass from the Irish-Italian-Polish-Jewish machine to the blacks and Chicanos within a decade or two. Just as power has passed to the blacks in cities where they have a clear population majority (Washington, Cleveland, Gary, Detroit); many other cities will have black majorities within the foreseeable future.[20] It takes time to build a political organization, but when the new emigrants do so, the machines will prbably be black and Chicano and significantly different in terms of functions. The new machines will probably be confined to those cities that have majorities or near-majorities of blacks and Chicanos, and the machines will allow them to control their own institutions and neighborhoods. The basic incentives will be similar to those of the classic machines: preferments to businessmen, social status to downtrodden minorities, and power over their own governmental structures. The old material benefits (such as jobs and economic assistance) will not be as important as in the past; the new incentives will be information and access to governmental benefits. In an increasingly complex and bureaucratic society, the machine can reestablish the old ties between neighborhood and government that were eliminated by the reformers. The party organization can serve as a link between the lone citizen and his remote government. Chicago may well be the first of these new-style machines, and it could serve as a model for such organizations in other similar cities.[21]

Party Competition—Toward More Equality

One indication of the relative vigor and power of party organizations is their ability or inability to compete effectively for various public offices. Actually, the signs of effective party competition go hand-in-hand with other variables associated with strong party organizations. Competitive party systems are more likely to have more party cohesion in the state executive and legislative branches and sometimes even more control over the nomination of their candidates. One index developed by Richard Dawson and James Robinson focuses on state governmental offices and measures the proportion of votes for each party in statewide and state legislative races, the duration of control by the parties of these offices, and the frequency of divided party control of government. From these pieces a raw data, an "index of interparty competition" can be determined, giving us an indication of the party balance in each state.[22] As the material in Table 4.1 shows, the Democratic Party is the dominant party. However, one should not infer that all of the individual states have been steadily marching toward the Democratic Party's standard. Twenty states have moved toward the Republican Party since 1946, but note that most of these moves were just slight shifts in one-party Democratic states to something less than complete Democratic domination. The mountain states of Colorado, Idaho, and Wyoming together with the sunbelt states of Arizona and Florida have experienced significant shifts toward the Republican Party. However, these few points of slippage toward the Republicans have been more than matched by a broader shift toward the Democrats. Old Republican bastions like Iowa, Maine, New Hampshire, and Wisconsin have joined the ranks of the two-party states, and two-party states like California, New Jersey, and Hawaii have shifted from Republican-leaning to Democratic-leaning. The over-all composite index has changed from .544 to .585, reflecting a gain for the Democrats since the early 1960s.

This type of index may categorize a state's over-all pattern over a number of years, disregarding what is happening now. Take, for example, the transformation of the South Dakotan political party system. South Dakota is indexed as .337 in the 1962-1973 period, making it the third most Republican state in the nation. However, since South Dakota entered the Union in 1889, the Republican Party has won close to 90 percent of all the statewide partisan elections;[23] but, as of mid-1976, the Democrats had won the governorship, both U.S. Senate seats, 19 out of 36 state senate seats, and 33 out of 70 state house of representatives seats. This is not the pattern of a modified one-party Republican state, but one of competition—at least during the middle third of the 1970s. Much of the credit for this Democratic Party revival must go to its U.S. Senator, George McGovern. As Neal R. Pierce has written:

> When McGovern forsook the security of his political science professorship at Dakota Wesleyan College in Mitchell. . . to become executive secretary of the state Democratic party, that organization was little more than a shell. It had won scarcely any elections since a brief interlude in New Deal days, and many of its officials were patronage hunters like the old "Post Office Republicans" in the South. . . . At the time, McGovern recalled, many people were even afraid to admit publicly that they were Democrats. But he went on to build the party almost single-handed, and the Democrats began steady gains. . . . [24]

Despite the steady decline in Republican members of Congress, it is only on the federal level that the Republicans can claim to be a national party. In 1976, out of Alabama's total of 140 state leiglsators, the Republicans could not claim a single member.

However, in 1976 Republicans won 3 out of Alabama's 7 seats in the U.S. House of Representatives. Democratic dominance in Southern state legislatures has changed from the total exclusion of Republicans to some token opposition by a handful of Republicans. In the 1977-1978 legislative sessions, Arkansas had 5 Republicans out of 135; Georgia, 27 out of 236; Louisiana, 5 out of 144; Mississippi, 5 out of 173; North Carolina, 10 out of 170; South Carolina, 15 out of 170; and Texas, 21 out of 81. Actually, some Northern legislatures are dominated by the Democrats as much as those in the South. In 1978 Rhode Island's 5 Republican state senators were far out-numbered by its 45 Democratic senators. Republicans were also a beleaguered mi-nority in all of Maryland's and Massachusetts's legislative chambers during the 1977-1978 sessions:

	Democrats	Republicans
Maryland state senate	39	8
Maryland state house	126	15
Massachusetts state senate	33	7
Massachusetts state house	194	43

Perhaps the most misleading of all are those states that have been labeled "modified one-party Republican" during the 1962-1973 period such as Wyoming and Vermont. In 1977-1978 the Wyoming state house had only 3 more Republicans than Democrats, and the Republicans in Vermont State House had only 2 more state representatives than the Democrats out of a total of 150 state legislators.

The plight of the Republican Party should be quite clear from this evidence. In the so-called Republican states, the GOP is barely able to control the state legislatures—the foundation of party politics; in many of the so-called two-party or competitive states, the Republicans in the mid-1970s were becoming less of a real opposition party and more a token force. In the Democratic stronghold states, there was still no mean-ingful Republican presence except in national-level elections. Even in the South, where the Republican future seemed to be so bright at the beginning of the 1970s, the tide has shifted back in favor of the Democrats—especially at the state level. In 1972 the Republicans held 15 percent of the state legislative seats in the South, but by 1976 this had been reduced to 10 percent. The GOP controlled a respectable 43 percent of the nation's state legislators in 1938. By 1948, the Republicans had climbed to 53 percent of the total, but in 1977, their total was only 32 percent. In their 1976 state-by-state analysis of party politics. Barone and Ujifusa noted the growing Repub-lican erosion in several states: "[In Michigan] at the House level, in state legislative races, even in contests for local offices, the Republicans seem almost to be vanishing from the political picture here." Or in their analysis of Massachusetts politics—once a GOP stronghold: "The Republican Party here, like so many of the elderly Yankees who were the most solid supporters, seems simply to have disappeared."[25]

Over-all state patterns of competition often hide widespread traditions of one-party dominant areas. In Illinois, the Democratic candidates have about as much chance to win in some downstate Republican bastions as the Republican sacrificial candidates do in the city of Chicago. An examination of electoral history maps in most states would disclose many districts where the minority party has not won in more than 50 years. Although many districts may have had a minority victory in an extraordinary year, such as 1932, 1952, 1964, or 1974, the office was quickly returned to the dominant party.

What factors account for this lack of competition in so many areas of the country? Part of the explanation can come from examining the historical patterns of each area. Much of the tradition of Democratic dominance in the South is due to the Civil War and the infamous carpetbag Republican governments that were established during the Reconstruction period. As soon as possible, Southerners got rid of the Republicans and black politicians, and then they "voted the way they shot" for a century. Some areas such as the major Eastern cities shifted from the Republican Party to the party of F.D.R. as a result of accepting the New Deal programs. Other areas of dominance can be accounted for by the presence of large numbers of members of certain ethnic or religious groups. As Americans continue to migrate and mix, these historical patterns will probably deteriorate. Part of the revival of the Republican Party in the South is due to the large migration of Northern whites to new jobs or retirement in the South.

There seems to be a significant amount of evidence supporting the thesis that the two parties often do not care about having a competitive two-party system in all parts of a given state. Political scientist Dr. Milton Rakove, who belongs to the Cook County Democratic machine, argues persuasively that the Chicago Democrats do not challenge the Republicans in downstate Illinois since the Republicans offer only token opposition in Chicago.[26] Others say that the "post office Republicans" phenomenon is found in the South because its Republican party leaders would rather be a big fish in a very small pond and thus be able to pick up all of the patronage crumbs tossed to their paper organization than run the risk of building a viable party and perhaps losing control of it. State legislatures frequently draw up legislative district and even congressional district boundaries to guarantee a specific division of the various seats among the two major parties. These arrangements are often made with the concurrence of the minority party, which accepts its long-term minority status but knows that its survival is assured.

Thus, it is important to remember that when scholars and party officials speak of the contemporary increased party competition in glowing terms, such competition is really found in only a few scattered places and on a few levels of government. Although the Republicans can compete in national elections, they are often overwhelmed in state contests. Finally, even in those states with an over-all competitive balance, there is little intrastate competition.

Statistically, how do the competitive states compare with the relatively noncompetitive party systems? Two-party states are far more urbanized than those with the least competition. They are also blessed with the highest levels of per capita income, the highest percentage of nonagricultural workers, and the most heterogeneous populations.[27] Economic, historical, and social factors seem to be correlated with the competitiveness of a state's two parties. The degree of competition found within a state is also strongly related to the nature of that state's party organizations. In one-party states, the minority party has almost no organization. Although there may be an organizational chart hanging on the wall in the state chairman's office, only the very highest offices will actually be filled, and there will be almost no organization at the grassroots level. Without real challenge from the minority party, the dominant party has no incentive to organize effectively. If you can win elections without spending much effort or money, you will continue to do so until compelled by the opposition to mobilize. The more competitive a state's parties are, the better organized they will be. However, even in the most competitive, urban states, some party organizations leave much to be desired. Often a party will be relatively well organized only in its strongholds and in the most significant swing areas, leaving the rest of the state to the opposition. Creating a party organization in "enemy territory" requires great patience and persistence. Attractive candidates must be recruited and money must be secured, despite the fact that parties are reluctant to put money into a hopeless cause; thus, parties often help to perpetuate their own defeat in certain areas. Hopefully, workers can be lured to work for good candidates and that there will be electoral victories before frustration and hopelessness set in.

Interparty Competition by Office Levels Across the Nation

If one collects information on the competitiveness of the two major parties for various elective offices throughout the country in recent years, the plight of the Republicans is quite clear. (See figure 4.1 on p.109) With the sole exception of the presidential contest, the Republicans have lost strength almost to the point of isolation from political power. In presidential politics since 1952, the Republicans have captured the White House in four out of seven elections. If one totals the major party votes for president between 1952 and 1976 inclusive, the Republicans have outpolled the Democrats by 248 million (51.8 percent) to 231 million (48.2 percent). In the 1976 contest, the Republican presidential ticket attracted enough votes to fall just short of victory. However, the GOP is in serious trouble on every other level of American politics. For the second congressional election in a row, 1976 saw the Republicans win very few seats: they had 38 U.S. Senate seats out of a total of 100, and 145 out of a total of 435 U.S. House of Representatives seats. Congressional seat distribution patterns since 1960 offer little hope to the Republicans for gaining control of Congress in the near future.[28]

In 1976, the Democrats added an addtional state house to their 1975 totals, holding an all-time historical high of 37 to 12 held by the Republicans; plus one an independent governor of Maine. Traditionally the state houses have been quite significant in national politics as building blocks for national-level campaigns. The Republicans no longer have what was once a virtual monopoly (outside of the South) of state houses.

The situation in the 50 state legislatures seems to be even more grim for the Republicans. Despite the solid performance by Gerald Ford, in 1976 the Democrats

Table 4.2 Inter-Party Competition 1962-1973, 1946-1963

	1962-1973	1946-1963	Category Change
One-Party Democratic (.850+)			
Louisiana	.993	.987	None
Alabama	.952	.957	None
Mississippi	.915	.981	None
South Carolina	.894	1.00	None
Texas	.878	.959	None
Georgia	.871	.995	None
Arkansas	.865	.943	None
Mofidied One-Party Democratic (.650 to .849)			
North Carolina	.775	.879	From 1 PD to M1PD
Maryland	.765	.714	None
Virginia	.754	.880	From 1PD to M1PD
Tennessee	.744	.872	From 1PD to M1PD
Florida	.741	.920	From 1PD to M1PD
Hawaii	.731	.490	From 2P to M1PD
Oklahoma	.730	.819	None
New Mexico	.711	.702	None
Missouri	.709	.660	None
Kentucky	.704	.765	None
West Virginia	.695	.722	None
Rhode Island	.686	.633	From 2P to M1PD
Massachusetts	.673	.523	From 2P to M1PD
Two-Party States (.350 to .649)			
Nevada	.606	.526	None
California	.602	.393	None
Alaska	.576	.677	From M1PD to 2P
Connecticut	.567	.442	None
Montana	.555	.470	None
New Jersey	.544	.361	None
Washington	.542	.565	None
Nebraska	.513	.388	None
Oregon	.508	.355	None

State			
Minnesota	.504	.461	None
Delaware	.495	.542	None
Michigan	.490	.377	None
Pennsylvania	.471	.405	None
Utah	.465	.460	From M1PD to 2P
Arizona	.438	.749	None
Illinois	.425	.385	From M1PR to 2P
Wisconsin	.425	.299	None
Indiana	.416	.355	From M1PR to 2P
Iowa	.411	.250	From M1PR to 2P
New York	.405	.317	From M1PR to 2P
Maine	.405	.241	None
Ohio	.369	.352	None
New Hampshire	.360	.268	From M1PR to 2P
Modified One-Party Republican (.150 to .349)			
North Dakota	.346	.186	None
Idaho	.345	.378	From 2P to M1PR
Colorado	.339	.483	From 2P to M1PR
Kansas	.338	.242	None
South Dakota	.337	.232	None
Vermont	.331	.176	None
Wyoming	.321	.347	None

One-Party Republican (.000 to .149)
No states in this category.

Source: These figures are adapted from material presented by Austin Ranney in "Parties in State Politics," in *Politics in the American States*, 1st and 3rd eds., edited by Herbert Jacob and Kenneth Vines. It should be noted that between these two editions Ranney adjusted the parameters of his various categories. The authors have used the third edition categories for both the 1946-1962 and 1962-1973 data in order to have comparable categories.

Table 4.3   Partisan Divisions in Congress 1960-1976

Year	Congress	House of Representatives		U.S. Senate	
		Dem.	Rep.	Dem.	Rep.
1976	95th	293	142	61	38
1974	94th	291	144	61	37
1972	93th	242	192	56	42
1970	92nd	255	180	54	44
1968	91st	243	192	58	42
1966	90th	248	187	64	36
1964	89th	295	140	68	32
1962	88th	258	176	67	33
1960	87th	263	174	64	36

Source: Clerk of the House of Representatives. Partisan totals of less than 435 or 100 in the House and Senate, respectively, indicate other parties or independents.

gained control of both houses in 36 states, a decline of one from their 1974 totals. The Republicans dominated the legislatures of only five states, a loss of three from their 1974 totals. The five states with Republican dominance in 1976 were South Dakota, Idaho, Wyoming, New Hampshire (the state senate is tied 12-12, but the Republicans have organizational control), and Colorado—hardly the states upon which a party would want to build a power base. The Democrats won control of the Kansas house for the first time since 1912, the North Dakota house for only the second time in that state's history, and the Vermont house for the first time since the Civil War. In California, the 1974 Democratic legislative landslide majority was increased in 1976, while the elctorate was voting for Ford and Hayakawa at the national level.[29] And finally, it is clear that, except for a handful of medium-sized cities, almost all of the largest metropolitan areas are governed by Democrats.

We will now examine three major state party systems in detail in order to highlight some of the special characteristics and problems found in various political settings and their implications for party organizations. Texas, Illinois, and California all illustrate the workings of state party organizations with distinctive traditions that shape the practices of politics and the parties. Texas represents the Southern pattern of competition and the problems of the Republican Party in trying to build a party organiza-

Table 4.4   Party Control of State Legislatures 1965-1977

	1965	1967	1969	1971	1973	1975	1977
Legislatures where Democrats control both houses	33	24	20	23	27	37	36
Legislatures where Republicans control both houses	7	16	20	16	16	5	5
Split control	8	8	8	9	6	7	8

Source: National Conference of State Legislatures, Press Release, November 4, 1976.

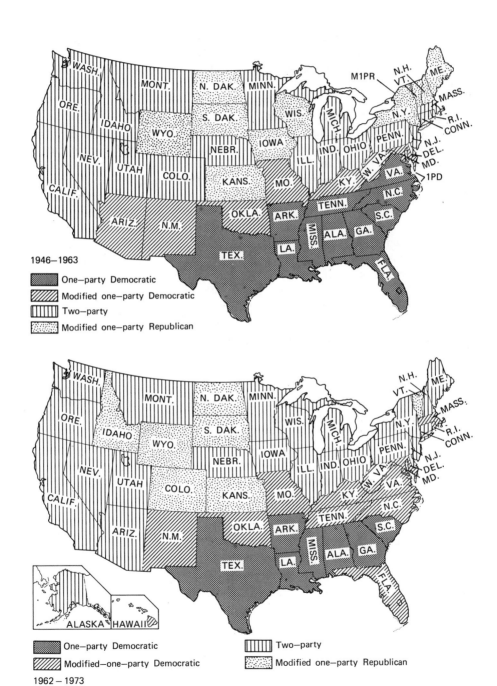

tion in a hostile environment. Machine politics and restrained competition have been the hallmarks of Illinois party politics during this century. And California exemplifies almost no-party politics and may provide a glimpse into the political future of this country.

Texas: Where Are the Republicans?

Among the ten most populous states, only Texas can claim to be a one-party state. From the end of the Reconstruction period to the present, the Republian Party has had virtually no impact on Texas politics. The first and last time the Republicans captured the state governorship was in 1869, and they had no U.S. Senate seats from 1877 to 1961, when John Tower won a special election to fill the seat that had been vacated by Lyndon Johnson when he became vice president. Tower was reelected to that seat in 1966 and 1972 under the same unusual circumstances, which we will discuss later on. The Texas state legislature has often met without the presence of even one Republican in either chamber, although since the 1960s the Republicans have secured 3 senate seats out of a total of 31, and 18 house seats out of a total of 150. There are almost no Republican city or county officials, reflecting the ongoing, serious grassroots problem. Only at the federal level has the GOP had any cause for joy. In 1976, the Republicans held one of the two U.S. Senate seats and 2 of the 24 House seats. Only 3 of the 22 seats won by the Democrats in 1976 would fall within the 55-45 percent classification as being competitive seats.[30]

Some scholars who specialize in Texas politics have argued that Texas actually has a three-party system. The weakest of the three is the Republican Party, which displays all of the characteristics of a patronage motivated group of entrenched politicians who do no care about winning elections if this would endanger their control of the party organization. There are two Democratic parties operating in the state: the Democratic Party and the Liberal Democrats of Texas.[31] The former is the conservative faction, and the latter represents the state's liberal elements. Each of these three parties has its own rather distinct geographical power base; Republican power is concentrated in the large cities to such a degree that fully half of the total Republican vote is found in the seven most populated counties. Another Republican stronghold is the Panhandle, whose people and economy closely resemble those of Kansas and northern Oklahoma rather than the rest of Texas; many former residents of those states helped to settle the Panhandle. The area is white, Anglo-Saxon, and Protestant—unlike much of the rest of the state. Another area of Republican strength is in the so-called German counties around in San Antonio. This region was settled in pre-Civil War days by German migrants who were Unionists and who have thereby tended to vote Republican for the following 100 years.[32]

When viewed objectively, the Texas Republican Party continues to be so pathetically weak that one textbook on Texas government and politics calls it an "interest group." Kraemer, Grain, and Maxwell trace the history of the Republican Party in Texas and the rise of R. B. Creager of Brownsville, who served as Republican national committeeman between 1923 and his death in 1950.[33] This one man ruled and used the hollow shell of the party for patronage advantages for nearly three decades. Creager made little or no attempt to build the party into an effective electoral organization, for he and his supporters were quite content to exchange their votes at the Republican National Convention for patronage preferments whenever possible. "As Creager and his colleagues saw it, their primary purpose was to control the political plums that dropped in the state when the Republicans occupied the White House."[34] Despite the great changes that have occurred in Texas politics since 1950, this "post office patronage" attitude is still strong among organizational Republicans. In 1972, for example, the Republican Party did not run candidates against the Democrats in 9 of 13 statewide races, in 11 of 24 U.S. House of Representative races, or in half of the state legislative contests.[35] In commenting on the Republicans, Francis Farenthold, a Democratic Party leader in Texas, said: "It leaves a real question in my mind how much they are committed to a genuine two party system. With all of their screaming about the one party system, they seem pretty satisfied with the rule of the Democratic establishment."[36]

There are many problems in trying to build a party beyond the "post office" mentality. First, although officially listed as a closed primary state, Texas allows a voter to decide which primary he will vote in on primary election day. Those who vote "Republican" in November may vote Democratic in the primaries because that is where the real action can be found. This practice leads to divided support patterns and inhibits the establishment of a real base of those who identify with the Republican Party.[37] Being shut out of the governor's office in this century has prevented the significant appointment powers of that office from being used to build a base for the party. Few attractive candidates can gain valuable experience and recognition at the lower levels of Texas politics under the Republican label. Consequently, most higher level candidates must be marketed to the voters on the candidate's merits in each election. This type of campaigning means hoarding the scarce party resources and concentrating them in a few targeted statewide races. Lastly, the extreme conservatism of the Texas Republican Party, as shown by Ronald Reagan's primary victory there over President Ford in 1976, has limited the range of its appeal throughout the state.

It is still probably too soon to know if the conversion of former Democratic Governor John Connally to the Republican standard during the Nixon Administration will have any significant effect on the party's feeble organization in the latter part of the 1970s. But it appears that Governor Connally has not inspired a significant number of Democrats to join the GOP on the state level; thus, the Republican Party will probably continue to be essentially a patronage-oriented political group as it has been since the 1870s. Probably more will be required than John Connally to change the Republican image as that of the party of Reconstruction, carpetbaggers, and the Yankees. While many Southerners (and especially Texans) are "presidential Republicans," they will probably continue to vote Democratic on state and local levels for the foreseeable future.

The liberal faction of the Texas Democratic Party continues to be a minority group. Its ideological heritage goes back to the Grange and Populist movements, which were the liberal factions of the 1800s. However, these older liberal movements were never quite able to defeat the entrenched conservative Democrats, who gained control in the 1870s. During the New Deal a liberal trend began in Texas, and it blossomed in the 1950s. A convention victory in 1956, Ralph Yarborough's U.S. Senate victories in 1957 and 1958, and an increasingly liberal-moderate state legislature gave the liberals hope in the 1960s. However, the main liberal organization, "Democrats of Texas," did not survive a bitter defeat at the 1960 state convention, and the liberals have not fared well since then. The occassional defection of Mexican-American support to the Chicano third party, La Raza Unida, and increased friction among the other segments of the faction have prevented the liberals from achieving any major statewide successes. In spite of this, the liberal Democrats won control of the state legislature in the mid-1970s, and otherwise indicated to the conservative faction that their support was essential against a strong Republican like John Tower. Nevertheless, the conservatives continued to control the party apparatus. The liberals tend to be concentrated in the southeast region, with significant numbers in the extreme south and in the Austin-San Antonio area; the major liberal groups are the urban dwellers, blacks, labor, and to some extent, Mexican Americans.[38]

There is a considerable overlapping in the geography of those who support the arch-conservative Republicans and conservative Democrats in Texas. The latter group has dominated state politics, with the exception of an occasional liberal governor, since the end of Reconstruction. The weakest area of conservative Democratic support is in the state's large cities. Of the 25 largest, only one city (Lubbock) is strongly conservative.

What explains the tremendous strength of the conservative Democratic faction? First, there is the tradition of Democratic dominance in what is essentially a conservative state. Then, the true opposition party, the Republicans, have not been able to put together an effective organization that could challenge the Democrats from a conservative position. The conservative faction also has awesome resources in the form of talent, money, and energy. Its intraparty rival has suffered from rather low voter turnouts among its chief supporters: blacks, Chicanos, and the relatively poor. The liberals have also lost strength because of black outmigration since the 1940s and formation of the Chicano third political party, La Raza Unida. And finally, as noted earlier, the Texas primary allows the Republicans to vote in it, thereby defeating the liberal candidates and preventing the Republicans from constructing an organizational base for themselves.

Certain trends can be seen that may encourage the opponents of the conservative faction. First of all, the cities are gaining population, and since the cities have been opposition strongholds, there may be a further deterioration in the conservatives' position. Between 1960 and 1970 75 percent of the state's total population increase occurred in the Dallas and Houston metropolitan areas. Secondly, there are indications that the Republicans are beginning to field attractive candidates in statewide elections; if they can exploit the Democratic factional divisions, they may be able to win the governorship that they lost by only 100,000 out of 3.1 million votes cast in 1974. With the governorship, the Republicans might be able to develop into a real opposition force.

Texas Party Organization and the Electoral Laws

Much of the credit for the long-term dominance of the conservative Democrats in Texas is due to the laws that they enacted to protect their power. The so-called white primary was created by Texas conservative Democrats to prevent blacks from participating in the all-important Democratic party primary. From 1923, when the legislature voted to ban blacks from primary elections, to 1944, when the U.S. Supreme Court ruled the ban unconstitutional, the liberals had no voting support from blacks. A poll tax law was enacted in 1902 (requiring the voter to pay about $1.75) in order to discourage blacks, Chicanos, and the poor from voting, and it succeeded remarkably well until it was ruled unconstitutional in state elections by a federal court in 1966. A third restrictive measure was the annual voter registration law that required yearly re-registration until it was declared unconstitutional in 1971.

Texas electoral laws establish a hierarchy of party organizations and structures, which are both temporary and permanent in nature. The permanent party organization is based on a precinct chairman who is chosen in the primary election and also serves as a member of the county executive committee. Each county party organization has a chairman who is also chosen during the primary election. On the state level, there is a state executive committee and a state chairman who is elected for a 2-year term at the state convention and usually serves at the pleasure of the party's gubernatorial nominee. The state executive committee, also chosen at the state convention, consists of the chairman and vice chairman, together with one male and one female from each of the 31 state senate districts.

In Texas, as in most other states, the real excitement occurs during the period when the temporary (or election year) party organization is in effect. During even-numbered years (election years in Texas), there are various conventions that culminate in the state convention. The first is the precinct convention which represents several hundred party voters. Attendance at this grassroots convention is usually light. The main purpose of this convention is to select delegates to the county conventions on the basis of one delegate for every 25 votes cast in the precinct for the party's gubernatorial nominee during the last general election. Here the liberal-conservative schism within the Democratic Party is quite clear. One faction or the other may walk out of the precinct or the county conventions and hold its own "rump convention" in the hope of winning a credentials battle at the county or state conventions. If one faction is clearly in control of a precinct or county convention, it may railroad its motions through and complete the business of the convention in 5 or 6 minutes. According to Wilbourn E. Benton, "All too frequently nothing is more undemocratic than a Democratic convention in Texas."[39] Another practice that excluded minority viewpoints was the "unit rule," which required all delegates to support the position of the majority. In 1968 the National Democratic Party Convention forbade states to use the unit rule.

County conventions build platforms and elect delegates to the state convention. Here one delegate is chosen per 300 to 600 votes for governor in the last general election. Democratic Party state conventions have frequently been the battlefield for bitter confrontations between the liberal and conservative factions. The state convention certifies the party nominees (the primary victors), constructs the party platform, and selects the members of the party's state executive committee.[40] Each faction will caucus and plan its strategies. At these caucuses and in other "smoke-filled rooms," the real decisions of the convention are hammered out. "Much that transpires on the convention floor is anti-climactic. Unless one gains admittance to the small councils, there is little chance to play an active role in decision-making within the party, at least the state level."[41]

As of 1974, a Texas political party must nominate its candidates by direct primary if its gubernatorial candidate won at least 20 percent of the total gubernatorial vote in the last general election. Parties that receive less than 20 percent of the gubernatorial vote (La Raza Unida party) must use the convention to nominate its candidates. Since the Republican Party secures significantly more than 20 percent of the gubernatorial vote, it must use the primary process, thereby exposing its weak base. In 1972, 54 counties had no Republican primary. Only 57,000 votes were cast in Republican primaries, and of this total 49,000 came from 17 counties. In the state's remaining 237 counties, there was an average of 33 Republican votes per county. Nearly 2 million votes were cast in the Democratic primary in 1972.[42]

In sum, Texas is essentially a tri-factional state, with the two minority groups affecting state politics by periodically joining or bolting the dominant conservative Democratic group. The prospects of developing a true two-party system in Texas do not seem optimistic for the near future.

Illinois: Where Is the Competition?

Political observers have often described Illinois as not only a state with strong political parties, but one with long-term competition between the two major parties. However, like most other states, such over-all competition conceals patterns of one-party domination. As in the case of other industrial states, Illinois is neatly divided into a metropolitan Democratic stronghold and a nearly solid Republican suburban and rural area. Consistent competition between the Republicans and Democrats can be found only in the statewide races for national or state executive positions.

Competition between the parties in Illinois has often followed national political patterns at certain historical periods. In the nineteenth century, Illinois experienced a post-Civil War style of politics, with those persons who came from the South or border states supporting the Democratic Party and the rest of the state voting Republican. Thus, the Democratic Party dominated the rural south and central parts of the state, as well as a small group located in Chicago. Like most of its non-Southern sisters, Illinois experienced a period of Republican dominance from the late 1890s until the early 1930s. From 1856 to 1932, Illinois elected a Democratic governor only twice—

in 1892 and 1912. The Roosevelt New Deal helped to revitalize the Democractic Party's fortunes at the presidential level and bring about a more even balance at the state level. The party made tremendous gains in the urban areas, especially Chicago; meanwhile, many long-time Democrats in the southern part of the state reacted to the urbanized nature of the new Democratic coalition by defecting to the Republicans.[43]

The post-Depression period seems to have brought about a balance between the two major parties. In almost every presidential election, the state is considered a tossup— neither party can count on its electoral votes. United States Senate seats are normally divided evenly between the parties, as are the seats in the state legislature; in fact, the lower chamber is often so evenly balanced that a single vote (or at most a handful of votes) separates the parties. This type of balance is partially achieved through a unique electoral measure called "cumulative voting," which was discussed in Chapter 3.[44]

Cumulative voting is just one of the electoral laws and traditions that give Illinois parties great discretionary power. For, unlike California, where the reformers enacted various laws that were hostile to the parties, almost every electoral law in Illinois protects the two major parties from third parties, independents, and other outside political forces. Another example is the law stipulating how a candidate must file for the lowest elective party office in Chicago—ward committeeman. A candidate must submit a petition with the signatures of registered voters equal in number to 10 percent of the party's vote in the preceding primary election. This percentage is five times higher than the signature totals required for alderman—the lowest elected city government office—and twenty times higher than the petition requirements for state representative or congressman.[45] Since this number of signatures can be accumulated only through the party organization, the crucial grassroots organizational leadership posts are protected from reformers or independents.

In order to understand party politics in Illinois, one must appreciate the relationships among the three major subdivisions in the state: Chicago, Cook County, and downstate. There are 102 counties in Illinois—Cook County and 101 so-called downstate counties. Cook County, which includes Chicago, has about 5.5 million inhabitants, or about 53 percent of the state's total population. One can subdivide Cook County into Chicago (3.3 million persons divided among 50 wards) and suburban Cook County (2.2 million persons divided among 30 townships). In each ward and township, a committeeman is elected in each party, and they meet as the Cook County central committees of each party. These committees are tremendously powerful because of their functions as specified by state law. Each party's central committee selects its candidates to run for public office in the county, handles thousands of patronage jobs, controls the party's financial resources, and concentrates various other political powers into the hands of a few politicians. Another unique provision of the Illinois electoral law gives each committeeman the number of votes in the county central committee equal to his ward's or township's party vote in the preceding election. This normally means that those committeeman who represent the respective party strongholds—the Democratic Chicago inner wards and the Republican suburban townships—have great power.

The state legislature has thoughtfully allowed Chicago party organizations to select their representatives to the state convention in a way that differs from the downstate organizations. Downstate parties select their delegates to the state convention at county conventions, but in Chicago, the party ward committeemen have the power to designate delegates. Illinois political parties have a complex web of party committees in addition to the ward/township committees and the state conventions. There are congressional district committees, municipal committees, and state central committees. Some (state central committees and county committees) are chosen during the primary elections for 4-year terms, while the rest are made up of party officials chosen at lower levels. One crucial point to remember is that this is the type of structure desired by the parties; it was not imposed upon them by reformers.

For the Democrats, real power lies in their stronghold of Chicago and the Cook County Central Committee. Republican strength is found in the downstate Republican counties (such as DuPage) and in the state governor's mansion. The Chicago political scientist Milton Rakove has observed that there seems to be collusion between Republican and Democratic leaders, which results in the effective division of the state into separate fiefdoms, so that there can be no assault from the other party.

> *There is evidence that an undestanding has existed from time to time between the two parties, an understanding by which the Democratic organization keeps control of Cook County and the city of Chicago, and the Republican party is allowed to keep control of the state government. Since Cook County is half the state, with at least the equivalent number of patronage jobs and other perquisites that the state government in Springfield has to dispense to the party faithful, such an arrangement can be advantageous to the professionals in both parties.*[46]

In fact, Rakove argues that it is in the interest of the Cook County Democratic machine to prevent other Democrats from winning the governorship and establishing a rival Democratic organization based on the Springfield patronage jobs. Evidence to support this viewpoint can be found in the curious events of the 1976 gubernatorial races. The incumbent, independent Democratic state governor, Daniel Walker, was dumped by the Daley Democratic machine and replaced by the significantly weaker candidate, Mike Howlett, who easily lost to the Republican Jim Thompson in the general election. There is equally strong evidence that the Republicans have no desire to build up the remnants of their party in Chicago. For 40 years the Republican Party has nominated rather unattractive candidates in Chicago who go on to lose without adequate funding or support from the downstate party. The 1975 mayoral election demonstrated the lack of effort made by Chicago and downstate Republicans. John Hoellen, the lone Republican on the 50-member Chicago city council, managed to win the Republican mayoral nomination, while at the same time losing his seat on the city council. After Hoellen saw the awesome Daley primary victory, he promptly decided to give up. Although his name remained on the ballot for the general election, he did not campaign; eventually he received 20 percent of the vote to Daley's 78 percent.

Even presidential contests are relatively insignificant when compared with the vital interests of the machine. The machine will support the national ticket and candidates for statewide offices if it believes that benefits can be obtained by such support, but most organizational efforts are focused on city and county races.

Rakove observes that an effective party organization needs five resources—offices, jobs, money, workers, and votes—and all of these are amply available in Illinois for building a powerful party system. But these resources (and thus party power) do not coexist in the same parts of the state.

Thus, Illinois's party politics appears to be well balanced and competitive when the election data are viewed as a whole. Upon closer examination, however, the state has many counties with one-party patterns similar to those found in the South. The Democratic party is alive and relatively healthy in Chicago, but the Republicans (while powerful as officeholders and supported by their own patronage army in Springfield) demonstrate little of their opponents' discipline and organization. As one political expert reported during the 1976 Illinois Republican presidential primary election, "There is no Republican organization in Illinois." In short, Illinois has political competition only when it serves in the interests of the parties.

California: Where Are the Parties?

The nation's largest and most influential state also has the weakest political party system. Since the early part of this century, California parties have been systematically reduced in power and influence.

As shown in Table 4.1, California was heavily dominated by the Republican Party from 1940 to 1960. This was just the most recent period of Republican control, for historically the state has been Republican-leaning and sometimes one-party Republican. California started its first decade (the 1850s) as a Democratic state. However, the impact of the Civil War shifted political sentiments toward the Union and the Republicans. The post-Civil War era was a fairly evenly balanced period which ended abruptly with the economic turmoil of the 1890s. Between 1867 and 1894, for example, the state governorship alternated without exception between the Republicans and Democrats. The Republican Ulysses S. Grant won California's electoral vote by a margin of 500 votes in 1868, and 24 years later, the Democratic standard-bearer Grover Cleveland secured California by a mere 124 votes. However, California, like most of the nation, responded to the economic turmoil of the 1890s by shifting its political support to the Republican Party. From 1898 to 1938, all of California's governors were Republicans. Winning the state legislature in the 1890s, the GOP did not relinquish control of the state assembly until 1937 or the state senate until 1959. Yet, to claim that the Republicans were running the state in the late nineteenth and early twentieth centuries would be to ignore the role of the Southern Pacific Railroad in the state's politics. With its tremendous financial resources and its eagerness for political power, the Southern Pacific Railroad constructed a sophisticated and ruthless political machine. "It made little difference which party was in power, the railroad still ruled. . . . In 1900, the Republican Party ran California and the Southern Pacific Railroad ran the Republican Party."[48] The Southern Pacific often functioned like a political party—recruiting legislative candidates, financing the campaigns, and organizing their victors in the state legislature.

In 1910 Progressive reformers under the leadership of Hiram Johnson launched an attack against the power of the railroad and the establishment of the Republican Party. With Progressive Johnson in the governor's chair and effective Progressive majorities in both houses of the legislature, a series of reform laws was enacted that nearly destroyed California's parties. With the twofold goal of reforming the state's style of politics and eliminating the parties as powerful actors, the reformers established nonpartisan elections in all local contests, forced the parties to adopt certain organizational structures, and stripped the parties of many of their vital functions. The Progressive period lasted scarcely more than 10 years in California, but it had a profound effect on the two parties by weakening them significantly.

After the glow had worn off the reform movement (by 1920), California's voters again supported the conservative Republicans who regained nearly complete control of the state. The Democrats reached their nadir in 1924, when they held only 7 out of a total of 120 seats in the legislature.[49] During the 1920s the Republican Progressives (rather than the almost nonexistent Democrats) actually served as the opposition party. "There was no Democratic politics to speak of in California throughout the 1920s. Republican nomination was tantamount to election." Between 1920 and 1930 a total of 555 offices were up for election within the state; the Democrats won only 25 or 4.5 percent. No Democrats were elected to statewide executive office, and no Democratic gubernatorial candidate received more than 36 percent of the vote.[50]

As a result of the Depression of the 1930s, the Democratic Party in California (as elsewhere) experienced a resurgence. From 1930 to 1936, 1.5 million registered voters were added to the Democratic total, while the Republicans lost nearly 400,000. The Democrats won the governorship in 1938 and control of the assembly in 1937, but they could not take full advantage of the unsettled political situation to become the dominant party; thus, California entered into a period of two-party competition.

The Progressive Legacy and the Weakness of California Parties

The major reforms of the Progressive period in California included: strict party organization requirements, cross-filing in primary elections, and adoption of the direct primary. The statutes pertaining to the activities and organization of California parties are perhaps the most detailed and restrictive in the nation; the parties have almost no flexibility in tailoring their organizations to fit their needs. Each party must have a state convention, a state central committee, and a complete set of county committees. Winston Crouch has described the party organizational structure as "resembling a pyramid in shape—and sometimes as lifeless."[51] Required to meet yearly in the state capital, Sacramento, the state conventions seem dull and insignificant. Here, the 170 delegates who are either incumbents or party nominees for the various state and federal offices in California adopt their state party platforms. And in California these platforms have even less significance, if that is possible, than elsewhere in the nation. The party state central committees, with between 1000 and 1500 members, are made up of delegates to the state convention as well as chairmen of the 58 party county central committees and their appointees. Serving on the party state central committee is often given as a reward for financial contributions; it reflects little real power. Of course, a committee of this size cannot exercise any real leadership. Any leadership would have to be exercised by the state party chairman and the state executive committee. The chairman cannot succeed himself, and the post must be rotated between representatives of northern and southern California. In short, the reformers designed such a large state central committee that it was bound to be ineffective, gave it no real executive, assigned it no meaningful functions, and finally made it nonrepresentative and undemocratic in its member selection.

Only the bottom layer of the party organization is chosen by the general electorate. The county central committees are elected by popular vote during the primaries for a 3-year term. Yet even these committees were designed to be impotent. The Los Angeles County central committees have a total of 217 members each. It is significant that California has no party organizations on the city or precinct levels as found in Illinois, Texas, and almost every other state. Since the reformers made local politics nonpartisan, they saw no reason for parties to organize at the grassroots level.

The over-all effect of the mandatory party organization was to undermine the vitality of the parties. There is no continuity between the top two levels (made up of officeholders, nominees, and their appointees) and the bottom level which is elected by the public.

> *A party organization in California hence really consists of a letterhead, offices in San Francisco and Los Angeles with skeletal staffs, and a dispersion of unpaid spare-time officers who have no way of mobilizing efforts on behalf of the party except through unpredictable tides of sentiment. . . . The reformers, while solemnly preserving conventional political nomenclature, left little in substance that a voter could attach himself to.*[52]

With party organizations (in California and elsewhere) largely resembling Hollywood movies sets, it should not be surprising that the parties do not perform an important role in campaigning. Each candidate whether for statewide or local office, puts together his own personal campaign organization and thus owes nothing to the party if he wins. Modern campaign management firms, now so prevalent throughout the country, emerged in California during the 1950s to fill the void left by the parties in helping their candidates' campaigns.

Ironically, parties are the only state organizations that cannot endorse various candidates before the primaries. Therefore, a number of unofficial political organizations informally attached to the two major parties have emerged since the 1930s. First, the California Republican Assembly (CRA) was formed in 1934 to try to counter the New Deal Democratic revival. Because these groups are not political parties, they do not have to meet the stringent provisions aimed at the parties. In many ways, though, the informal organizations function as California's real political parties: they organize voting precincts, enlist voter support, recruit candidates, make preprimary endorsements, do such "drudgery" work as fund-raising and envelop-stuffing, and offer many of the services of a viable campaign organization.[53]

The CRA, representing a more liberal faction of the Republican Party, achieved a great deal from the late 1930s to the mid-1950s, with almost all Republican nominees carrying the CRA endorsement. The conservatives within the party counterattacked in the early 1960s and gained control of the CRA in 1964—the year of Goldwater's California primary victory. A year earlier, some arch-conservatives formed their own organization—the United Republicans of California (UROC), which is still an extreme ultraconservative faction within the party. After the liberals lost control of the CRA, they decided to build their own organization—the California Republican League (CRL)—and allowed the conservatives to keep the CRA.

The Democrats began to organize informally after the Republican victories of 1952, with the establishment of the California Democratic Council—a statewide federation of local Democratic clubs; many of these clubs had been established to help Adlai Stevenson's 1952 presidential campaign in California. A tremendously vital, volunteer political organization, the CDC reached a peak in 1958 when all of the Democratic primary winners and all of the Democratic candidates except the one for secretary of state won in the general election. At that time the CDC had more than 100,000 members; this figure has now dwindled to about 10,000 or less.[54]

Cross-filing, or the practice of permitting a candidate to enter the primaries of both major parties and thus secure the nominations of both, has also contributed to the long-term mailaise of California parties. From the early 1910s to the 1950s names would appear on the primary ballots without any indication of party affiliation. Thus, Republicans could win not only in their own nomination but that of the Democrats as well, thereby overcoming the numerical advantage held by the Democrats since the 1930s. Cross-filing reached its peak effectiveness in congressional races in 1940, when 55 percent of the state's seats were filled in the primary election by candidates who had secured both major-party nominations. In the 1944 primaries for the assembly and senate, 80 and 90 percent of the seats, respectively, were won in the primary election.[55] Needless to say, the tradition of cross-filing served to reduce the meaning of parties to insignificance. After cross-filing was abolished in 1959, a party could finally call its nominees its own.

The Progressives also enacted an effective civil service law that eliminated nearly all of the material incentives for supporting the parties. In his classic study of volunteer Democratic political clubs, James Q. Wilson discovered that Pat Brown, Senior, had only about 600 political jobs under his control as governor, and most of these were honorific and thus unpaid.[56]

No discussion on the weakness of parties in California would be complete without mentioning the fundamental hostility of Californians toward parties. Gelb and Palley speak of "antiparty trends" as a fundamental aspect of American political culture.[57] As a result of corruption during the time of the Southern Pacific—Republican Party closeness, the party was viewed as the epitome of bad government and a legitimate target for destruction. This attitude, which prevailed during the early part of this century, still exists to some extent in California's political culture. Few people seem to favor any substantial changes that would enable the parties to function as effective political organizations. Today, California exemplifies a new style of non-party politics, where the candidate alone is of any importance. Although there are signs of a revival of party power in the state legislature, it appears that there will be little party influence in California politics in the near future.

If, indeed, as John R. Owens has remarked, California is the place where the future patterns of American politics first unfold themselves. California's un-party system may soon prevail throughout the rest of the country.[58] In responding to a question from James Reston about California's political contribution to the rest of the nation, Gladwin Hill said:

> It offers the example of a large number of people who have scrapped the party system in its orthodox form, and have got along fairly well nevertheless. It has demonstrated that with the most ramshackle, illogical arrangements for Party politics, citizens can keep closely in step with national political trends and state government can be kept honest and progressive.[59]

Intraparty Factionalism in the South

Real political competition in the South is among intraparty factions within the Democratic Party, In the 100 years since the end of the Reconstruction period, the Democrats have almost completely dominated electoral politics in the 11 former states of the Confederacy. The feeble Republican Party there is made up of a patronage-motivated group of professional politicians who are nourished by the periodic crumbs thrown their way when a Republican occupies the White House. The GOP often does not run a candidate for lower-level offices, although recently they have offered more candidates for statewide offices, these people seldom win.

Since the general elections in November seldom have much electoral significance, one must look to the Democratic Party primary election where the real decision-making occurs. Here, candidates from rival factions within the party fight the real political battles of the South. Intraparty Democrtic factions were researched by V. O. Key in his classic study, *Southern Politics*.[60] Some of these factions will coalesce around a particularly charismatic leader and will survive as long as he has influence within the state. Others are built around family ties, economic considerations, regionalism, and rarely, ideological differences. Key did not view factions as an adequate replacement for two-party competition in the South. Factions do not reduce voter confusion because they have no continuity in name, voter base, or organization, as parties normally do. Rival candidates are difficult to distinguish because their allegiances are not mentioned on the primary election ballots. Candidate recruitment is often chaotic because acceptable procedures have not been established, and candidates running under the same label must resort to unusual campaign tactics in order to win primary victories. Consequently, demagoguery and buffoonery have often been the norm in Southern primaries. Last, but not least, factions seem to be amorphous structures and have not functioned as initiators of governmental policies.

Key described both bifactional and multifactional systems. In the bifactional states, the Democractic Party has two major factions—usually the state's dominant political family and its major opponents. In Louisiana, Georgia, and Virginia politics has been dominated by the Long, Talmadge, and Byrd families. Alabama has been bifactional in congressional elections and multifactional on the gubernatorial level, while, Texas's bifactionalism consists of liberal and conservative wings of the Democratic Party. Factionalism can also be found in the few stronghold Republican states: Vermont exemplifies bifactionalism through family ties (pro and anti-Proctor family) and Maine has multifactional patterns similar to those found in Florida and Arkansas.

Factional politics is quite typical of the South. It continues with surprising vigor in Louisiana and Virginia so long as the Longs and Byrds still dominate state politics. Texas continues to be ideologically fragmented, and various types of multifactionalism will prevail where the Republicans cannot challenge the incumbent Democrats. Although V. O. Key concluded that "the South really has no parties,"[61] Giovanni Sartori believes that the South's politics resembles the two-tiered federal system:

> The South is not politics without parties, but a case of party system atrophy resulting from historical conditions and also a two-tier structuring of American party politics which allows for the deficiencies of one level to be compensated at the other level.[62]

The Decline of Party Control over Candidates

It can be argued that of all the functions performed by parties in a democracy, nominating and providing campaign support are most essential to the continued existence of parties as meaningful political structures. Since the 1940s parties have gradually lost their nomination function; moreover, the dynamics of the primary process have diminished the role of party organizations in general election campaigns.

Over the years candidates have been selected in different ways. Soon after the Revolutionary War, nomination was largely by an informal self-selection process. Local notables would sound out other influentials, and names would be placed in the race by a simple announcement in local newspapers or on bulletin boards. However, as the first parties began to organize in the late 1790s, they attempted to concentrate their efforts on certain candidates. The caucus was devised so that party members could gather together and select a candidate for public office. Candidates for statewide offices were usually chosen by caucuses held in the state capital, but due to transportation difficulties at that time, most caucus participants lived in or near the capital city. Consequently, by 1800 most states had switched to the *legislative caucus* to select candidates for governor and lieutenant governor. However, since a party's legislative contingent did not always include members from all parts of a state, some delegates elected by caucuses in the unrepresented parts of a state were added. This was called a *mixed-caucus* selection system.

Congressional caucuses came into being in 1800 for selecting U.S. presidential and vice-presidential candidates. They continued to be used until the controversial election of 1824, when the Republican congressional caucus could not agree on a successor to James Monroe and split its vote among five serious contenders. The potential losers boycotted the nominating session and used such alternative methods as state legislatures, state conventions, and mixed caucuses to nominate themselves. This confusion continued through election of 1828. Then, in 1832, the Jacksonian forces used a *national convention* to nominate Martin Van Buren for vice president.

Actually conventions had been used on the state level since 1824 to nominate candidates for governor, with the number of delegates usually equaling the number of state legislators. Stair-step conventions were created to select candidates on all levels of American politics. It was felt that conventions would reduce factionalism, facilitate balanced tickets, open nominations to more persons, and democratize the party process.

Conventions did not significantly democratize the candidate selection processes, for they proved to be perhaps even more unrepresentative than the old caucus system. They became dominated by local party bosses, who pushed forward slates of their own delegates. But, most important, conventions never appealed to the public. Despite these weaknesses, conventions might have continued as the principal way of selecting candidates if it had not been for the ambitions of a young man from Wisconsin at the end of the 1890s. Robert M. La Follette wanted the Republican nomination for governor of Wisconsin in 1896, but he lost it at the state convention because of the opposition of the party bosses. When he was denied the nomination a second time in 1898, La Follette, vowing to destroy boss rule, promoted the idea of the *direct primary* to accomplish that end. His quest for the direct primary became the central plank in his crusade against the Wisconsin bosses; when he finally won the nomination and governorship in 1900, the most important part of his legislative program was to secure direct primary law. In 1903 the Wisconsin legislature finally passed the first mandatory and comprehensive primary law. Austin Ranney has called this law the most radical party reform in American history.[63]

By 1917, only four states had not yet enacted a direct primary law; 32 were both mandatory and comprehensive. Reformers like La Follette hoped to purify the parties by means of the direct primary; others who opposed parties even more hoped that the direct primary would destroy them. The reformers had great expectations for the direct primary: they hoped that it would end boss rule forever, that it would revive the public's interest in politics; that it would attract better candidates to run for public office, and that it would translate the public's desires directly into political reality. Almost by fate the United States had been swept by a reform movement that, among other things, included a candidate-selection device that would make our party system unique among democratic nations.

Today, without a doubt, the direct primary is the principal method for selecting candidates in the United States. It is interesting to note that although many of our institutions and governmental structures have been copied by other nations, not one has ever adopted the direct primary. Elsewhere, party organizations have retained complete control over those who will represent the parties on election ballots.

All 50 states use the direct primary for nominating candidates on at least some level of government. Thirty-six states use it for all statewide offices and most lower-level offices. Three Southern states require it for the Democratic Party but allow the Republicans to select their candidates by conventions. Nine have mixed systems that combine conventions and primaries in various interesting patterns, which will be discussed later on. Two states use primaries for some statewide offices and conventions for others.[64]

There are three major types of direct primaries, as well as a number of subtypes:

1. *The Closed Primary*: Most states use this type of primary, which is least objectionable to the parties. In 40 states, only those voters who are willing to declare their party affiliation are allowed to vote in their party's election. These declarations must be made months before the primary election, the voter cannot change his mind at a later date. In some states like Texas the voter can declare his party choice at the polls and then receive the ballot for that party. Thus, closed primaries try to limit a given party's nomination to those who are willing to disclose their preference for that party.

2. *The Open Primary*: Eight states (Idaho, Michigan, Minnesota, Montana, North Dakota, Utah, Vermont, and Wisconsin) allow their voters to select their party primary in the privacy of the voting booth. The usual procedure is to give each voter the ballots of both parties and then let the voter fill out the ballot of his choice. Understandably, party organizations oppose this type of primary because it permits "raiding." Say, for example, that a two-term incumbent governor is running unopposed (or with insignifcant opposition) in the Democratic primary and there is a hotly contested race between two Republican candidates in their primary. Republicans are afraid that many Democrats will not vote in their own primary because there is no real contest but will vote instead in the Republican race—perhaps for the weaker candidate, thereby helping the Democrat in the general election. Such fears do not seem to have much foundation; the best examples of a crossover effect, but not raiding, seem to be in the presidential nominations and are based on a real preference for the candidate of the opposite party rather than on an effort to hurt that party.[65] Sometimes, party organizations try to get rid of open primaries and replace them with closed primaries. When Utah tried to do this, the public protested the restriction

on its freedom of choice and the parties were obliged to bring back the open primary in the next election.

3. *The Blanket Primary*: This is the third type of primary, but it is found only in Washington, Louisiana, and Alaska. In Washington State, the blanket primary became law by means of initiative despite the parties' objections, and there has been enough popular support to keep it on the statute books. In essence, the blanket primary, allows each voter to participate in *both* party primaries so long as he does not do so for the same office. Thus, a voter can select his favorite among the Democratic nominees for governor, but if Democratic U.S. Senator Jackson has no opposition in his bid from other Democrats, the voter can select among the Republican nominees for the U.S. Senate post. It is assumed that this type of primary leads to frequent "raiding"— the nomination of weaker candidates in one party due to supporters from the other party. In fact, the evidence seems to indicate that the electorate in Washington is rather sophisticated, for when voters have "crossed over" on a certain office, they have generally selected the better candidates—perhaps thinking, "if my candidate loses, then it won't be a complete disaster for the state."

The following are subtypes of primaries:

1. *The Runoff Primary*: Found in nine Southern states plus Oklahoma, the runoff primary is a natural outgrowth of the one-party Democratic domination. One example of this type of primary occurred in Alabama in 1968. The result of the Democratic primary for a U.S. senate election was:

		Percent
Jim Allen	224,483	*(40)*
John Crommelin	10,926	*(2)*
Jim Folsom	32,004	*(6)*
Armistead Selden	190,283	*(34)*
Mrs. Frank Stewert	5368	*(1)*
Bob Smith	92,928	*(17)*

Since Jim Allen failed to obtain more than 50 percent of the vote, he and the second-ranked candidate, Armistead Selden, faced each other in a runoff primary several weeks later, which Allen barely won.

Runoff Primary 1968

Allen	196,511	*(51)*
Selden	192,446	*(49)*

The November general election was just a ritual:

Allen (D)	638,774	*(70)*
Hooper (R)	201,227	*(22)*
Schwenn (3rd party)	72,699	*(8)*

A primary runoff is needed in order to make sure that one candidate receives a majority of the vote. Another reason for the runoff primary in the South in years past was to prevent black voters from winning elective office with a small percentage of the vote in a crowded field.

2. *Challenge Primaries*: Several states that use direct primaries have attempted to combine the democratic features of primaries with the organizational supporting aspects of conventions. Connecticut, which was the last state to adopt primary elections, still placed main responsibility for candidate selection in the hands of the state party convention. If a loser for a party nomination had at least 20 percent of the total vote at the state convention, he could challenge the party's choice in a primary election. It should be noted that this is not mandatory, but is up to the defeated convention candidate. It is a tribute to the persuasive powers of the Bailey-led Democratic primary Party machine that the first statewide challenge primary occurred in 1970—15 years after the law went into effect. Occasionally, the party's choice will be defeated by voters in the challenge primaries; for example, Charles Tisdale lost to insurgent Geoffrey Peterson by 1100 votes in the 1976 Connecticut Democratic congressional primary. Delaware specifies that a candidate must win at least 35 percent of the convention vote in order to challenge the nominee in a primary. New York State uses the state party central committee to make nominations, and a losing candidate can demand a primary if he has won 25 percent of the committee vote or can gather 20,000 petition signatures.[66]

Utah's convention-primary system deserves special mention. That state's nomination process begins with mass meetings in all of the state's voting districts or precincts. Each voting district selects delegates to county and state conventions. At these conventions, the delegates vote to nominate candidates for office at all levels within the state. If a candidate wins more than 70 percent of the total vote, his name is automatically placed on the general election ballot. If this does not occur, then the top two candidates will enter a primary election in September. The Utah two-step system has several significant advantages: it opens the electoral process to as many citizens who want to participate and gives the party organization a chance to control its nominations. One disadvantage is that the mass meetings may be packed with loyal supporters of a candidate who really does not have statewide strength.

3. *Nonpartisan Primaries*: Another anti-party device that stemmed from the Progressive Movement was the nonpartisan primary in which all the candidates try to place first or second in the field and thus advance to the general election ballot. Since party labels are not allowed, Republicans, Democrats, third-party candidates, and independents are all grouped together on the primary ballot. Many candidates for local offices, frequently state-level judges, and the Nebraska state legislature are selected in nonpartisan primaries. Some of these nonpartisan primaries are actually independent of parties and political organizations; others are so heavily permeated with party endorsements or unofficial party interventions that they are nonpartisan in name only.

Despite the popularity of the direct primary, the party convention has not disappeared at the state level. Almost every state allows minor parties to select their candidates by conventions of party supporters. In fact, in the state of Washington, a minor party must hold a convention on primary day, attendeded by at least 100 members, in order to get on the general election ballot. Indiana, a relatively strong party state, requires a convention for the nomination of all persons to statewide office. Michigan uses a primary to nominate gubernatorial candidates. As noted earlier, New York, Connecticut, Delaware, and Utah still use state conventions (although New York has now switched to state central committees) together with primaries, if necessary.

Direct Primaries: A Serious Continuing Threat to Party Organization

How much of this decline in the parties' vitality can be directly attributed to the adoption of the direct primary? We tend to agree with V. O. Key, the dean of American party scholars:

> *The adoption of the direct primary opened the road for disruptive forces that gradually fractionalized the party organization. By permitting more effective direct appeals by individual politicians to the party membership, the primary system freed forces driving toward the disintegration of party organizations and facilitated the construction of factions and cliques attached to the ambitions of individual leaders. The convention system compelled leaders to treat, to deal, to allocate nominations; the primary permits individual aspirants by one means or another to build a wider following within the party....* [67]

Another party scholar has concluded:

> *If the advocates of the direct primary wanted to aim beyond the nomination process and strike the parties themselves, they found their target. In many instances the direct primary has weakened the parties' control of nominations, robbed their organizations of an important raison d'être, and liberated their officeholders. It has in many important ways made the American political parties what they are today.* [68]

The United States is the only democratic nation in which political parties have been stripped of their basic function—candidate selection. Sorauf believes that the direct primary best explains most of the differences between the American and other Western nations' party systems. [69] Many nominations for local government are made on a nonpartisan basis; the county, state, and congressional nominations are often made by direct primary, where the parties have little influence. Even the main prize of American politics—the presidential nomination—has almost completely slipped away from party control, since party conventions merely rubberstamp the collective decisions of the presidential primaries. In the early 1900s, many Progressive reformers

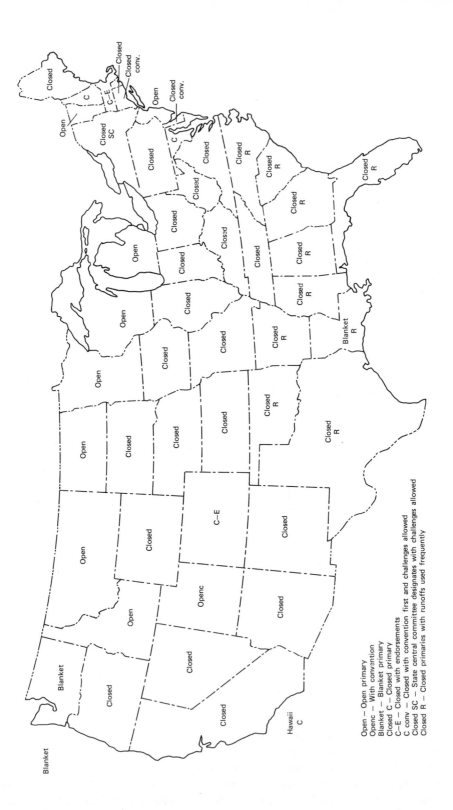

Open – Open primary
Openc – With convention
Blanket – Blanket primary
Closed C – Closed primary
C–E – Closed with endorsements
C conv – Closed with convention first and challenges allowed
Closed SC – State central committee designates with challenges allowed
Closed R – Closed primaries with runoffs used frequently

hoped that the direct primary might cripple, if not destroy, the corrupt party organizations of that time. It is quite clear that party organizations have been badly
wounded; for every party organization that can usually impose its candidate choices
in a primary (for example, the Cook County Democratic Party), there are hundreds
whose candidate choices are ignored by the primary voters. In 1974 the New York
Democratic Party State Central Committee put together an ethnically balanced slate of
candidates for statewide offices. That slate was completely rejected by the voters
in the Democratic primary, and the insurgent candidates were nominated. Ramsey
Clark was nominated for U.S. Senator after winning only 1 percent of the vote at the
state Democratic convention. There are countless examples in which a candidate selected by the party leaders is defeated in the primary by a challenger who has put
together a non-party, personal political organization.

What, then, are the consequences for the party organizations? Parties cannot select
their own candidates, they cannot expect to be able to influence these people once
they have been elected to public office. Unless there are meaningful sanctions, such
as the threat of denying future nominations or campaign support, why should a candidate pay any attention to the party leadership? Furthermore, the parties no longer
have incentives and rewards for party workers or followers. Traditionally, such workers have been rewarded for thousands of hours of behind-the-scenes work by giving
them a chance for public office. This reward is no longer meaningful when many
others can seek the nomination with a reasonable chance of success through the direct primary.

The prospects for responsible party government also seem dim. Low levels of party
cohesiveness in Congress, the rise of mavericks, and the weakness of congressional
leadership are related in part to the independence of congressmen from their party
organizations. Since congressmen can be nominated and win elections without party
help, why should they follow the party leaders in Congress?

Sometimes a party is embarrassed when a candidate gets its nomination but none of
the party leaders want that candidate. This is what happened to Congressman Allan
Howe (D-Utah). In 1976 Howe was convicted on charges of sex solicitation; the Utah
State Democratic Party, finding that Howe had no opposition in the party primary, did
not know how to replace him as their candidate unless he would voluntarily withdraw.
Consequently, the party tried to disavow Howe's candidacy and encourage a hopeless
write-in candidacy—thereby conceding the election to the Republican candidate.

Primaries are also very expensive in the sense that they divert money from the
general election. Millions of dollars can be spent in statewide primary races; this is
much more than would be spent for selecting candidates at a convention or at a closed
party meeting. Generous party contributors are so often tapped during the primaries
that few sources of money are still available for the general election campaign. Of
course, the primary expenditures are not totally wasted because extending the length of
the campaign often helps the candidate to become better known among the electorate.

Hard-fought primary battles may increase intraparty strife and bitterness. Hard
feelings are not necessarily overcome by the joint support statement issued the day

after the primary election, and sometimes the losers sit out the general election or even decide to support the other party's candidate. Although such splits also occur in a more closed selection process, they seem to be exacerbated by the media politics that exists on the higher levels of today's primary campaigns.[70] Some scholars have argued that direct primaries encourage one-party dominance in many parts of the country. V. O. Key pointed to the Democratic Party Primaries in the South, the place where the real action takes place, and thus the place where all new voters turn. Researchers since Key have noted the decline of one-party dominance in the South and elsewhere and thus have discounted the effect of the primaries on party competition.

The adoption of direct primaries has also helped to undermine the parties' campaign support for candidates. Although party organizations are supposed to be neutral in primary contests, they do intervene in some parts of the country—usually with subtle assistance to incumbents. However, each candidate, even an incumbent, is usually compelled to put together his own personal campaign organization composed of specialists if he hopes to win the primary election. This personal organization is notable because of the staff's personal or professional ties to the candidate. The lucky candidate who wins the nomination with his own "team" is not likely to abandon the combination that has already proved its worth for a group of party advisers whose value and loyalty are unknown. Actually the primary winners have not yet faced this particular dilemma because party organizations cannot now offer an alternative package of specialists and services. Thus, the candidate's need to organize in order to win primary elections leads him even further away from the party organization.

Primaries and Parties: The Over-all Impact

To say that some party organizations have learned to live with the direct primary and have adapted their tactics accordingly seems to ignore the over-all negative impact of this method for selecting candidates on our party organizations. Few defenders of the primary would argue that they have successfully achieved the goals put forth by the Progressives in the early part of this century. Since voter turnouts are normally low in primary elections, the candidate-selection process has not become substantially more democratic. In many states a primary election turnout of 30 percent of the eligible voters is considered good. Often a candidate can win the nomination with the support of between 10 and 15 percent of a party's registered voters. This may be even fewer persons than the number of party members who participate in a statewide party convention, starting with precinct mass meetings. Despite pleas on the editorial pages of newspapers to vote in the primaries, 70 to 80 percent of the electorate do not do so unless there is a particularly important intraparty fight or an important office is at stake. Neither has the objective of increased competition for the nomination been achieved. Approximately 60 percent of congressional nominations in 1972 were unopposed, and more than 80 percent of the candidates were nominated with little or no real opposition. This lack of competition extends down to the lowest levels of state government—the primaries for the state legislature. Research done in Pennsylvania and Wisconsin has shown that approximately 60 percent of their state legislative nomintions were unopposed. There is generally more primary competition in urban areas where an incumbent is not seeking renomination.

Since the primary has weakened party discipline and undercut party government, one can ask if parties serve any useful purpose anymore. It seems unlikely that anything will replace the direct primary in the foreseeable future; in fact, trends seem to indicate that primaries will be used even more (30 states used the presidential primary in 1976). Unfortunately for the future of our parties, the electorate has been persuaded that the primary is the "American way" to choose candidates. Perhaps the only way in which the parties could hope to alleviate the adverse impact of primaries would be to try to encourage convention-primary or convention-challenge primary combinations where more selection decisions could be made by the party leadership and actual supporters at a convention. However, since the general public is somewhat anti-party, taking a small step toward a decreased emphasis on primaries seems highly unlikely. Therefore, American political parties will probably have to learn to live with the primary system and without having any real control over those who run under their various banners.

Conclusions

In every other modern democratic nation except West Germany, political parties are not regulated by restrictive laws; they control their own membership, choose their own leaders, draft programs, and select their nominees with little or no governmental interference. In the United States, however, parties are closely regulated by both state and federal laws.[71] We have the type of party system we seem to want—very weak and politically ineffective. And there is very little indication that anything could be changed in the near future. The non-party style of politics found in California may eventually spread to other parts of the nation.

FOOTNOTES

1. In 1968 50 percent of the precincts in Kansas had no candidates at all for the post of precinct committeeman. Contests were found in 3 percent of the precincts, and the rest had only one candidate for each post. John S. Saloma and Frederick H. Sontag, *Political Parties* (New York: Vintage, 1972), p. 159.

2. Ibid., p. 271.

3. One such giant county committee is that of the Bronx (New York) with 3750 members.

4. Saloma and Sontag, op. cit., Chapter 5.

5. James McGregor Burns, *The Deadlock of Democracy* (Englewood Cliffs, N.J.: Prentice-Hall, 1963), pp. 236-237.

6. Gordon G. Henderson, *An Introduction to Political Parties* (New York: Harper and Row, 1976), pp. 116-117.

7. Frank B. Feigert and Margaret Conway, *Parties and Politics in America* (Boston: Allyn and Bacon, 1976), p. 143. In one midwestern state in 1960, a Republican national committee-

man was expected to contribute a minimum of $25,000 to the party each year. For specific empirical research on party organization, see David W. Abbott and Eward T. Rogowsky, *Political Parties: Leadership. Organization, Linkage* (Chicago: Rand McNally, 1971).

8. Henderson, op. cit., p. 119.

9. Ralph de Toledano, *The Washington Post*, September 21, 1976.

10. Saloma and Sontag, op. cit., p. 92.

11. Ibid., p. 100; and Feigert and Conway, op. cit., p. 41.

12. Cornelius P. Cotter and Bernard C. Hennessy, *Politics without Power* (New York: Atherton, 1964); and see Hugh Bone, *Party Committees and and National Politics* (Seattle: University of Washington Press, 1958).

13. See Alfred Steinberg, *The Bosses* (New York: Signet, 1972). For more about the urban machines in American history, see: John A. Gardiner and David J. Olson, *Theft of the City* (Bloomington, Ind.: University of Indiana Press, 1974); Charles N. Glaab and A. Theodore Brown, *A History of Urban America* (New York: Macmillan, 1976); Fred I. Greenstein, "The Changing Pattern of Urban Party Politics," *The Annals* 353 (1964); Robert K. Merton, "The Latent Functions of the Machine: A Sociologist's View." In *Social Theory and Social Structure*, edited by Robert K. Merton (New York: Free Press, 1957), pp. 71-82; William L. Riordon, *Plunkitt of Tammany Hall* (New York: Knopf, 1948); Raymond E. Wolfinger, "Why Political Machines Have Not Withered Away and Other Revisionist Thoughts," *The Journal of Politics 34*, No. 2 (May 1972), pp. 365-398; and Harold Zink, *City Bosses in the United States: A Study of Twenty Municipal Bosses* (Durham, N.C.: Duke University Press, 1930).

14. Mike Royko, *Boss: Richard J. Daley of Chicago* (New York: Signet, 1971); and Milton Rakove, *Don't Make No Waves, Don't Back No Losers* (Bloomington, Ind.: University of Indiana Press, 1975).

15. See Royko, op. cit.; and Rakove, op. cit., pp. 112-113.

16. Theodore J. Lowi, "Machine Politics—Old and New," *The Public Interest*, No. 9 (Fall 1967), pp. 83-84.

17. The New York submachines and their bosses are Joseph Crangle (Buffalo), Meade Esposito (Brooklyn), Matthew Troy (Queens), Pat Cunningham (Bronx), and Frank Rossetts (Manhattan). Neal R. Peirce, *The Megastates* (New York: Norton, 1973), p. 57.

18. Alexander B. Callow, Jr., *The City Boss in America* (New York: Oxford University Press, 1976), p. 267.

19. V.O. Key, Jr., *Southern Politics* (New York: Vintage, 1949, pp. 274-75).

20. Rakove, op. cit., pp. 256-284.

21. By 1984, the following United States cities are expected to have black majorities. New Orleans, Richmond, Baltimore, Jacksonville, Gary, Cleveland, St. Louis, Detroit, Philadelphia, Oakland, and Chicago. This list includes seven of the nation's ten largest cities. *Report of the National Advisory Commission on Civil Disorder* (Washington, D.C.: U.S. Govt. Printing Office, 1968), p. 216.

22. Austin Ranney, "Parties in State Politics," in *Politics in the American States*, edited by Herbert Jacob and Kenneth Vines (Boston: Little, Brown, 1976).

23. Neal Peirce, *The Great Plains States of America* (New York: Norton, 1973), p. 178.

24. Ibid., p. 183.

25. Michael Barone et al., *The Almanac of American Politics 1976* (Boston: Gambit, 1975). See descriptions of the political backgrounds of Massachusetts and Michigan.

26. Rakove, op. cit., p. 141.

27. Austin Ranney concluded that the two-party states were substantially more urbanized than the others and that the Republican-dominated states were the most agricultural and rural. Ranney, op. cit., p. 91. Trends seen in the 1976 election confirm this observation; the Republican stronghold is increasingly being centered in the region of the upper mountain states, Idaho, Wyoming, and Utah.

28. In 1977 special elections for congressional seats resulted in Republican victories in three out of four contests.

29. National Conference of State Legislatures, press release, November 4, 1976.

30. Nelson Polsby, ed., *Guide to U.S. Elections* (Washington, D.C.: Congressional Quarterly Press, 1975). See relevant Texas House elections.

31. Wilbourn E. Benton, *Texas: Its Government and Politics*, 3rd ed. (Englewood Cliffs, N.J.: Prentice-Hall, 1972), p. 86.

32. Clifton McCleskey, E. Larry Dickens, and Allan K. Butcher, *The Government and Politics of Texas*, 6th ed. (Boston: Little, Brown, 1978), p. 102.

33. Richard H. Kraemer, Ernest Crain, and William E. Maxwell, *Understanding Texas Politics* (New York: West, 1975), pp. 67-68.

34. Ibid., p. 68.

35. Peirce, *The Megastates*, op. cit., pp. 309-310.

36. Ibid.

37. McCleskey, op. cit., p. 54.

38. According to the 1970 census, 12.6 percent of Texas's population was black and 16.8 percent was Mexican American. As of June, 1976 161 blacks were elected in public offices (1 congressman, 9 Texas house members, 6 mayors, 63 city council members). As of 1971 736 Mexican Americans were in elected offices, including 2 congressmen, 2 state senators, 10 state house members, and a wide variety of local government positions. However, it should be kept in mind that there are more than 23,000 elected state officials in Texas. McCleskey, op. cit., pp. 119-121.

39. Benton, op. cit., p. 84.

40. Eugene W. Jones et al., *Practicing Texas Politics*, 2nd ed. (Boston: Houghton Mifflin, 1974), p. 69.

41. Benton, op. cit., p. 79.

42. Jones, op. cit., p. 64.

43. See David Kenney, *Basic Illinois Government* (Carbondale, Ill.: Southern Illinois University Press, 1974).

44. George S. Blair, "The Case for Cumulative Voting in Illinois," *Northwestern University Law Review*, July 1952, p. 351. See also: Austin Ranney, *ILlinois Politics* (New York: New York University Press, 1960); George S. Blair, "Cumulative Voting: Patterns of Party Allegiance and Rational Choice in Illinois State Legislature Contests," *American Political Science Review LII* (March 1958), pp. 123-130; and Jack Sawyer and Duncan MacRae, Jr., "Game

Theory and Cumulative Voting in Illinois: 1902-1954," *American Political Science Review LV* (December 1962), pp. 936-946.

45. Rakove, op, cit., p. 107.

46. Ibid., p. 144.

47. Winston W. Crouch, John C. Bollins, and Stanely Scott, *California Government and Politics*, 5th ed. (Englewood Cliffs, N.J.: Prentice-Hall, 1972), p. 42.

48. John R. Owens, Edmond Costantini, and Louis F. Weschler, *California Politics and Parties* (New York: Macmillan, 1970), pp. 32-33.

49. Gladwin Hill, *Dancing Bear: An Inside Look at California Politics* (New York: World, 1968), pp. 77, 108, 113.

50. Royce Delmatier's research, quoted in Michael P. Rogen and John L. Shover, *Political Change in California* (Westport, Conn.: Greenwood, 1970), p. 113.

51. Crouch, op. cit., p. 71.

52. Hill, op. cit., pp. 111-113.

53. Ruth A. Ross and Barbara S. Stone, *California's Political Process* (New York: Random House, 1973), p. 67.

54. Membership totals in the early 1970s for the Republican informal organizations were *CRA*, 12,000; *URC*, 9000; and *CRL*, 4000. Hill, op. cit., p. 243.

55. Crouch, op. cit., p. 73.

56. James Q. Wilson, *The Amateur Democrat* (Chicago: University of Chicago Press, 1962), reprinted in part in Eugene C. Lee and Willis D. Hawley, **The Challenge of California** (Boston: Little, Brown, 1976), p. 112.

57. Joyce Gelb and Marion L. Palley, *Tradition and Change in American Party Politics* (New York: Crowell, 1975), p. 7.

58. Owens, op. cit., p. 324.

59. Hill, op. cit., p. 268.

60. Key, op. cit.

61. Ibid., p. 299.

62. Giovanni Sartori, *Parties and Party System* (New York: Cambridge University Press, 1976), p. 87.

63. Austin Ranney, *To Cure the Mischiefs of Faction* (Berkeley: University of California Press, 1975), p. 121.

64. Ibid., p. 123.

65. Hugh A. Bone, *American Politics and the Party System* (New York: McGraw-Hill, 1971), p. 271.

66. New York City has now adopted runoff primaries if no candidate receives 40 percent of the vote. If no candidate gets 35 percent of the vote in Iowa and South Dakota, a party convention will select the candidate. Sorauf, op. cit., p. 218.

67. V.O. Key, Jr., *Politics, Parties and Pressure Groups* (New York: Crowell, 1964), pp. 342, 386.

68. Frank Sorauf, *Party Politics in America* (Boston: Little, Brown, 1976), p. 233.

69. Ibid., p. 210.

70. Robert A. Bernstein, "Divisive Primaries Do Hurt: U.S. Senate Races, 1956-1972", *American Political Science Review LXXI* (June 1977), pp. 540-545.

71. Ranney, *To Cure the Mischiefs of Faction*, op. cit., p. 47.

5
The Changing American Electorate

Since the 1960s voters have shown their disdain for parties and candidates either by crossing party lines or by staying at home. In 1974 only about one in three Americans of voting age bothered to vote. Among those who did, ticket-splitting was at an all-time high. The electorate of New Braunfels, Texas, displayed their contempt by voting for Mickey Mouse for county judge; he just barely lost.[1] The 1976 elections continued this trend. Voting participation declined from 63 percent of those eligible in 1960 to 54.4 percent in 1976—the lowest percentage since the Truman-Dewey race of 1948. The voters of 1976 were not a stable group with fixed party affiliations. The pre-election polls showed that the electorate, at first highly critical of the Republican Party, swung back to give President Ford more support than he could have expected right after the Republican National Convention. But even though the electorate gave Ford a substantial number of votes, there was no indication that this meant support for the party. Of those voters who had initially favored Carter but then switched to Ford, 17 percent did so because "Ford was the better man." Only 1 percent switched in order to "stay with my party."[2]

Significant third-party movements have threatened both major parties in the 1960s and 1970s. Eugene McCarthy and George Wallace tried to appeal to an independent-minded populace. Ronald Reagan claimed that the 1972 presidential election indicated a conservative mandate and said that, if the two major parties failed to represent the "real will" of the American people, he might lead a third party in 1976. Although Reagan lost the Republican presidential nomination in 1976, a Gallup poll taken in May 1976 found that 25 percent of all the voters said they would support a party that was more conservative than the Republicans.[3] A democratic political system cannot survive for long without the support of its citizens. When citizen support wanes, the potential for changing that political system is enhanced. Both the Democrats and Republicans are minority parties; neither party has a majority of the electorate. Only 21 percent identify themselves as Republicans, and 44 percent claim to be Democrats.[4] Empirical evidence also indicates a general shift away from the established parties, especially from the Republican Party. As young people begin to vote or refrain from doing so, they may affect the shape of American politics. This chapter discusses the changing American electorate—the new independents, the ticket-splitters, and the non-voters—as well as party reforms in delegate selection, and the new party activists.

PARTIES AND LIMITED POLITICAL PARTICIPATION

Parties depend upon their external environment. The general electorate is a major determinant of party activities and services. By providing (or not providing) the parties with skills, resources, and personnel, and by articulating demands (or not doing so), the electorate shapes the parties' political performance. Thus, in evaluating the criticism of party services and activities, we should remember what resources are available to the two major parties. Complaints are made that the parties are overly concerned with winning elections and not with formulating policies; the parties seem to be bent on "examining their navels." At the same time, voter turnout is low and other types of political activity are even lower.

Many people hold that it is important to participate in the political process that selects those who will be making major decisions affecting us all. Most Americans believe that people should be involved in the activities of their communities. In a national sample, 83 percent of those interviewed said that ordinary people ought to be participating in politics.[5] Academicians also extol the virtues of citizen participation. In building a case for citizen involvement, political scientists have suggested a wide range of social and personal benefits. They argue that citizen involvement is important because participation can make the individual a "better" person and participation results in "better" decisions. Defining participation as "citizen political activity that influences what the government does,"[6] political scientists have selected certain activities that they believe indicate participation and measured the percentage of the eligible public that engages in these activities. A landmark, Milbrath's *Political Participation*,[7] is an early example of an attempt to find out who is actively involved in politics and to what degree. Milbrath constructed a scale of political involvement, ranging from the lowest degree—voting—to the highest—holding public and party office.

Hierarchy of Political Involvement

Holding public and party office	
Being a candidate for office	
Soliciting political funds	Gladiatorial
Attending a caucus or a strategy meeting	Activities
Becoming an active member in a political party	
Contributing time in a political campaign	
Attending a political meeting or rally	Transitional
Making a monetary contribution to a party or candidate	Activities
Contacting a public official or a political leader	
Wearing a button or putting a sticker on the car	
Attempting to talk another into voting a certain way	Spectator
Initiating a political discussion	Activities
Voting	
Exposing oneself to political stimuli	
	Apathetics

Source: Lester Milbrath, *Political Participation* (Chicago: Rand McNally, 1965), p. 11.

Using Milbrath's categories, political scientists have done enormous amounts of research on who engages in these activities and how often. From their large collection of data, one can infer why parties concentrate mainly on securing votes at election time and why they cannot give candidates either strong financial or volunteer support for their campaigns.[8] They irony of the parties' situation has been well summed up in a political science tongue-in-cheek essay question:

> *It has been said that to be elected President of the United States, one must occupy the middle of the road, and middle-of-the-road candidates have been defined as men who do not want to make substantial changes in American life. In an essay of 25 words or less, explain why an electorate which is so vocally unhappy with so many aspects of American life prefers to vote for candidates who promise not to change anything.*[9]

Although most Americans seem to believe that one ought to participate in the political decision-making process, only a limited number actually do engage in some type of political activity. Even fewer do more than vote. A profile of citizen participation is presented in Table 5.1.

Those activities requiring more effort, such as contributing money and time to the parties, are generally performed by 10 to 15 percent of the eligible voters. Verba and Nie concluded that even in 1972, "It is quite clear that most acts of political participation are performed by only a small segment of the citizenry."[10]

DECLINING PARTY SUPPORT

Voting Turnouts

The historical record of voting turnout demonstrates that some of those who feel that a good citizen is one who votes, must have had a good excuse themselves on election day. Figure 5.1 indicates that voter participation has generally declined since the early 1960s.

In presidential elections generally no more than 65 percent of the eligible voters go to the polls; in nonpresidential elections only 40 to 50 percent cast a ballot. In the 1970s it seems that even fewer citizens are going to the polls. The Census Bureau's figures indicate that only 55 percent of the electorate voted in 1972; that only 45 percent of the 141 million eligible voters went to the polls in 1974.[11] Some 81.5 million Americans voted in the 1976 presidential election; although this was a record turnout in numbers, it represented only 54.4 percent of the electorate.

David Broder of *The Washington Post* has interpreted decreasing voter turnout as a sign of discontent:

> *When people who sell and service cars start talking in Detroit about their customers' reluctance to buy those "lemons," it's a pretty good sign the automobile business is in trouble. Something like that happened in Washington this week—but it happened to this town's major industry, which is not automobiles, of course, but politics.*[12]

Table 5.1 A Profile of Citizen Involvement

Type of Political Participation	Percentage
1. Report regularly voting in presidential elections	72
2. Report always voting in local elections	47
3. Active in at least one organization dealing with community problems	32
4. Have worked with others in trying to solve some community problems	30
5. Have attempted to persuade others to vote	28
6. Have actively worked for a party or candidates during an election	26
7. Have contacted a local government offical about some issue or problem	20
8. Have attended at least one political meeting or rally in last 3 years	19
9. Have contacted a state or national government official about some issue or problem	18
10. Have formed a group or organization to attempt to solve some local community problem	14
11. Have given money to a party or candidate during an election campaign	13
12. Presently a member of a political club or organization	8

Source: From Sidney Verba and Norman Nie, *Participation in America: Political Democracy and Social Equality* (New York: Harper and Row, 1972), p. 31.

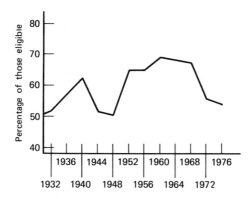

Sources: Figures for 1930 to 1968 in the U.S. Bureau of the Census, *Statistical Abstract of the United States 1969*, p. 368. Data for 1972 provided by the U.S. Bureau of the Census and Congressional Quarterly, Inc. Data for 1976 provided *Congressional Quarterly Weekly Report 34*, No. 45 (November 1976).

Alarmingly, the evidence shows that the citizens who have turned away from politics are both concerned and capable. A 1974 study of non-voters indicated that among people under 35 years of age, those with a college background outnumbered those with less education. Even among the older stay-at-homes, almost one-fourth had gone beyond high school. The new stay-at-homes are those who have decided there is nothing to be gained by voting. "We used to think that apathy and ignorance led to nonvoting," commented Walter DeVries, a North Carolina consultant and political scientist. "Now, we're finding that information and education lead to a deliberate decision not to vote."[13]

American citizens' dissatisfaction with the government extends to the two major parties. The public seems to be unhappy with the major-party candidates, the lack of policy differences between the parties, and the parties' non-representation of specific constituent needs. A Gallup poll taken of non-voters after the 1972 election indicated that 6 million eligible voters failed to vote because they were dissatisfied with the major party candidates.[14] The voter in 1976 was equally un-enthusiastic about the political parties and their candidates. A pre-election survey revealed that many of those who had decided not to vote believed that the "candidates say one thing and do another." Others in the sample refused because "it doesn't make any difference who is elected, because things never seem to work out right." A majority of the sample explained their decision to not vote because "Watergate proved that elected officials are only out for themselves."[15]

Although most non-voters claim that their lack of participation in presidential elections is due to their failure to register, since 1972 a significantly larger percentage of non-voters is saying that they have either no confidence or no interest in the electoral system. The percentage who said that they were "not interested in politics" increased from 4 percent in 1972 to 10 percent in 1976. The percentage of non-voters who said they were unhappy with both presidential candidates also increased during this 4-year period. Those claiming that they "did not like the candidates" increased from 10 percent in 1972 to 14 percent in 1976. Even those who voted did not necessarily *favor* any one candidate; 16 percent of Ford's supporters voted for him because he was "the lesser of three evils."[16] Although parties and candidates have never been able to appeal to all voters, it is apparent that now they are appealing to, and able to mobilize, even fewer voters.

Waning Party Identification and the New Independents

The 1970s have seen a decrease in the number of voters with a strong party affiliation and an increase in the number of independent voters. By the end of 1973 the Democrats had lost their national majority of party supporters; only 47 percent of the electorate claimed to be Democrats at that time. The Republican electorate had dropped to 25 percent. Then, in June 1975, a Gallup poll revealed that only 21 percent of all adults called themselves Republicans, 44 percent classified themselves as Democrats, and 35 percent claimed to be independents.[17] Figure 5.2 depicts the waning party identification among voters.

Robert Lane has suggested that people participate in politics to advance their economic well-being, to understand the world, to satisfy their need for friendship, to relieve intrapsychic tensions, to obtain power over others, and to defend and improve their self-esteem.[18] It appears that although many people in the past looked faithfully to the party as an avenue of political involvement, this is no longer true. Figure 5.2 indicates a number of trends.

First of all, identification with the two major parties has declined since 1940 until today one-third of the electorate classify themselves as politically independent. In 1940 both parties were about equal in strength: 38 percent of the electorate claimed to be Republicans, 42 percent identified themselves as Democrats, and 20 percent were independents. But since that time, the Republicans have lost substantial electoral support, most of which was picked up by the Democratic Party until 1964. From

Figure 5.2 Party identification in the American population.

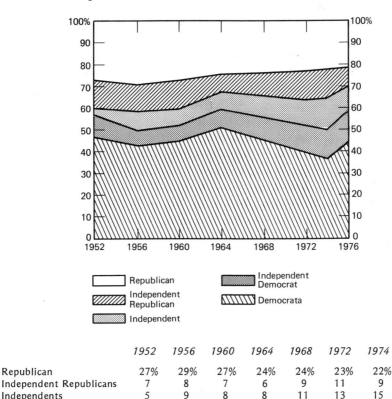

	1952	1956	1960	1964	1968	1972	1974	1976
Republican	27%	29%	27%	24%	24%	23%	22%	22%
Independent Republicans	7	8	7	6	9	11	9	8
Independents	5	9	8	8	11	13	15	11
Independent Democrats	10	7	8	9	10	11	13	14
Democrats	47	44	46	51	45	40	38	45

Source: Survey research center, Institute For Social Research, The University of Michigan, Ann Arbor, Michigan.

1964, however, many voters have fallen away from both major parties and become independents. Since 1972 the number of independents has outnumbered the Republicans; in 1976, 22 percent of the electorate identified themselves as Republicans, while 33 percent considered themselves independents.

Secondly, although the Republican Party has borne the brunt of the shift away from party affiliation, the Democratic Party has also lost support. In 1964 the Democrats had 51 percent of the electorate's support, in 1976 it had only 45 percent. In the 1964 presidential election, the Democratic candidate, Lyndon B. Johnson, received the largest electoral percentage margin in history. This triumph, however, was followed by 8 years of division among the Democratic coalition; confronted with the Vietnam war, racial issues, and urban riots, the public elected Richard Nixon, a Republican, by a narrow margin in 1968 and by a landslide in 1972. In 1976 Jimmy Carter, who successfully reunited the Democratic Party, received 82 percent of the Democratic vote—more than enough to recoup those losses of party support attributable to the 1968 and 1972 elections.

In third place, although partisan affiliation has declined, it is still the most stable predictor of the electorate's voting behavior. As Figure 5.2 indicates, while partisan affiliation has gradually declined since 1952, the division of the electorate between the two major parties has remained remarkably stable. From 1952 to 1976 the Republicans never enjoyed less than 21 nor more than 29 percent of the electorate's support. Both the magnitude and frequency of the Democratic Party's fluctuations have surpassed the Republicans'. Yet, those who identify themselves with a political party seem to be quite consistent in supporting their party's candidates. Less than one-third of the Democrats who defected to Nixon in 1972 also voted for a Republican candidate for the U.S. House. A majority of the Democrats who voted against McGovern did vote for other Democratic Party candidates.

And finally, regardless of their stated non-affiliation, the majority of independent voters support the same political party year after year, just as the Republicans and Democrats do. Although one-third of the electorate claims to be independent, Gallup found that most of this group admitted leaning toward one of the two major political parties; when these people were reclassified as either Republicans or Democrats, only 11 percent of the electorate remained actually independent. Similarly, another study redistributed the independents according to the party they supported most of the time; with the redistribution, only 13 percent of the sample was equally likely to vote for either party.[19]

Despite the decline in partisan affiliation, the 1976 elections indicated that possibly the decline in the Republican Party has ceased; in fact, Republican Party identification seems to have stabilized—there was a drop of only 1 percent in Republican support since 1972.[20] And the fact that the Republican Party has been a minority party has not prevented it from showing remarkable strength. Since 1952 the Republicans have been in the White House for 16 years, though they never had a membership of more than 29 percent of the electorate. Much of this apparently disproportionate power may be due to the relative concentration of Democrats in a few states and the wider distribution of Republicans nationwide. In addition, the Republicans seem to have demonstrated an ability to select presidential nominees who appear to be closer to the center of American politics than such Democratic nominees as Stevenson or McGovern. While President Ford's party has the membership of only 22 percent of the electorate, Ford himself received 49.2 percent of the popular vote and 45 percent of the Electoral College vote.

Table 5.2 indicates that those who have deserted the two major parties are predominantly white, college educated, under 30 years of age, and from the West and Midwest. The Democratic Party has lost its hold on Catholics, those 30-49 years of age, white collar workers, and farmers. Republican losses are most heavily concentrated among the college educated and manual laborers. The Republican-turned-independent is described as a "young, middle-class, college-educated, Protestant suburbanite in a large metropolitan area of the Northeast who left the party sometime between 1960 and 1964."[21] Voters have not been changing parties; they have simply been joining the ranks of the independents—the most significant force in politics right now. Accounting for about one-third of the electorate, independents comprise a potential base for a strong third-party effort or influence close races. Eugene McCarthy's independent presidential candidacy in 1976, for example, may have made it more difficult for Carter to get the nomination by draining away Democratic support.

Depending upon one's explanation for the decline in party loyalty, one will make different predictions about the future of the two major parties. Walter Dean Burnham believes that lowered party loyalty indicates the "onward march of party decomposition."[22] Sundquist is much more optimistic about the parties' future.[23] He believes that the decline in party allegiance and the rise in the number of independents are due to the social turmoil of the mid-1960s—a short-term influence:

> The rise in independent attitudes in the 1960s coincides with the rise to a dominant position of the three powerful and related issues . . . race, Vietnam, and the social issue. By cutting across the existing line of party cleavage these issues blurred the distinction between the major parties and created polar forces that found no satisfactory expression through those parties.[24]

Independents used to be viewed as those who were less politically involved, who were not well informed about the issues, and who had only a marginal effect on election outcomes. This profile has been challenged by the new independents of the 1970s. As David Broder pointed out, "The new independents are not the rather indifferent, inattentive, inert citizens described in voting behavior studies of the 1950s."[25] DeVries and Tarrance discovered that the independent voter of the 1970s knows just as much about American politics and government, is just as concerned about public issues, and is just as likely to vote as professed Republicans and Democrats.[26]

Table 5.2   Changes in Political Affiliation of Various Population Groups, 1966 to 1976 (in percentage)

Group Identification	1966			1976			Change		
	D	R	I	D	R	I	D	R	I
Over-all party identification—all voters	50	26	24	48	23	29	-2	-3	5
Sex									
Men	49	25	26	46	22	32	-3	-3	6
Women	52	26	22	49	25	26	-3	-1	4
Race									
White	47	28	25	44	26	30	-3	-2	5
Non-white	x	x	x	78	7	15	x	x	x
Religious Afflilation									
Protestant	41	35	24	45	28	27	4	-7	3
Catholic	60	16	24	54	18	28	-6	2	4
Jew	x	x	x	55	11	34	x	x	x
Age									
Under 30	46	22	32	43	19	38	-3	3	16
30-49 years	53	22	25	49	22	29	-4	0	4
50 and older	50	30	20	50	29	21	0	-1	1
Size of Community									
1,000,000 and over	56	21	23	46	26	28	N/A	N/A	N/A
5000,000-999,999				53	16	31	N/A	N/A	N/A
50,000-499,999	48	25	27	51	22	27	3	-3	0
2500-49,999	45	33	22	42	26	32	-3	-7	10
Under 2500, rural	49	28	23	48	24	28	-1	-4	5
Region									
East	49	28	23	47	26	27	-2	-2	4
Midwest	45	30	25	41	26	33	-4	-4	8
South	58	16	26	62	11	27	4	-5	-1
West	49	31	20	46	28	26	-3	-3	6
Education									
College	38	34	28	39	27	34	1	-7	6
High school	50	25	25	49	22	29	-1	-3	4
Grade school	58	22	20	59	22	19	1	0	-1
Occupation									
Professional and business	42	30	28	40	29	31	-2	-1	3
White collar	48	29	23	38	27	35	-10	-2	12
Farmers	50	33	17	44	33	23	-6	0	6
Manual workers	54	21	25	53	17	30	-1	-4	5

Source: Gallup Opinion Index, February 1966, p. 14, and *Gallup Opinion Index*, December 1976, p. 50. "X" signifies no data collected. "N/A" signifies not ascertained.

Ticket-Splitting

Both party members and independents are splitting their tickets with increasing freedom. Throughout American history up until the mid-1960s, a majority of voters (60 to 80 percent) voted a straight ticket. In 1968, however, Gallup found that only 43 percent of the electorate reported that they had voted a straight ticket. This trend has continued, with a marked rise in the percentage of voters who were splitting their tickets. Even with the 1972 Nixon landslide, there was a heavy wave of ticket splitting. Table 5.3 traces the history of ticket splitting in gubernatorial and U.S. senatorial elections.

From 1914 to 1958 (the end of the Eisenhower era) less than 30 percent of the states simultaneously elected governors and senators of opposite parties with the exception of 1940. Beginning in 1960, the number of states that split their gubernatorial and senatorial winners between the parties increased significantly. Table 5.3 shows that, in four of the last seven elections, a majority of the states simultaneously electing a governor and a senator have chosen men of opposite parties. The high-water mark for ticket-splitting in America came during the 1968 elections. This practice coincides with Broder and Johnson's 1970 finding that it is "rare to encounter a voter—anywhere—who thinks of politics in terms of political parties."[27]

The trend since 1968 still supports the viewpoint that parties are salvageable and that voters will reidentify with the two major parties unless an extremely important issue arises. Although not declining to pre-1960 levels, ticket-splitting has declined somewhat since 1968. The data on ticket-splitting also reveal a remarkable degree of party durability. Despite Mr. Gallup's belief that the future of the parties is bleak and the opportunity is "so ripe for a third party to emerge" because "disenchantment with both major parties has never been so high,"[28] one should note that in 1974 only one independent candidate was elected to office,[29] and that no independent senators, representatives, or governors were elected in 1976.

CHANGES FROM WITHIN: THE ELECTORATE IN THE PARTY

The Identifiers

While the number of people calling themselves either Democrats or Republicans has declined significantly, the typical party member today has the same general characteristics as the one back in the mid-1960s. A comparison of those who identify with the two major parties indicates differences in education, occupation, place of residence, age, religious affiliation, and race. Republicans are likely to have a college education; be from an agricultural, professional, or business background; come from the West or Midwest; and attend a Protestant church. Democrats are primarily from the South and the big cities of the North and East, have high school or grade school educations, and are manual laborers. Young people, Catholics, and Jews are more likely to identify with the Democratic Party. There are no significant differences between the sexes in their partisan identification. Nor, with the exception of the large Northeastern

Table 5.3   Split Outcomes in Gubernatorial and U.S. Senatorial Elections: 1914-1974

Year	States with Simultaneous Elections	Number of Split Outcomes	Percent: Split Outcomes
1914	22	6	27.3
1916	24	5	20.8
1918	22	1	4.5
1920	24	0	0.0
1922	22	5	22.7
1924	26	1	3.8
1926	24	4	16.7
1928	24	4	16.7
1930	24	5	20.8
1932	23	3	13.0
1934	22	3	13.6
1936	24	2	8.3
1938	24	4	16.7
1940	26	11	42.3
1942	23	3	13.0
1944	22	6	27.3
1946	24	1	4.2
1948	22	4	18.2
1950	24	5	20.8
1952	22	6	27.3
1954	25	6	24.0
1956	20	3	15.0
1958	22	4	18.2
1960	19	5	36.3
1962	27	12	44.4
1964	18	10	55.6
1966	22	13	59.1
1968	15	9	60.0
1970	24	11	45.8
1972	12	6	50.0
1974	25	11	44.0
1975	10	3	30.0
1976	9	3	33.3

Source: Data for 1914-1970 are from an unpublished paper by Howard Reiter, Harvard University, John Fitzgerald Kennedy School of Government, March 1969. Cited in Walter DeVries and Lance Tarrance, Jr., *The Ticket Splitter,* p. 31. Data for 1972-1974 are from the *Congressional Quarterly Almanac,* 1972 and 1974. Data for 1976 are from *Congressional Quarterly Weekly Report 34,* No. 45 (November 6, 1976).

cities, does community size have a significant impact on party identification.

The Republicans have been notably unsuccessful with racial minorities; only 7 percent of all non-whites consider themselves Republicans. By contrast, the Democrats have enjoyed sizable support from non-whites; in 1976, 78 percent of all non-whites declared themselves to be Democrats. Numbering 8 million in 1976, the registered black voters represent a significant voting force.

The New Party Activists

The major parties are faced with two challenges arising from the influx of a new type of worker within the party organization: (1) the types and goals of party activists have changed over time; and (2) party organizations have been entered by the young, the inexperienced, women, and racial minorities. These new workers have succeeded in bringing about comprehensive changes in the delegate-selection procedure for the national nominating conventions.

The newcomers have become political participants because of ideological or social concerns, rather than because of acquisitions of material gains, status, or prestige. These new activists are demanding a larger role in party decisions than their predecessors did. They are calling for party reorganization to ensure intraparty participation and wider representation at the national convention.

In the past many people were attracted to the parties because of material incentives and nonideological appeals; they wanted to help the party gain or maintain control of the government. Now it seems that party activists are more ideologically oriented and are more concerned with governmental reform. This contrast between the new party activist and the former party worker was described by James Q. Wilson in his dichotomy between "professional" and "amateur."[30] Wilson said that the "professional" was oriented toward material rewards or a career in government, with little concern for issues. The "amateur" party worker, on the other hand, was not interested in material rewards, tended to be of higher occupational and educational status, and participated in politics because he or she was concerned about particular issues.

A case study of the personal characteristics and motivations of party workers by Conway and Feigert supports Wilson's contentions.[31] They concluded that the amateur model appropriately describes contemporary activists. Eighty-seven percent of the suburban Republicans and 80 percent of the suburban Democrats interviewed cited ideological and other impersonal (nonmaterial, nonstatus) reasons for becoming politically active.

Table 5.4 on page 148 shows some interesting differences in the motivations for doing political work.

Suburban county activists cited civic duty and a desire to "influence policies" more frequently than rural precinct leaders.

The New Participant

Historically, delegates to the national conventions have been middle aged, white, male, and wealthy. But since the 1960s, many of the delegates have not fit this pattern.

Table 5.4   Party Activists' Reasons for Political Participation

Reason	Montgomery County (Suburban)		Knox County (Rural)	
	Democrat	Republican	Democrat	Republican
	Percentage		Percentage	
Personal friendship with a candidate	6.6	1.5	10.3	10.8
Way of life	11.7	4.5	20.5	8.1
Attachment to party	10.0	16.7	23.1	18.9
Enjoyment of social contacts	—	—	2.6	10.8
Enjoyment of campaign excitement	1.7	—	—	8.1
Build personal position in politics	—	—	2.6	—
Influence policies	30.0	42.4	17.9	16.2
Be close to people doing important things	—	—	2.6	2.7
Business contacts	—	1.5	—	—
Community recognition	—	4.5	—	—
Civic duty	40.0	28.8	20.5	16.2
No response	—	—	—	8.1
	100.0	99.9	100.1	99.9

Source: These data were presented in M. Margaret Conway and Frank B. Feigert, "Motivation, Incentive Systems, and the Political Party Organization," *American Political Science Review*, No. 4 Vol LXII (December 1968), pp. 1159-1173. This information comes from interviews with precinct workers, 1966-1967.

There have been significantly more women, youth, racial minorities, and inexperienced participants. A review of the delegate representation at the 1968, 1972, and 1976 national conventions indicates that both parties may eventually become "open doors." See Table 5.5.

The white, wealthy, well-educated businessman who voted for Richard Nixon at the 1968 Republican National Convention has now been joined by a more diverse group of delegates. Looking at the newly enfranchised 18-year-olds and recognizing that occupying "the White House doesn't guarantee that we will later," the Republican Party has changed its delegate-selection process. For example, in response to the suggestion that "It's been a mistake for the Republican Party to write off blacks," there were 46 black delegates at the 1972 convention as compared with 26 at the 1968 convention. Changes in Democratic delegate-selection rules since 1968 have significantly altered the composition of the convention. In 1972 only 10 percent of the delegates could be classified as politicians; most delegates were attending their first convention. In 1972, 15 percent of the delegates were black, as compared with 5 percent 4 years earlier.

Table 5.5   Changing Delegate Representation at the National Conventions, 1968-1976

	Republican		Democratic		
	1968	1972	1968	1972	1976
	Percentage		Percentage		
Youth (Under 30 years of age)	1.0	8.7	4.0	21.4	14.8
Blacks	1.9	4.0	5.5	15.2	9.0
Women	17.0	30.1	13.0	38.0	34.0
Delegate inexperience[a]	65.3	65.3	62.7	81.4	N.A.

[a]Inexperience means delegate is attending his/her first convention.

Sources: Data for 1968 are taken from Joseph H. Boyett, "Background Characteristics of Delegates to the 1972 Conventions: A Summary Report of Findings from a National Sample," *Western Political Quarterly XXVII* (September 1973), 469-478. Data on the 1972 convention delegates are taken from *Congressional Quarterly Weekly Report* (August 12, 1972), p. 2002. Data on the 1976 Democratic convention delegates are from the *New York Times*, July 12, 1976, p. C5.

The late Mayor Daley asked, "Do you want to follow the rules [rules for delegate selection designed to make party conventions more democratic], or do you want to win the election in November?" It appears that the parties have decided that the two are not incompatible. The way in which the parties have made the conventions more representative of the electorate at large is to change the delegate-selection procedure.

Changes in the Delegate-Selection Process

Before 1968 there were factions in both major parties who believed that the way in which delegates were chosen needed to be revised.[32] During the 1960s the democratization of political processes was an important issue. Social unrest and the unpopular war in Vietnam drew attention to the importance of the nomination procedure. Groups within both parties claimed that the delegate-selection process was biased against their interests. Senator McCarthy and his followers claimed that they would not have a fair chance at a convention that was largely made up of delegates selected by the party leaders in smoke-filled rooms. Rockefeller contended that the Republican convention did not reflect the general electorate's preference in its nomination of a presidential candidate. In response to these and other charges, both the Democratic and Republican parties have made substantial changes in how delegates are chosen.

At the chaotic 1968 Democratic National Convention in Chicago, the liberal minority of the Rules Committee presented various proposals designed to change the delegate-selection procedure. The convention adopted the following resolution:

It is understood that a state Democratic Party, in selecting and certifying delegates to the National Convention, thereby undertakes to assure that such delegates have been selected through a process in which all Democratic voters have had full and timely opportunity to participate . . . [further] the

convention shall require that: (1) The unit rule shall not be used in any state
for the delegate selection process; and (2) All feasible efforts have been made
to assure that delegates are selected through the party primary, convention
or committee procedure open to public participation within the calendar
year of the National Convention. [33]

Early in 1968 the Democratic National Chairman, Fred Harris, appointed two commissions to study the matter of reform: the Commission on Party Structure and Delegate Selection (popularly known as the McGovern Commission) and the Commission on Rules. The McGovern Commission recommended 18 specific guidelines requiring the states to "adopt explicit written party rules governing delegate selection." These guidelines forbade proxy voting and use of the unit rule; required state parties to "eliminate all vestiges of discrimination" because of age, sex, race, color, or creed; urged state parties to remove restrictive voter registration practices; declared that no party member could be assessed more than $10 to participate or to run as a delegate; and required adequate public notice of the time, places, and rules for all public meetings of the party. The states were also expected to repeal the laws that allowed certain public or party officeholders to be delegates simply by virtue of their official positions. The McGovern Commission guidelines were intended to enlarge the grassroots base of the Democratic Party and to ensure the opportunity for all to participate. Although not using the term "quota system," the commission ordered the state party organizations to demonstrate their efforts to "overcome the effects of past discrimination" and suggested affirmative steps that state parties could take to encourage participation by the young, women, and minorities.

The Democratic National Committee adopted these guidelines unanimously in February 1971. Simultaneously, the Commission on Rules increased the size of both the convention and the standing committees in the hope of facilitating wider representation of the entire convention. The 1972 delegates agreed to create a new commission to "review the guidelines for delegate selection . . . after due consideration of their operations in 1972." In October 1973 a new commission, the Commission on Delegate Selection and Party Structure, recommended several revisions of the McGovern Commission's guidelines. Basically, however, the new commission reaffirmed the move toward greater participation and representation within the party organization. The rules for the 1976 Democratic convention modified the controversial quota system by stating clearly that the affirmative action programs "shall not be accomplished either directly or indirectly by the party's imposition of mandatory quotas at any level of the delegate selection process." Meanwhile, the 1976 Democratic apportionment formula continued the practice of apportioning delegates on the basis of Democratic strength within the states and of requiring the election of a majority of delegates at the grassroots level. The 1976 delegate-selection rules specified that state committees must apportion their delegate seats according to one of the following four criteria: [34]

1. A formula giving equal weight to the total population and to the average of the vote for the Democratic candidates in the two most recent presidential elections.
2. A formula giving equal weight to the vote for the Democratic candidates in the most recent presidential and gubernatorial elections.
3. A formula giving equal weight to the average of the vote for the Democratic candidates in the two most recent presidential elections and to Democratic Party registration or enrollment as of January 1, 1976.
4. A formula giving one-third weight to each of the formulas in the first three items.

These reforms have significantly changed the makeup of the Democratic Party. The Republicans claim that "Many of the reforms the Democrats are just now getting around to discussing were accomplished without fanfare years ago by our own party."[35] Actually the Republicans abolished the unit rule before 1968; yet, unlike the Democrats, they recommended rather than required the state party organizations to reform their delegate-selection procedure.

In 1968, the Republican National Convention approved a resolution prohibiting discrimination in the selection of future delegates and established a Delegate and Organizations Committee. This committee recommended (among other things) that states have equal numbers of men and women delegates to the national convention and that each state "should include delegates under age 25 in numerical equity to their voting strength."[36] The committee stressed that each delegation should have a balance of women, youth, and minorities, but it avoided establishing a quota system for any group.

The 1972 Republican convention adopted the "California Compromise," a new delegate selection formula for state representation at the 1976 convention. The plan favored small Southern and Western states, and it ensured a larger contingent of conservatives than had been the case in 1972.[37]

CONCLUSION

A recurrent theme in the literature is the imminent collapse of the two-party system. Regrettably, those who predict the demise of the party system fail to see parties as flexible entities, responding (although admittedly in a cumbersome fashion) to and reflecting the attitudes of the leaders. In criticizing Burnham's grim scenario of the parties' future, James Ward, is justifiably optimistic:

> What seems unlikely is the disappearance of parties. Burnham consistently confuses parties as institutions with parties as functions of the perceptions and behavior of the electorate. What replaces parties as organizations that nominate candidates for office? ... Even partisanship seems unlikely to decline into insignificance.[38]

Despite their pronounced disdain of the parties, voters continue to rally around the candidates of the two major parties at election time. It also appears that declining party support has stabilized, and the parties have demonstrated their capacity for structural change. These factors point to an extended life span for the two major parties. The parties also have certain "built-in" advantages provided by electoral law; these were discussed in Chapter 3. In the next chapter, we will examine the effects of modern campaign techniques upon the parties.

FOOTNOTES

1. Application for a temporary injunction was filed in the 207th District Court to stop a recount in precinct 18 to determine how many votes were cast for the mouse. County election officials claimed, "The said Mickey Mouse is an idiot, lunatic and minor and very possibly an unpardoned felon and is therefore, according to the laws of the state of Texas, ineligible to hold office." The five county officials moved to block the recount contending that "Mickey Mouse is not and has not been a resident of Comac County for 6 months as required by law." *The Salt Lake Tribune*, Thursday, November 28, 1974.

2. *The Gallup Opinion Index*, December 1976, p. 20.

3. Gallup Poll, "Public Opinion Poll: Independents Gain," *Salt Lake Tribune*, May 21, 1976.

4. Gallup Poll, ibid.

5. The most widely used source for American civic attitudes is Gabriel Almond and Sidney Verba, *The Civic Culture* (Princeton, N.J.: Princeton University Press, 1963). Others include, Lester Milbrath, *Political Participation* (Chicago: Rand McNally, 1965); Robert Dahl, *Who Governs?* (New Haven, Conn.: Yale University Press, 1961); Angus Campbell et al., *The American Voter* (New York: Wiley, 1960); William Flannigan, *Political Behavior of the American Electorate* (Boston: Allyn and Bacon, 1972); William Mitchell, *Why Vote?* (Chicago: Markham, 1971); Robert E. Lane, "What Conscious Needs Are Served by Participation in Political Life?" In *Power, Participation and Ideology*, edited by Calvin Larson and Philo Wasburn (New York: McKay, 1969), pp. 201-217.

6. Sidney Verba and Norman H. Nie, *Participation in America: Political Democracy and Social Equality* (New York: Harper and Row, 1972), p. 8.

7. Lester Milbrath, *Political Participation* (Chicago: Rand McNally, 1965). The second edition did not include this table of progressive development.

8. Political parties are criticized for not supporting the candidates' campaigns, yet the electorate fails to provide its skills and effort. See James McGregor Burns, "Coming to the Aid of the Parties," *Newsweek*, December 2, 1974.

9. Russell Baker, "American Studies Final Exam," *New York Times, Seattle Post-Intelligencer*, June 6, 1972. This is a hilarious satire on politics; the following is an excerpt: "This is the final examination in American studies. Each correct answer is worth 10 points. Grade your own paper. Students scoring less than 70 points should leave the country immediately. MULTIPLE CHOICE QUESTIONS: 1. You want to be shot. The best way to go about it is to: (a) Run for office, (b) Join the police force, (c) Buy a pistol and leave it in the drawer next to the liquor cabinet where your wife can easily find it on Saturday night."

10. Gabriel Almond and Sidney Verba, op. cit; Reviewing the percentage of the electorate that participates in various political activities, the authors state: "Six of the twelve activities are performed by fewer than 20 percent of the citizens, and only presidential and local voting have frequencies of performance significantly greater than 30 percent," p. 31.

11. *Congressional Quarterly Almanac XXX*, 1974. Previous survey experience has shown that people tend to overreport voter participation. In the 1974 congressional elections the reported estimate of 45 percent compares with 39 percent from a preliminary count of actual votes cast. *Congressional Quarterly Weekly Report XXXII*, No. 45 (November 9, 1974).

12. David S. Broder, "Politics Reach Sad State," *The Washington Post,* January 2, 1975.

13. Walter DeVries, consultant and political scientist, as quoted by David S. Broder in *The Washington Post,* January 2, 1975.

14. *Gallup Opinion Index,* Report No. 90, December 1972, p. 11. Sixty-two million eligible Americans did not vote in the 1972 election; the Gallup poll published the following reasons they gave for not voting (percentages from the Gallup sample are projected into numbers of people): 24 million did not register or were prevented by residence requirements; 18 million were not interested in politics; 6 million said they did not like either major-party candidate; 6 million were sick or disabled; 4 million said they could not leave their jobs; and 4 million were away from home. Cited in Milton C. Cummings, Jr., and David Wise, *Democracy under Pressure* (New York: Harcourt, Brace, Jovanovich, 1974), p. 285.

15. Released September 5, 1976, this survey was conducted by Peter D. Hart Research Associates Inc. for the Committee for the Study of the American Electorate.

16. *Gallup Opinion Index,* December 1976, p. 12.

17. The Gallup poll of June 1975 was included in "Gallup Opinion Poll Index," *Salt Lake Tribune,* October 19, 1975. Arlen J. Large made a valuable commentary on declining party loyalty in "The Fading Importance of Party Loyalty," *Wall Street Journal,* November 9, 1972, p. 26. See also Howard Flieger, "Don't Start the Wake," *U.S. News and World Report,* June 16, 1975.

18. Robert Lane, *Political Life* (Glencoe, Ill.: The Free Press of Glencoe, 1959).

19. "Loss of Life in the 2-Party System, Studies Show," *Deseret News,* August 20, 1976, p. A1.

20. The January 7, 1975, special election in Louisiana's sixth congressional district had a record turnout and a Republican victory. The implications of this first election in 1975 were summed up by Ben R. Miller: "The defeat of so many officeholders in November was largely due to dissatisfaction with all incumbents. In addition, Republicans were hit by a Watergate backlash. But the special election in January showed the backlash was short-lived—and that the mood of the electorate is far more 'conservative' than it is 'liberal' when distractions are removed from the basic issue." Quoted in Howard Flieger, "Sign of the Times," *U.S. News and World Report,* February 3, 1975.

21. James L. Sundquist, "Whither the American Party System?" *Political Science Quarterly 88* No. 4 (December 1973), p. 569.

22. Walter Dean Burnham, *Critical Elections and the Mainsprings of American Politics* (New York: Norton, 1970). Also, "The End of American Party Politics," *Transaction 7* (December 1969), p. 22. An excellent summary and analysis of Burnham's thesis is presented by James F. Ward, "Toward a Sixth Party System? Partisanship and Political Development," *The Western Political Quarterly XXVI.* (September 1973), pp. 385-413.

23. Sundquist, op. cit.

24. Ibid., p. 578.

25. David Broder, *The Party's Over* (New York: Harper and Row, 1972), p. 200.

26. Walter DeVries and V. Lance Tarrance, Jr., The *Ticket-Splitter: A New Force in American Politics* (Grand Rapids, Mich.: William Eerdmans, 1972).

27. *The Washington Post,* October 9, 1970.

28. "Pollster Records Own Views," *Salt Lake Tribune,* November 14, 1974.

29. James B. Longley, elected governor of Maine, 1974.

30. James Q. Wilson, *The Amateur Democrat: Club Politics in Three Cities* (Chicago: University of Chicago Press, 1962).

31. M. Margaret Conway and Frank B. Feigert, "Motivation, Incentive Systems, and the Political Party Organization," *American Political Science Review*, No. 4 (December 1968), pp. 1159-1173.

32. For a review of the reasons for changing the delegate-selection process, see: Judith A. Center, "1972 Democratic Convention Reforms and Party Democracy," *Political Science Quarterly LXXXIX*, No. 2 (June 1974), pp. 325-350; William Cavala, "Changing the Rules Changes the Game: Party Reform and the 1972 California Delegation to the Democratic National Convention," *American Political Science Review LXVIII*, No. 1 (March 1974), pp. 27-42; and Austin Ranney, "Comment," *American Political Science Review LXVIII*, No. 1 (March 1974), pp. 43-44.

33. Commission on Party Structure and Delegate Selection, *Mandate for Reform* (Washington, D.C.: Democratic National Committee, 1970), pp. 14-15.

34. The reforms of both parties are set forth in the *Congressional Quarterly Almanac XXXII*, 1972.

35. Anne Armstrong, Co-Chairman of the Republican National Committee, quoted in *Congressional Quarterly Weekly Report XXX* (August 12, 1972), p. 1999.

36. Review of the 1972 Republican National Convention presented in *Congressional Quarterly Weekly Report XXX* (August 12, 1972).

37. *Congressional Quarterly Weekly Report XXX* (August 26, 1976), p. 2119.

38. James F. Ward, op. cit., p. 412.

6
Parties and Campaigns: An Altered Role

Parties are not only being brushed aside by independent candidates and professional consultants; they are in danger of being supplanted. During the 1976 presidential campaign, *Newsweek* gave almost as much attention to the Spencer-Roberts consulting team as to the candidates themselves. Milton Shapp's successful challenge of the Democratic Party's organization man (which was carried out by a hired professional consultant) is no longer unique. In 1976 the incumbent president was seriously challenged for the Republican nomination. The Ford-Reagan race, described as a "heroic struggle for control of the bridge of the Titanic," was the closest since Eisenhower battled Taft in 1952. Outsiders have made significant inroads into the Democratic Party; the 1976 presidential nomination went to a man who achieved prominence without the help of the party's kingmakers. Both Ronald Reagan and Jimmy Carter ran personalized campaigns and were relatively new to the traditional party organizations. Among the growing list of those who have employed campaign specialists are Ronald Reagan, Nelson Rockefeller, Hubert Humphrey, and Gerald Ford. The 100 professional firms that regularly manage political campaigns generally work exclusively for either Republican or Democratic candidates and have indeed made considerable advances against both parties.

Contrary to the warnings of several scholars that "if neither the Democrats nor the Republicans come out with a program that inspires widespread confidence . . . election year 1976 may bring a serious third party challenge,"[1] this did not happen. Although the parties are no longer the center of campaign politics, they are still important actors; most voters rally around the party banners. Now that there are laws limiting campaign expenditures, the volunteer assistance that the parties can sometimes muster has become important, although not absolutely necessary for electoral success. In this chapter we will discuss the changes that have taken away the parties' dominance of campaign politics and evaluate their present role.

INCREASING PRESSURE AND DECLINING VISIBILITY
The ground rules for nominating presidential candidates have been altered substantially. According to one commentator:

Running for the Presidency has always been an intricate affair. But the new rules for choosing convention delegates, raising campaign funds and running in a proliferating array of primaries have made the Presidential game almost as hard to understand as it is to survive.[2]

Because of primaries, campaign-spending regulations, and delegate-selection procedures, there have had to be modifications in campaign strategy.

Since the mid-1960s presidential campaigns have begun earlier than they used to. George Romney announced that he would run for president several years before the 1968 election, and Gerald Ford publicly announced his candidacy for reelection much earlier than previous presidents. Representative Morris Udall of Arizona formally announced his candidacy a full 2 years ahead of the election. The making of a president has become an exercise in the politics of exhaustion. The number of presidential primaries has doubled between 1968 and 1976—from 16 to 31. In 1976, for the first time, the ten most populous states (with the largest blocks of convention delegates) used the primary system; primary-selected delegates now constitute three-fourths of all those chosen for the national conventions. Apparently the days are gone when a candidate, with a moderate effort and the support of the boys in the backroom, could make a few public appearances in a limited number of states and be touted as a nationwide favorite.

The candidates are under substantially more pressure. Besides the increasing number of primaries is the lessened importance of any single one. A candidate must now make a strong showing in several primaries in order to develop the momentum he needs to emerge as a clear frontrunner. Furthermore, the candidate cannot select which state primaries to concentrate on, since 15 states now require all nationally recognized presidential aspirants' names to appear on the primary ballot. In 8 of those 15 states, a candidate must file a legal affidavit in order to be removed from the ballot; this, of course, would then eliminate him as a serious contender in any other primary contest. Thus, a candidate is obliged to spend time and money in the compulsory primaries or gamble on an outcome that might taint his image as a contender.

The widespread use of primaries has further burdened the candidates by increasing the likelihood that no one will emerge from the primaries as the clear-cut leader; all contestants, therefore, must scramble for uncommitted delegates. When history's longest primary season ended in June 1976, none of the candidates in either party had enough delegates to secure the nomination; all contenders were forced to begin the post-primary, pre-convention search for additional support. Carter, although the leading Democrat at the end of the primary season, had to put an end to a stop-Carter movement by winning the support of additional delegates. Reagan and Ford each had the difficult job of personally wooing several hundred individual GOP delegates at a time "when you have to pick them up at retail rates, in ones and twos."[3] The large number of primaries today has increased the likelihood that the delegates will be divided among several competitors and that party conventions will be deadlocked. Candidates who anticipate such difficulties have turned for help to the professional. Clifton White, of the campaign management firm of Clifton White Associates and the mastermind behind Goldwater's 1964 nomination, was signed on by the Ford team to develop a *modus operandi* for securing convention delegates.

The Democratic Party has adopted new rules for selecting delegates; at least 75 percent of all delegates in each state must be elected in voting units that are no larger than congressional districts, and no more than 25 percent of the delegates may be selected by state central committees—in short, the "winner-take-all" rule has been abolished. These changes also make the campaign more difficult for the candidates, increasing the likelihood that the delegates will divide their support among several contenders and thus weakening the candidate-party relationship. The purpose of these changes was to open up the delegate-selection process in non-primary states and "to bring the business of choosing a President out of the backroom;" but, as the Republican Dean Burch suggested, these reforms may represent "a case of democracy gone mad."[4] The primaries have turned presidential politics into a punishing marathon, in which a media superstar could eliminate a traditional party candidate by winning landslide victories in early primaries and thus carry a winner's aura into the subsequent primaries. According to one observer:

> The primaries alone have turned into a mind-numbing cross-country obstacle race.... Their order is entirely arbitrary.... The rules of play vary dizzingly from primary to primary. Losers claim moral victories. Winners, particularly in the crowded Democratic field, may be impossible to determine.[5]

Large-scale use of the primary and new delegate-selection procedures, together with two additional phenomena—the limitation on campaign spending (and the use of federal money) and the noncommital attitudes of the voters—have left the party vulnerable. The two major parties are threatened on two fronts: the personalized, media-oriented campaigns that ignore the party organization, and by the various revitalization movements that might take over the party apparatus.

It is not clear what the effect will be of using federal money for presidential campaigns. This money might tempt some to enter the race, which otherwise would be out of the question. Some observers believe that "losers," having no real public support and no possibility of victory, are lured into a crowded field by the prospect of federal money. Others believe that the law's stringent provisions for obtaining federal money have forced some of the best-qualified candidates into premature retirement. Acceptance of government money disqualifies the candidate from receiving private funds over and beyond a legal limit. These restrictions compel candidates to try to obtain the most for their campaign dollars. Joseph Napolitan, one of America's best-known professional political consultants, argues that regulating campaign spending will further increase the demand for a packaged professional campaign service, thus making it an even more lucrative element in politics; he contends that regulation should take the form of giving equal (and free) television and radio time to all candidates for major offices.[6]

Limits on campaign spending have actually created a greater demand for a CREEP-style, centralized political campaign, divorced from party control. The repercussions for the party-campaign organization relationship are substantial. Present-day campaign organizations are likely to be monolithic and dependent upon professional consultants. The 1974 law requires candidates to have a single, central campaign committee that will file reports with the Federal Election Commission. Campaign contributions and expenditures must be disclosed, and there is a firm ceiling on spending. These provisions make it necessary to have precise accounting, excellent management skills, and centralized managerial control over every detail of the campaign. Although the drafters of the reform bill were convinced that they were "ensuring the renewal of the parties by allowing them to solicit independent contributions and make independent expenditures,"[7] this is not the way it has worked out in practice. Parties and volunteer labor have become subordinate to the central campaign organization. The leading expert on campaign finance, Herbert Alexander, speculates that the law may even dampen political participation by the middle class. He reasons that if the national campaign organization doesn't give the volunteers the authority to carry out specific activities that they believe will be effective, they will drop out of the politically active group. Alexander contends that campaign centralization is also discouraging volunteer workers by causing them to feel that they are being manipulated into programmed activities.[8] Since campaign managers need large numbers of volunteers to mobilize support through the traditional precinct-level canvassing, voter registration, telephone solicitation, and get-out-the-vote drives, fewer volunteers will mean that the party has an even smaller role in campaign politics.

The electorate's attitude of indifference has also added to the parties' burdens. Indifference, however, is somewhat easier to cope with than active hostility. Fortunately, there is no widespread enthusiasm for a third party at this time. Voter apathy has dampened enthusiasm not only for the parties, but for any possible rival movements.

NEW CAMPAIGN POLITICS

The decline of the parties' roles in campaign politics is particularly evident in three areas. First, many of those seeking office are relative newcomers to politics, and thus they do not have extensive past ties with the major parties. Second, campaign organizations are now built around the candidate, not the party organization, and are staffed by experts—specialists trained in marketing skills and not party politics. Third, candidates and their staffs are carrying their campaign messages directly to the voter without filtering them through the party structures.

The Candidate

A review of the reasons why people decide to run for public office helps us understand why parties no longer dominate the recruitment process. Each office-seeker must weigh the matter of resources and opportunities. Since parties are now only one source of campaign help, they cannot very well limit nominations to the party faithful.

Even a cursory examination of the price of defeat, both financial and otherwise, raises the question, "Why run?" Congressman Byron G. Rodgers, who lost by only 27 votes in a Colarado Democratic primary, and the one-term Congressman Samuel Young who lost to Abner Mikva in Illinois demonstrate the heartbreak of politics—no matter how close one comes to winning, there is no substitute for victory. Mikva, the incumbent Democratic congressman, was defeated by Young in the 1972 election by a 52 percent to 48 percent margin. In 1974, Mikva challenged Young for the Illinois tenth district House seat and won by a handful of votes out of the several hundred thousand cast. Mikva and Young then squared off again in the 1976 race; the results were not determined until several weeks after election day, when Mikva was again declared the winner by only 201 votes. During the course of these three elections the two candidates spent more than $1 million.

For a political novice to run against another novice is a challenge, but facing an incumbent is substantially more difficult. The incumbent, because of his position, staff, and public recognition enjoys enormous financial and manpower advantages over all challengers. The great majority of incumbents who seek reelection are successful; 95 percent of the congressmen who chose to run again in 1976 were reelected, and 90 percent of the incumbent House members who were up for reelection in midterm elections during the period 1958-1970 were successful. According to Fishel, new candidates running for a House seat "collectively have about one chance in five of electoral success."[9] Because of these odds, one's decision to run for public office—particularly against an incumbent—is an intriguing matter. What motivates a person to cross the threshold from being "only interested" to candidacy? Is the individual concerned with a particular issue—as the "peace" candidates in the 1970 congressional campaign claimed—or is the ego involved? In studying the "why" of candidacy, researchers have taken a sociological approach, a psychological approach, and a structural approach.

Assuming that background, particularly one's occupation, facilitates entry into public office, researchers have classified public officials according to occupation, educational experience, and their fathers' occupational status. It is assumed that certain occupations and social backgrounds carry with them a socialization process that sets before the individual a "nonstop highway from their birthplace to Washington." Both Matthews, in his analysis of the Senate, and Senator Clark, in Congress: The Sapless Branch, conclude that a particular type of social environment will produce a candidate.[10] They maintain that, given a background of position, wealth, security, and a family tradition of activism, a candidate will emerge. Their perspective applies quite well to the Kennedys, the Rockefellers, and the Roosevelts. Data collected on the characteristics of people in public office indicate that they certainly do not typify the population at large. A disproportionately large number of elected public officials come from the professions and from the middle or upper social classes. Table 6.1 shows the occupational background of Members of Congress in 1977.

Table 6.1 Members of Congress by Occupation, 1977

Occupation	House			Senate			Congress
	D	R	Total	D	R	Total	Total
Agriculture	6	10	16	3	6	9	25
Business or banking	69	49	118	14	10	24	142
Education	57	15	72	8	4	12	84
Engineering	0	2	2	0	0	0	2
Journalistm	10	4	14	3	1	4	18
Labor Leader	6	0	6	0	0	0	6
Law	155	68	223	46	22	68	291
Law Enforcement	7	0	7	0	0	0	7
Medicine	1	1	2	1	0	1	3
Public Service/politics	34	26	60	12	14	26	86
Clergyman	4	2	6	0	1	1	7
Scientist	2	0	2	0	1	1	3

Source: Congressional Quarterly Almanac, 1977.

A second approach to understanding why certain people decide to run for public office is the psychological—the individual's personality traits and personal ambitions. Joseph Schlesinger[11] has argued that personal ambition is both a motive to seek office, and a determinant of what level of office will be sought. "Ambition lies at the heart of politics." Schlesinger identified three degrees of ambition: (1) the *discrete* office-holder, who aspires only to a local office, and then to retire; (2) the *static* officeholder, who wants a particular office and to make a career there; and (3) the *progressive*, who plans to use his position simply as a stepping stone to higher office. Because of the high turnover among state legislators who do not move on to other offices, this group apparently has only discrete, or limited, political ambitions. The political progressives—the John Kennedys and the Richard Nixons—lie at the other end of the scale. John Kennedy served first in the House of Representatives, and then defeated the Republican incumbent, Henry Cabot Lodge, Jr., for a Senate seat in 1952; he was reelected to that seat 6 years later. His attempt to win the Democratic vice-presidential nomination in 1956 failed, but he was successful in the 1960 presidential election. Richard Nixon entered politics shortly after his return from naval service by winning a congressional seat. From there, he moved to the Senate and then on to the vice-presidency. Unsuccessful in his first bid for the presidency, he also lost the 1962 gubernatorial election in California. Six years later, he was finally elected president and then was reelected in 1972.

Some researchers have tried to analyze the intensity of the Democratic and Republican candidates' career commitment to politics. Are Democrats more likely than Republicans to perceive their candidacy for public office as a stepping stone in their political career? Jeff Fishel found that Democrats and Republicans do differ significantly in their levels of personal ambition; Democrats were much more likely to view their candidacies as stepping stones:

> *Because the differences between Democratic and Republican challengers cannot be explained by the higher social status of Republicans, nor by a*

greater degree of social mobility among Democrats . . . one is left with an
unfashionably simple conclusion: Democrats, as Democrats, are simply more
careerist in their orientation to politics than are Republicans.[12]

A third approach to understanding why people become candidates emphasizes political opportunities. The structural approach contends that one's political ambitions are molded by the "opportunity structure" presented to the office-seeker. Running for office is perceived as a risk, with the magnitude of the risk partially determined by the structural characteristics of the electoral system. Opportunities for political candidacy and electoral success vary according to political circumstances beyond the control of the individual. Structural factors, such as the size of the election district and the degree of party competition within that district, affect one's chances for moving up the political ladder. "The theory rests on the idea that office-seekers attempt to behave in a rational manner in selecting among alternative offices," explains Gordon Black. "Rather than being driven by excessive ambition, they tend to develop ambition slowly as a result of their changing circumstances."[13] The structural approach, therefore, emphasizes the immediate circumstaces of an individual at the time of his decision to seek office, rather than his background or his personality. Ambition is believed to develop in relation to political opportunities. For example, large districts require large campaign expenditures, and there is usually more intraparty competition.

Another important factor affecting one's chances for election is the relative strength of the parties in the district. Obviously, there are more political opportunities for a candidate in a "safe" district (where his party usually wins) than for a candidate in a more competitive district. Table 6.2 summarizes some of the advantages and disadvantages that are structurally determined.

None of these three approaches claims to be a total explanation. Barber suggests an approach that combines personal ambition, opportunity, and resources. He points out that all three elements should be considered in deciding to seek public office, and suggests that potential candidates must give an affirmative answer to the following questions:[14]

1. Do I want it? (Ambition)
2. Can I do it? (Resources)
3. Do they want me? (Opportunity)

Noting that these factors are interrelated, Barber says that if any one of them is missing, the prospective candidate usually will not enter an election race.

Resources, ambition, opportunity, and background are obviously important, but what is the relative importance of each? Trying to understand why people become candidates involves mental gymnastics, a bit of amateur psychology, and an imaginative mind. Serving as House minority leader, Gerald Ford's ambitions appeared static—"once a congressman, always a congressman." Then, in a twist of fate, he became vice president, and observers speculated that he would be the Republican presidential

Table 6.2 Incumbent and District Advantages and Disadvantages

	Incumbent	Nonincumbent	Large District	Small District
Candidate Recognition and Media Use	Has already received media exposure and has easy access to the media for campaign purposes	Needs to make name known (assuming he or she has not previously held public office)	Requires large campaign expenditures	Media often cover more than one district, so candidate must purchase unnecessary coverage
Funds and Workers	Services provided while in office bring candidate into contact with many politically valuable groups and possible campaign contributors	Needs to build up following and contributors Usually has not had access to sources required for favor-trading	Requires large expenditures for media Because there are many competing groups, resources are more easily available to non-incumbents	Campaign expenses can be small. Circulars, organizational activity, and word-of-mouth usually prove to be fairly effective Candidate can more easily monopolize support of most important political and economic groups
Issues	Has knowledge of politics and issues from experience in office and an established public record Can create issues by making official remarks, holding press conferences, proposing legislation	May have knowledge of politics and issues, but has no official record on which to run for office Needs to develop dramatic or timely issues with which he or she can be identified	Many issues available to select from, especially if there are many different groups in the district Must find a few issues affecting most voters to emphasize in campaign Too varied a district may force campaign to concentrate on personal images rather than on issues	Issues are few and are well known to voters; candidates must demonstrate specific knowledge of district's problems Organizational support for candidates may become more important than election issues

Source: Editorial Staff, American Government Today, 1974, p. 415.

candidate in 1976. But Mr. Ford denied this speculation, saying, "I think I can do a better job for the Administration and the party by not involving myself in the prospects of a personal campaign for the presidency." He clarified his position even further in a press interview:

Q. Does this mean that if—for any reason—you become president before 1976, you would step aside and not run to stay in that office?
A. Yes, that is what I am saying.[15]

When Nixon resigned in 1974 and Ford became president, his earlier declarations became moot; in July 1975 Ford made his early, but anticipated, announcement of his candidacy for election. Gerald Ford, for so many years seemingly satisfied with a career in politics much like the *static* officeholder described by Schlesinger, became a *progressive*, willing to use the leverage of the White House to be elected president in his own right. Did structural changes increase the personal ambitions of Mr. Ford? Is opportunity the key factor as claimed by Plunkett of Tammany Hall: "I seen my opportunities and I took 'em"?[16] Contrast the gradual rise of Gerald Ford's ambitions with those of Sam Yorty, former mayor of Los Angeles:

> *Samuel W. Yorty: successful candidate for the assembly of the California Legislature in 1938. In April, 1939, ran unsuccessfully for Los Angeles City Council. Ran unsuccessfully for U.S. Senate 1940. Ran again for the California Assembly in 1942, once again met with defeat. Ran sixth among thirteen candidates in the 1945 Los Angeles mayoralty election. In 1949, successful in winning a seat in California Legislature. In 1950, won seat in Congress, but in 1954 ran for Senate and lost. Unsuccessful in 1956 bid for the Democratic nomination for U.S. Senate and returned to the practice of law. In addition, Yorty sought the Democratic nomination for president on several occasions. A review of Yorty's political career indicates that on several other occasions prior to 1961 he entertained the idea of running for mayor of Los Angeles. In 1961 Yorty was elected mayor of Los Angeles.[17]*

Gerald Ford's political ambitions grew as opportunities came along. By contrast, Yorty refused to give up his ambition for political office, despite negative feedback. Why do some people continue to pursue public office with the exhaustion of campaigns, the cost in time and money, and the countless insults? One of the jokes about Carter during the 1976 campaign dealt with his personal politics of expediency. "They were going to put Carter on Mount Rushmore," teased comedian Pat Paulsen at a social affair, "but they didn't have room for two more faces." President Ford heard many remarks that challenged his competence: "Ford finished a typical day of campaigning; he kissed a snowball and threw a baby." Although researchers have not yet reached a conclusion, it seems certain that the decision to seek political office is as complex as the individual making it.

Before the 1960s, party resources were the predominant means of support, and a successful candidacy required a "thumbs up" commitment from the party organization. Although today's candidates usually cannot afford to alienate the party organization, they do not look to it for campaign help.

THE PROFESSIONALS AND THEIR SKILLS

As the candidate-party relationship has deteriorated, office-seekers increasingly rely on the services and skills of "outside" professionals. These outsiders have the skills and perspective that they acquired in such non-political fields as communications and journalism. They see the parties as only one of many potential campaign resources. The professionals' growing role in campaigns has been astounding, and their prospects for the future seem even more promising.

Although the number of campaigns in which professionals have participated since 1970 has been variously estimated, it appears that the trend is still increasing. Most major campaigns have become battles between management firms that almost equal in magnitude the battles between the candidates; the only difference is that the managers never completely lose, since the candidates have to pay for their services regardless of the outcome. In the 1970 U.S. Senate race in Michigan between Romney and Hart, two professional consultants squared off against each other. Harry Treleaven was hired by Mrs. Romney and was paid $20,000 for a biographical film of the candidate. Charles Guggenheim was hired by Hart, the Democratic incumbent. Although Romney was defeated, Treleaven collected his fee. The cost of hiring political consultants is rarely ever revealed by the candidates or the consultants themselves. However, their expenses are reported to be about $500 a day. A Democratic consultant reports that his firm of 12 persons needs $1200 per day, or approximately $80,000 for an average U.S. House campaign.[18]

The professional campaign manager of today differs from his traditional counterpart in two distinct ways: in his relationship with the party organization and in the sophistication of the skills he employs. The traditional campaign manager, who had many years of party experience, relied heavily on the organization and the skills of the party workers for the traditional vote-getting procedures—door-knocking, canvassing, and personal voter contact in the precincts. The professional, however, operates largely from an established, private, profit-making firm that is relatively independent of the political party. He sees himself as primarily a businessman, not a party man. Bill Roberts, of the Spencer-Roberts team, emphasized this at a meeting sponsored by the Republican National Committee:

> As a campaign manager, your sole purpose is to win. There is absolutely no other goal. You are not trying to prove a cause or sell a philosophy. You are trying to win a campaign in the most expeditious manner possible, using every legal and moral way to do so.[19]

Although the professional is generally aloof toward the party organization, he must rely on it to some extent. He may profess general dissatisfaction with a weak party organization and with the party's inability to marshal the forces necessary to assure victory on election day, but he has a vested interest in the continuation of the two major parties as a factor in campaign politics.

The professional campaign manager also differs from the traditional one in his personal background, which will determine the skills he uses. The professional is well-versed in marketing, public relations, and communications rather than door-knocking and backroom dealing. The traditional campaign manager and his relation-ship with his constituency is perhaps best exemplified by Vito Marzullo, a Chicago ward committeeman. Marzullo, one of the last of a dying breed, marshaled party support for the late Mayor Richard Daley. He reminded a newspaper columnist of the effectiveness of this method of campaigning, contending that the new avenues of politicking are unnecessary: "You can take all your news media and all the do-gooders in town and move them into my 25th Ward, and do you know what would happen? On election day we'd beat you fifteen to one." What is the key to Marzullo's success? He relies on his precinct captains and on his own personal contact with residents of the ward. His address to precinct captains on the eve of the 1971 mayoralty election implies that traditional campaign methods simply communicate political reality.

This ward [is] not depending on the kind of publicity given to trouble-makers and the nitwits and crackpots. [Rather, the 25th Ward was] depend-ing on the record for sixteen years of our great mayor and the people who will put their shoulder to the wheel because they love Richard J. Daley and what he has done for the city of Chicago with the help of the Democratic Party.

Marzullo admonished his precinct workers to carry this message personally to their neighbors in their own language, and to continue to serve and communicate with their people. Marzullo reinforced this prod with a personal commitment:

Anybody in the 25th who needs something, needs help with his garbage, needs his street fixed, needs a lawyer for his kid who's in trouble, he goes first to the precinct captain. . . . . If the captain can't deliver, that man can come to me. My house is open every day to him.[20]

The twenty-fifth ward committeeman also writes to all new residents, expressing the Democratic Party's and his own concern for them:

Dear Friend:
   As you know, the City Council of Chicago has redistricted the Wards, and you are now a resident of the 25th Ward. As the Ward Committeeman and Alderman of the 25th Ward, I take pride in welcoming you into the official family of our Ward.
   The 25th Ward is fortunate in being represented at all levels of government by people of all ethnic backgrounds. We are truly a cosmopolitan organization. As members of our organization, we have the Honorable Frank Annunzio, who is Congressman for the Seventh Congressional District; Honorable Thaddeus V. Adesko, Judge of the Appellate Court; Honorable Charles S. Bonk, County Commissioner; Honorable Anthony Kogut, Judge

of the Circuit Court of Cook County; Honorable Sam Romano, State Senator; Honorable
Matt Ropa, State Representative; and Madison Brown, Con-Con Delegate.

I would like to point out to you that the next nonpartisan aldermanic election will be
held on February 23, 1971. At that time I am sure you will be visited by your Democratic
Precinct Captain who will be most anxious to discuss any problems of mutual interest.

Our organization has always endeavored to meet the needs and wants of our people. I
personally await the opportunity, on behalf of all of the officials of the 25th Ward and myself, to be of assistance. Do not hesitate to let us know what your problems are, and if we
can help, we are more than willing to extend our services.

                                          Sincerely,
                                          Alderman Vito Marzullo
                                          25th Ward Committeeman[21]

Marzullo, one of the late old-line ward bosses in the Democratic Party organization,
maintained political leverage through service and communication. By contrast, most
professional campaign managers (as described by David Rosenbloom in *The Election
Men*) were not trained in party politics; 67 percent of those studied had a background
in either public relations, advertising, journalism, or radio and television, while 11 percent came from a traditional political party or campaign staff position.[22]

The *Congressional Quarterly* list of campaign consultants includes the names of
Squier, Ailes, Cerrell, Reese, and Spencer-Roberts. Robert D. Squier, president of the
Communications Company, whose past clients have included Hubert Humphrey, the
Democratic National Committee, and the reelection bid of Governor John Burns (D-
Hawaii), has a background in television. Both Baus and Ross, whose California firm
is one of the few that handle every phase of the campaign for both Republicans and
Democrats, have a background in public relations. However, not all prominent campaign managers are from a non-political background. Matt Reese, a campaign consultant
specializing in techniques of voter registraion, telephone banks and "get-out-the-
vote" drives, has been active in Democratic Party politics since 1954. The Spencer
and Roberts team, probably the best-known management firm in the nation, handles
all aspects of campaigning exclusively for Republicans; they met while doing volunteer work for the Young Republicans in the 1950s. These men, credited with the turnabout of President Ford's 1976 pre-convention campaign, are both experienced party
workers; ironically, in 1976 they worked against Ronald Reagan, who had first
achieved political prominence through their efforts.

CAMPAIGN ORGANIZATION AND SKILLS: SPECIALIZATION AND DIVISION OF LABOR

Most candidates try to maximize their chances to win, since they realize that there is
no magic formula for success. In trying to get the greatest return for their time and
money, candidates have sought the specialist and his professional techniques. Special-
ization and division of labor have become key principles in the campaign strategy for
most major offices. Figure 6.2, a model of an "ideal" campaign organization, illustrates these principles since the work is divided into at least ten staff tasks.

Figure 6.1 Organizational Chart of Campaign Personnel

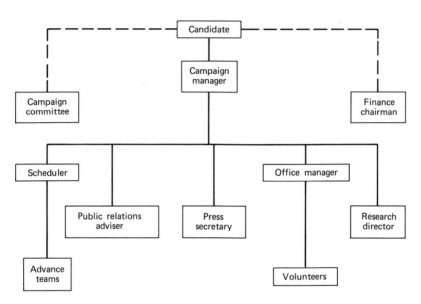

Of course, very few campaign organizations resemble this model; most of them are exercises in frenzy, described by one consultant as "a Marx brothers movie without a laugh track."

Campaign organizations vary in size from a group of three or four who are trying to elect a friend to a minor office, to the team of thousands who work in a presidential campaign. In some cases, the candidate himself is the entire campaign "staff," while in others he may have a separate staff member for each major task. Whatever the size or complexity of the organization, the basic task remains the same: to coordinate the efforts of the three groups of campaign workers—the professionals, the party workers, and the non-party volunteers. The candidate relies on these groups to carry his message to the voters; coordinating *all* of these groups, therefore, is extremely important. While the contribution of the campaign organization is difficult to assess accurately, analysis has shown that an effective campaign organization is essential to election victory and that organizations that include professionals generally fare better at the polls—for both national and local offices. Winners in the 1972 Illinois state legislative races reported that their organizations were of fundamental importance; by contrast, the losers in those elections were not sure about the importance of good organizations. The victors in these elections also paid much more attention to political advisers than their defeated opponents.

Political campaigns have been likened to wars, athletic contests, and games; the contest is played with certain rules and requires the formulation and execution of many game plans in order to win. One of the top political management teams, Baus and Ross, entitled their book of successful campaign tactics the *Politics Battle Plan.*[23] Napolitan spells out the "rules" of victory in his book, *The Election Game and How to Win It.*[24] Journalists are especially inclined to view elections as athletic events; the losers are spoken of as "posting poor batting averages." Regardless of these analogies, the essence of successful politicking remains the same: "The process of acquiring and using the political resources that can secure votes."

Since most resources are acquired and utilized by the campaign organization, the effectiveness of the organization is extremely important to the candidate. Both experts and nonexperts alike attributed Senator Henry Jackson's smashing 1976 presidential primary victory in Massachusetts to a creative campaign organization that mobilized Massachusetts voters with novel campaign tactics. Jackson's campaign staff came up with the idea of pairing all of cities having identical names in both Washington and Massachusetts, and persuading the registered voters of the Washington city to write supportive letters to residents of their Massachusetts counterpart. Thus, residents of Quincy and Belmont, Washington, wrote to the voters of Quincy and Belmont, Massachusetts, urging them to vote for the Senator in the Massachusetts primary. Workers in the campaign organization matched the cities, compiled the voting lists, and put together a cover letter asking Jackson supporters in Washington for a few minutes of their time and a 13¢ stamp to write a letter to their Massachusetts neighbors. Similarly, Jimmy Carter's defeat of George Wallace in the 1976 Florida primary is also attributed, in large part, to a cohesive, efficient campaign organization. The Florida primary was particularly important in the Carter drive for the Democratic presidential nomination, since a victory there would demonstrate Carter's appeal to both moderates and conservatives in the South.

Candidates have usually found that parties cannot adequately and consistently provide the funds, media coverage, and constituency research that are necessary for a successful campaign. While some candidates may envision the party as a vast network of workers who blanket the nation at election time, this conception is false. Statistical data indicate that fewer than 1 in 20 voters is actually visited by a party worker, and only about 25 percent receive any type of party-oriented literature. Without a central organization, parties cannot very well serve national campaigns. At the state level, the typical state party organization has become a paper tiger, but there are rare exceptions. For example, in 1974 the Republican Party of North Dakota supplied state legislative candidates with professional services to develop newspaper, radio and television advertising; issue information; successful campaign operations; billboard campaigns; absentee ballot programs; and a comprehensive voter issue survey. Thus, in an election year in which Republicans did not do very well nationwide, they made substantial gains in the North Dakota legislature.

Candidates are begging, borrowing, or buying a variety of skills; the following is a list of the types of specialists now employed in campaign work:

Specialists Employed in Campaigning

Management	Information	Media
Accountant	Marketing researcher	Journalist
Public relations	Public opinion pollster	Media advance man
Counselor	Political scientist	Radio and TV writer
Advertising agent	Social psychologist	Radio and TV producer
Advance man	Computer scientist	Film documentary
Fund-raiser	Psychologist	producer
Management scientist	Computer programmer	Radio and TV time buyer
Industrial engineer	Demographer	Newspaper space buyer
Telephone campaign	Statistician	Television coach
organizer		Radio and TV actors
Campaign management		Graphic designer
consultant		Direct mail advertiser
Election Legal Counselor		Computer printing
		specialist
		Speech coach
		Speechwriter

Source: Robert Agranoff, The New Style in Election Campaigns (Boston: Holbrook Press, 1976), p. 25.

Because specialists have proved valuable, candidates for national office have generally accepted Jesse Unruh's observation that "in politics, as in everything else, you tend to get what you pay for."[25] A New York politician has described the *ad absurdum* rush of some of the current politicians who seek professional help much like a consumer behaves at a moonlight madness sale:

> *If they have money, they try to buy security by hiring all the expert advice they can. They're faddish, like mutual fund managers: They buy whoever was hot last year. Very few candidates know exactly what they want and who the best consultant is to do it. The consultants are in business, you know, and politics is very seasonal—they have to make their money, and some are really thieves. But the good ones are more than worth their money—you just have to make sure you pick the good ones, and for the services "you" really need, not those "they" think you need.*[26]

Hiring expert advice and building the campaign organization around the candidate, rather than around the party structure, is not new. As early as 1952, the Republicans used professional experts in planning the advertising for Eisenhower's presidential campaign. Nelson Rockefeller's 1966 reelection campaign for the governorship of New York was not only one of the most expensive nonpresidential campaigns, but also one of the most professional. His campaign specialists included the Gallup organization of professional pollsters and Tinkers and Partners, who are now known for their successful marketing of Alka-Seltzer and Rockefeller. Hubert Humphrey's 1968 presidential campaign is perhaps the best example of the transition from a traditional campaign organization to reliance on the professional. Winning the nomination amid party strife and chaos, Humphrey began his bid for the presidency by leaning primarily for help on a divided Democratic Party. By September 1968, his campaign was obviously stumbling; the issue of Vietnam had irreparably divided the national party, and the polls showed that Humphrey was trailing Richard Nixon by 16 percentage points. At this point the professionals were called in to try to resurrect the Democratic campaign.

Napolitan and his team of filmmakers, television producers, advertising men, and pollsters organized the campaign around the theme "Humphrey and Muskie—Men the Voter Can Trust." Under this new management, Humphrey was able to substantially close the gap with his opponent; despite his failure to win the presidential race, Humphrey learned how a campaign ought to be run. His 1970 bid for election to the U.S. Senate leaned heavily on the professional firm of Sherman, Valentine and Associates, an organization that did not ignore the Minnesota Democratic Party, but simply reduced it to a secondary role in the campaign. Humphrey's campaign experience in 1968 and 1970 illustrates two things: first, the transition from party-oriented politics to candidate-centered, professionally run campaigns; and second, the importance of a campaign organization. Humphrey's rapid recovery in the polls after he retained Napolitan and his team was emphasized when the Nixon leadership told Theodore White that, "had the election been held on Saturday or Sunday [two or three days later], Nixon might have lost; had it been a week later than it actually was, their [the Democratic] margin of victory might have run as high as 2,000,000 to 5,000,000 votes."[27]

Despite the substantial assistance of the professional, both party workers and volunteer help are still important in campaign politics. Norton Simon's 1970 campaign to win the California Republican Party's U.S. Senate nomination demonstrates the importance of these groups in successful campaigning. Simon launched his race against the incumbent George Murphy in defiance of the party bosses; since he was unknown to the party regulars, he was forced to rely on commercial advertising. Hiring the film specialist Charles Guggenheim, Simon spent nearly $2 million in trying to persuade the public that Senator Murphy was suspect because of his continuing connections with Technicolor, Inc., the firm from which he was drawing $20,000 a year for consulting fees, $4000 for his services as a director of the company, and half the rent for his Washington apartment. This approach failed; Murphy won easily. But one should not assume that Simon's defeat was due solely to his lack of party support, for Milton Shapp was able to obtain the Pennsylvania Democratic Party's gubernatorial nomination without being a party regular; in any event, party assistance is usually a valuable resource in campaign politics. Although there was a correlation between the amount of money spent upon Shapp's campaign and his victory, this is not always the case. In some instances, party and volunteer help are able to offset financial deficiencies.

AVENUES OF RESEARCH AND COMMUNICATION

Research

Campaigns have been described as exercises in mass persuasion. Innovative techniques of gathering information about the voters, together with new means of transmitting the candidate's campaign message to the public, are now quite important. Information-gathering and information-dissemination can produce a very tailored, issue-oriented campaign that selects a certain group of voters and then zeroes in on the issues that would most appeal to that group. The techniques for gathering information about a constituency give the candidate a candid profile of his district. This, in turn, suggests guidelines for making key strategy decisions. Although the lists vary, most campaign specialists agree on a minimum of five factors with which a candidiate should be familiar:

1. Voting behavior patterns such as voter turnout, ticket-splitting, and party competition.
2. Demographics—racial, income, educational, occupational, age, and residential characteristics.
3. Party affiliation—strength of the voters' party identification, participation in party organization and activities.
4. Issue position and concerns—his own priorities and issue stands.
5. Profile of the opposition—group support, issue positions, skills, strengths and weaknesses with the voters, and advertising tactics.

Methods of collecting information used by adherents of the "old" party politics are easily distinguished from those used by the followers of the "new" politics. In the past, a profile of the electorate would be drawn, based upon the party politicians' guesses and the wardheelers' insights. Candidates now rely on experienced behavioral scientists to collect reliable data. Research consultants use several methods for determining the constituency profile, including recorded statistical data and the opinion poll.

Recorded Statistical Data. Statistics of past elections are important in predicting future voting behavior, identifying the relative strength of party registration in a particular district, and determining voter-turnout levels. Demographic characteristics suggest possible issues of concern to voters. A district with a large proportion of aged citizens would probably be interested in federal subsidies to the aged. Similarly, districts with a low per capita income would probably want more job opportunities and social welfare benefits. Election statistics—voter turnout, registration lists, and candidate totals—are available from county, municipal, state, and federal governments. Demographic information pertaining to the city block, census tract, standard metropolitan statistical area (S.M.S.A.), and state (compiled by the U.S. Bureau of the Census), is available from the U.S. Government Printing Office. Using this information, one can quickly put together a profile of the educational, occupational, and ethnic characteristics of the population in a city or an individual election district. From the Census Bureau books, one can learn about such details as the population per occupied housing unit; the value and monthly rent of housing in a district; toilet facilities; the number of white-collar workers; the number of foreign-born; and the number of foreign-born, white-collar workers who live in $100 per month housing with only one toilet per housing unit. Analyzing this type of data enables the candidate to have a comprehensive picture of his district and thus understand the interests and needs of the people living within it. Such information is invaluable in planning campaign strategy.

Public Opinion Polls. Polling, or survey research, is the most common means of gathering up-to-date information about the electorate. Candidates for public office rely on polls for identifying voter priorities and preferences, assessing voter expectations of the officeholder, and measuring voter familiarity with the candidates and issues. The polls' reliability has made them potent weapons, since a poor showing tends to demoralize volunteers and discourage potential contributors. In September 1968, when the polls showed that Humphrey trailed far behind Nixon in voter popularity, his fund-raising efforts were seriously hampered. The big contributors who usually give to both candidates to ensure a friendly reception by the victor, felt no need to support a sure loser. A favorable poll before a party nomination has been used to pressure both party delegates and potential financial contributors, since it would indicate the potential strength of the candidate in the future election.

The importance of polls goes far beyond gathering information about who is "winning" and who is "losing." Agranoff has compiled a list of the kinds of information that are available from polls that may be useful for campaign planning. Although not exhaustive, his list indicates a broad range of material: important issues to stress during the campaign; how to campaign among various groups; where to place the campaign's geographic focus; candidate personality information, including which personality factors to stress in advertising; how much emphasis needs to be given to familiarizing people with the candidate's name; what is known and unknown about the candidate's past record; potential areas of appeal that might increase the number of vote-switchers; which voters are undecided—their characteristics and issue preferences; the characteristics and issue preferences of ticket-splitters; and the media that each voter group utilizes most often. In an effort to test the political climate for Illinois Republicans in 1974, John Anderson commissioned a private poll in November 1973 to determine which issues were of most concern to the Illinois voter. Anderson was thinking of running for the U.S. Senate seat of the incumbent Adlai Stevenson, III, in 1974. After receiving the results of the poll, however, Anderson changed his mind: the poll showed that 46 percent of the Illinois voters thought Watergate was the most important issue of the time. Anderson decided that a Republican contender would be at a distinct disadvantage.

Polls are also used during a campaign to dramatize a candidate's standing. Announcing the results of candidate preference polls almost automatically gets coverage in newspapers, radio, and television. Aside from the polls commissioned by the candidates and those undertaken by magazines, newspapers, and other media, the public is continually being asked: "If the election were being held today, which candidate would you vote for?" If the respondent refuses to answer or seems undecided, he or she is not dismissed; the second question is: "Well, is there one candidate you lean to more than the other?"

Despite the allegation that candidates are using polls to gain more media coverage or to encourage reluctant donors to contribute, polls are widely accepted as accurate instruments for measuring popular sentiments. They have been criticized for exerting an undesirable influence on elections (the so-called bandwagon effect) and for distracting public attention from more important issues. Sometimes the polls are wrong, though this is rare. Pollsters are continually being reminded of their 1948 prediction that Thomas Dewey, rather than Harry Truman, would win the presidential election. This specific error was largely due to the pollsters' failure to detect a last-minute shift in the preferences of the electorate because of the time delay between asking the question and publishing the results.

Although polls have their occasional shortcomings in both accuracy and how they are used, they are still widely read, quoted, and believed by politicians and the public. They are also widely in demand and very expensive. A single, statewide poll for a candidate costs about $12,000 to $15,000, or approximately $10 per interview. Costs increase with depth: a Louis Harris and Associates, Inc. survey conducted for a Senate subcommittee, with a sample of 1596 respondents in 200 different places nationwide, cost the government $25,000. Telephone polling is rapidly becoming more popular because it is less expensive and the data can be collected much more quickly. With this type of poll, overnight surveys can be taken to get an approximate measure of public reaction to a very recent event. Richard Nixon often used overnight polls to ascertain public reaction to his presidential speeches.

For a poll to be accurate, the audience surveyed must be representative of the constituency, and the interviewers must know the purpose of the poll. The skills required for effective polling are not available from party organizations, nor are campaign volunteers of any particular help. As polls have become more important to elections, therefore, more businesses have been established specifically to run private polls for candidates; as of 1976, there were more than 200 firms in this field. In 1974, 80 percent of all candidates for the U.S. Senate and 25 percent of all candidates for the House used polls. The Republican George Romney used polls to monitor his media efforts during one of his Michigan gubernatorial campaigns in the 1960s. First, he polled the state to learn which issues were important in which regions and then constructed regional media campaigns that were later checked for effectiveness by polling and adjusted, if necessary.

Computer-Simulated Data. The joining of technology and politics has transformed the computer into a valuable political tool. Computers are being used in politics for three different tasks: (1) housekeeping tasks—maintaining an account of the resources accumulated and spent; (2) personal communications with the voters by means of typed letters that look as though they had been typed individually; and (3) maintaining a large and detailed data bank, through which intricate analyses of the subtle shifts in voter behavior can be chronicled. The new politicians are systematic, and data processing by means of sophisticated computer analysis has become an essential tool of the trade.

The techniques that have proved so effective in business management are now being applied to politics with a vengeance. Candidates have four resources that are often extremely limited—time, money, manpower, and talent. Computers help to determine how and where these resources should be allocated; they are valuable in measuring the effect of these resources when applied. Electronic data processing helps in making difficult policy decisions. Computer programs can be designed to spell out the implications of each alternative. The computer program enables the candidate to keep track of his campaign resources and evaluate strategy alternatives.

The computer's capacity to store, sort, and print information has helped to reduce the enormous volume of clerical work that most campaigns require; the computer is also being used for voting analysis, election simulations, and detailed voter and issue identification. Using the great storage capacity of computer data banks, candidates can combine several types of voter information and put together a detailed profile of the voter in his district, such as the number of school-age children per family, the major occupations, and the percentage of newspaper readers. No longer dependent on the party's informal channels of information, party leadership instinct or hearsay, candidates are gathering their own information and assessing the political climate themselves. Candidates are also communicating their message to the voter directly and bypassing the party organization.

Communication

Many of the television spots utilized in previous campaigns have been extremely clever. Rockefeller's TV spots in his 1966 New York gubernatorial campaign have been labeled 60-second classics: The candidate was never seen, and his voice was never heard. This type of advertising never acknowledges the opposition, but generally emphasizes the accomplishments of the incumbent. A different advertising approach, which does identify the opposition, was used by Reagan and Brown in their 1966 contest for the governorship of California. Reagan, a newcomer to politics, capitalized on his amateur status and attempted to rally voters around the theme "You and Me versus the Professional Politicians." His opponent, Edmund Brown, Sr., assailed Mr. Reagan's inexperience in politics and his past career as a movie actor. Brown hired Charles Guggenheim and Associates to produce some 22 different short spot commercials, which were then aired on television. These satirical spots reveal some of the tactics of campaigning via television:

The Scene: Tight closeup of the printed ballot listing the name and present occupation of the candidates for office in the upcoming election. (Camera pans up from bottom of printed form, stopping at Reagan's name. There is no occupation or present position listed.)

Voice of Narrator: When you vote, you'll notice that under every candidate's name he'll list his occupation as a guide to his experience and qualifications for office. Every candidate but one. If Ronald Reagan can't find anything in his background to qualify him for office, how can he expect the rest of us to find it?

The Scene: A press conference. (Newsreel shot of Reagan as he replies to question by reporter.)

Reagan: Um . . . I feel that I had ah . . . well, if I didn't feel that I'd had experience that qualifies me to seek this job, I wouldn't do it. Now, mine was not in politics. (Quick cut to old Reagan movie; the actor is dressed in cowboy costume, holding rifle.)

Cowboy Reagan (to mob of vigilantes): You wanted law and order in this town, you've got it. I'll shoot the first man who starts for those steps. (A man steps forward and Reagan guns him down with a blast from the hip.)
(Quick cut to slip from TV film with Reagan giving a commercial. He holds product as he talks directly to TV audience.)

Salesman Reagan: And here's exciting new Boraxo waterless hand cleaner. Watch. (Cut away to film clip from old movie as Reagan pushes mud pie into face of man at bar. Sound effects of "splat." Cut back to continuation of previous commercial.)

Reagan (smiling): New Boraxo waterless hand cleaner removes the toughest dirt or stains. Gets hands clean and smooth fast anytime. What a convenience. That's new Boraxo waterless hand cleaner. (Cut to clip from old Reagan movie: the actor, playing an ex-convict, is in a shabby hotel talking to a woman.)

Down-and-Outer Regan (piano music in background): I see beyond this joint. Right through the dirty wallpaper.
(Cut to preview trailer for old Reagan movie: the actor stands in a jungle looking through a surveyor's transit.)

Announcer's Voice: Ronald Reagan as the tight-lipped soldier of fortune, whose past was a mystery. (Sound fades under.)

Voice of Narrator: Over the years, Ronald Reagan has played many roles. This year he wants to play governor. Are you willing to pay the price of admission?[28]

Since the 1950s candidates have turned increasingly to the media to advertise their candidacy and qualifications. Parties, recognizing their own limitations, are encouraging candidates to seek out communication specialists; according to Rogers C. B. Morton, former chairman of the Republican National Committee: "We at the National Committee encourage our candidates to seek help from advertising agencies as the best guarantee of quality work in this important area." Candidates generally rely on six types of advertising: (1) television spots and programs, (2) radio spots and programs, (3) newspaper ads and flyers, (4) printed material, (5) display advertising, and (6) direct mailings. Thus, many more voters can be reached and more frequently than ever before.

Where do voters get their information on candidates and issues? Which sources of information carry most influence with voters, particularly those who are undecided? Research indicates that television is the primary source of information about candidates. Interestingly, television news, documentaries, and talk shows are ranked as more influential than the candidates' spot commercials. Newspaper editorials are more influential than television editorials or talk shows. Radio newscasts are ranked higher than political brochures, billboards, or magazine stories. Table 6.3 shows why candidates rely so much on television.

Television and Radio Advertising.   Political commercials do have some influence on the voters' reactions to candidates and issues; they have their greatest impact when the message is simple, direct, and believable. Television is particularly useful in conveying a compressed 20-, 30-, or 60-second message to large audiences, because it gives the viewer the illusion of being a favored spectator at a special event; he finds himself involved in the audiovisual presentation:

> *Television has an inherent mobility. It moves. It captures time and makes a record of it. . . . A still photograph or a printed word is static, it does not*

Table 6.3   Relative Importance of Sources That Influence the Voting Decisions of the Undecided

Very Important	Important	Not Important
Television newscasts	Talks with friends	Magazine advertisements
Television documentaries	Radio talk shows	Television entertainers
Newspaper editorials	Magazine editorials	Billboards
Television editorials	Talks with political	Telephone campaign
Television talk shows	party workers	messages
Television educational	Talks with work asso-	Movies
programs	ciates	Stage plays
Talks with family	Radio editorials	Phonograph records
Radio educational	Political brochures	
programs	Talks with neighbors	
Radio newscasts	Magazine stories	
The Democratic Party	Newspaper advertisements	
Contacts with candidates	The Republican Party	
Newspaper stories	Television advertisements	
	Books	
	Political mailings	
	Membership in religious	
	organizations	
	Membership in professional	
	or business organizations	
	Radio advertisements	

Source: Walter DeVries, "Taking the Voter's Pulse," in *The Political Image Merchants*, by Ray Hiebert, pp. 72-73.

move forward or backward. Furthermore, it takes a much more willful effort to ignore that which stimulates two of our senses than that which strikes only one. In other words, that which I see and hear involves me more than what I just see. Once I am involved, I become a participant and add something of myself to what I see and hear. I add my own impressions and attitudes. I have become part of a circle of communication.[29]

Several types of TV political programs—editorials, talk shows, educational programs, documentaries, and specials—rank as more influential than talks with friends, contacts with candidates, or discussions with party workers or one's own family. Alert producers have already learned that spot ads using news formats, when placed in time slots adjacent to newscasts, benefit from the aura of credibility attached to the network news program. They have learned to avoid the hard-sell approach; instead, they prefer a softer, more indirect touch: "Friends of ———— believe that he can do the job."

The use of tactics such as these, however, has raised charges of creating false candidate images, distorting the issues and candidate-issue preferences—in short, the unethical marketing of the candidate as one would market a box of cereal or a deodorant. Some complain that voters are being entertained and duped, rather than informed: They believe that the purpose of the short TV spot is to sell the voter an illusion, to move him to act without analyzing the material before him, to "con" him psychologically. Those responsible for the commercials reply that they do not fabricate a message; they simply attempt to communicate what is really there. They claim that the candidate himself is the subject matter for advertising: "To the extent that advertising can help illuminate those virtues, we play a role. But the notion that we are able to 'create' winners, or even remove warts, is nonsense."[30]

The costs of television campaigning seem to be exorbitant, but one needs to examine the cost-per-home-reached. Thirty-second spots can run as high as $3,000 or as low as $50 for a spot after the late-late movie. A one-minute prime time commercial on network TV costs $50,000. Sometimes the purchase of expensive prime time will bring in handsome profits for the candidate. Ronald Reagan's half-hour televised speech in 1976, just before the North Carolina primary, on his position as a presidential candidate netted his campaign $300,000 and a crucial first victory over President Ford.

Radio ranks third in importance as a source of voter campaign information, following television and newspapers. Despite this lower ranking, however, radio remains an important avenue of candidate exposure. Although network radio broadcasting expenditures have lagged far behind the expenditures for television, the amount of time purchased on radio is much greater. For example, in the 1970 general election both major parties bought a total of 2123 hours of non-network program radio time. Radio advertising differs from that of television in terms of the expense, the profiles of the two audiences, and the ease in production and acquiring premium airing time. Radio spots are much less expensive: Four radio spots can be purchased for the cost of one television spot. Various radio stations offer programs that appeal to narrow, homogeneous segments of the population, but the major television channels compete for similar broad audiences on a national scale. Radio offers the advantage of available prime advertising time, and requires less technical and expensive production equipment. A candidate can quickly and inexpensively respond to a recent event, the polling results, or his opponent's last-minute campaign attacks. Radio is particularly effective as a "reminder"—reminding the voter to vote for a specific candidate. The costs and benefits of radio programs make them accessible and desirable to most candidates. As with television, the cost of radio time varies—30 minutes of evening or daytime programming may be purchased for $200 or $300, while only 5 minutes of prime time programming will cost from $75 to $100. Some professionals have argued that in certain commuter markets such as Southern California, radio ads can be more effective than television.

Expenditures for radio and television candidate exposure have increased markedly since 1960—from $20 million in 1962 to $60 million in 1970. The 1970 total represents an 85 percent increase since 1966. And one observer estimated that, if all the production costs were taken into account, a comprehensive figure for broadcasting in the 1972 election might have been as high as $90 million.[31] Heavy spending for political broadcasts, however, has not guaranteed success. Incumbency has proved to be a more important—if not the single most important—factor in determining one's election success. Republican candidates for the U.S. Senate spent $4.4 million in 1974 on broadcasts during their campaign, as compared with $4.2 million spent by the Democratic candidates. The Democrats won 22 of the Senate seats; the Republicans won only 11.[32]

Newspaper Advertising. All too often, candidates are attracted to the dramatic and expensive medium of television, and fail to utilize the enormous potential of the newspaper. Newspapers are excellent means for disseminating in-depth information on the candidate's background and issue positions. Those working in campaigns must be careful not to underestimate newspapers—particularly editorials—as avenues of communication. Voters rate newspaper editorials as more influential than television editorials, following only television newscasts and documentaries in significance. Perusal of the newspaper is a regular part of most voters' daily lives. More than 70 percent of the adult public report reading a newspaper every day. Unlike radio programs, newspapers attempt to appeal to a broad segment of society. Past research indicates that newspaper advertising enjoys the attention of a very large and diverse audience of men and women of all age, income, and educational groups.

Newspaper campaign advertising is generally one of three types: (1) that which attempts to establish candidate name identification; (2) endorsements, usually from prominent citizens, or a list of well-known citizens who support a particular candidate; or (3) that which gives a biographical or issue sketch of the candidate. The cost of such advertisements varies with the size of circulation, the size of the ad, and its location in the newspaper. Newspaper ads vary in price from $300 per page in a small-town newspaper to $9000 for a full-page ad in the Sunday *New York Times*.

To get the most mileage out of a newspaper ad, candidates are cautioned that it must be "different." In a typical daily newspaper, there will be at least 300 ads competing for the reader's attention. The candidate's ad must catch the reader's eye as he makes his way to the comics or sports section. Good art work, "catchy" headlines, and large ads attract attention. The typical ad usually shows a picture of the candidate and says a few words about his experience, integrity, and community activities. The more creative ads may start with a cartoon or a slogan for a headline, such as Richard Nixon's "Bring Us Together." "Catchy" headlines give the reader an incentive to read the ad.

Historically all candidates have complained about an unfair press. Describing his arduous task of campaigning, Goldwater cited the press and its negative attitude—"most of them were against us"—as one of the factors that kept him on edge. After losing the gubernatorial race in California, Richard Nixon lambasted the press for unfair coverage: "You won't have Nixon to kick around anymore because, gentlemen, this is my last press conference...."[33] Former Vice President Spiro Agnew, a vocal opponent of the press, repeatedly accused it of having excessive influence in molding public opinion. The Vice President protested the "instant analysis and querulous criticism ... by a small band of network commentators and self-appointed analysts ... who wield a free hand in selecting, presenting and interpreting the great issues in our nation.... A tiny, enclosed fraternity of privileged men elected by no one."[34] David Brinkley's rebuttal summarized the press's position that it reports, and doesn't create, the news: "To politicians on an ego trip, which is most of them most of the time, any piece of journalism not filled with overwhelming and obsequious flattery is biased on its face."[35]

Two complaints traditionally lodged against the electronic and printed media are that it has undue influence on election outcomes and that it operates with a distinct conservative or liberal bias and favors one party over the other. Can the media create a candidate? Do the Broders or the Cronkites exert undue influence? Of course, correspondents and columnists do play a significant role in interpreting political events and in analyzing candidates, but how much influence they exert is somewhat ambiguous, and opinions differ. Some people worry that the media enjoys too much credibility and not enough critical evaluation by the voters. These critics point out that 95 percent of all American homes have television sets, and almost four out of every five adult Americans claim to read a newspaper daily. Critics of the media believe that it molds public opinion, shapes voter preferences, singles out its own preferred candidates, and creates an aura among the voters that its chosen candidate is the nation's favorite son. On the other hand, the media can destroy a candidate's chances by focusing unduly on his mistakes; Romney's "brainwashing" statement during the 1968 New Hampshire primary is but one example of a candidate's tongue slips that has been repeated again and again, through print and airwaves. Governor George Romney's (R-Michigan) charge that he had experienced a "brainwashing" while visiting Vietnam quickly became a "word that went around the world" and, according to the candidate himself, a word so publicized that "nobody will forget it."[36] This brainwashing charge, so well covered by the media, evoked considerable criticism and was followed by a sizable drop in his ratings in the polls. A Louis Harris presidential preference poll before the "brainwashing" statement predicted that President Johnson would win over Romney by a 52 to 48 percent margin. After the statement President Johnson's strength increased to a 58 to 42 percent margin.

Those who support the media argue that voters are individuals who have their own predispositions and opinions, not vacuums waiting to be filled by journalists or television newscasters. They believe that voters screen out most material that conflicts with their own views, listen selectively, and evaluate the content of the message. From this perspective, the media simply conveys cues to an already predisposed audience, so that voter opinions are not altered, but simply reinforced and stabilized.

Do the "big" names in journalism set the theme, decide the issues, and plot the candidates' futures? Rumors of "pack" journalism—of hierarchies among media men, in which the campaign reporters from prestigious papers and positions set the tone for a candidate's coverage—are rampant. Crouse describes the loss of individuality in the coverage of the 1972 presidential elections:

> *A group of reporters were assigned to follow a single candidate for weeks or months at a time, like a pack of hounds sicked on a fox. Trapped on the same bus or plane, they ate, drank, gambled, and compared notes with the same bunch of colleagues week after week.*[37]

Campaign journalism is, by definition, "pack" journalism: "to follow a candidate, you must join a pack of other reporters; even the most independent journalist cannot completely escape the pack."[38] Those who believe that the media is neither reasonably objective nor intellectually independent point to the 1968 and 1972 presidential elections. Those who are convinced that, on the whole, campaign reporting remains objective and competitive claim that the nation was only passing through an unfortunate period during those two presidential election years.

Direct Mailings and Computer "Votergrams."   Direct mailings are effective campaign tools for both influencing voter decisions and raising funds. Meyer, author of *The Winning Coalition*, considers mailings the most effective campaign publicity; he credits the Lodge victory in the 1964 New Hampshire primary to this factor.[39] Bella Abzug's campaign manager attributes her reelection in 1974 in part to a mass direct-mail campaign. Volunteers were put to work for 5 months writing prepared campaign appeals on personal stationery. Held until 2 weeks before the election, thousands of letters, personally written and addressed, were then sent to voters' homes.

Survey research indicates that 75 percent of those receiving a letter read it. Although voters have a high threshold of apathy, personal letters have apparently been able to penetrate it. All other things being equal, a candidate who uses direct mailings will usually pick up a 7 percent vote advantage over an opponent who does not.

First of all, one must compile lists of large numbers of voters, their addresses, and more detailed personal information about each name on the list. Direct mailings concentrate on certain groups—members of the National Rifle Association, party members, school teachers, residents of a small township—and the message is tailored to the interests and needs of each group. Individual members receive "personalized" letters: "People in —— occupations are concerned about ——. Congressman —— agrees that this is an important issue and will support legislation dealing with this problem." Thousands of letters, printed by computers that can handle more than 1000 letters per hour, are then mailed out. A candidate needs only a number of mailing lists, which can readily be purchased. In fact, the selling of mailing lists has in itself become a lucrative business. Lists of active and retired military personnel, conservative Republicans, contributors to the United National International Children's Fund, and taxpayer rolls are just a few of the many lists of names and addresses that are available from various sources. An extensive range of personal data can be obtained from mail-list brokers—information on the types of publications an individual reads, the types of charitable organizations he contributes to, the party he belongs to, and his possible views on various issues. With such information, candidates, interest groups, and others are able to raise money or address their appeals to a particular type of voter. The timing of these personal appeals is very important; those scheduled to arrive either on election day or the day before tend to be most effective. One clever technique, the "Votergram," has turned out to be a significant election day tactic. Resembling the telegram in size, shape, and color, the personally addressed note reminds the receiver to vote, mentions the polling place, and promotes the candidate. Printed by a computer, the personal touch is painstakingly maintained:

> *Vonna and William Wilbur*
> *220 West 4th Avenue*
> *Denver, Colorado 80204*
> *May I remind you that your polling place for the election Tuesday is Baker Jr. High School at 574 West 6th Avenue.*
> *If you need a ride to the polls, a baby-sitter or any information, please call your McNichols Volunteer Headquarters at 733-2497.*
> *Based upon my 14 years of experience as a Democratic State Senator, Lt. Governor, and Governor of Colorado, I can go to work immediately in the Kennedy tradition for you and all the people of Denver County.*
> *Vonna and William Wilbur, I hope I have your trust and that I can count on your votes. Please pull lever 2B.*
> *Steve McNichols[40]*

The cost of direct mailings varies according to the price of the mailing lists. A printed mailing to 1000 households costs between $150 and $200, or approximately 15 cents per unit.

Direct mailings are also useful for raising money. Because the economic recession and competition from various charitable organizations has made it difficult to secure funds, candidates armed with computers have turned to mass-mail solicitations; this approach has proved highly lucrative. Politically independent fund-raising groups were quite successful with direct mailings during 1969-1970. During this period the Committee for the Democratic Process, relying primarily on a letter carrying McGovern's (D-South Dakota) signature, raised $730,000. Viguerie, the professional political direct-mail fund-raiser, collected $4.8 million for George Wallace: "We got an average $9.20 donation on the prospect mailings, and an average $14.00 from house mailings."[41] The Viguerie Company, with an average mailing of more than 600,000 pieces a week, has mastered the science of direct mailing: "We know the importance of the color of the envelopes, length of letters, personalized variables in letters, because we've tested all of these variables. The results are analyzed . . . and the success of each variation is measured."[42] Reaching the voter through the mails has apparently become as much a science as public opinion polling and media campaigns.

MEDIA MIX

The advertising experts are learning the importance of mixing the media. Recognizing that some channels of communication are more effective with some groups than with others, they are also finding that it is worthwhile to use several avenues to reach one audience. For example, a message for women may be scheduled for television during the afternoon "soap opera time" and a similar advertisement placed on the social page of the local newspaper. A winning candidate is usually one who establishes an appropriate blend of the avenues of communication for a particular constituency. This blend includes not only the electronic and print media, but also informal, personal types of communication. Some candidates have placed too much emphasis upon television as their exclusive or prime means of communication; but most candidates use varied channels of communication, including buttons, bumper stickers, brochures, hats, kitchen utensils, and billboards. The cost of these miscellaneous items is often high and, except for publicizing the candidate's name, their effectiveness is relatively uncertain. These items are distributed largely among the most intense supporters, and it is reported that they boost the workers' morale. Governor George Wallace came up with a way of using these items to help his personal fund-raising attempts; he set a campaign "first" in signing a contract with his own campaign organization that permits him to draw $150,000 in personal royalties over the following 10 years for the campaign's use of his likeness on pennants, watches, and other materials.

"Politics is not an exact science" summarizes the various warnings given by experienced campaigners to newcomers. Despite the voluminous research done on the media and its effects on electoral results, the findings are not conclusive. Our total store of knowledge about the precise effects of campaign appeals is limited. Investigations of the voter decision-making process have only served to emphasize the complexity of that process. Analysts would like to have a much more thorough understanding of the external stimuli that influence the voter, as well as more insight into the psychological factors that cause the voter to be drawn to a particular candidate.

PARTIES AND CAMPAIGN POLITICS: AN ALTERED BALANCE

Several years ago a team of well-known political observers recommended the following campaign strategy to the then-underdog Republican Party: (1) deemphasize party identification as a cue for voting, and focus on broader voting cues; and (2) play down the importance of party identification in the minds of the voters. At present most campaign strategy is not developed around the party but does include the party organization. "Candidates who pursue new politics campaigns still prefer to have parties and groups with them rather than against them."[43]

A successful candidate today generally combines the old methods of campaigning with the new; a party organization, when it is available, can be an important source of personal contact with the voters—through door-knocking, canvassing, and telephoning. Consultants, despite their public denouncements of the party structure, still rely on the organization when it is advantageous; they are available for party employment and align themselves with one or another party by working exclusively for its candidates. Napolitan, who managed the Humphrey campaign in 1968, did not ignore the Democratic Party; instead, he simply took it over. The present is an uncomfortable period of transition for parties, candidates, and professionals in campaign politics.

FOOTNOTES

1. A. James Reichley, "Both Parties Need Restyling for the Political Road Ahead," in *Readings in American Government,* 76/77 (Guilford, Conn.: Dushkin Publishing Group, 1976), p. 182.

2. Peter Goldman, *Newsweek,* January 12, 1976, p. 19.

3. William Rusher, "GOP Was Quite a Horse Race," *Daily Breeze,* July 15, 1976.

4. *Newsweek,* January 12, 1976, p. 27.

5. Ibid.

6. Joseph Napolitan, *The Election Game* (New York: Doubleday, 1972).

7. Bruce F. Freed, "This Time Everybody's Got a CREEP," *Washington Monthly* (November 1975).

8. Herbert Alexander, as quoted in Bruce F. Freed, ibid., p. 36.

9. Jeff Fishel, "Ambition and the Political Vocation: Congressional Challengers in American Politics," *Journal of Politics 33* (1971), pp. 25-56.

10. D. R. Matthews, *U.S. Senators and Their World* (Chapel Hill: University of North Carolina Press, 1960); Joseph S. Clark, *Congress: The Sapless Branch* (New York: Harper & Row, 1965).

11. Joseph A. Schlesinger, *Ambition and Politics* (Chicago: Rand McNally, 1966).

12. Fishel, op. cit., p. 34.

13. Gordon S. Black, "A Theory of Political Ambition: Career Choices and the Role of Structural Incentives," *Journal of Politics 33* (1971), p. 145.

14. James David Barber, *The Lawmakers* (New Haven, Conn.: Yale University Press, 1965).

15. "Will Ford Change His Mind about Running in 1976?" *U.S. News and World Report*, August 26, 1974, p. 17.

16. George Washington Plunkett, "Honest Graft and Dishonest Graft," *The City Boss in America*, edited by Alexander B. Callow, Jr. (New York: Oxford University Press, 1976), pp. 149-151.

17. Conrad Joyner, *American Politician* (Tucson, Ariz.: University of Arizona Press, 1971).

18. "Campaign Management Grows into National Industry," *Congressional Quarterly Weekly Report XXVI*, No. 14 (April 5, 1968), p. 708.

19. Quoted by David Lee Rosenbloom, *The Election Men: Professional Campaign Managers and American Democracy* (New York: Quadrangle Books, 1973), p. 104.

20. Milton Rakove, *Don't Make No Waves—Don't Back No Losers* (Bloomington, Ind.: University of Indiana Press, 1975), p. 118.

21. Ibid., pp. 119-120.

22. Rosenbloom, op. cit., p. 68.

23. Herbert M. Bauss and William B. Ross, *The Politics Battle Plan* (New York: Macmillan, 1968).

24. Napolitan, op, cit.

25. John Deandourff, "Most Important Campaign Tool Is Good Preliminary Planning," *Campaign Insight 1*, No. 6 (September 1970), p. 1.

26. Ibid.

27. Theodore White, *The Making of the President, 1968*, (Paterson, New Jersey: Atheneum Press, 1969), p. 417.

28. Ernest Rose and Douglas Fuchs, "Reagan vs. Brown," *Journal of Broadcasting 12* (Summer 1968), pp. 254-255.

29. Joseph Napolitan, "Zeroing in on the Voter." In *The Political Image Merchants*, by Ray Hiebert, Robert Jones, John Lorenz, and Ernest Lotito (eds.) (Washington, D.C.: Acropolis Books Ltd., 1971), pp. 48-49.

30. Federick Papert, "Good Candidates Make Advertising Experts," in ibid., p. 97.

31. Herbert E. Alexander, *Financing Politics: Money, Elections and Political Reform* (Washington, D.C.: Congressional Quarterly Press, 1976), p. 29.

32. Ibid.

33. Richard Nixon, *Facts on File, 1962* (New York: Facts on File, 1962), p. 390.

34. Spiro Agnew speech, quoted in *Facts on File, 1969* (New York: Facts on File, 1969), p. 745.

35. Ibid.

36. George Romney, as quoted in *Facts on File, 1967* (New York: Facts on File, 1967), p. 395.

37. Timothy Crouse, *The Boys on the Bus* (New York: Ballantine Books, 1972), p. 7.

38. Ibid.

39. D. S. Meyer, *Winning Candidate: How to Defeat Your Political Opponent* (New York: James H. Heinman, 1966), p. 102.

40. Peter Iovino, "Some Candidates Win with Just One Worker—Computer," *Campaign Insight 1*, No. 8 (November 1970), p. 1.

41. For a discussion of the Richard Viguerie direct mail business, see *Dollar Politics*, op. cit., *Congressional Quarterly Staff*, 1974, pp. 4-5.

42. Ibid., p. 5.

43. Robert Agranoff, *The Management of Election Campaigns* (Boston: Holbrook Press, 1976), p. 8.

7
Political Money and the Role of the Parties

"Money is the mother's milk of politics." This frequently cited statement by Jess Unruh, when he was the boss of the California state assembly in the 1950s, accurately sums up the significance of money in modern politics. The political money scandals of the 1972 presidential election have focused attention on the matter of how we finance our parties and candidates and the implications of these methods. Are our elections too expensive? Are the post-Watergate reforms effective? And, given the present and probable future patterns of political financing, how will these patterns affect the future viability of American political parties?

Are American Campaigns Too Expensive?

Political spending during 1972 for all campaigns on all levels of American government totaled a record $425 million, including $138 million just for the presidential race. The total spent in 1976 for the federal level campaigns, was $212 million—$61 million for House campaigns, $38 million for Senate campaigns, and $113 million for the presidential primaries and general election campaigns. Since many observers believed that these were "excessively expensive" campaigns, the federal campaign finance laws of 1974 and 1976 were enacted. The costs of campaigning have sharply risen since the 1960s. Herbert E. Alexander, the foremost scholar on the subject of campaign finances, has reported these increases in presidential election years beginning in 1952, when the total spending for all levels of government hit $140 million; these totals rose rose to $155 million in 1956, $175 million in 1960, and $200 million in 1964. The sharp jump occurred in 1968, when a 50 percent increase raised the total to $300 million.[1] When these gross totals are converted into cost per vote, the 1912-1952 period was relatively cheap, with the cost per voter ranging from 10 cents in the 1944 election to 31 cents in the hotly contested 1928 and 1936 elections. However, beginning in 1964, the costs per voter rose to 35 cents and reached 60 cents in 1968 and $1.36 in 1972.[2] The gross total of $425 million may seem to be a terribly expensive way of selecting political leaders; however, a per capita cost of approximately a $1 a vote appears to be quite reasonable, considering the scope of government activities in our society. In 1972 all levels of American government spent a total of $350 billion, or 40 percent of our gross national product; by comparison, we spent only .037 percent of the GNP in selecting more than 500,000 officials. Perhaps it might be worthwhile to realize that in 1972 the two largest corporate advertisers (Procter and Gamble and General Motors) spent more in advertising than the total cost of all of the 1972 campaigns. The $425 million spent in 1972 includes the following subtotals:

1. $138 million to elect a president, including pre-convention campaigns and the campaign of minor-party candidates
2. $98 million to nominate and elect congressional candidates, including contributions from labor, business, professional groups, party, and miscellaneous committees, as well as these committees' fixed expenditures for their own maintenance and operation
3. $95 million to nominate and elect governors, other statewide officials, and state legislators; and to campaign for and against state ballot issues and constitutional amendments
4. $95 million to nominate and elect hundreds of thousands of county and local public officials.[3]

There are many reasons why political expenses have risen sharply since the 1960s. Between 1968 and 1972 the electorate increased by 16 million (the right to vote was extended to 18-year-olds in 1971) and the task of communicating with these new voters required additional expenditures. Furthermore, inflation, the greater use of professional campaign organizations (including television, computers, polling, and data processing), increased competition in many formerly one-party regions, and the increase in wealthy candidates all contributed to higher campaign spending.[4] Self-financed candidates such as Nelson Rockefeller, Howard Metzenbaum, Milton Shapp, P. S. DuPont IV, and H. J. Heinz III ran unusually expensive campaigns in their efforts to win public office.

Richard Nixon's 1972 reelection campaign may have been the model of a high cost, money-is-no-object campaign. His assistants raised nearly $70 million (more than twice as much as had ever been raised for an American presidential campaign), and they paid for many services that had previously been supplied by volunteers. Salaries alone accounted for $3 million during the general election period, between August 1 and October 1, 1972, more than 1900 storefront headquarters were set up by CREEP (Committee to Re-Elect the President). Nixon's network media costs totaled more than $7 million and, as can be seen in Table 7.1, more than $2.7 million was spent on campaign paraphernalia.

It should noted that campaigns may vary substantially in cost. A seat has been won to the state legislature from a competitive district in Utah for as little as several hundred dollars, whereas a candidate for the Democrat Party nomination for a San Francisco seat in the California state senate spent $230,000 *and lost*.[5] Large sums of money do not guarantee victory for a candidate; although it can buy many useful

Table 7.1 Pre- and Post-Convention Expenditures of the Committee to Re-Elect the President and Related Organizations, 1971-1972

Expense Category	Dollars (in Millions)
Advertising (broadcast, including production costs and fees)	7.0
Direct mail to voters (not including fund-raising)	5.8
Mass telephone to voters	1.3
State organizations (primary elections, personnel, storefronts, locations, travel, voter contact, etc.)	15.9
Campaign materials[a]	2.7
Press relations, publications, and literature	2.6
Headquarters (campaign, personnel, rent, telephone, travel, legal, etc.)	4.7
Travel and other expenses of President, Vice President, surrogates, and advance men	3.9
Citizen group activities	1.9
Youth activities	1.0
Polling (including White House-directed surveys)	1.6
Convention expenses	.6
Election night	.2
Fund-raising (direct mail—$4 million, and major events—$1 million)	5.0
Fund-raising (national administration and gifts for contributors)	1.9
Legal fees	2.1
Democratic settlement (Watergate)	.8
Democrats for Nixon	2.4
Total	61.4

[a]The Nixon campaign of 1972 purchased 25 million buttons, 16 million bumper stickers, 100,000 posters, 40 million brochures, 10,000 tee shirts, 40,000 straw hats, and 300,000 balloons.

Source: Herbert A. Alexander, *Financing the 1972 Election*, p. 82; *Financing Politics*, p. 198.

resources, it can seldom overcome a candidate's handicap. S. I. Hayakawa, president of San Francisco State College during the student riots in the late 1960s, easily defeated two well-financed opponents in the 1976 Republican U.S. Senate primary in California. Hayakawa spent less than $100,000 and used little television, while his two opponents—former California Lt. Governor Robert Finch and Congressman Alphonzo Bell—spent $500,000 and $681,752, respectively, in trying to overcome Hayakawa's favorable public image.

The candidates for Congress during the 1976 election spent more than $60.9 million. The new record for "the most money spent by both candidates for a House seat" was set in California's hotly contested 27th district in 1976 by Republican Robert Dornan and Democrat Gary Familian—a total of $1,040,755.[6] In 1972, there were 24 congressional districts in which the combined spending exceeded $250,000, in 1976, these were 63 districts in that category. On the other hand, the Democrat David W. Evans in 1974 spent only $15,846 in defeating the incumbent Republican William Bray for the sixth district in Indiana. In the 1976 congressional elections, the House winners averaged about $80,000 per campaign and their opponents less than half that amount. Senate campaigns are considerably more expensive than House seats because of the larger size of their constituencies. Successful Senate candidates in 1976 averaged $617,000 in general election expenditures.[7]

Among the 100 U.S. Senate seats that are up for election on a 6-year basis, there is also a wide range of costs. The two candidates for Utah's Senate seat that was being vacated by Wallace Bennett in 1974 spent a total of only $808,662. On the other hand, Senator George McGovern, running for reelection to the Senate, spent $1,172,831 to win a modest 53 percent of the final vote. McGovern spent nearly $10 per vote in a state whose population is about half that of Utah's. Senator Allan Cranston's 1974 reelection campaign in California cost a little more, but this averaged out to only 50 cents per vote.

When the average cost per vote in the United States is compared with election campaign expenses in other democracies, the comparison usually favors the United States. The Swedes, for example, spend four times as much as we do on a per capita basis.[8] The total true expenditures have never been calculated in Japan's general elections (due to inaccurate reporting procedures), but these expenditures are probably many times the amount spent in the United States.[9] Thus, from a broader perspective, our campaign expenditures may not be excessive; however, it should not be inferred that there are no serious problems in this area. There are serious problems, and they affect our party system.

IT WASN'T ALWAYS SO EXPENSIVE

In the early years of our history, political campaigning was incredibly cheap. The predominant style of colonial campaigning could be labeled "whiskey campaigning." When George Washington ran for the Virginia House of Burgesses from Fairfax County in the election of 1757, he spent nothing on advertising, buttons, bands, polls, consultants, traveling, or primaries and conventions. His campaign expenses were 28 gallons of rum, 50 gallons of rum punch, 34 gallons of wine, 46 gallons of beer, and 2 gallons of ciderroyal—for 391 voters in his district. Two decades later, when another future president, James Madison, lost a bid for reelection to the Virginia legislature partly because he refused to have a "whiskey campaign,"[10] a fundamental principle of political campaigning became clear: "Don't abandon campaign techniques which are expected by the voters to be part of the minimal standards of the contest." Even with today's emphasis on the media, political buttons and banners are still a major expense even though no one knows if they are really productive. In order for major California candidates to be taken seriously, they must purchase at least a certain number of billboards.

Early presidential elections were also quite inexpensive. George Washington's first two elections cost nothing—not having an opponent in either election certainly helped. However, as the size of the electorate increased and elections became competitive, the costs of campaigning also rose. Newspapers became the primary mode of political communication, and parties and political leaders attempted to establish their own newspapers in order to support their cause. Thus, until the late 1820s newspapers and rallies were the predominant campaign techniques, and these costs could easily be borne by the candidate and his close friends.

Andrew Jackson's election to the White House in 1828 changed the pattern greatly. The electorate had mushroomed to more than a million potential voters, and the costs of reaching this many people increased. Parties had become permanent structures and required continuing support. Many public offices that had been appointive were made elective during the Jackson era. All of these changes required money, and the spoils (or patronage system) helped fill the campaign coffers. Governmental jobs were tied to the success or failure of the party or candidate. If your candidate won and you received a government job, you were expected to "kick back" a percentage of your salary to help the party stay in power. The famous Tammany Hall machine in New York City required 6 percent of the city employees' weekly pay. Vote buying during the 1830s increased the costs of campaigning:

> Getting out the vote now meant, in many cases, buying it. The price of an uncommitted vote in New York City in 1832 was approximately five dollars, which was two or three days wages for an ordinary laborer. In the 1838 mayoralty race, both Whigs and Democrats paid "floaters" to vote early and often. The Whig bid of $22.00 for the first vote and $18.00 for each additional vote was sufficiently high to ensure the reelection of the Whig incumbent. . . . Edgar Allan Poe was one victim of this corruption. He died on October 7, 1849, four days after an election in Baltimore. He appears to have died of alcoholism brought on by liquor he purchased with money received for selling his vote.[11]

It should be noted that one of the few futile attempts to raise money by regular dues was tried by the Whigs during this period. Their 1 cent a week dues failed to raise enough money, and so other sources had to be found. By the 1840s the relationship between politicians and business began to develop. With election costs rising sharply, the wealthy were a logical source of funds for candidates who couldn't finance their own campaigns. The honor of being the first "fat cats" in America went to the DuPonts of Delaware who from 1839 were the chief financial supporters of the Whig Party.

The Civil War closed a period of relatively inexpensive campaigns and moderate corruption. By the 1870s, election costs rose dramatically, with U.S. Grant's 1868 presidential campaign expenditures ($200,000) doubling those of Lincoln in 1860. George Thayer refers to the 50 years after 1876 as the "Golden Age of Boodle": "No office was too high to purchase, no man too pure to bribe, no principle too sacred to destroy, no law too fundamental to break."[12] Much of this corruption was found in the various state legislatures and their handpicked representatives to the federal government—U.S. Senators. For, until 1918, U.S. Senators were selected by the state legislatures, and these seats were sometimes sold to the highest bidders. Often legislatures were virtually owned by powerful interests; the most publicized examples were Montana (Anaconda), Illinois (Illinois Central RR), and California (Southern Pacific RR). It was said that Standard Oil did everything to the Pennsylvania legislature except refine it.

In an attempt to stop the collection of campaign funds from government employees, the Pendleton Act of 1883 was passed; it forbade such solicitations, but actually strengthened big business as the main source of political funding. The solicitation of the business community reached a peak of efficiency during Mark Hanna's management of William McKinley's presidential campaign in 1896. That campaign has been called the first modern one in our history. Millions of posters, billboards, pamphlets, and buttons were distributed, including more than 300 million pieces of campaign literature in more than a dozen languages. More than 1400 speakers stumped the nation in support of the Republican McKinley. Obviously such a campaign costs a tremendous amount of money, and estimates place the total at $6 or $7 million. His Democratic opponent, William Jennings Bryan, spent only one-tenth that amount. Big business, fearful of the radical nature of Bryan's campaign, gave huge sums of money to help defeat him. Hanna made assessments on various industries; banks, for example, were asked to give ¼ of 1 percent of their capitalization, and Standard Oil contributed $250,000, not because of specific promises, but simply to continue the Republicans in office and guarantee a general pro-business administration.

Three changes occurred in the second decade of this century to further raise campaign spending. The 17th Amendment shifted the election of U.S. Senators from state legislatures to the voting public; the 19th Amendment doubled the size of the electorate by enfranchising women; and the establishment of direct primaries multiplied the number of elections that had to be contested.

In the 1920s radio began to be utilized as a campaign tool, again raising the amounts of money needed for campaigns. A new source of political money—the underworld— was not created, but was certainly enhanced by the prohibition laws of the 1920s. Politicians needed money and the gangsters needed protection, so the ties were established that continue up to today. Beginning in 1936, labor unions began to raise money and campaign—largely for liberal candidates of the Democratic Party. The main sources of political money—labor, business, organized crime, interest groups, fat cats, and individual citizens—were firmly established by the late 1930s, and there has been only one major change since then, federal matching funds for presidential elections.

The Rise and Fall of the Fat Cats

"Fat cats" (individual contributors who give very large sums of money to a politician) may have reached a peak of influence in American politics during the two presidential campaigns of 1968 and 1972. Such wealthy supporters have been a part of politics for as long as there has been politics. Machiavelli, writing in *The Prince* some 500 years ago, noted, "As a general rule, those who wish to win favor with a prince offer him the things they most value and in which they see that he will take most pleasure. . . ."[13] It has already been noted that the original American fat cats (such as the DuPonts, Astors, and Vanderbilts) contributed an extraordinary proportion of party campaign expenses in the 1840s. However, in the twentieth century, the nature of the reporting law has been such that most modern fat cats escaped detection until the 1968 and 1972 elections. Without a doubt, the fattest cat of them all was the Chicago insurance magnate, W. Clement Stone, who gave or loaned $7 million to various conservative politicians between 1968 and 1972. Stone's Democratic counterparts were Stewart Mott (General Motors) and Max and Joan Palevsky (Xerox) who gave $400,000 and $337,190, respectively, to McGovern's 1972 campaign.

Campaigns in the late 1960s and early 1970s were often begun and nurtured by the seed money given by big contributors. Eugene McCarthy's 1968 campaign was financed by a few who gave a lot and many who gave a little; 50 fat cats gave McCarthy $2.5 million. Nixon's 1968 campaign fund received $8 million from 285 contributors, while in 1972 he received more than $20 million from 153 fat cats. The number of fat cats increased greatly between the 1968 and 1972 campaigns. In 1968 there were a total of 15,000 contributors who gave more than $500 and 424 who gave more than $10,000. In the 1972 campaign these totals had increased to 51,230 and 1254. Over $51 million was contributed by individuals giving $10,000 or more in 1972.[14] As expected, presidential candidates have sought to make these large contributions a permanent politician-contributor pattern. Lyndon Johnson and Richard Nixon each had their own version of "the president's club," in which large contributors exchanged their money for regular access to the White House. During his campaign, George McGovern set up the Woonsocket Club, consisting of 35 members who had each given a minimum of $25,000; it was named after the town where McGovern met his wife.

The problem with financing election campaigns with fat cats lies in the expected quid pro quo nature of the contribution. A prominent supporter who raised $500,000 for Hubert Humphrey's 1968 election eve telethon by making six telephone calls to big givers rejected a $50,000 offer from a businessman who wanted advance information on aerospace contracts. Large contributors also can place tremendous pressures on candidates to adopt specific policies that they favor.[15] Hubert Humphrey's fund-raising experiences during 1968 indicate how such pressure can be applied. Desperate for media money soon after the August convention, Humphrey's fund-raisers flew to Houston to ask for support from a group of oil millionaires at the Petroleum Club. First, however, the oil men wanted to know what Humphrey's position was on the oil depletion allowances—the special tax loophole that has greatly benefited oil investors. Humphrey's position was that he couldn't promise anything. In a second meeting with Humphrey at his home in Minnesota, the oil men offered several million dollars for the campaign if Humphrey would agree not to recommend or support a cut in the allowance if elected. Since Humphrey refused to make such a promise, the oil men gave their money to Richard Nixon, who accepted their condition.[16] Humphrey then turned to some of the former supporters of Senators Eugne McCarthy and Robert Kennedy for financial support. One of these, Stewart Mott, wrote to Humphrey that he and his friends would

Give you a hearing—a personal, private interview of an hour's length . . . we have the capacity to give $1 million or more to your campaign—and raise twice or three times that amount. But we will each make our own individual judgments on the basis of how you answer our several questions and how you conduct your campaign in the coming weeks."[17]

The quid pro quo was millions of dollars in exchange for greater opposition to the war in Vietnam. With these fund-raising experiences, it was not suprising that Humphrey remarked in 1974: "Campaign financing is a curse. It's the most disgusting, demeaning, disenchanting, debilitating experience of a politician's life. It's stinky, it's lousy; I just can't tell you how much I hate it."[18]

Hopefully this type of political fund-raising is a thing of the past; accounts of the 1976 campaign seem to indicate a substantial reduction in fat cats at the federal level. The $1000 limit on contributions to candidates for federal offices, enacted in 1974, seems to have had some effect. The Democratic hopeful, Jimmy Carter, went all the way to the convention without incurring the heavy financial obligations that had burdened most nominees in the past. H. E. Alexander announced during that campaign that "the fat cats are dead." They were killed by the $250 matching fund requirement for a candidate to qualify for federal money.[19] Since fat cats like W. Clement Stone and Stewart Mott could give only $1000 per candidate, they shifted their attention in part to non-federal races. It is one thing for a wealthy person to write out a check for $100,000 to a candidate; it is quite a different thing to ask such a person to solicit 99 friends to give $1000 each. According to Max Pelevsky, who stopped raising money for Jimmy Carter in 1975, "It's very annoying." The time and talent required to raise many small contributions has turned off many of the former fat cats. W. Clement Stone's major contribution to Gerald Ford's 1976 campaign seems to have been his signing a letter to ask fellow businessmen to give $1000 to the Ford treasury.[20] The biggest fat cat of the 1976 federal elections was a Texas businessman who spent $63,000 for advertising for Reagan's primary campaigns in Texas and Michigan. It seems as though most of the old fat cats ignored the loophole of independent spending that the Supreme Court had opened for them in its January 1976 decision on the federal election law.

Direct-mail solicitors largely replaced the big contributors during the 1976 presidential primaries. Thus, the necessity of raising money in amounts of $250 has made those technicians who can bring in many such contributions indispensable. Carter's direct-mail specialist, Morris Dees, observed that it cost $200,000–$225,000 to send out a million letters asking for contributions. Gerald Ford's counterpart, Robert Odell, established state-by-state quotas for their contact men, usually well-known businessmen.[21] Of all the candidates in the 1976 presidential race, those who did this type of fund-raising best—Ford, Carter, and Reagan—had the fewest money problems by the end of the primaries.

Until 1972 and 1976 the sources of the millions of dollars spent in political campaigns were seldom disclosed. Both politicians and their financial supporters went to great lengths to conceal the ties that bound them together. However, the strengthened federal disclosure laws of 1971 and 1974 and new statutes in a number of the states have revealed the magnitude of the role played by special interests in funding election campaigns.

The Organizational Fat Cats

Common Cause's survey of political funding during the 1976 congressional campaigns disclosed that special interest groups poured an unprecedented $22.6 million into House and Senate campaigns—nearly twice the $12.5 million they had invested in 1974. These organizational fat cats can be broadly categorized as labor, business, professional, and ideological contributors. Table 7.2 summarizes the contributions by special interests to congressional candidates in the 1970s.

Organized labor's entry into the political money game in the 1930s was one of the more significant changes in American politics.[22] Since its first contribution to Roosevelt's 1936 campaign, Big Labor has poured tens of millions of dollars into the coffers of the Democratic Party and its various candidates. Its contribution to congressional candidates alone in 1976 totaled more than $8.2 million. In the 1976 congressional campaign, 96.5 percent of Big Labor's money went to Democrats.

Much of labor's money is spent on a few selected ("target") congressional districts; in 1974 there were 83 target districts that received a disproportionate share of the money. A typical contribution from labor might be about $5000, but then it gave $168,700 to Senator Howard Metzenbaum, who was defeated by Glenn in the 1974 Ohio Democratic primary for U.S. Senator. In his study of the 1968 election, Herbert Alexander noted that while labor provided only 5 percent of the Republican financing at the national level, it accounted for more than 60 percent of the Democratic funding.[23] The 1972 presidential campaign was unusual in that labor contributed heavily

Table 7.2 Special Interest Contributions to Congressional Candidates in 1976 and the 1972-1976 Period

Special Interest	1972-1976[a]	1976
American Medical Association	4,098,096	1,790,879
Dairy associations	2,194,434	1,362,159
AFL-CIO COPES	3,023,465	996,910
Maritime unions	1,981,823	979,691
United Automobile Workers	2,098,337	845,939
Coal/Oil/Gas associations		809,508
National Education Association	1,207,420	752,272
National Association Realtors		605,973
Financial institutions		529,193
International Association of Machinsts	1,147,234	519,157
United Steelworkers Union	1,090,633	463,033
American Dental Association		409,835

[a]The 1976 totals are included in 1972-1976 figures.

Source: Common Cause, "Report to the American People on the Financing of Congressional Election Campaigns," April-May, 1977. Reprinted with permission of Common Cause.

to Richard Nixon's campaign. After being read out of the party by McGovern's supporters at the 1972 Democratic Convention, a number of traditionally Democratic-leading unions sat out the presidential election. Still other labor groups turned to Nixon and made substantial contributions; for example, the Seafarers Union gave $100,000 and the Teamsters gave about $600,000. However, despite these well-publicized contributions. organized labor eventually gave about $900,000 to McGovern, almost twice the amount it gave Humphrey in 1968.[24] Actually the money organized labor gave McGovern was consistent with its policy of not becoming heavily involved in financing Democratic presidential campaigns. Most of labor's political contributions go toward helping to elect a pro-labor Congress, especially selected races in key states. In any event, the real impact of labor on elections often occurs in areas that cannot be measured in terms of dollars and cents. In 1972 the AFL-CIO Industrial Union Department and affiliates may have spent up to $5 million in their citizenship programs, including voter registration drives. In 1976, labor estimated its support to be worth an equivalent of $11 million to Carter's campaign. It is assumed that these will tend to favor Democratic Party candidates. Drawing on their strongest resource, manpower, such registration and get-out-the-vote drives have helped the Democratic Party overcome the Republican advantage with respect to money.

The fund-raising activities of corporations achieved much public attention due to the Watergate-related trials of many of the nation's largest corporations on charges of making illegal campaign contributions during the 1972 elections. Using corporate funds for political candidates had been made unlawful in 1907 and reaffirmed in 1925. However, like most of the laws on political funding, this one had been completely ignored until brought to light by Watergate. Both corporations and unions had been able to evade the prohibition on making political contributions by establishing separate political action committees (PACs). These committees enable corporations (as well as labor unions and other interest groups) to establish a special fund to finance the campaigns of preferred candidates. PACs are very easy to establish, and they have been encouraged by rulings of the Federal Election Commission in 1975 and 1976. An officer of a PAC must first register it with the FEC; then it can collect up to $5000 per employee or member and contribute up to $5000 per candidate per election, with no over-all limitations. Different types of organizations solicit their funds quite differently. Texaco asked its employees for donations of under $100 because the contributors' names would not have to be reported; Coca-Cola said that it asked its 100 top executives to give 1 percent of their annual salary—it also reported a 100 percent participation as it expected. By December 1977 there were 1298 PACs—double the number of only 3 years earlier. Seventy-five percent of these new committees were affiliated with corporations or labor unions; apparently, the political potential of such committees is tremendous. In its 1976 report on PACs, Common Cause said that once they got into full swing, they would be able to amass "untold millions of dollars" for political campaigns. Early in 1977 the Republican National Committee formed a special PAC Division. As chairman William Brock explained, "Recognizing that PACs are the newest and fastest growing factor in American politics . . . [the new division] will attempt to assist in motivating corporations, professional, and vested interest groups to institute and activate their own PACs."[25]

Business PACs gave almost $7.1 million in 1976 to congressional candidates, a $4.6 million increase over the 1974 totals. Labor union PACs contributed more than $8.2 million; dairy industry PACs alone gave $1.4 million; and the American Medical Association's PACs gave $1.8 million.

Generally labor's money has flowed to the Democrats and business's money to the Republicans, but there are very significant exceptions. Both sources are often more interested in helping incumbents rather than new challengers. In the 1974 congressional elections, business groups gave $1.9 million to incumbents and only $182,000 to challengers; health groups $1.4 million to incumbents and $137,000 to newcomers; and labor gave $2.8 million to incumbents and a relatively large $1.7 million to challengers because they wanted to build up the pro-labor contingent in the Congress. In 1976 the maritime-related unions, seeking to obtain favorable changes in federal laws affecting the shipping industry, contributed to 24 of the 27 Democrats and 6 of the 13 Republicans on the House Committee on Merchant Marine and Fisheries. Such bipartisan support can also be found in the dairy industry, the American Medical Association, and others. Agricultural interests invested most heavily in incumbents in the 1976 congressional elections, with a 7.3 to 1 ratio of funding in favor of incumbents. The 1976 average of all the major interest groups favored incumbents by a ratio of 3.1 to 1; only the so-called ideological money favored nonincumbents in 1976.

Interest groups that are trying to preserve or enlarge their favored tax treatment continue to contribute heavily to members of the House Ways and Means Committee, which originates all tax legislation. These include such industries as oil and gas, real estate, securities, banking, public utilities, and trucking. Each has been concerned with the impact of federal tax laws on its industry and feels that well-placed contributions can facilitate desired changes or stall any disliked changes.[26]

Narrower interest groups have also become a significant factor in financing federal elections in recent years. In the 1974 congressional elections, the American Medical Association (AMA) gave money to 223 members of the House of Representatives and a total of $1.5 million to more than 300 congressional candidates between the 1972 and 1974 elections. By 1976, the AMA's contributions had risen to $1.8 million. The National Education Association (NEA), the de facto school teachers union, claimed that 22 of the 28 candidates it supported for the U.S. Senate were elected, as well as 225 of the 282 candidates for the U.S. House of Representatives. Education money may be even more effective on the state government level. The Utah Education Association supported 69 out of 75 state house candidates, and 56 of them were elected. No wonder the UEA fares so well in the Utah legislature and has been called the most effective lobby organization in the state. Today hundreds of interest groups are helping to finance political campaigns. In the 1970s, some of these groups had begun to target their key opponents very carefully for defeat. One such organization, Environmental Action, has issued a list of the "Dirty Dozen"—those Congressmen most opposed to environmental legislation. Between 1970 and 1976, 41 members of the U.S. House of Representatives appeared on the list, and 25 were defeated and an additional 6 have retired. EA works with better financed lobbies, such as the League of Conservation Voters, which provides campaign money to opponents of the Dirty Dozen.[27] Other groups that have claimed such victories on a regular basis include the National Rifle Association, which took credit for defeating 5 U.S. Senators in 1972 because they voted "wrong" on a handgun control law.

Ideological money has grown in importance since the 1960s, particularly on the left. Among the various left-of-center groups funding political campaigns have been the National Committee for an Effective Congress, Council for a Livable World, Democratic Study Group, Congressional Action Fund, and the League of Conservation Voters. In 1974 the National Committee for an Effective Congress budgeted $1 million to give to 80 candidates with the contributions averaging about $15,000 and $3,000 in Senate and House races, respectively. All together these groups contributed about $1.7 million in 1972, with 91 percent going to Democratic candidates. The conservative organizations are characterized by very large budgets and small direct campaign contributions to candidates. In 1976, conservative PACs such as National Conservative Political Action Committee (NCPAC), Committee for Survival of a Free Congress (CSFC), Gun Owners of America (GOA) and others raised $10.7 million and gave less than $1 million to candidates. Compared to the National Republican Congressional Committee, these ideological PAC have very high overheads, plus expenses for general proselytizing activities. The NRCC, for example, in 1976 raised $8.5 million and gave $2 million directly to candidates plus another $2.6 million in indirect aid.[29]

Contemporary Fund-Raising Techniques

Unless the candidate is a multimillionaire or running for a low-key, low-cost political office, modern campaigns require someone on the staff who can arrange special events that will bring forth money from potential supporters. On June 31, 1976, Jimmy Carter appeared at a series of parties in Houston, Philadelphia, Pittsburgh, and Washington, D.C. and collected $415,000 in contributions. Five hundred people paid $250 each to meet the candidate at one hotel, and a short time earlier 150 paid $1000 to attend a fund-raising party together.[29] Campaign dinners have long been a popular method of soliciting funds; during the 1968 campaign, for example, more than $43 million dollars was raised. One dinner alone—the "Victory 72" dinner in September 1972—generated $4.6 million with a closed circuit TV program in 28 cities.[30] It is a truism that it takes money to raise money. Some methods of raising funds require spending as much as $2 to raise $3. One thousand dollars a plate dinners have the lowest overhead (5-10 percent), while $10 a plate dinners often have an overhead of up to 50 percent.[31]

One of the newer techniques of fund-raising has been the television telethon. The Democratic telethon of July 8-9, 1972 lasted 19 hours on network television, cost $1.9 million to produce and broadcast, brought in pledges of $4.46 million, and netted $2 million for the party. That telethon was so successful that the Democrats had another one in June 1974 that netted $2.7 million, 85 percent of the amount pledged.[32]

However, the major fund-raiser in 1976 was the direct-mail solicitor. An expert in these techniques can bridge the gap between the candidate and the vast majority of Americans who never get invited and would not even go if invited to the $500 per plate dinners. While more than 45 percent of the population believe that citizens should make political contributions, statistics show that very few Americans actually do so.[33] Polling data indicated that only 8 percent of the electorate contributed money to the 1976 campaigns. Since the 1960s a number of notable presidential campaigns have relied heavily on small contributors—Goldwater in 1964, Wallace and McCarthy in 1968, and McGovern in 1972, but it should be noted that all of these candidates were defeated.[34] In 1972 McGovern was largely isolated from the organizational fat cats and traditional Democratic supporters such as organized labor, so that he had to rely upon direct-mail solicitations. His postal fund-raising drive (masterminded by Alabama lawyer Morris Dees) raised more than $15 million at a cost of about $3.5 million. Issue or ideological candidates tend to be significantly more successful in direct-mail solicitation than the center or middle-of-the-road candidates. During the 1973-1975 pre-campaign period, George Wallace's fund raising operation spent $2 million on 12 million pieces of mail and raised more than $4 million.[35] A direct mailing can either be addressed to a specific group that has already supported a candidate, or the mailing can be viewed as "prospecting."

> *Prospecting is a high-cost, low profit operation. It entails massive mailings, running about 10 million letters in Wallace's case, and generally producing contributions from only 1 to 3 percent of the recipients. . . . Prospecting begins with rental of lists of names, which cost anywhere from $20 to $60 per thousand, and are available from direct mail companies . . . or more specialized firms called list brokers. Tens of thousands of lists are on the market. There are lists of magazine subscribers, charity donors, contributors to Republican and Democratic campaigns and backers of conservative or liberal causes. They range in length from a few thousand names to half a million or more. In political prospecting, cross sections of larger lists are·tested first to see how productive they are likely to be. Names can be fed into a computer which prints a letter with a personal salutation. . . . The names of those who contribute in the prospect mailing are filed in the computer and become part of what is known in the trade as "the house list." The big profits in direct mail come from tapping the house list, time after time. [Wallace's house list numbers about 200,000 names.][36]*

President Ford used a selective strategy early in his 1976 campaign. Mailgrams were sent out to a "gilt edge" list of 7000 contributors to previous Republican campaigns. At a cost of just under $10,000, more than $400,000 was received from about 600 persons. The direct-mail specialist has now become an indispensable part of a national campaign; he is replacing the fat cats in importance.

Patronage used to be the single most important source of political funds. Even today some states finance their party work largely through contributions from state and local officeholders and patronage employees. Illinois, especially Cook County (Chicago), has financed Democratic Party activities from such sources, as have both parties in neighboring Indiana. However, a 1976 U.S. Supreme Court decision against the patronage job system in Cook County may eventually bring such funding to an end.[37]

Celebrity fund-raising has also proved to be an extremely lucrative source for those candidates who can arrange such affairs. Some of the more successful efforts in 1976 were Jimmy Carter's use of the Allman Brothers Band, and Ronald Reagan's tour with Efrem Zimbalist, Jr. ("F.B.I.") and Ken Curtis ("Festus" on "Gunsmoke").

Five concerts held by George McGovern in 1972 raised a total of $1 million. His April 15th Los Angeles concert starred Barbra Streisand, James Taylor, Carole King, and Quincy Jones and the ushers in the $100 per seat section included Warren Beatty, Shirley MacLaine, Jack Nicholson, Julie Christie, James Earl Jones, and about two dozen other movie stars.[38]

The Failure of American Campaign Finance Laws

Most attempts to legislate reforms in political financing have been failures. Every significant piece of legislation before 1974 was written in such a way that it left loopholes for anyone who wanted to use them; further, the key element to any effective reform—an attentive public—was lacking.

Four major methods can be used to control the role of money in politics. First, limitations may be placed on the amount of money that can be given to candidates or parties. Second, limitations can be placed on expenditures by political actors either by restricting their total expenditures or by restricting specific categories of expenditures (for example, television). Third, disclosure laws may be adopted to reveal who contributes money and how that money is spent in campaigns. Finally, the government may assume some or most of the costs of campaigning and thus reduce the need for private contributions.

The American experience has been one of filling a large number of offices (more than 500,000) with as little regulation as possible. During most of our history, there have been no effective federal laws on financial improprieties in elections. The 1883 Pendleton Act did reduce the "kickback" system (where, in order to keep one's job in the federal bureaucracy, a "contribution" to the party in power was regularly required). Such a limited objective was relatively easy to achieve, and the significance of this type of funding declined greatly. The Tillman Act of 1907 outlawed corporate contributions, and 3 years later Congress required multistate committees active in congressional elections to register and disclose their contributions and expenditures. In 1911 candidates for the Senate and House were limited in their campaign expenditures to $10,000 and $5000, respectively.

Between 1925 and 1971, the Federal Corrupt Practices Act was the principal law regulating political finances. Covering only general elections, the law limited candidates to maximum expenditures of $25,000 and $5000 for Senate and House races, respectively. Another law passed in 1939, the Hatch Act, prohibited active participation in national elective politics by federal employees. As amended in 1940, it prohibited federal contractors from contributing to federal candidates, extended the coverage to primary elections, established a $5000 yearly individual limit to any federal campaign, and established a $3 million limit on expenditures by a multistate political committee. One last provision of note is a section of the Taft-Hartley Act of 1947 that made labor union contributions to political campaigns illegal.

By the beginning of the 1970s only the most naïve and uninformed could imagine that the various political finance laws made any difference. Corporations and labor unions often calculated correctly (until Watergate, that is) that the possible benefits of making contributions far outweighed the chances of being caught and prosecuted. Most embarrassing was the massive disregard for the campaign expenditure limitations by congressional candidates. It was an open secret that everyone exceeded the the unrealistically low ceilings, and Congress was reluctant to raise the ceilings to a reasonable level because the legislators might then be pressured to comply. Furthermore, the various pre-1974 laws contained enough loopholes so that even the most inept politician could evade the proclaimed intent of the laws. Committees could be set up in Washington, D.C. or in a single state and not have to report to federal authorities. Even for the required reports, the Secretary of the Senate and the Clerk of the House would not anger any potential or current employer by doing anything dangerous with them. For example, in the 1970 election campaign of U.S. Senator Lloyd Bentsen (Texas), he reported zero spending to the Secretary of the Senate while reporting $459,330 to the Texas Secretary of State; the legal maximum was $25,000 at that time. Most politicians could pretend that they had no "knowledge and consent" of their expenditures and thus they could not report them.[39] "Over these decades, no legislative action to rationalize political finance was effective. Violations have been commonplace and enforcements at best sporadic, at worst, nonexistent."[40]

The Reforms
In 1971, Congress enacted a set of significant reforms that, together with amendments in 1974 and 1976, have greatly affected the nature of federal level campaigns. The keystone of these new laws was the Federal Election Campaign Act of 1971. Among other things, it repealed all of the previously ignored expenditure ceilings and established a comprehensive system of disclosure rules. All committees spending more than $1000 and all contributions over $100 had to be reported. It also placed a ceiling on

contributions made by any candidate or his family to his own campaign for a federal elective office and established spending limits on the use of the media. A companion law, the Revenue Act of 1971, provided for tax credits or deductions for those who contributed to campaigns on any level of American politics. This act also established the checkoff fund that financed the 1976 presidential campaigns.[41]

The disclosure provisions of the 1971 reform law also proved to be marginally useful in controlling the impact of money on politics. There is little evidence to indicate that even if all of the contributions were reported accurately before the election, the information would have much impact on the public. In analyzing the 1971 law, Adamany and Agree asked "Is anybody listening?"[42] Apprently, the answer to this question is "Very few!" The essential factor in financial reform is communication that will attract the attention of the voting public, which is expected to evaluate such information and use it to help decide which candidates to support. Unfortunately, the key assumptions have proved to be false. The volume of reporting forms has simply inundated the reporting offices: in 1972, the House candidates filed more than 117,000 published pages, and an estimated 69,500 were filed by Senate candidates.[43] With respect to individual contributors to presidential candidates, more than 84,000 contributions in amounts exceeding $100 were given by 70,000 persons. Clearly such a large volume of reports can only be analyzed long after the elections are over, and thus the impact of disclosure is insignificant because it will appear in the newspapers too late to affect the election. The 1976 congressional disclosure reports were not completed and made public until well into 1977. Even if the data could be gathered together before election day (many contributions are reported just before the election and thus cannot be evaluated until long afterward), who is responsible for interpreting these mountains of reports? Clearly, the media cannot adequately explain what the 1972 numbers really meant. Often interest group contributions to certain candidates were reported without comment, or lists of the largest contributors were printed in the smallest size type.

> If the nation's major newspapers are overwhelmed by the torrent of data unleashed by disclosure and are unable or unwilling to give the kind of repeated, in-depth coverage needed, political finance reporting in smaller papers, which serve most voters and do not have Washington or state capitol correspondents, must conform even less to the model required for a working disclosure system.[44]

Finally, the experiences of 1972 and 1976 indicate that even when the public has the data in reasonably clear form, such information seldom has much effect on an election.

> The electoral impact of the complex political finance issue [in the 1972 presidential election] was non-existent. Despite the highly publicized $9 million Democratic debt as the year began, the continuing reports of vast

*Nixon fund raising successes, and periodic reports about McGovern's dif-
ficulty keeping his campaign from floundering financially, 47 percent of the
people [interviewed by the Harris Survey] thought neither party had "an
unfair money advantage over the other."[45]*

A Twentieth Century Fund survey of voters right after the 1972 election discovered
that:

1. Only 55 percent of those polled had heard or read anything about Republican
    campaign financing.
2. Only 50 percent of the sample could cite something specific about Republican fi-
    nancing. Only 29 percent mentioned anything about GOP financial sources. Only
    22 percent noted anything about the amounts of Republican spending. This was
    the public impact of the best-reported, best-investigated campaign in U.S. his-
    tory.
3. Of those polled, only 51 percent could remember hearing anything about Demo-
    cratic financing. Only 11 percent mentioned anything about the sources of Dem-
    ocratic funds.[46]

Most of the respondents indicated that the information they remembered about political financing had not led them to change their attitudes about the two parties.

The Federal Election Campaign Act of 1971 should not be viewed as a failure.
It mandated many changes in the style and activity of American electoral campaigns
that have, at the very least, opened up our politics for public study. The real value
of the 1971 law was in the reporting requirements of both contributions and expenditures, and the first step toward possible effective control of money in politics.

The 1974 Amendments

Watergate, especially the money-raising aspects of the scandal, compelled a reluctant
Congress to revise substantially its 1971 campaign reforms. The media restrictions
were all repealed, and a series of restrictions were placed on both contributions and
expenditures (see Table 7.3).

Table 7.3 Major Provisions of the 1974 and 1976 Amendments to the Federal Campaign Act
1971[a]

Limits on Contributions

- Each individual can contribute up to $1000 for each primary, runoff, or general
  election to any federal level candidate. An individual is limited to an aggregate total contribution of $25,000 to all federal candidates in any year.
- Each organization or PAC is limited to $5000 maximum to any candidate to
  federal office. There are no aggregate limits on the totals an organization can
  contribute as long as the $5000 per candidate per election limit is observed.
- Cash contributions over $100 and foreign contributions are prohibited.
- An individual may give only a maximum of $5000 a year to a PAC and $20,-
  000 to a political party's national committee.

Table 7.3 continued

- The Democratic and Republican senatorial campaign committees may give up to $17,500 a year to a candidate.
- All PACs established by a company or international union are considered a single PAC for contribution purposes, with the $5000 per candidate ceiling.

Spending Limits

- Each candidate for a major party presidential nomination is limited to $10 million total for all the primaries.
- Each major party is limited to $2 million in expenditures for its presidential nominating conventions.
- Presidental nominees of major parties are limited to $20 million expenditures in the general elections.
- Each national party organization may spent up to $10,000 to support House general election campaigns, $20,000, or 2 cents per vote, whichever is greater, for candidates in Senate general elections, and approximately $3 million in presidential general elections. These expenditures are in addition to the candidate's spending limits.
- Presidential, vice-presidential candidates, and their families are limited to no more than $50,000 expenditures of their own money.

Public Financing

- In presidential general elections, the major party candidaters automatically qualify for full funding. Other candidates are eligible for partial funding based on votes received in the general election. If the public financing is accepted, no private contributions are permitted.
- In presidential primaries, a candidate can qualify for up to $5 million in matching public funs after reaching a "threshold" of collecting $5000 in small amounts in each of 20 states. Only the first $250 of individual contributions will be matched by federal funds. Candidates receiving less than 10 percent of the total vote in two consecutive presidential primaries entered would lose the federal matching funds.

Federal Election Commission

- A six-member FEC is appointed by the President and confirmed by the Senate. Congress retains the powr to veto any regulation proposed by the FEC.
- The FEC is to administer federal election laws and the public financing program.

Disclosure Provisions

- Essentially, all contributions and expenditures of $50 or more must be reported periodically to the FEC.
- Each candidate has to establish one central campaign committee that administers all contributions and expenditures.

[a]Provisions deleted by the U.S. Supreme Court are not included.

Public Financing of Presidential Elections

The 1976 presidential election was the first federally subsidized election in American history. Major party candidates collected more than $23 million in matching federal money to help finance their pre-convention campaigns. President Ford secured a little more than $4.7 million while his challenger, former California governor Reagan, received $5.1 million. Thirteen candidates for the Democratic nomination collected varying amounts of federal money, from Jimmy Carter's 3 million to Governor Jerry Brown's $373,578. Such matching federal funds up to $5 million are available to a candidate after he has raised $5000 in each of 20 states, with $250 being the maximum individual contribution that will be matched by the federal money. When a candidate accepts the federal matching money for the primaries, he must agree to spend no more than $10 million for the pre-convention period.

Each of the major party presidential nominees then received $21,820,000 in federal funds for the general election campaign. No private contribution could be used by either Carter or Ford during the general election campaign. However, a limited amount of private money—about $3.3 million—could be raised and spent by the Democratic and Republican National Committees on behalf of their respective candidates. By accepting the federal grant, Carter and Ford agreed to report all of their campaign expenses to the newly formed Federal Election Commission (FEC), make all of their other records available, and submit to a post-election audit. Besides agreeing not to accept any private contributions, each campaign was committed to spend no more than $21.8 million. These federal subsidies were collected by the U.S. Treasury in accordance with the Revenue Act of 1971 which permitted a $1 checkoff per taxpayer for this purpose. By 1975, 24 percent of all taxpayers were checking off $1 to finance the 1976 presidential elections.

An unlikely coalition led by William F. Buckley and Eugene McCarthy opposed the 1974 law. Ultimately, the challenge was heard by the U.S. Supreme Court which, on January 30, 1976, issued a decision in the case of *Buckley* v *Valeo*. The court ruled that limitations on the personal spending by candidates for the U.S Senate and U.S. House were unconstitutional. The court also threw out spending limitations which had been imposed on federal candidates for the House and Senate. The 1974 law had stipulated that candidates for the U.S. House of Representatives could spend only $70,000 in the primary and the same amount in the general election. Most observers viewed these figures as an ironclad incumbents' protection act. The advantages of incumbency in Congress are so great that in 1974, for example, it generally required the expenditure of more than $100,000 by anyone who hoped to unseat a sitting congressman.

Upheld by the Court were the restrictions on individual contributions to a candidate's campaign organization, but the court said that individuals could spend unlimited amounts of money in independent efforts to support a candidate or cause in federal elections. Such independent efforts had to be uncoordinated and truly independent of the candidate's own efforts; the court viewed these efforts as constitutionally guaranteed as part of an individual's right to freedom of speech and expression. Lastly, the court ruled as unconstitutional the composition of the six-member Federal Election Commission which was empowered to issue rulings and to enforce the above restrictions. The commission had been constituted with two members appointed by the president, two by the president of the Senate, and two by the speaker of the House. This, the court ruled, violated the constitutional principle that the executive branch appoints and the legislative branch confirms. A 30-day grace period was granted by the court; if Congress and the president did not act to reconstitute the FEC properly, it would lose its power to make rulings and to authorize federal matching subsidies. Thirty days passed, and Congress failed to pass the reconstituting bill. Representative Wayne Hays, Chairman of the House Administration Committee, which was responsible for the committee work on the new bill, was opposed to these reforms and delayed the bill as long as possible. By March 1976, the FEC had lost its powers and the federal matching funds stopped; however, the fund-raising restrictions such as the $1000 limit and $25,000 aggregate total to federal candidates in one year still remained. Many candidates dropped out of the Democratic race, undoubtedly due to the lack of federal money. Ronald Reagan's campaign was in such severe financial straits by the eve of the important North Carolina primary that it was reported that he seriously considered withdrawing from the race. Carter, the early front-runner after his victories in New Hampshire and Florida, was able to continue his fund-raising, as was President Ford, but all of the other contenders had serious financial problems. March and April passed; finally there was a new bill that was signed into law in May by President Ford.

Among the changes authorized by the 1976 amendments was a procedure for business PACs to solicit their employees for political funds, and a cutoff of federal matching funds to any presidential candidate who failed to win 10 percent of the party's primary vote total in two consequent primaries. This last provision allowed the FEC in May to cut off money to some of the less successful Democratic candidates such as Ellen McCormick, who had been running for president in the Democratic primaries to publicize her anti-abortion stand. The 1976 amendments permitted these candidates to reestablish their eligiblity with a 20 percent share of the vote in a future primary.

Implications of the Federal Election Reforms

The reforms instituted between 1971 and 1976 have accomplished a great deal. First, the influence of the fat cats has been greatly reduced by the $1000 limitation on contributions to a federal level candidate. No longer can a Clement Stone give several million dollars to a presidential candidate and bankroll a string of congressional aspirants to victory. The new hero is the person who can arrange a fund-raising network for a candidate that will produce a number of relatively small individual contributions. With money no longer available from the fat cats, presidential and congressional candidates must rely increasingly on such non-party technocrats as the direct-mail fund-raisers.[47].

A second accomplishment of the reforms was a reduction of interest group financial support of presidential elections. As Common Cause noted after the 1976

Sanders in The Milwaukee Journal

"Don't you feel much better now that presidential
candidates are no longer dependent on special
interest financing?"

A second positive outcome of the finance reform was the reduction
of interest group financial support in the presidential election
(Reprinted with permission of the Milwaukee Journal).

election, "A President . . . was finally free from crippling indebtedness to large contributions from special interests."[48] On the negative side, it appears that most of the
money that used to go to presidential candidates has now been shifted to congressional and state level campaigns. The reform laws have encouraged the establishment
of PACs, which have greatly increased their contributions to state and local politics.
The National Education Association, for example, gave only $30,000 in political con-
tributions in 1972, but in 1976 it gave $2.5 million. In 1977 President Carter sent
to Congress a request to extend public financing to congressional elections. This proposal was killed in the Senate because Southern Democrats and conservative Republicans objected to the use of federal funds to finance their own challengers. As the
House Republican Conference Chairman, John B. Anderson, noted: "About 95

percent of the incumbent House members were re-elected in 1976. They're pretty well satisfied with the present system."[49] Although this measure was defeated in 1977, it will probably continue to be an issue in future sessions of Congress.

Initially, there was some fear that the public subsidy of presidential elections would eliminate all but the best-known candidates. "A very dark horse would not even get to the track,"[50] because the $1000 contribution limit would prevent the big loans and contributions (seed money) from the fat cats. However, Jimmy Carter's darker-than-dark-horse campaign seems to have quieted this fear.

The 1974 reforms have continued the previously discussed bias of American election law in favor of the existing two major political parties. Not only have the existing minor parties been hurt by the $1000 individual contribution limits, but they have been carefully excluded from the federal presidential subsidies for the general election. Minor or third parties can qualify for the federal subsidies only after the election is over and if they have collected at least 5 percent of the total vote. Thus, a new third party would have to run its own campaign under the very restrictive contribution rules and hope to do well enough to receive its subsidy retroactively, which would then qualify it for federal money in the next presidential election—when the party might no longer exist, if past trends continue. Other aspects of the reforms could eventually strengthen the position of the party organizations vis-a-vis their candidates. With limited general election money for the presidential campaigns, the party organizations could become more significant in supporting such campaigns. On the other hand, the general election subsidies go directly to the candidates, making them even more independent of the regular party organizations than in previous years.

It may turn out that the contribution limitations ($1000 for individuals and $5000 for PACs) are too restrictive for contemporary media campaigns. As former U.S. Senator John V. Tunney (D-California) remarked during his victorious 1976 primary campaign against the former antiwar leader Tom Hayden, "This $1000 limit is just killing us. I have to spend 75 percent of my time going around with a tin cup. It makes me feel so dirty."[51] Such experiences were common in 1976 and prompted some observers to recommend an increase in the individual contribution limits to $5000.

Spending limits of $10 million in the presidential primaries and $20 million for the general elections may be too low for effective, comprehensive campaigns. During the Ford-Reagan pre-convention fight, both candidates were so close to the $10 million limitation that they had to close their headquarters or curtail state level campaigns in many states during the crucial last 2 weeks. In 1976 Reagan collected and spent $16.1 million and former President Ford approximately $14 million. Both of these totals exceeded the legal limit because of an automatic inflation subsidy and a 20 percent allowance for fund-raising that were added to the $10 million base. Most of the $22 million ($20 million plus an allowance for inflation) received by both Ford and Carter for the general election went toward mass media appeals. Few dollars were left for many of the traditional features of presidential campaigns such as buttons, bumper stickers, and printed literature. Consequently, volunteers had little material to distribute door-to-door, and so there was a sharp decline in citizen participation in 1976. Common Cause has recommended increasing the general election presidential subsidies to $30 million plus inflation adjustments.

One possible loophole created by the Supreme Court's decision was permitting individuals to spend unlimited amounts of money in independent efforts to support a candidate. At least 50 groups or individuals spent money under this loophole. One organization, the Friends of the First Family, spent $24,783 to help President Ford in the Michigan primary; and one individual, Joseph Coors of Golden, Colorado, spent $32,671 to assist Reagan's campaign. Various independent groups, such as Farmers for Carter and Illinois Consumers for Carter-Mondale, spent small sums of money for support during the general election.

Political Finance and the States

Many states acted before Watergate to curb the influence of money on state elections: 43 states required pre-election reporting; 25 had bipartisan election commissions; 22 had limits on individual contributions to candidates; and 34 had ceilings on campaign expenditures.

Eight states have checkoff provision on their state income tax forms and the money raised is given to the parties or to the individual candidates (Minnesota). In 1977 Utah gave its checkoff money to all parties on the state's ballot. The Democrats received $17,925; the Republicans, $14,086; the Libertarians, $685; and $1435 was authorized for the American Party, but was rejected because of ideological objections to government involvement in political finance. This money is typically used to defray state party headquarters or convention expenses.[52]

Those states (Maine, Maryland, Massachusetts) that opted for the surcharge method of raising money found it very difficult to secure enough funds to finance the activities originally envisaged by the sponsors. The Maryland experiment in public financing of state election campaigns appears to be headed for failure. With 25 percent of the 1975 state income tax returns filed, only 3.5 percent of the taxpayers had contributed to the fund—a total of only $40,000.

Historically, state campaign finance laws have been a toothless tiger. Seldom have there been any prosecutions for violations, and the data collected have rarely been presented to the voters during the election period in a meaningful fashion. However, the post-Watergate laws have been more serious and could, at least, lead to some guidelines that would reform money-raising and spending on the state level.

The Party as a Money-Raiser

Party organizations have generally been relatively weak fund-raisers. For every Cook County Democratic Party organization with its overflowing coffers, there are thousands of party organizations that are trying to find a few thousand dollars in order to keep their state or county office open on a year-round basis and give the image of a full-time professional party organization. Robert Strauss, former National Chairman of the Democratic Party, observed that the national party organizations have trouble raising money because they appear to be inanimate, headless, and soulless bodies that cannot arouse the same emotional reactions that a candidate can.

The Democrats have had a continuous debt since the 1952 election, with the exception of McGovern's 1972 campaign. During the late 1960s, they did not hold a single successful fund-raising event because of the anti-party attitudes of many Democrats who disagreed with the party leaders over Vietnam. The DNC began 1972 with a debt of $9.3 million, but, through a series of successful fund-raising events, managed to end the year with a reduced debt of about $4 million. From the McGovern nominating convention to the November election, the DNC raised about a half million dollars. Much of this was due to the DNC Associates program, which built up a regular membership by November of 143 members who each contributed $98 a month ($1176 a year) which was largely used to cover headquarters expenses. Various Democratic congressional committees collect money from interest groups and contributors (usually in $500-a-plate Washington, D.C., dinners) and distribute it to candidates for both the House and Senate. In 1976, the early reports indicated that the Democratic Senate Committee was averaging about $5000 per selected candidate in contributions.

Other Democratic sources of money since the 1960s have been the President's Club, formed by 4000 supporters of Presidents Kennedy and Johnson in 1961, which raised $4.3 million between 1961 and 1964. Program advertising at the Democratic National Convention has also proved to be profitable. In 1972 the party raised $1 million by selling full-page ads at $12,000 a page. The Republican National Convention program ads cost almost the same, and they brought in $1.6 million in 1972. Ninety corporations placed ads in both programs, and a total of 281 corporations placed ads in one or the other convention programs.

The Republican National Committee established a series of special projects in the 1970s to ensure a continuing source of money for its operations. Expenditures by the RNC and its associated committees were budgeted at $6.8 million in 1972, and much of this money was raised by a mail and telephone solicitation campaign that focused on the small contributor. The Republican National Sustaining Fund, which asked for a $15 per year contribution, brought in almost $5.3 million in 1972 (a general election year), and a little less than $4 million in the off-year 1973. Two additional programs were established by the RNC in 1969: the Republican Campaigner Program and the Republican Victory Associates. The former asked for annual contributions in the $100-$500 range and the latter for contributions in the $500-$1000 range, with the $1000+ range filled by the Richard Nixon (or RN) Associates. These two new party programs raised a total of $2.3 million in 1972; however, when this is compared with the $70 million that Nixon raised in 1972, one can see the actual role of the party. Republican congressional campaigns are helped by two special committees—the National Republican Congressional Committee for the House and the Republican Senatorial Campaign Committee. Direct-mail solicitation and an annual joint dinner raised money that was distributed to Republican candidates in amounts of up to $10,000 and $30,000 for the House and Senate races, respectively. House Republican candidates receive more financial assistance from their party than do House Democratic candidates. In 1976, 39 percent of House Republican candidates received over $10,000 from party sources, while only 11 percent of Democratic candidates received comparable assistance. Party contributions also account for a larger proportion of Republican candidates' total funds. One third of Republican House candidates reported that party funding accounted for over 10 percent of their total campaign funds. Democratic candidates receiving party funds accounting for over 10 percent of their funds totaled only 6 percent.[53]

Reports on the state of national party finances released by the Federal Election Commission in 1978 point to the continuing financial difficulties of the Democratic Party and the relative affluence of the Republican Party. During 1977, the Democratic Naional Committee raised $6 million and the Republican National Committee a total of $16.9 million. The Democratic House and Senate Campaign Committees collected only $1.3 million; their Republican counterparts amassing over $10 million. During the year all national level Republican organizations raised $28.2 million and had a $9.4 million surplus in early 1978. All national level Democratic organizations raised $7.9 million and faced a $1.5 million deficit in 1978.[54]

Conclusions

The future of political parties as major fund-raisers for their respective candidates does not seem to be especially bright. Direct subsidies to the candidates for the presidential primaries and to the party nominees in 1976 have completely circumvented the party organizations. Also, the few provisions of the 1974 political finance law that seemed to enhance the party's role in congressional campaigns were declared void by the Supreme Court in 1976. Clearly, the current trend is toward a continued flow of power to the candidate and his personal organization and a continued decline of party organizations in both campaign services and campaign finances. What the parties need is source of funds for the party organization so that it can finance essential services to its candidates and reestablish its influence on campaigns again.

The 1976 election marked an important turning point in the American pattern of financing electoral campaigns. For the first time, federal money financed the general election campaigns for the presidency and so the candidates did not have to sell themselves to the highest bidders as they had in the past. These reforms, hopefully, will lead toward the eventual federal financing of congressional campaigns and guarantee access to the all-important media time for all significant and serious candidates.

FOOTNOTES

1. Herbert E. Alexander, *Financing the 1972 Election* (Lexington, Mass.: Heath, 1976), p. 78. Herbert E. Alexander is, without doubt, the most prolific modern scholar on the subject of political money. His most recent book, *Financing Politics* (Washington, D.C.: Congressional Quarterly, 1976), covers the 1976 primaries. In addition to his pioneering book, *The Costs*

of Democracy, Alexander was the author of the financial studies of the 1960, 1964, and 1968 elections as well as the 1972 election noted above. The Citizens Research Foundation, located at Princeton University, and its president, Alexander, have published dozens of other titles dealing with election finances on the state and federal levels, media expenditures, foreign money expenditures, and other related subjects. Perhaps the second most prolific scholar in this field is David Adamany; in addition to his work coauthored with Agree, Adamany has published two volumes dealing with the finance of politics on the state level: *Financing Politics: Recent Wisconsin Elections* (Madison: University of Wisconsin Press, 1969), and *Campaign Finance in America* (North Scituate, Mass.: Duxbury Press, 1972). Dozens of other valuable studies have been written in recent years on the problems of political finance, and the authors gratefully acknowledge their contribution to this chapter even though space limitations prevent the listing of each individual effort.

2. Alexander, *Financing the 1972 Election*, op. cit., pp. 80-81.

3. Ibid., p. 78.

4. David W. Adamany and George E. Agree, *Political Money* (Baltimore: Johns Hopkins, 1975), pp. 21-24.

5. By 1970, about 25 percent of the California state senate campaigns were in the $50,000-$100,000 category, and one candidate for the state assembly spent $120,090. California *Journal*, December 1970, January 1971.

6. *Congressional Quarterly Weekly Report XXXV*, No. 44, pp. 2299-2311.

7. Common Cause, "Report to the American People on the Financing of Congressional Election Campaigns," April-May 1977.

8. Adamany and Agree, *Political Money*, op. cit., p. 9.

9. For a very informative and interesting description of election campaigning in Japan, see Gerald L. Curtis, *Election Campaigning Japanese Style* (New York: Columbia University Press, 1971).

10. George Thayer, *Who Shakes the Money Tree?: American Campaign Financing Practices from 1789 to the Present* (New York: Touchstone, 1973), p. 25.

11. Ibid., pp. 29, 37-38.

12. Ibid., p. 37.

13. Lester A. Sobel, *Money and Politics* (New York: Facts on File, 1974), Chapter 4.

14. Herbert Alexander, *Financing the 1972 Election*, p. 372.

15. Max McCarthy, *Elections for Sale* (Boston: Houghton Mifflin, 1972), p. 14.

16. Morton Mintz, *America, Inc.* (New York: Dell, 1971), pp. 232-234.

17. McCarthy, *Elections for Sale*, op. cit., p. 14.

18. *The New York Times*, October 13, 1974.

19. *The Washington Post*, April 16, 1976.

20. Ibid.

21. Ibid.

22. In 1936 the United Mine Workers gave $500,000 to the Democratic Party and started the trend of union support of the party.

23. Herbert E. Alexander, *Money in Politics* (Washington, D.C.: Public Affairs Press, 1972), p. 131.

24. Alexander, *Financing the 1972 Election*, op. cit., p. 503. It should also be noted that several of the big 1972 labor contributions were made by unions that needed help from the federal government. The Seafarers' president had been indicted in 1970, and the case was dismissed in 1972 by the Justice Department. Also, the Teamsters' former president, Jimmy Hoffa, was paroled from federal prison by Nixon in December 1971.

25. Common Cause, "Report to the American People," op. cit.

26. *The New York Times* News Service article carried in *Salt Lake Tribune*, September 20, 1974.

27. The New York Times, July 22, 1976 and February 1, 1976. Associated Press release, June 5, 1978.

28. *The Washington Post*, March 21, 1978, "Conservative Groups Raise Millions, But Candidates Get Little."

29. *The Washington Post*, July 1, 1976.

30. *The New York Times*, October 25, 1972.

31. Congressional Quarterly, *Dollar Politics*, Vol. 1, (Washington, D.C.: Congressional Quarterly Press, 1972), p. 5. On January 20, 1956, President Eisenhower spoke on closed circuit TV to 53 banquets simultaneously in 37 states. The net was between $4-5 million for the Republican Party.

32. Alexander, *Financing the 1972 Election*, op. cit., p. 304.

33. Alexander, *Money in Politics*, op. cit., p. 287.

34. Thayer, *Who Shakes the Money Tree?* op. cit., pp. 80-90.

35. *The Los Angeles Times*, August 15, 1975.

36. Ibid.

37. *Elrod* vs. *Burns* (1976).

38. Alexander, *Financing the 1972 Election*, op. cit., p. 125.

39. McCarthy, *Elections for Sale*, op. cit., pp. 147-148.

40. Alexander, *Money in Politics*, op. cit. p. 8.

41. By 1974 the incentives for individual citizens to contribute to political parties were increased by permitting a tax credit of $25 per taxpayer ($50 on a joint return) or $100 deduction ($200 on a joint return).

42. Adamany and Agree, *Political Money*, op. cit., p. 106.

43. Alexander, *Financing the 1972 Election*, op. cit., p. 12.

44. Adamany and Agree, *Political Money*, op. cit., p. 106.

45. Louis Harris, *The Washington Post*, October 19, 1972.

46. Twentieth Century Fund Survey of Political Finance, reported in Adamany and Agree, *Political Money*, op. cit., pp. 107-108.

47. *The Washington Post*, April 16, 1976, p. 1.

48. Common Cause, "Report to the American People," op. cit.

49. UPI, March 5, 1977.

50. Cris Lyndan, *The New York Times*, November 16, 1975.

51. *The Los Angeles Times*, May 8, 1976.

52. Alexander, *Financing Politics*, op. cit., Chapter 7.

53. *Congressional Quarterly Weekly Report XXXVI*, No. 11, p. 718.

54. *Associated* Press release, April 9, 1978.

8
Selecting the President:
The Decline of Party Influence

We Americans have managed to construct a process to select our president which has become the longest, most complicated such process in the world. Once the parties occupied the central role in the process, but increasingly in this century they have lost their influence over the electorate and control over their own nominations. In this chapter we will examine the road to the presidency with special attention to the changing role of the political parties in the process.

MANY ARE ELIGIBLE, BUT FEW ARE CHOSEN
In the late 1970s, the population of the United States stood at approximately 215 million. It is, perhaps, interesting that out of such a large population pool, so few people are singled out for consideration for the highest political office. William Keech and Donald Matthews have studied the informal "availability rules," which have sharply restricted the pool of potential candidates.[1] Between 1936 and 1972 a total of 923 persons held either elective or appointive offices that could be viewed as having presidential potential; 434 were state governors, 368 U.S. Senators, 8 Vice Presidents, and 113 cabinet officers. Ninety percent of all those who polled 1 percent or more of support for a presidential nomination in Gallup Polls held public offices. Only 62 Democrats and 47 Republicans gathered the minimum 1 percent public support during the 36 years of this study. Thus, during almost four decades of the most turbulent period in our history, a little more than 100 persons composed the pool from which presidential candidates were selected. All persons nominated for the presidency were on this list.

Clearly, some offices have proved to be better bases from which to run for the White House. Perhaps the office with the best potential is the vice-presidency. All vice presidents during this period received substantial support for stepping up to the presidency. The vice president has the tremendous advantage of operating within the context of the executive branch. Many recent occupants of the office have had a chance to win the top office: Truman, Nixon, Johnson, Humphrey, and Ford. Almost co-equal with the vice-presidency as a presidential route is the position of United

States Senator. Ten percent of the Senate appeared on the list of potential presidential candidates during the period of the study. The Senate has certain structural features that offer tremendous advantages on its members. Senators serve 6-year terms, and this often allows them to try for the White House without having to give up their seat. Only one Senator has lost his seat in such an attempt since the beginning of the century—Barry Goldwater in 1964. Another tremendous advantage of U.S. Senators is their perceived expertise in the area of foreign policy. Whether a specific Senator actually has any great knowledge about foreign affairs is not really as significant as the public's belief that he does. In the post-World War II period, most Americans feel that any man who aspires to the presidency must have a background in foreign affairs. In the nineteenth century state governors were the main presidential contenders, but until Jimmy Carter's success, the last governor elected to the presidency was Franklin Roosevelt in 1932. Although the governors of large states can claim an important political base, they have certain handicaps: a background in provincial issues, lack of foreign policy experience, and an inability to campaign for long periods outside their states.

Other significant officeholders, while receiving some poll support, are almost never serious contenders for the nomination. Only one Supreme Court Justice has won a presidential nomination—Charles E. Hughes in 1916. Judges have sufficient prestige, but the appointive nature of the position and the unwillingness of many judges to give up life tenure on the bench has generally excluded them from the pool of serious presidential possibilities. Cabinet appointees suffer from the lack of a political base and the short term of their office. The House of Representatives has not produced presidential prospects on a regular basis since the early nineteenth century. Its size, 435 members, prevents most of them from ever rising to public prominence. Big city mayors have never won a nomination, despite the attention given by the national media to at least "the big three" (New York, Chicago, and Los Angeles). Unfortunately for these mayors, the political problems they face seem to be unsolvable and so they have little opportunity to build a national following. Of recent presidential aspirants, only Hubert Humphrey had once been a mayor (of Minneapolis).

At one time in the not so distant past there was an understanding that served to discourage potential candidates who failed to fit certain specifications. Convention prescribed that the perfect presidential candidate was a white, Anglo-Saxon, Protestant who came from a small town background in a large state. Consequently, no Southerners, Catholics, divorcees, women, minority-group members, or persons from large cities and small states would not get very far. John Kennedy and Jimmy Carter ended the myths that Catholics and Southerners could not become president. Adlai Stevenson won the nomination as a divorced politician and the increasing number of divorces among U.S. Senators appears to have effectively eliminated that restriction. Finally, the "small" states of South Dakota, Georgia, Minnesota, Maine, Arizona, Alabama, Oklahoma, and Washington have produced nominees or major contenders since the 1960s. As Gerald Pomper discovered, three-quarters of the nominations before 1928 were won by contenders who fit the availability qualifications. Since then, less than half have fit these qualifications.[2] Certainly, Jimmy Carter managed to smash some of them by proving that a Deep South candidate and former governor could secure the White House. Even more significant is the pattern of anti-party establishment candidates who have won their party nomination since the 1964 campaign. Goldwater, McGovern, and Carter all represented insurgent candidacies that successfully outwitted and outmaneuvered the party mainstream, reflecting the growing weakness of the party organizations in determining who would carry their banner in the presidential contest. Women and racial minority groups have yet to break the barriers that have kept them off major party tickets; however, there is evidence indicating that having one of them on the ticket as a vice-presidential candidate might be an asset.[3]

One should mention the role played by the nation's mass media in determining who is considered qualified for the presidency. Political columnist Russell Baker of *The New York Times* has called these president-makers "the great mentioners." They comprise the key political commentators on the most prestigious media across the nation, but especially in New York City and Washington, D.C. Foremost among this élite are David Broder of *The Washington Post*, and Tom Wicker, Joseph Kraft, and James Reston of *The New York Times*. These commentators, as well as the nature of the television coverage, tend to develop a set of criteria for presidential candidates. Jimmy Carter was found acceptable in 1976, while George Wallace, Edmund Muskie, and a host of others were found wanting in 1972 and 1976.[4]

Primaries and Parties: The Rise and Decline

At present, the presidential primary season begins in late February and ends early in June. It is a path along which a candidate can collect the most valuable commodity of the presidential selection process—convention delegates. Presidential primaries were first introduced in Florida just after the turn of the century. In 1910 Oregon adopted the first dual preference primary, in which voters could express their preference for the party presidential candidate and also elect delegates to the national convention. By 1912, 12 states had adopted these institutions. However, that year proved to be a setback for the primary as a method of delegate selection; since former President Theodore Roosevelt challenged his hand-picked successor, William H. Taft, for the Republican nomination in 1912. Roosevelt chose to challenge (and thereby discredit) his party's incumbent president in the newly developed primary elections. Roosevelt defeated Taft in nine primaries, lost to Taft in one, and both lost to Robert LaFollette in two. All in all, Roosevelt won 221 of the 388 delegates who could be selected in the primaries. However, Taft as president controlled the Republican delegates from the Democratic South, and the convention renominated Taft; Roosevelt then bolted the convention, and Taft eventually placed third in the November election. Ironically, the Democrats were learning the same lesson about the value of the primaries that year. Champ Clark, Speaker of the House of Representatives, split ten primaries equally with Governor Woodrow Wilson, and Clark led with 413 delegates to Wilson's 274 at the beginning of the convention.[5] Wilson eventually won the nomination and then beat both Roosevelt and Taft in November 1912. Thus, both parties managed to choose candidates who had clearly been defeated in terms of winning delegates in primary elections. Disillusionment with the presidential primary soon set in, and state after state began to abandon it. Georgia ended it in 1916, Iowa and Minnesota before the 1920 election, North Carolina after the 1920 election, Montana after 1924, and Michigan and Indiana by 1928. After reaching a high of 22 states using the presidential primary in 1916, the number of states remained at 15 until the 1950s. In 1952, due to intensely contested nomination battles in both major parties, the electorate's interest in the primary increased sharply.[6] The biggest jump in the number of states using the presidential primary occurred between 1968 and 1976, when it doubled from 15 to 30 (plus Washington, D.C.).

It is said that the long ordeal of the primary season tests presidential candidates in quite specific and, some feel, desirable ways. First, a string of 31 such events (as of 1976) tests the physical stamina and determination of the candidate. Weaker, less-motivated candidates will drop out leaving the truly dedicated to finish the race. The candidate's organizing ability, or at least his skill in selecting a staff, will be tested by the effectiveness of his multiple state organization. Other more personal characteristics may also become apparent during the course of the campaign. From this perspective, the primaries serve as a screening device to eliminate the less-qualified candidates before the convention. The primaries seem to have served this purpose well in 1976, with the elimination of Shriver, Shapp, Harris, Bentsen, and Wallace.

It is very difficult to make generalizations about the 31 primaries, since their rules differ a great deal from one state to another. There are three basic ways a candidate can have his name placed on a state's presidential primary ballot, according to that state's election laws: by gathering a minimum number of registered voters' signatures on a petition, by action of the state's secretary of state, and by action of a special board that controls access to the ballot.[7] As of 1976, four different kinds of presidential primaries were in use:

1. *The electorate chooses only delegates, not candidates.* New York is, perhaps, the best-known example of this type of primary. In the 1976 Democratic primary the voters could choose between slates of four to six delegates who were pledged to specific candidates. Each of the state's 39 congressional districts had a separate election, and the slate that secured a plurality won all of the Democratic delegates in the district. In 1976, 206 Democratic delegates were chosen by the districts and another 68 selected later on a statewide level but in proportion to the district results. There were really 39 "mini-primaries," but none of the major candidates had slates on the ballot in each of the 39 districts. A candidate needed 1250 petition signatures in a congressional district to secure a slate on the district's ballot. This proved to be quite difficult: Udall led with slates in 37 districts, Jackson in 35, Carter in 26, and Wallace in 3. Jimmy Carter, incidentally, did quite poorly in New York, winning only 33 of the 274 delegates available. Texas and Alabama also used this form of primary.

2. *Voters indicate their preference for president, but this vote is only "advisory."* Delegates are selected in a separate election. New Hampshire's first-in-the-nation primary abides by these rules. Technically it is possible for a candidate to win a plurality in the preference poll and lose in the delegate-selection election. A more frequent occurrence is a deadheat in the preference election such as Reagan's 1317 (out of 108,000 total) vote loss to Ford in New Hampshire and then Reagan's near shutout by Ford with respect to delegates elected (Reagan 4, Ford 17 delegates). Other states using this type of primary are Illinois, Nebraska, New Jersey, Pennsylvania, Vermont, and West Virginia.

3. *The electorate votes for candidates for a party's presidential nomination, and the results are converted into delegates.* In this increasingly popular type of primary, the voters choose their preferred candidates, whose names appear on the ballot, and then delegates are awarded to the candidates according to a formula based on the popular vote totals. California has a mixed type of primary; the Republicans use the nearly extinct *winner-take-all* principle, according to which the candidate who wins the plurality vote secures all of the delegates. California is the only large state that still uses this type of primary. Since the Democratic Party has banned the winner-take-all principle, the Democratic primary in California used a proportional system that awarded 210 delegates among the congressional districts to all candidates who polled at least 15 percent of a district's vote. An additional 70 delegates were distributed according to the proportion of delegates won by each candidate at the district level.

4. *Voters select their preferred candidate, and the winner takes all within a specified district.* This is called a *loophole primary*. The Democrats in Pennsylvania and five other large states used this type of primary in 1976. Pennsylvania used state senate districts (as did Texas) while others used congressional districts; the candidates who win the plurality vote in each district are awarded all of the delegates allocated to that district. The 1976 Democratic National Convention banned the use of loophole primaries for 1980.

Pre-Convention Strategies and the Primaries. Certain understandings have emerged over the years on strategies and tactics to be used in the pre-convention period. One such understanding is that whoever works for the party will be rewarded. The electoral successes of Richard Nixon in 1968 and Jimmy Carter in 1976 were due in part to strategic decisions made at least 3 years in advance. Both Nixon and Carter campaigned extensively for their party's congressional candidates who were running in the off-year elections of 1966 and 1974, respectively. Their efforts won the support of many of the congressional victors as well as the support of lesser politicians they met during their extensive travels.

Each presidential candidate must develop a strategy that will allow him to maximize his advantages so that he can arrive at the convention with the greatest strength. Traditionally, strong candidates have been advised not to enter primaries; this advice worked for Hubert Humphrey in 1968, but Richard Nixon felt he had to enter all of the primaries in 1968 and 1972. Candidates far behind the front-runner or with severe handicaps certainly have little or nothing to lose from entering the primaries. Victories in early primaries gave credibility to Goldwater, McGovern, and Carter; and key victories by John Kennedy in West Virginia and Barry Goldwater in California helped reduce their handicaps—Catholicism and narrowness of support.[9] Conventional wisdom argued that a candidate who chose to follow the primary path should carefully select only those primaries where he had a reasonable chance of success. In 1972 George McGovern declined to enter the West Virginia, North Carolina, Indiana, and Illinois primaries. In 1976 Jimmy Carter ran in all of the Democratic primaries except West Virginia, where the favorite son Robert C. Byrd won with nearly 90 percent of the vote. But his opponents selectively chose their primaries: Jackson skipped New Hampshire, Vermont, Illinois, and the District of Columbia; and Udall passed up Vermont, Illinois, Indiana, West Virginia, and New Jersey. Carter's strategy was to establish his credentials quickly and force his opponents out of the race one by one.[10] Since the new rules permitted delegates to be awarded to other than the first-place finishers, Carter picked up delegates in nearly every state of the union.

A second strategy that can be followed by a presidential aspirant is to wait until the early group of candidates has eliminated one another and then step in as a fresh, new face. Senator Frank Church began his campaign with the 1976 Nebraska primary on May 11, and California Governor Jerry Brown entered his first primary in Maryland on May 18. By early May, Carter had edged Bayh, Shapp, Shriver, Harris, and Jackson completely out of the race; and Wallace and Udall were barely hanging on. Between May 11 and June 8, Carter and the new challengers entered a total of 9 primaries. Governor Brown won in Maryland, Nevada, and California; Senator Church was victorious in Nebraska, Idaho, Oregon, and Montana; and Carter won in only two of these late-season primaries. Unfortunately for both Brown and Church's campaigns, it was too little and too late. With Carter's June 8 victory in Ohio, the stop-Carter movement totally collapsed and his nomination was assured; this was surely one of the finest pre-convention efforts in American political history.

Hubert Humphrey decided to follow a third strategy in his last attempt to win the White House. Several times in 1976 Humphrey appeared to be on the verge of announcing his active candidacy, but then he finally decided to wait until the convention, hoping that the Carter juggernaut would run out of steam and that a deadlocked convention would turn to him as a compromise choice. However, this was not to be in 1976. Richard Nixon also followed this general course during the 1964 pre-convention campaign. Their strategies were quite similar: be a friend to all, an enemy to none, and the second choice of many—while hoping for the delegate leader to stumble.[11]

Ronald Reagan took the selected primary route in his challenge to President Gerald Ford in 1976. Reagan did not oppose Ford in New Jersey, New York, and Pennsylvania, and presented only half-hearted challenges in several other Eastern states.

Although it is difficult to ascertain if greater efforts by Reagan in these states would have weakened him significantly elsewhere, his failure to make any important inroads in these larger state delegations cost him the nomination at Kansas City.

Other pieces of conventional wisdom that have proved to be less than successful since 1968 pertain to challenging an incumbent president from inside his own party. It was thought that only by defeating a president early could a challenger hope to establish his credibility as a candidate for the nomination. Governor Ronald Reagan lost the first five primaries to President Ford, although sometimes only by a very slim margin, as in New Hampshire; Governor Reagan did not manage a victory until North Carolina's March 23 primary—more than 4 weeks and 5 defeats later. It had been more than 60 years since a rival had seriously challenged an incumbent president (Roosevelt's challenge to Taft in 1912), and never had a rival suffered such a string of initial defeats and still forced a president to scramble among uncommitted delegates to construct a first ballot victory. It has always been argued that money was the key to the middle campaigns. In 1976 the failure of Congress and President Ford to reconstitute the Federal Election Commission quickly reduced the amount of money Reagan could use during the middle primaries, but Reagan prospered during this time. Judging from the 1960 and 1972 campaigns, it would appear important for a candidate to close with a string of primary victories. John Kennedy won his last ten primaries in 1960 and George McGovern won his last six in 1972. But in 1976 both Ford and Carter lost most of the primaries during the last phase of their campaigns, including "the Super Bowl" of the primary season—California on June 8.

Another campaign tactic is the write-in candidacy. For a candidate who is running far behind, the write-in tactic seems worthwhile. If nothing happens on primary election day with write-ins, the candidate can point to the inherent difficulties of write-ins and lose nothing. But if he draws a large proportion of the vote, the write-in can be hailed as a great victory. The best-known presidential primary write-in victory in recent years was that of Henry Cabot Lodge over Nelson Rockefeller and Barry Goldwater in New Hampshire in 1964. Governor Brown tried the same ploy in the Oregon primary in 1976 and polled a respectable 24.7 percent—a third-place finish. Another tactic that is quite difficult to use is to persuade voters of the other major party to cross over and vote in one's own party primary. Ronald Reagan apparently benefited from this tactic with primary victories in Indiana, Texas, and Georgia since he received the support of many conservative Democrats. One of the 1976 Democratic reforms was aimed at trying to prevent such crossover voting from affecting the Democratic presidential primary results.

Democratic Party Delegate-Selection Reforms

Selecting delegates in 1976 was quite different from what it had been in past years because of new rules that had been promulgated at the 1972 and 1974 Democratic National Conventions. The form of 13 Democratic and 5 Republican primaries was changed for 1976, largely from winner-take-all to proportional-type primaries. Only eight states (including California) kept some type of winner-take-all primary, and these were all Republican primaries. One of the reasons for the Democratic reforms was the perceived inequality of the winner-take-all primaries that gave McGovern 65 percent of all of the primary states' delegates with only 25 percent of the vote.[12] Changing to a proportional allocation of delegates gave Jimmy Carter 43 percent of the delegates on the basis of winning 42 percent of the primary states' vote as of the last primary week in 1976.[13]

The 1980 Democratic presidential candidate will be chosen under a different set of rules that were recommended by the 58 member Winograd Commission in 1978. The major changes will be:

1. A shortening of the presidential caucus and primary session from the 20-week period in 1976 to 13 weeks between March and June 1980.
2. The use of at-large delegates to make affirmative action corrections in the makeup of the various state delegations.
3. An increase in the size of state delegations of about 10 percent and the granting of voting rights to state party officials and elected officeholders.
4. The establishment of an escalating minimum vote in primaries for a candidate to receive delegates. Up to the second Tuesday in April, the minimum vote in order to win delegates will be 15 percent. It will increase to 20 percent on the second Tuesday in May and 25 percent after that date.

As the authors have argued elsewhere in this book, the delegate-selection rules significantly affect the distribution of rewards. Table 8.1 shows how different sets of rules would have affected the 1972 primary results. If the winner-take-all principle had been in effect in 1972 (as it was in 1968), Humphrey would have been the primary winner, while Wallace would have had pluralities under either the proportional or districted systems. Comparable data for 1976 indicate that Jimmy Carter benefited greatly from the "loophole" primary, which allowed him to win 100 delegates more than he would have if the loophole states had had proportional primaries.[14] Forty-two percent of the 1976 Democratic National Convention's delegates were chosen in loophole primaries, but the Democratic Rules Committee—by a 58½ to 58¼ vote— has abolished this type of primary for 1980. At that time, all Democratic presidential primaries must be proportional, and so the various candidates will have to make the necessary adjustments. James Lengle and Byron Shafe point out that these rule changes mean

> Choices about the types of candidates who would bear the party's standard, the type of voters who would have the power to choose those standard bearers, and the type of issues with which both groups would try to shape history. They were, in short, decisions on how to reconstruct the Democratic Party. . . . Primary rules matter a great deal.[15]

See Table 8.1.

Table 8.1   The effect of Delegate-Selection Rules in Fifteen 1972 Democratic Primaries

Candidate	Winner-Take-All	Proportional	Districts	Actual
Humphrey	*446*	314	324	284
Wallace	379	*350*	*367*	291
McGovern	249	319	343	*401½*
Muskie	18	82	52	56½
Others	0	27	6	59

Source : James Lengle and Byron Shafe, "Primary Rules, Political Power, and Social Change," *American Political Science Review* 70 (March 1976), p. 29.

The Importance of the Primaries

In their 1976 study of presidential nominating politics, William R. Keech and Donald R. Matthews concluded that the primaries were not very important in deciding who will get the nomination.[16] They argue that the "primaries are secondary to the ability of a candidate to become accepted as a front-runner" before the primaries begin. Between 1936 and 1968 in 13 cases out of a total of 13, the front-runners have eventually won the party nomination. Keech and Matthews believe that the primaries simply serve as an arena in which to challenge the front-runners, an opportunity that offers little chance of success. Usually the primaries just confirm the status of the front-runner or provide such an ambiguous situation that nothing is significantly altered. Perhaps when there were only a dozen or so primaries, their significance was slight when compared with the campaigns in the other states. However, with 31 primaries in 1976 (and the prospect of many more to come in the near future), they should probably not be dismissed as insignificant. George McGovern rode his primary victories to the 1972 nomination defeating the pre-primary front-runner, Senator Edmund Muskie. A similar situation occurred in 1976 when Carter, a newcomer to national politics who held no political office, defeated better-known opponents in one state after another. With additional opportunities to demonstrate strengths and weaknesses, the conditions that destroyed the candidacies of Senator Edmund Muskie in 1972, Governor George Romney in 1968, as well as many other candidates, will probably be significant in selecting future party nominees.

One must remember that the primary results are always evaluated in terms of the expectations of the observers—both political and mass media. It is not enough for a candidate to defeat his opponents; he must do so in a manner that is acceptable to his critics—especially those in the press. For example, President Lyndon Johnson and Senator Edmund Muskie won pluralities in the New Hampshire primary in 1968 and 1972, respectively. However, the press reported that each had suffered a serious defeat since he did not attract as many votes as the media felt he should. Johnson defeated Senator McCarthy 49 percent to 42 percent, but within a month the president had announced his decision not to seek renomination. The press decided that Senator Muskie should get at least half of the 1972 New Hampshire vote, and when he defeated George McGovern 48 percent to 37 percent, it described the primary as a "moral victory" for McGovern.

The media attach more importance to some state primaries than to others; for example, it singles out the first primary held in New Hampshire in late February. Although all political observers acknowledge that New Hampshire does not typify national Democratic Party sentiment and the state represents only three-tenths of 1 percent of the United States population, *The Washington Post* editorialized, "Happiness is not getting wiped out in New Hampshire."[17] Other states, while offering a signifi-cant number of delegates to the winning candidates, are seldom perceived as part of the election process. California primary winners do not often win the presidency;[18] neither California victor in 1976 (Brown and Reagan) secured his party's nomination. Nevertheless, the Democratic candidates who won the most delegates in the primaries in 1972 and 1976 went on to be nominated, and so the reliance on primaries is likely to continue in the foreseeable future.

Should the Presidential Primaries Be Further Reformed?

Despite the great increase in presidential primaries since the 1960s, many students of presidential politics oppose them. Hubert H. Humphrey commented in 1974 that "Presidential primaries are a curse . . . the primaries are all run under different sets of state laws. They are expensive, debilitating, and subject to misinterpretation by the media. This is an outrage, to be in 12 or 25 primaries. You run around like a chicken with your head cut off."[19] Others point out that the average voter knows very little about the candidates at the time of the primaries. An Associated Press poll in June 1976 showed that half of Jimmy Carter's supporters did not know where he stood on the issues; another quarter had incorrect ideas about his stands; and only about one-fifth had correct impressions.[20] Many others agree with Humphrey's point that there are too many primaries. David Broder, political columnist of *The Washington Post*, concluded that 30 primaries in a single campaign are about 20 too many.[21] Vice President Walter Mondale, after giving up his presidential campaign in 1975, noted that "the system doesn't make any sense at all anymore," and historian Arthur Schlesinger,

Table 8.2   Results of the 1976 Democratic Presidential Primaries

Candidate	Primaries Contested	Finished			Percent of Total Democratic Primary Vote
		1st	2nd	3rd	
Carter	26	17	8	0	39
Wallace	24	0	9	4	12.5
Udall	22	0	7	6	10.1
Jackson	22	1	1	3	7.1
Harris	18	0	0	1	1.5
McCormack	18	0	0	0	1.5
Church	12	4	1	4	5.3
Shriver	9	0	1	1	1.9
Brown	3	3	0	1[a]	12.5
Byrd	3	1	0	0	2.0

[a]Write-in vote.
Source: Congressional Quarterly, June 26, 1976.

Jr., concluded that "the system is out of control."[22] More significantly, the rise of presidential primaries has reduced the power of the political parties to control their single most important product—the presidential nomination. Candidates can win a state's delegates despite the almost unanimous opposition of the state party organization and leadership. Ronald Reagan won the 1976 GOP Indiana primary although "nearly all of the state's well organized Republican machine was behind Ford, including Republican Governor Otis Brown and 95 percent of the county chairmen."[23] Donald Fraser, former chairman of the Democratic reform commission, called the cumulative effect of the 30 primaries "terrible" and "destructive of party responsibility."[24] Finally, David Broder, one of the strongest defenders of the party who supports major reforms to enhance the roles of the parties, concluded after the 1976 primaries were finished:

> The political parties—whose nominations are still the prizes in this primary game—are increasingly irrelevant to its outcome. They have lost their old role as mechanisms for recruiting, evaluating and selecting candidates for successively higher levels of government responsiblility. Increasingly, they are viewed by the contestants as vestiges of the past, obstacles to be overcome on the way to the great plebescite in November.[25]

George McGovern and Jimmy Carter demonstrated conclusively that the Democratic nomination can be secured quite easily by an anti-party issue or personality candidate. Jimmy Carter's nomination triumph completely bypassed the old Democratic Party structure.[26]

National Primaries—the Next Major Reform?

A Gallup Poll announced in February 1976 reported that 68 percent of the nation favored the establishment of a national primary to replace the chaotic 31 primaries. From Gallup's first survey on this issue in 1952, the public has consistently favored this reform by ratios of 6 to 1. It is supported by 71 percent of the Democrats, 65 percent of the Republicans, and 69 percent of the independents.[27]

Advocates of a national presidential primary argue that it would cost less, the campaign would be nationally focused, the candidate could better coordinate his campaign, and the process would be easier for both politicians and the electorate to understand. Opponents counter that probably such a media-oriented election would cost more and that name recognition or ethnicity might become quite important in building national support. Political unknowns on the national level, such as Eugene McCarthy in 1968, George McGovern in 1972, and Jimmy Carter in 1976, could not gradually build momentum by piling up small victories. If the field is crowded, it is possible that a minority-wing candidate could secure the nomination despite opposition from a majority of the party's supporters. Lastly, opponents charge that a national presidential primary would be a serious blow to the survival of the political parties; it would eliminate them as viable bodies. "A winning candidate could totally disdain the party organization, using its *label* in his election campaign."[28]

One frequently suggested reform, less radical than a national primary, is the adoption of a series of regional primaries. This plan sees perhaps four or six such primaries which would allow candidates to concentrate their campaigning in one whole region at a time (for example, New England or the Pacific Northwest), thus saving energy, time, and organizational resources. It would eliminate situations such as New Jersey, Ohio, and California primaries all being held on the same day—June 8, 1976. Since media coverage is sometimes regional in nature, this might save money, not to mention the time saved by not having the candidate crossing the nation several times in the same week. A Harris Survey in May 1976 found that 54 percent of the public favored a plan of four regional primaries at 3-week intervals.[29] The same poll showed that the public was not satisfied with the present system of primaries; only 17 percent wanted to see it continued.

Two regions attempted to establish regional primaries in 1976. A mini-New England regional primary was held on March 2nd, with Massachusetts and Vermont voters balloting on the same day, and Oregon, Nevada, and Idaho holding their primaries on May 25. Such reforms have generally been well received by state officials; the Southern Governor's Conference voted unanimously to support regional primaries as a means of bringing "some order and rationality to the overall nomination process."[30] However, it seems that an ad hoc development of such regional primaries (where several adjacent states hold their primaries on the same day) will be quite difficult to accomplish. For political reasons individual states like to be in the spotlight, and New Hampshire has shown great reluctance to conform to any such plan. On May 4, 1976, Indiana and Illinois were to hold their primaries together, but then Illinois decided to change its date to the middle of March. Washington State was to be part of the May 25 Pacific Northwest primary, but could not decide if that would be best for its candidate—Senator Henry Jackson—and so it declined to participate. Although regional primaries might bring some order out of the chaos, such a reform will be difficult to achieve in the foreseeable future; the party organizations might first concentrate on establishing a more uniform set of delegate-selection rules and then move gradually toward regional uniformity.

The Caucus States

In a formal sense the 1976 presidential campaign did not begin in the snowy fields of New Hampshire, but in the cornfields of Iowa. Although 30 states and the District of Columbia held presidential primaries in 1976, 20 states chose another route for selecting national convention delegates—the caucus-convention method. Iowa held the first step in this process—the precinct meeting—on January 19, 5 weeks before the New Hampshire primary. Jimmy Carter was adjudged to be the winner at that time in the Iowa delegate-selection process, and this helped to propel him toward his New Hampshire primary victory. About one-tenth of Iowa's Democrats participated in the 2530 precinct meetings around the state and, although two-thirds of them voted to remain uncommitted, Carter received a 20 percent plurality. Doing well in these early caucus states was probably responsible for much of the later success by both George McGovern and Jimmy Carter.

The guidelines for delegate selection discussed earlier helped to reduce the number of caucus states since the party leaders felt that the guidelines could best be met by establishing primaries. In 1968, 28 states used caucus-conventions for selecting delegates, accounting for more than 51 percent of all of the Democratic delegates. By 1976, only 20 states used this method, selecting less than 25 percent of the Democratic delegates. Most of the states that still cling to this more traditional method are found in the Middle West and mountain areas, since many Southern states abandoned the caucus system between 1968 and 1976.

Procedures and rules, like those of the primary elections, differ among the various convention states. In general, however, voter meetings are held on the precinct level, which elect delegates to the county or congressional district conventions. The county conventions, in turn, select delegates to the state convention and, depending upon the individual state, the county or state convention selects delegates to the national convention. The new Democratic delegate-selection rules of 1976 mandate that all such meetings be open and publicized, that all delegate candidates announce their preference for the party's presidential nomination, and that national convention delegates be awarded proportionally to the caucus vote.[31] The Republicans have not made these changes.

Caucuses usually attract far fewer participants than primary elections. In 1972 when George McGovern won the Iowa caucuses, only 35,000 Democrats turned out to vote in January (7 percent of his November total).[32] Three-quarters of a million Democrats attended caucuses in 22 states and 4 territories to select their presidential nominee in 1976. The turnout ranged from 600 in Wyoming county meetings to an estimated 120,000 in Louisiana. Although the best caucus turnout was 19 percent in Connecticut, this was less than half of the average turnout in the 30 primary states (43 percent).[33] One source estimated that the average 1972 caucus turnout was about 6 percent.[34] Caucuses tend to be filled with "the court house crowd, government people and party activists."[35] T. R. Marshall argues that those who attend caucuses are even less representative of the party rank-and-file than primary voters; since caucuses attract the highly active, highly motivated, highly educated, ideologues, and extremists.[36]

Achieving a triumph in caucus states is largely due to the efficiency of a candidate's organization. Jimmy Carter visited 110 Iowa towns and cities in 1975.[37] In 1964, 1972, and 1976, the supporters of Goldwater, McGovern, and Carter, respectively, simply out-organized and outworked their opponents. When measured in terms of the cost per delegate won, the caucus states are a tremendous bargain for candidates who must now operate under the new federal expenditure limitations. McGovern, for example, spent an average of $25,000 per delegate in the primary states but only

$300 per caucus state delegate.[38] One major change in the candidates' campaign style between 1972 and 1976 was their greater emphasis on the caucus states in the latter contest. McGovern spent almost no time in the caucus states in 1972; Carter and the other candidates of both parties gave a large amount of their time, energy, and resources to the caucus states. In 1964 Goldwater did well in both the caucus and primary states, but ran considerably stronger in the caucus states. Humphrey nearly swept the caucus states in 1968, while Nixon did well in both. In 1972, Mc-Govern ran better in the primary states, while in 1976 Carter won 221 caucus state delegates, as opposed to fewer than 120 for his combined opposition.[39] In short, caucus states offer another arena for presidential nomination candidates to prove themselves, but the skills necessary for caucus victories are quite different from those valued in primary contests. In this period of resource shortages, the relative inexpensiveness of campaigning in the caucus states should attract more of the attention of the candidates.

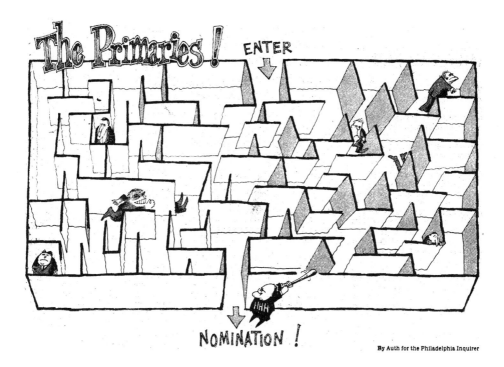

By Auth for the Philadelphia Inquirer

There are two paths to the nomination: the primaries or waiting at the convention for a fortuitous ambush. In this 1976 cartoon, Carter races through the primary maze while Udall and other candidates have lost their way and Humphrey waits at the end hoping to knock off Carter, but in vain. . . . .

National Conventions: The National Parties in Action

The convention had a total of 40,000 visitors, and the delegates and press were jammed into the convention hall trying to figure out what was happening behind the scenes in the smoke-filled rooms where the politicians were meeting. As each state delegation arrived, the reporters tried to take quick polls as to which way the delegates were leaning. The high powered staffs of the candidates—"hustlers, evangelists, salesmen, pleaders, exhorters, schemers"[40]—and political friends fanned out from the head-quarters hotel, bargaining and collecting political debts. After the convention began, the candidates' managers attempted to manipulate the rules to gain tactical advantages and even resorted to "dirty tricks" such as counterfeiting seat tickets in order to control the galleries for their candidate.[41] This is a description of a Chicago national party convention; it is not the infamous 1968 Democratic convention, but rather Abraham Lincoln's 1860 Republican convention. Clearly, little has changed at our national conventions in a century except that the media have increased power and delegates are now selected differently. Although the general patterns of behavior at political conventions have not changed greatly since Lincoln's time, several trends are evident. First, the convention used to be the actual place where it was decided who would get the presidential nomination; now the convention simply ratifies the decision. Second, there has been a gradual democratization of the delegate-selection process, and this has weakened the power of the old political bosses who once domi-nated (and made the key decisions at) the conventions. And lastly, the convention has become a media event—not the crucial end of the nomination process—but the first step of the general election campaign.

Although it would be correct to say that a convention has not chosen a presidential nominee since the 1952 Democratic convention, this does not mean that the conven-tions do not perform significant functions. First, by ratifying decisions made earlier, conventions *legitimize* the new party standard-bearer. The plurality winner from the primaries or caucuses becomes the majority's choice through a rollcall of the states. However, this attempt at legitimization is not always successful. Since the 1960s three convention nominees (Goldwater, Humphrey and McGovern) were not accepted by the majority of party identifiers and they later suffered crushing defeats. Second, conventions *influence* the vice-presidential nomination decision. David Broder believes that the convention provides "the environment in which the successful presidential nominee makes his decision." For example, in 1976 neither Gerald Ford nor Jimmy Carter had decided on running mates before the convention began, but they both responded to loud signals from the floor. Carter was obliged to make a more liberal choice than he might have otherwise, and Ford was influenced in the opposite di-rection.[42] Broder sees the runner-up in the presidential sweepstakes as nearly value-less except in his power to influence the choice of running mates.

The Organization and Structure of the Convention

Planning for a national party convention actually begins at the previous convention 4 years earlier but comes to public attention when the "convention call" is issued by the party's national committee. The convention call, issued about a year before the actual convention is scheduled, includes a listing of the major committees on credentials, rules, and platform; the appointment of the temporary convention officers; and the allocation of delegates among the various states and territories.

Delegate allocation has caused considerable conflict among the Republicans since the conservative faction became dominant in 1964. During the nineteenth century delegate allocations were based on the electoral vote totals of each state. However, after the 1912 convention, when President Taft won renomination thanks to the "paper" Republican organizations in the South, the party adjusted the delegate strengths to reduce the number of Southern Republican delegates. The first bonus system was adopted in 1924, giving extra delegates to those states that had supported Republican presidential nominees. Later the bonus was expanded to include gubernatorial candidates, U.S. Senators, and Congressmen. As of 1976, half of the delegate-allocation formula was equally based upon the states' electoral vote and upon the states' support of party candidates. Therefore, each state received 6 at-large delegates, 3 delegates for each congressional district, 1 delegate for a Republican governor and/or U.S. Senator, and 1 delegate for a congressional delegation that was more than 50 percent Republican; finally, if the state voted for Richard Nixon in 1972, it received 4½ delegates plus a percentage of its electoral vote total. This presidential support bonus discriminates against the larger states, since the ten largest states gave Nixon 55 percent of his total vote in 1972, but received only 44 percent of the 1976 Republican delegates—a net disadvantage of 327 delegates. Meanwhile the ten smallest states gained 119 delegates over their fair share as determined by votes cast in 1972. The way in which this presidential bonus operated in 1976 probably cost Ronald Reagan the nomination. Since Nixon's 1972 reelection was such a landslide, the bonus factor in 1976 was extraordinarily large. Analyzing the effect of the bonus at the 1976 convention, *The New York Times* concluded that if the bonus had been smaller, Reagan would have entered the convention with a 33 vote lead instead of the reverse.[43] The Ripon Society, a liberal Republican group, challenged the 1976 delegate-allocation formula, but it was rejected by the United States Supreme Court early in 1976 as was a similar challenge to the California winner-take-all presidential primary. The Democrats adopted bonus delegates in 1944 and established a new formula in 1971 that balances a state's population almost equally with the popular vote for the Democratic presidential candidate in the three preceding elections.

With respect to convention size, the Democratic trend has been toward larger and larger conventions. Between 1960 and 1976, the number of Democratic delegates increased from 1521 to 3008. During the same period the typical Republican conventions were usually smaller (around 1350 delegates), but the bonus provisions and other political considerations increased the 1976 allocation to 2259 delegates. There is usually a great deal of grassroots pressure for a large convention so that more local workers can be rewarded as delegates.[44]

The makeup of the convention committees and the temporary offices is determined by the national committees of the two parties. As Theodore Roosevelt, Ronald Reagan, and Eugene McCarthy discovered, this power of selection can be used in a devastating manner by an incumbent president. The crucial planning and decision-making at the convention are controlled by the incumbent, and the challenger must expect a number of unfavorable decisions on his behalf.

The Key Committees of the Convention
As in the case of many institutions, most significant decision-making at a convention takes place in the permanent standing committees and not on the convention floor. Both parties have three traditional standing committees: credentials, rules and platform.

The Credentials Committee. This committee determines the validity of challenges to the legitimacy of members of the various state delegations. On occasion the victory or defeat of a candidate for the party's presidential nomination is decided by a vote of this committee. Most of the bitterest conflicts have been over the legitimacy of Southern delegations, especially in the Republican Party. Historically the Republican Party in the South has been merely a patronage party, that is, Washington-oriented party regulars who were just puppets for an incumbent Republican president. At the 1912 Republican convention former President Theodore Roosevelt's challenge to incumbent President William H. Taft was defeated by a vote of the party's national committee, which awarded 235 of 254 contested Southern delegates to Taft who controlled the national committee with 37 of 53 seats. Roosevelt brought 72 delegate challenges to the floor of the convention, the final arbiter for all disputed committee decisions. All of the challenges were decided in Taft's favor, with the disputed delegates allowed to vote on all cases but their own. A similar series of events occurred in 1952 when Robert Taft and Dwight Eisenhower battled over disputed delegates from Georgia, Texas, and Louisiana. The Credentials Committee voted to seat the Taft delegates, and the convention reversed the decision and seated the Eisenhower delegates, thereby assuring him the nomination.

Since 1952 the Democratic Party has had more Credentials Committee conflicts. The first major conflict occurred in 1964 on whether an all-white delegation or a rival mixed group should be seated as the legitimate Mississippi delegation. A floor vote proposed the compromise of seating the regular delegation, two members of the challenger group, and the rest of the challengers as honored guests. Both sides rejected the offer, but the vote also mandated that at all future conventions delegations would be barred if racial discrimination was evidenced. The McGovern convention of 1972 saw an unprecedented number of credentials challenges: a total of 1289 delegates were challenged, representing more than 40 percent of the convention's total delegates. Eighty-two separate challenges involving 30 states and one territory were processed, with 80 percent of them being filed on the ground of noncompliance with delegate-selection guidelines.[45] The most controversial challenges involved Mayor Richard Daley's Illinois delegation and McGovern's winner-take-all victory in California. The Credentials Committee stripped McGovern of 151 of the 271 California delegates and unseated Daley's delegation. The convention subsequently voted to return the rest of McGovern's delegates to him and sustained the decision to expel Daley's delegation. As it turned out, the decision to overrule the Credentials Committee's decision on McGovern's California delegates proved to be the crucial decision that gave McGovern the nomination.

For the 1976 Democratic convention, a special Judicial Council was established to help decide credentials challenges. However, there were only 40 such challenges; the Credentials Committee handled them without producing a single minority report.[46] The absence of serious conflict in credentials challenges in 1976 reflected the harmony of the Carter-dominated convention.

The Rules Committees. The rules of the convention game, as they have developed over the years, have significantly affected the nature of modern conventions. Actually, the Democrats waited until 1972 to adopt a formal set of rules, but they relied upon two rules that their Republican counterparts never adopted: the unit and two-thirds rules. The unit rule, which was abolished by the 1968 Democratic convention, authorized a majority of a state's delegation, if permitted by the state party, to cast the entire state's vote for a single candidate or issue position.[47] The two-thirds rule, a relic of the earliest Democratic conventions, set the threshold for the nomination at two-thirds of the delegate total. It provided a de facto Southern veto over the party's nominees until it was abolished in 1936. The two-thirds rule produced some turbulent Democratic conventions, the most notable being in 1924 when John W. Davis was nominated on a record 103rd ballot. The Roosevelt-dominated 1936 convention voted to end the two-thirds rule, and a special rule change in delegate allocation was made to increase Southern representation at the convention. Since the abolition of the two-thirds rule, only one Democratic convention (that of 1952 with 3 ballots) has experienced a multiple-ballot nomination.

Since then the rule changes have dealt with delegate selection, a new delegate allocation formula, enlargement of the three major committees, banning of floor demonstrations for presidential candidates, and ending the traditional alphabetical order of roll calls. It could be argued that the cumulative effect of these and other rule changes has produced a major reformation in convention composition and behavior patterns.

Ronald Reagan's challenge to President Gerald Ford brought about a major rules battle in 1976. First, Ford's backers, fearful of the possible "softness" in their delegate totals, passed a "fair play rule," requiring all bound delegates to follow the directions of their states' voters as indicated by the primary or caucus results. Reagan countered with his new Rule 16C proposal to require each presidential candidate to announce to the convention his choice for vice-presidential nominee; failure to do so would unbind the delegates. Ford had enough votes in both the Rules Committee and on the convention floor to defeat Reagan's proposal (which might have forced Ford to make a damaging political decision). Traditionally Republicans have been quite reluctant to change their party convention rules. Few reforms were made at the 1976 convention because Ford strategists prevented any from being made on the apportion-ment of delegates, the composition of the National Committee, or Rule 32 (on partic-ipation).[48] One change modified Rule 9 to increase from three to five the number of states that must nominate a candidate. This change will prevent favorite sons or one-state candidates from being nominated. There has been little pressure on the Repub-licans to make meaningful reforms since few of the militant reformer groups are found within the party. In the 1970s Republican rules battles have dealt with the delegate-apportionment formula; challenges from the Republican liberals have been beaten back in the party and in the courts. In 1972 a Rule 29 Committee (Steiger Committee) was formed to study the party rules and make recommendations. However, in 1976 the party conservatives replaced the committee members with National Committee members and selected an anti-reform chairman. Thus, there appears to be little prospect that the Republicans will soon adopt the type of reforms instituted in the Democratic Party.

Building a Platform:

In addition to selecting presidential and vice-presidential nominees, the convention's next most visable task is to construct a party platform. The platform summarizes the party positions on major and minor issues of the day. First used by the Democratic Party in 1840, the early platforms were relatively brief (1000 words in 1840). However, George McGovern's 1972 platform, *For the People,* was a 25,000-word document that almost certainly would not be read by any but the most masochistic party loyalist.

Platform fights have often served as important early tests of strength for the presi-dential candidates. Those conventions with large numbers of issue-oriented delegates have often experienced bitter and divisive platform battles. Such battles have usually occurred among the Democrats (rather than the more staid Republicans), with notable conflicts in 1924 (Ku Klux Klan), 1932 (Prohibition), 1948 and 1960 (Civil Rights), 1968 (Vietnam), and 1972 (Guaranteed Income and Abortion). However, in 1976, the Republicans (rather than the Democrats) came into conflict over their foreign policy and defense planks. Such platform battles can seriously injure a party's chances in the general election. In 1948 the Dixiecrats walked out and this nearly cost Truman the election, and the liberal dissatisfaction with Hubert Humphrey's unwillingness to compromise on the Vietnam plank contributed to his narrow loss to Richard Nixon in 1968. In the contemporary media-oriented conventions, prolonged platform fights, such as during the 1972 Democratic convention (20 separate minority planks were brought to the floor of the convention for consideration), can use up valuable prime television time, relegating the more important nomination activities into a less desirable time period.

Political commentators generally agree that the platform has only symbolic value. According to David B. Truman:

> *The platform is genuinely regarded as a document that says little, binds no one, and is forgotten by politicians as quickly as possible after it is*

adopted. . . . Considered as a pledge of future action, the party platform is almost meaningless and is properly so regarded by the voters.[49]

Writing in the *Chicago Tribune*, Louis M. Kohlmeier criticized the 1976 party platforms as being "built of thin cardboard planks. . . . intended not to address but to obscure the issues . . . not for presidential candidates to run on but to hide behind."[50] Others note that the platforms hold out unrealistic promises: the 1976 Republican platform reflected the policy desires of the amateur/purist Republican delegates and not the realities of the Republicans-in-power. According to *The Wall Street Journal*: "The Republican platform you see is not quite the Republican government you get."[51] Yet, at least one American party scholar has studied the political role of the platform and concluded that these criticisms are too harsh. Gerald Pomper claims that the platforms are not ignored by the parties once they achieve power; more than half of the party's pledges are eventually redeemed and only one-tenth completely ignored.[52] In studying 12 party platforms between 1944 and 1964, Pomper discovered that one-tenth of the pledges were in direct conflict with other major planks in the platform, and that there was substantial agreement only on foreign policy and civil rights issues. Typically, one-fifth of a platform is general rhetoric, two-fifths is an evaluation of the party's past record, and the rest consists of policy criticism and future promises. There are differences in the types of issues emphasized by the two parties: the Democrats focus on labor and welfare, while the Republicans emphasize defense and the role of government. Pomper also noticed that the party that was leading in the campaign at convention time tended to make ambiguous generalities, while the trailing party was more specific and emphasized future promises. A well-run convention will usually produce a platform that the presidential ticket can speak of without embarrassment, that compares its party history favorably with that of the opponent, that includes several planks that a majority of voters already support, and that avoids minority controversial positions and issues that are still somewhat vague in the public's mind.

In 1972, 15 percent of the Democratic delegates perceived the platform as "the most important thing they wanted to see done at the convention."[53] These delegates tend to be "purists"—those who see principles as being more important than selecting a winning candidate and beginning a campaign with every possible political advantage. Therefore, the convention nominee must sometimes compromise his positions in order to accommodate the issue-oriented delegates. A platform can serve as an integrative device "bringing about harmony among factions and cementing their allegiance to the party."[54]

The Nominee's Big Decision: Selecting the Vice-Presidential Candidate

After the presidential nominee has been chosen, the next major event is to select the vice-presidential nominee. Only once in recent history has this matter been turned over to the convention to decide. In 1956, during a rather lackluster Democratic convention that nominated former Governor Adlai Stevenson for his second contest with Dwight Eisenhower, Stevenson asked the convention to choose his running mate, perhaps in hopes of invigorating the convention. Stevenson hoped that a young U.S. Senator from Massachusetts, John F. Kennedy, would be chosen as his running mate, but the convention decided on the Tennessee Senator, Estes Keeefauver. Somewhat ironically, when Jimmy Carter reportedly toyed with the same idea in 1976, Stevenson's son, at that time a U.S. Senator from Illinois, strongly urged Carter not to make the mistake his father had made 20 years earlier. "It would be dangerous and irresponsible for the 1976 presidential nominee to allow the Democratic National Convention to dictate the second spot on the ticket. . . . "[55]

What criteria are used by the nominee to select the man who, if elected, stands as the party's most logical choice to succeed to the White House after the president retires? With slight tongue-in-cheek, *The New York Times* offered this advice to Jimmy Carter as the convention was turning to this matter in 1976:

> He should announce that he seeks a person of high moral caliber, superior judgment, formidable intelligence, and adequate experience. All presidential candidates say that they select their running mates on these criteria. And the system has produced a remarkable collection of lintheads, knaves, and non-entities.[56]

The actual decision-making has to do with practical political considerations. In the early years of our Republic, the vice president was whoever received the second highest number of votes for the presidency, but then this selection method backfired in 1800 when Aaron Burr, the Democratic-Republican vice-presidential candidate, decided he wanted to be president instead. Since the 1840s, the vice-presidential candidates have been chosen at the national nominating conventions. One of the most common considerations for selection has been the desire to have an ideologically balanced ticket. Al Smith, the 1928 Democratic nominee (a Catholic, urban, New Yorker), balanced his ticket by selecting Joseph T. Robinson, the Senate Minority Leader, a "dry Protestant from Arkansas." Thomas E. Dewey, the 1944 Republican nominee, selected Ohio Governor John W. Bricker for a similar reason. Perhaps the most usual consideration over the years has been the perceived need for geographical balance. In 1952 Adlai Stevenson (Illinois) accepted Alabama Senator John W. Sparkman; Governor James M. Cox (Ohio), the 1924 Democratic nominee, selected New Yorker Franklin D. Roosevelt, the assistant secretary of the navy; and Jimmy Carter chose Walter Mondale of Minnesota for both ideological and geographical balance. Sometimes the vice-presidency is offered as part of a deal in order to gain enough support to win the presidential nomination. In 1932 Franklin D. Roosevelt was finally nominated on the fourth ballot after an arrangement had been made with House Speaker John Nance Garner's supporters; they switched their support to Roosevelt, and then Garner was selected unanimously as vice president. Another consideration in choosing a vice president is to heal party wounds and thereby increase the electoral strength of the ticket. In 1960 U.S. Senator Lyndon B. Johnson was offered the vice-presidential nomination in an attempt to bring the party together; he surprised the nominee, John F. Kennedy, by accepting the offer.

The more hopeless a presidential campaign appears at the time of the convention, the more difficult it will be to obtain a quality vice-presidential nominee. In 1904 the Democratic nominee, Alton B. Parker, facing a hopeless race against incumbent Theodore Roosevelt, chose former West Virginia Senator Henry G. Davis, then 80 years of age and quite wealthy in hopes that he would finance part of the campaign expenses.[57] George McGovern had extreme difficulty trying to find a vice-presidential nominee in 1972. On the other hand, the prospects of victory were so strong in the summer of 1976, that Jimmy Carter had a wide range of aspirants from which to choose his running mate.

It is usually assumed that vice-presidential nominees can help the ticket by carrying at least their home states. Carl D. Tubbesing has found that betwen 1836 and 1972 the vice-presidential nominees won their home states an average of 53 percent of the time, while presidential candidates won their home states an average of 62 percent of the time.[58]

The fact that the 1972 Democratic vice-presidential nominee, Thomas Eagleton, had to be replaced during the campaign, and that Vice President Spiro Agnew had to resign in 1973 because of tax evasion charges has led to considerable debate over how

By Mike Peters for the Dayton Daily News

Sometimes vice-presidential nominees are chosen because they can raise issues and attack the opponent in a manner the presidential candidate would prefer to avoid.

the selection process could be changed to produce better nominees. The Democrats established a Vice-Presidential Selection Committee in 1972, chaired by former Vice President Hubert Humphrey. The committee made three major recommendations: (1) establish a screening committee for prospective vice-presidential nominees, (2) extend the convention from 4 days to 5, and (3) give the presidential nominee the option of postponing the decision to a mini-convention to be held 21 days after the regular convention adjourns. In 1972 the Republicans established a Rule 29 Committee that heard testimony in 1974 on this subject, but since the chairman of the committee (Rep. W. Steiger, R-Wisconsin) opposed substantial changes, it is unlikely that the Republicans will accomplish very much in the near future.[59] It has been suggested that vice-presidential candidates be allowed to run for the nomination during the primaries; and several states have provisions that could accommodate such a campaign. Former Governor Endicott Peabody (D-Massachusetts) actually campaigned for the spot in 1972, but he was passed over by George McGovern.

The need for a more rational process of selecting a vice-presidential nominee was also apparent in 1976. Since Jimmy Carter had secured the nomination long before the convention, he had a great deal of time in which to evaluate prospective vice-presidential candidates. Carter's supporters felt that he chose deliberately and well. However, the chaos of the Republican convention reflected the way in which President Gerald Ford chose Senator Robert Dole (R-Kansas) to be his running mate. Challenged by Reagan's Rule 16C strategy, Ford had eliminated most of the more obvious choices— Senator Howard Baker, William Ruckelshaus, and Governor Reagan—and rejected the suggestion to turn over the choice to the convention. The original plan after the nomination was for President Ford to retire by midnight, but Ford was up until 6 A.M. trying to find a way to heal the wounds of the party. After a couple of hours of sleep, Ford arose and decided on Robert Dole to the surprise of some of his advisers. Ford's method was in the traditional manner: rushed, personal, and slightly irrational.[60] It should be noted that by late October Walter Mondale was adding 3 extra percentage points in the polls to the Carter ticket, while Dole was hurting the Ford ticket. Vice-presidential nominees rarely add to a ticket's strength; only Edmund Muskie and Walter Mondale have lent strength in recent years. By the last week of the campaign, Jimmy Carter was running on the coattails of Walter Mondale. "Remember," Carter said on October 27, 1976, "You're voting for a ticket, not just one man. . . . Carter-Mondale, that's our ticket. Ford-Dole, that's the other ticket."[61]

The Delegates and Convention Behavior
There was never a calmer and better organized convention in American political history than the extravaganza put on by the Republicans in Miami Beach in 1972. The nomination decision had long since been made, and so all the delegates had to do was to sit back and enjoy the show. That year the Democrats tore themselves apart at their convention, one that was so disorganized that the presidential nomination acceptance speech was delayed until after the national television audience had

retired for the night. Reversing roles in 1976, the Democrats demonstrated harmony and coordination, while the Republicans ripped themselves apart in Kansas City. The key factor in determining the dominant pattern of behavior at a national convention is whether the delegates have already decided who will be the presidential nominee. Paul T. David, Ralph Goldman, and Richard C. Bain have developed a typology of convention types that categorizes conventions according to the level of evident conflict. The lowest conflict type is the *confirmation* convention, in which the nominee is an incumbent or the accepted and recognized head of the party. Richard Nixon's renomination in 1972 and Lyndon Johnson's nomination in 1964 exemplify this type of convention. A second type of low conflict convention is when a *natural successor* is widely accepted among the party leaders and delegates. Natural successors are not common in this century, but Taft's 1908 and Nixon's 1960 nominations belong in this category. High conflict conventions occur when no leader has secured the nomination by convention time, or, if he has, there is still significant opposition. Examples of *non-consensual* nominations include Ford (1976), McGovern (1972), Humphrey (1968), Goldwater (1964), Stevenson (1952), Eisenhower (1952), Dewey (1948), and Willkie (1940).[62]

Over the years a classical model of convention political behavior has emerged; it is now being challenged as party scholars reevaluate the results of the 1968, 1972, and 1976 conventions. The classical model looked like this, as constructed by Sullivan and his colleagues in 1972:

1. The state delegations are the key units for bargaining and communication.
2. The party rank-and-file is manipulated by the leadership.
3. Leaders try to stay uncommitted as long as possible in order to maximize their political power.
4. The vice-presidential nomination is used to mollify the nominee's opponents.
5. After the convention, the various factions will rally around the ticket.[63]

The state delegations now have a major competitor for the allegiance of the delegates—the special interest caucuses. Women, Latins, blacks, youth, senior citizens, liberals, conservatives, and others regularly meet at the conventions to try to work out common strategies and issue positions. However, research on the 1972 and 1974 Democratic conventions indicated that while the caucuses played a significant role during the off-year meeting, they were relatively powerless during the nominating conventions. They simply could not compete with the more powerful candidate organizations when a crosscutting issue emerged. Delegates are still organized by, communicated to, and controlled by the state delegations.

With respect to the second point, delegates are no longer passive; more and more they are issue- and candidate-oriented and unwilling to follow the dictates of party bosses if there is any conflict with their own individual value systems. The rise of "uncontrolled" delegates is due to changes in the delegate-selection rules and an increase in the number of purist delegates, especially since the 1952 Stevenson Democratic convention and the 1964 Goldwater Republican convention.[64] Purist delegates are generally defined as those who are more interested in ideological or issue positions than in candidates or electoral success. Their counterparts, the professional delegates, emphasize the selection of "a winning candidate," rather than issue or ideological purity. Purists attended the 1964 and 1976 Republican conventions in great numbers, and they dominated the 1972 Democratic convention. Between 1972 and 1976 there was a significant increase in the percentage of professionals at the Democratic convention. Sullivan and his colleagues found that only 36 percent of the 1972 Democratic convention delegates had a professional outlook, whereas they made up 49 percent of the 1976 delegates. As one would expect, the proportion of purists or professionals who supported the different candidates varied greatly. The supporters of Carter, Jackson, and Humphrey were the most professional; the followers of Wallace and the leftist candidates were the most purist.[65] Much was made of the fact that 80 percent of the 1972 Democratic convention delegates were attending their first convention; this might help to explain the high percentage of purist (or amateur) delegates at that convention. However, Johnson and Hahn's study of more than 50,000 delegates who attended national party conventions between 1940 and 1968 found that 63 percent of the Democratic and 65 percent of the Republican delegates were attending their first convention and that most of the others had attended only one previous convention. They concluded that the turnover of convention delegates was a fact of political life and that liberalness (not inexperience) was the main difference between 1972 and previous conventions.[66]

The question still remains: Are the delegates generally searching for a winner or are they looking for an issue-articulator? Conventional wisdom holds that the delegates are looking for someone who can first of all win the nomination; second, win the election; and last, make a reasonably good president.[67] Observers of the Goldwater and McGovern conventions frequently noted the "I'd rather be right than win" attitudes of some of the more extreme delegates. Such an attitude was also found among the Ronald Reagan delegates at the 1976 GOP convention, where only one-fourth of his supporters preferred a winning candidate to purity on the issues, whereas nearly half of the Ford delegates wanted a winner first.[68] President Ford and Ronald Reagan met head on in 22 primaries in 1976, with the latter winning ten times and outpolling the president by 4.6 million to 4.5 million votes; but the public opinion polls showed Reagan as offering a weaker challenge to Jimmy Carter in November.[69] The delegates' desire to be with the winner are clearly illustrated by the events at the Democratic conventions of 1932 and 1976. Jim Farley, President Roosevelt's campaign manager, used as a criterion for patronage and other political favors the letters FRBC (For Roosevelt before Chicago). Thus, those who jumped on the FDR bandwagon early received special attention while latecomers had to wait. The week following the 1976 primaries, Governor Jerry Brown sought to win the support of Louisiana Governor Edwin Edwards and 14 Democratic delegates. Edwards refused to give Brown a full endorsement, which he noted would be "tantamount to buying the last ticket on the Titanic."[70]

With the increase in the number of independent delegates, there has been a corresponding decrease in the power of the old party bosses. Traditionally the bosses controlled blocs of delegates loyal to them, and these blocs could be shifted easily from one candidate to another as the boss decided. Governor Thomas Dewey (R-New York), Mayor Richard Daley (D-Chicago), and John Bailey (longtime boss of the Connecticut Democratic Party) demonstrated this power in their respective party conventions. However, the Daleys, Deweys, and Baileys are now gone from the political scene as is this style of politics. Now the only powerful political boss at a convention is an incumbent president. In 19 of the 21 conventions since the Civil War presidents have been successful in securing their own renomination or designating their successors.[71] Two examples are the nomination of Hubert Humphrey in 1968 and Gerald Ford in 1976. The president sets the date for the convention (the 1968 Democratic convention was scheduled for President Johnson's birthday in August), dictates the party platform, designates the officials of the convention, influences the selection of many of the delegates, and controls the special working committees of the convention by controlling the National Committee.[72]

The Convention as a Media Event.   Not for 25 years has a national convention actually chosen a presidential nominee. Rather than serving as the final step of the nominating process, conventions have become the first phase of the general election campaign. Conventions in the 1970s have included between 2000 and 3000 delegates, 10,000 guests and officials, and 11,000 media representatives who interpret the proceedings for the public. It is this one group—the media representatives—who have most changed the format of the conventions. No longer can a party afford to "waste" its media exposure on the endless speeches and demonstrations of the pre-television era. Both Democrats and Republicans, but especially the former, have taken steps to streamline their format so that their conventions are pleasing to the media. For example, the Democrats have banned all floor demonstrations, placed strict time limits on nomination speeches, and virtually eliminated favorite-son nominations.[73] In addition, both parties have adjusted their convention rules to make it more difficult for minority planks to reach the floor of the convention, thus avoiding long, boring debates during prime-time television.

Since the roll call of the states for the presidential and vice-presidential nominations lacks in any real suspense, the media highpoint has become the acceptance speeches by the nominees on the closing day of the convention. Gerald Ford's acceptance speech may well have been the highpoint of his 1976 general election campaign. No other campaign speech that year was as polished and well prepared as his acceptance speech. The president and six aides had been working on it for more than 6 weeks. Tested over and over again, the speech style was most advantageous to Ford; made up of short declarative sentences with a special rhythm and cadence, it was finally polished into a media event and then tested again in two videotaped trial runs.[74]

Increasingly, the parties are using multimedia presentations at the convention that are aimed at those present as well as the millions watching on television. In 1976, the Democrats used films on the Democratic Party and the Carter primary campaign. The 1972 Nixon renomination convention, the best organized and least spontaneous convention in American political history, was timed precisely down to the last second and films were used to set the proper mood for the convention.

The Candidates Organization. In order to control the floor action at a national convention, candidate organizations have become highly complex and effective. The prototype of the candidate organization was put together by John Kennedy in 1960. It boasted a comprehensive communications network and a wealth of data on each delegate. The delegate information was gathered as much as one year before the convention by people who did research on all those who *might* become delegates or have an influence on the convention process. At the convention one man was assigned to each state delegation and he kept in close touch with the communications center, providing information on changes in that delegation. Gerald Ford arrived in Kansas City with 200 aides and set up a trailer just off the main convention floor. The Ford organization consisted of 12 whips, a number of floor managers, and ten "floaters." Direct telephone lines were established from the communications trailer to the podium, party headquarters, the White House, Kansas City police, and the 12 whips. The whips, wearing red baseball hats, were stationed at telephones that flashed high intensity light to draw attention. The floaters, carrying walkie-talkies, were the moving trouble-shooters.[75]

Why the Conventions Will Survive. Despite the fact that conventions have not been important in the nominee-selection process for almost three decades, one should not conclude that conventions are meaningless and ought to be phased out of existence. Conventions still present the only highly visible public image of the party at the national level. They also serve an important communications function by bringing the party together at least once every 4 years (and perhaps every 2 years for the Democrats). Other significant functions include: drafting the party platform to indicate the party's stands on important contemporary issues, providing the opening phase of the presidential campaign, serving as one of the last remaining rewards to party workers and activists, and enabling the stress and conflicts that may have developed during the primary to be ameliorated.

The Race for the White House

While the nominees' acceptance speeches actually begin the real campaign to win the White House, there is usually a lull in the campaign right after the conventions as the candidates catch their breath and make plans for their intensive autumn effort. During this time the candidates make decisions about their organization and resource allocation that will set the basic strategy and tactics for the following 2 months. Time and money must be set aside for "studio days"—making the commercials that will appear on radio and television—which means many conferences and decisions. Human resource management is also important for contemporary presidential campaigns. Carter's staff took over the top three floors of an Atlanta office building, and from there they planned who was to be doing what.

One huge map of the United States has a plastic overlay, one for each week of the campaign. Travels are traced in grease pencil: a green line for Carter, blue for his wife, Rosalynn, orange for running mate Walter F. Mondale, and purple for the Carter children.

Each state was allocated so much in the way of human resources, depending upon the staff's estimate as to how much effort would be necessary to win that state in November. These allocations were converted into a point system according to the importance of each state in the over-all campaign strategy. New York, for example, was given 48 points (41 for electoral votes, 7 as the key state in the Northeast). Each principal campaigner was assigned a weighted value: a Carter visit 7 points; Mondale, 5; the wives, 3; and the candidates' children, 2. A state would then receive personal visits in certain planned combinations equal to the state's number of points.[76] By election day it was estimated that Carter had made a total of 1495 speeches in 1029 cities, covering 461,245 miles of travel, in the 2 years he had been seriously campaigning for the White House. The Carter headquarters also maintained an intelligence operation that divided the nation into ten regions and required each Carter state campaign manager to report through these regional coordinators.

Several scholars have developed the theory that candidates tend to allocate scarce campaign resources in proportion to a state's electoral votes.[77] Since all of the major states have been "swing states" in recent presidential elections, they have all received extraordinary attention from the candidates of both parties. Generally, both Carter and Ford campaigned coast-to-coast in 1976.[78] George Gallup maintained that the 1976 election was the closest in American history because a shift of only 3 percentage points in a record number of states, 28, would have changed the outcome.[79] It seems that, with the exception of just a handful of one-party leaning states, nearly every state was listed as a "possible" by the two major parties in 1976. Yet, each candidate develops a scenario for victory that combines the probable states with the possible states, adding up to an Electoral College majority. Jimmy Carter combined his solid base of the South with certain Northeastern and large urban Midwestern states, while Gerald Ford sought to add to his Western and Plains states a majority of the large Midwestern and Northeastern states.

Campaign organization and administration is a special problem for presidential candidates. Since they have to conduct a nationwide campaign, they must build an organization that can effectively administer their efforts in all 50 states and thousands of local subdivisions. The presidential campaign, although traditionally somewhat separate from the state party efforts, has become almost entirely separate due to the 1974 and 1976 federal election laws. Each candidate draws up an organizational plan that will best serve his needs and personality. Before Jimmy Carter, perhaps the most serious efforts to establish a rational, highly centralized campaign were made by Barry Goldwater in 1964 and Nixon in 1972.[80] Richard Nixon's Committee for the Re-election of the President (CREEP) was centralized in the extreme. Almost entirely administered from the White House and staffed by the president's loyal personal aides, CREEP left the Republican Party and its various committees to support congressional campaigns. Without discussing all of the aspects of the Watergate scandal, it can be said that the secretive nature of CREEP facilitated financial corruption, dirty tricks, and other reprehensible activities that would have been rejected by more professional party administrators.

After a 16-year absence, the Carter-Ford campaign saw the return of presidential campaign debates. When Senator John Kennedy debated Vice President Richard Nixon in 1960, an average of 70 million Americans watched, and this enabled Kennedy to establish his credibility as a presidential candidate. Carter and Ford had three debates in 1976 (one each on domestic, foreign, and general issues). Although these debates really resembled simultaneous press conferences held before panels of four reporters, they constituted the only highlight of the campaign. Public opinion polls favored Ford after the first debate; Carter was favored after the pivotal second debate on foreign policy, when President Ford said that Poland was outside the Iron Curtain. Perhaps more than anything, this slip of the tongue hurt Ford, and a tie between the candidates in the third debate allowed Carter to narrowly defeat Ford in November. Carter's "win" in the second debate was important to his campaign, for it boosted his credibility in the foreign policy area, in which he was assumed to be weakest. This campaign also saw the very first vice-presidential candidates' debates, and in the subsequent polls Democrat Walter Mondale easily defeated Republican Robert Dole, thereby greatly contributing to his party's ticket. An average of 80 million Americans saw the presidential debates, and well over half claimed that the debates had helped them decide how to vote. A Gallup Poll taken after the election showed that two-thirds of the American public want to see such debates again in 1980.[81] The fact that an incumbent president, Gerald Ford, requested the 1976 debates will make it quite difficult for President Carter to turn down such a challenge in 1980.

Summary

Presidential politics has been tremendously altered by the rule changes in the 1970s and the impact of modern technology. The increasing number of primaries has changed the strategic thinking of candidates; they must begin to organize very early in order to enter these primaries and to qualify for federal financial subsidies. Jimmy Carter began his campaign in September 1974 and continued throughout 1975, with more than 250 campaign days for Carter alone in 1975, not counting his wife's efforts.[82] With more proportional primaries, a candidate must enter all of them in order to maximize his delegate support. The complete federal financing of major-party nominees now requires a centralized, well-administered national campaign.

The influence of American political parties has declined since the 1950s in the matter of selecting presidential nominees. This has largely been due to the adoption of presidential primaries. Local party organizations no longer control the delegate-selection process. At present national party conventions simply ratify decisions that have been made elsewhere. Conventions have become media events that mark the beginning of the campaign for the White House; they no longer serve as the arena where crucial decisions are made. The political parties have also been gradually pushed aside during the presidential campaign. Most recent candidates have regarded the national party organizations as relatively insignificant with respect to resources, and thus have given the parties only a minor role in their campaign planning. This attitude has been reenforced by other contemporary trends such as the federal financing of presidential campaigns and the technological innovations and expertise that are now required for conducting national campaigns. Federal financing largely bypasses party organizations, which have not been able to adapt very well to the needs of media-oriented campaigns. However, parties must still be acknowledged in the selection and election of presidents. Any candidate's hope of becoming president must begin by securing the nomination of either major party. Thus, parties still function as the gatekeepers to the White House. Finally, the party's endorsement of a candidate is still the decisive factor affecting the voting decisions of millions of Americans.

FOOTNOTES

1. William R. Keech and Donald R. Matthews, *The Party's Choice* (Washington, D.C.: Brookings, 1976), Chapter 1.

2. Gerald Pomper, *Nominating the President* (New York: Norton, 1966), p. 127.

3. On May 24, 1976, the Harris Survey reported that 72 percent of the American public felt no objection to a black vice-presidential candidate, while 30 percent objected to a woman in that position, 20 percent objected to a Jew, and 20 percent objected to a Spanish American.

4. For the role of the media, see Timothy Crouse, *The Boys on the Bus* (New York: Random House, 1973); James M. Perry, *Us and Them: How the Press Covered the 1972 Election* (New York: Clarkson N. Potter, 1973); and David Broder, "Political Reporters in Presidential Politics." In *Inside the System*, edited by C. Peters and J. Fallows (New York: Praeger, 1976).

5. Donald R. Matthews, *Perspectives on Presidential Selection* (Washington, D.C.: Brookings, 1973), p. 40.

6. Ibid. In 1952 Taft won five primaries for a total of 458 delegates, while Eisenhower won four primaries securing 406 delegates.

7. In 11 states plus the District of Columbia by petition; in 9 states by the action of the state secretary of state; by nominating committees in 5 states; and in Alabama, New York, Ohio, South Dakota, and Texas the candidate's name never appears on the ballot.

8. An NBC news report on the Florida primary said that Jimmy Carter's staff had been in Florida so long before the primary on March 9, 1976, that it was listed in the telephone books.

9. Nelson W. Polsby and Aaron Wildavsky, *Presidential Elections* (New York: Scribner, 1976), p. 109.

10. Bayh was forced out on March 4; Shapp on March 12; Shriver on March 22, Harris on April 8, and Jackson May 1.

11. Polsby and Wildavsky, op. cit., p. 106.

12. *Congressional Quarterly Weekly Report*, June 5, 1976.

13. Ibid.

14. National Journal, *Politics, Parties and 1976* (Washington, D.C.: Government Research Corporation, 1977), p. 1030.

15. J. Lengle and B. Shafe, "Primary Rules, Political Power, and Social Change," *American Political Science Review 70* (March 1976), pp. 25-40.

16. *The Brookings Bulletin 13*, No. 1 (Winter 1976).

17. *The Washington Post*, February 25, 1976.

18. *San Francisco Chronicle*, June 19, 1976.

19. *The New York Times*, October 13, 1976.

20. Associated Press release, June 4, 1976.

21. *The Washington Post*, April 7, 1976.

22. Richard Stout, *The Deseret News*, February 26, 1976.

23. *Time*, May 17, 1976.

24. *Voters, Primaries and Parties* (Cambridge, Mass.: Institute of Politics, 1976), p. 27.

25. *The Washington Post*, June 10, 1976.

26. Walter Dean Burnham in *The New York Times*, July 12, 1976.

27. The Gallup Poll, *San Francisco Chronicle*, February 26, 1976.

28. Joyce Gelb and Marian Palley, *Tradition and Change in American Party Politics* (New York: Crowell, 1975), p. 260.

29. The Harris Survey, May 15, 1976.

30. *The Washington Post*, September 1, 1976.

31. When a candidate wins as much as 15 percent of the preference vote cast in a state's caucuses, he is then entitled to a proportion of that state's delegation to the national convention.

32. *Congressional Quarterly Weekly Report*, December 20, 1975.

33. *Congressional Quarterly Weekly Report*, July 10, 1976.

34. T. R. Marshall, *National Civic Review 65*, No. 8 (September 1976), pp. 390-393. Everett Ladd noted that "in the 28 states that held presidential primaries (1976) and kept statewide data on them, just 28 percent of the voting-age population went to the poles." In states where delegates were selected by caucuses, just 1.9 percent of the voting-age population participated. George F. Will, "GOP'S Weird Physics,"*Deseret News*, November 15, 1977.

35. *Congressional Quarterly Weekly Report*, December 20, 1975.

36. Marshall, op. cit., p. 390.

37. David Broder, *The Washington Post*, April 28, 1976.

38. *Congressional Quarterly Weekly Report*, December 20, 1976.

39. Ibid., July 10, 1976.

40. John S. Saloma and Frederick H. Sontag, *Political Parties* (New York: Vintage), pp. 52-53.

41. Ibid., p. 53.

42. David Broder, *The Washington Post*, September 1, 1976.

43. *The New York Times*, August 15, 1976.

44. The Canadian political parties apportion delegates to their national conventions among public officeholders; provincial party representatives; local organization representatives; and representatives of youth, women, and student organizations. For details, see Carl Baar and Ellen Baar, "Party and Convention Organizations and Leadership Selection in Canada and the United States," in Matthews, op. cit., pp. 49-84.

45. *Guide to U.S. Elections* (Washington, D.C.: Congressional Quarterly Press, 1976), p. 94.

46. *The New York Times*, July 12, 1976.

47. *Guide to U.S. Elections*, op. cit., p. 12.

48. *Kansas City Star*, August 29, 1976.

49. David Truman, *The Governmental Process* (New York: Knopf, 1951), pp. 282-283.

50. Reprinted in the *Salt Lake Tribune*, August 16, 1976.

51. *The Wall Street Journal*, August 16, 1976.

52. Gerald M. Pomper, *Elections in America* (New York: Dodd, Mead, 1971), p. 185.

53. Sullivan, op. cit., p. 71.

54. Ibid., p. 75.

55. *The San Francisco Examiner*, June 25, 1976.

56. *The New York Times*, July 12, 1976.

57. *The Washington Post*, July 13, 1976.

58. Carl D. Tubbesing, "Vice-Presidential Candidates and the Home State Advantage: or 'Tom Who?'" *Western Political Quarterly 26*, No. 4 (December 1973), pp. 702-716.

59. *Congressional Quarterly Weekly Report*, July 3, 1976.

60. President Ford referred to Senator Dole as a "team player," of similar philosophy with an abrasive wit. *The Washington Post*, August 20, 1976.

61. Patrick Caddel, *The New York Times*, October 29, 1976. Jules Witcover, *Marathon* (New York: Signet, 1977), p. 671.

62. Keech and Matthews, op. cit., pp. 179-180.

63. Sullivan, op. cit., p. 17.

64. See James Q. Wilson, *The Amateur Democrat* (Chicago: University of Chicago Press, 1966); Aaron Wildavsky, *The Revolt against the Masses* (New York: Free Press, 1971); and John Saule and James Clarke, "Amateurs and Professionals: A Study of Delegates to the 1968 Democratic National Convention," *American Political Science Review 64* (September 1970), pp. 888-899. For general works on convention behavior patterns, see Richard C. Bain and Judith H. Parris, *Convention Decisions and Voting Records* (Washington, D.C.: Brookings, 1973); Paul T. David, Ralph Goldman, and R. C. Bain, *The Politics of Party Conventions* (Washington, D.C.: Brookings, 1960); Judith H. Parris, *The Convention Problem: Issues in Reform of Presidential Procedures* (Washington, D.C.: Brookings, 1972); John Soule and

Wilma McGrath, "A Comparative Study of Presidential Nominating Conventions: The Democrats in 1968 and 1972," *American Journal of Political Science 19* (August 1975), pp. 510-511. See also Joseph Boyett, "Background Characteristics of Delegates to the 1972 Convention," *Western Political Quarterly* (September 1974).

65. *The Washington Post*, September 6, 1976.

66. Loch K. Johnson and Harlon Hahn, "Delegate Turnover at National Party Conventions, 1944-1968," in Matthews, *Perspectives,* op. cit., p. 13.

67. Saloma and Sontag, op. cit., p. 68.

68. *The Washington Post*, August 17, 1976.

69. Quote by Governor Thompson of New Hampshire in UPI release on July 27, 1976.

70. *Newsweek*, June 21, 1976.

71. Only four presidents, all in the nineteenth century, lost their nominations: Arthur (R) 1884, Pierce (D) 1856, Fillmore (Whig) 1852, Tyler (Whig) 1844.

72. See Polsby and Wildavsky, op. cit., p. 104.

73. In 1976 Adlai Stevenson, III and Robert C. Byrd ran as favorite sons in the primaries. The new rules of the Democratic convention require 50 to 200 delegates to sign a petition to place a candidate in nomination with not more than 20 from any one state. The first favorite son was George Washington, "freedom's favorite son." Others who ran as favorite sons were Van Buren in 1835, John Davis in 1924, and Harding in 1920—the last to win the presidency. *The Washington Post*, March 29, 1976.

74. *National Journal Politics, Parties and 1976*, (Washington, D.C.: Government Research Corporation, 1977), p. 1202.

75. *Newsweek*, August 23, 1976.

76. See Martin Schram, *Running for President*, (New York: Pocket Books, 1977) Appendix 3 and 4. See also Jules Witcover, *Marathon*, op. cit., Chapter 35, "The Carter Battle Plan." This latter book is the best account of a presidential campaign since Theodore White's, *The Making of the President—1960.*

77. See Steven J. Brams and Morton D. Davis, "The 3/2's Rule in Presidential Campaigning," *American Political Science Review 68* (March 1974), and C. Colantoni, T. Levesque, and P. Ordeshook, "Campaign Resource Allocation under the Electoral College," *APSR 69* (March 1975), pp. 141-1561.

78. From the beginning of the formal campaign until October 23rd, Jimmy Carter traveled 42,000 miles, visiting 35 states and 70 cities.

79. George Gallup, *The Deseret News*, November 9, 1976.

80. For two classic pieces of research on campaign organization, see Karl A. Lamb and Paul A. Smith, *Campaign Decision-Making* (Belmont,. Calif.: Wadsworth, 1968), and John H. Kessel, *The Goldwater Coalition* (Indianapolis, Ind.: Bobbs-Merrill, 1968).

81. Gallup Poll, November 28, 1976.

82. *Newsweek*, September 13, 1976. For the journalist's accounts of the presidential elections since 1960, see Theodore White's *The Making of the President, 1960 (1964, 1968, 1972)* (New York: Atheneum, 1961 [1965, 1968, 1973]).

9
Parties and Government: A Continuing Relationship

Parties still play a notable role in government,[1] although it is primarily through organization, appointment, and election procedures, rather than by governing. None of the branches of the state or federal government is insulated from party influence, although at times an election or appointment is claimed to be nonpartisan, or the influence is otherwise denied. The party affiliation of the members in Congress is the basis for organizing Congress; and it was the machinery of the congressional Democratic Party that successfully challenged the seniority system in the House of Representatives and brought about many other procedural reforms in 1975. At the state level, the parties are still influential in the legislative chambers of the nation, although this influence varies.

Parties also affect the executive and judicial branches of government via the appointment process. On taking office, a president must fill some 2000 appointive positions; partisanship is still an important consideration. Contrary to the myth of judicial nonpartisanship, 90 percent of all Supreme Court Justices have belonged to the appointing president's political party. In addition, party membership is a factor in both lower federal court appointments and state court elections and appointments.

The parties' role in government can best be illustrated by examining the organization and voting behavior of legislatures, executive appointments, and judicial decisions. It will be seen that party influence is pervasive; this will help to ensure the parties' survival in the immediate future.

PARTY INFLUENCE IN THE LEGISLATURES
Party influence is obvious in both the Congress and the state legislatures. The organization of Congress is based upon political parties and the committee system; these sometimes affect the shaping of public policy. The political skills of the House Democrats in the 94th Congress reinvigorated the party caucus, which challenged the seniority system and influenced various legislative matters as well. Because of the caucus's actions in 1975, changes were made in the power of committee chairmen, the Demo-

cratic Rules Committee members were instructed to support an anti-oil depletion allowance amendment, and the caucus went on record as opposing any further military aid to Indochina. Democratic conservatives—many of whom suffered at the hands of the generally liberal-controlled caucus—rebelled against the legislative role that the caucus had assumed and threatened to take the matter to the press and the public. Both conservatives and liberals felt that the caucus was becoming either too overbearing or too strong as a policy adviser; their views were expressed in such statements as, "We've got to stop this damn caucus from legislating."[2]

Despite the success of the caucus in influencing the organization and operation of the House, the Democrats could not extend this influence to substantive issues. Thus, they failed to secure the votes necessary for overriding the president's vetoes, despite a Democratic majority in both houses. Congress ended its 1976 session with only 12 successful overrides of presidential vetoes out of 27 attempts.

The influence of the parties in state legislatures varies widely. Therefore, one cannot generalize about the relationship between the parties and the legislature. In the urban-industrial states, where the political strength of the parties is competitive, or in those states where Democratic and Republican legislators represent different socioeconomic constituencies, the party most definitely influences decision-making. On the other hand, in those state legislatures where competition between parties is minimal (one-party states) and in nonindustrial states, there is little party influence. In state legislatures, party influence is often somewhat masked and difficult to ascertain; however, the parties are certainly important to state policy-makers.

Parties in Congress

The phrase "organizing by party and voting by coalition" aptly describes the main function of the parties in Congress. While parties and committees both help to organize Congress, each performs different functions. Committees facilitate a division of labor among congressmen, allowing for the careful scrutiny of many legislative matters, while parties help to direct and organize the committees' work.

Parties versus Committees. Parties perform several basic functions that are aimed at either promoting or blocking legislation:

1. They select leaders who are responsible for advancing the business of the chamber.
2. Party leaders help choose those who will fill subsidiary leadership positions.
3. The leaders appoint members to the various committees.
4. The leaders control the legislative agenda.
5. The leaders serve as a liaison between Congress and the executive branch.

In order to perform these functions, parties have developed an apparatus that includes both formal positions and informal party groups (see Table 9.1). Although both houses of Congress organize separately and differently, they do so for the same reasons.

Table 9.1 Party organization in 1976 Congress

House of Representatives

Democrats	Republicans
Speaker	Minority Floor Leader
Chairman of the Caucus[a]	Chairman of the Conference[a]
Majority Floor Leader	Minority Whip
Majority Whip	Regional Whips
Deputy and Assistant Whips	Committee on Committees
Steering and Policy Committee	Policy Committee
Democratic National Congressional Committee	National Republican Congressional Committee
Patronage Committee	

Senate

Democrats	Republicans
Majority Leader	Minority Leader
Majority Whip	Minority Whip
Chairman of the Conference[a]	Chairman of the Conference[a]
Policy Committee	Policy Committee
Steering Committee	Committee on Committees
Senatorial Campaign Committee	Senatorial Campaign Committee
	Personnel Committee

[a]The conference and caucus consists of all members of the given party.

Party Conferences (Caucuses)

A review of the activities of the party conferences underscores the gap between theory and practice in the workings of American political institutions. Theoretically the party conference (or caucus, as the Democrats call it), staffed by all members of the respective parties elected to Congress, is the governing agency of the party; in fact, it has generally been used by the elected leaders to further their own programs. The conference's tasks have been largely confined to selecting party leadership. The awkwardly large size of the conference, the inability to make decisions that will be binding on individual members, and the unwillingness of the leaders to share authority with the conference's general membership—all of these obstacles have seriously hampered the conference in trying to promote meaningful debate among members, and to become a deliberative body making party policy. Instead, the conferences select party leaders and serve as informal channels of communication between the leaders and the conference members.

Before the 1960s, the Democratic caucus exercised power for only a short period. During the Wilson Administration party loyalty and binding caucus decisions were the order of the day; thereafter, there was a steady decline in the power of the caucus. The Republican conference has consistently failed in its attempts to become a policy-making agent in government. Since the 1960s, the Democrats have turned again to the caucus as an instrument of reform and have attempted to develop a party legislative program. For 50 years the House Democratic caucus did nothing except elect the party leaders and nominate candidates for Speaker of the House or members of the Ways and Means Committee; then, in 1969, the Democrats began to revitalize the party caucus, which has now become a more powerful agent. In the middle and late 1960s moderate and liberal House Democrats began discussing how the party might be strengthened in the House; they decided that the caucus might be the most viable instrument. Agreeing on the need for regular discussion and exchange of information, the Democrats decided to schedule monthly meetings with the beginning of the 91st Congress in 1969.

In 1973 the caucus adopted a resolution permitting a secret vote for committee chairmen if one-fifth of the committee members requested such a vote. The Steering and Policy Committee was also created in 1973 to assist the House leadership in developing party and legislative priorities, scheduling floor debate, and working with Senate Democrats. The caucus then adopted a rule guaranteeing at least one major committee assignment to all Democratic Party members, and placed three new members on the Democratic Committee on Committees. The power of the caucus was further enhanced during 1974-1975, when it successfully transferred the power to make committee assignments from the Ways and Means Committee to the Democratic Steering and Policy Committee, required all committees with more than 20 members to establish at least four subcommittees, required that the chairmen of the Appropriations subcommittees be approved by the caucus, expanded the Ways and Means Committee from 25 to 37 members, and deposed three senior chairmen of powerful House committees.

House Democrats have had mixed reactions to this assertion of power by the caucus, and the future of the caucus is not clear. The conservatives were particularly upset by the fact that the caucus intervened in substantive issues, again raising the question of whether the party should provide and enforce policy guidelines for its members. As a consequence, several Democratic House members have threatened to open up the caucus to the press.

Democratic freshmen and liberals are afraid that party unity may be threatened by continued reliance on the caucus as an instrument for developing and enforcing party policy on specific legislative matters. Conservative members see the caucus as having only a limited role—serving as a safeguard against procedural abuses and as an arena for discussing only broad policy areas. These members feel that the caucus must carefully avoid undermining the committee system.

The Policy Committees

Policy bodies in name only, the policy committees have served as forums for discussions, channels of communication between party leaders and members, and most recently as research sources on important issues. Created for the purpose of developing comprehensive party policy for each party, they have not been able to enhance party influence in Congress:

> *They have never been "policy" bodies, in the sense of considering and investigating alternatives of public policy. The committees do not assume leadership in drawing up a general legislative program . . . and only rarely have the committees labeled their decisions as "party politics."*[3]

If the party committees had more authority, the independent power of the leaders of both houses of Congress would be threatened; the committees' influence over legislation would decline; and the freedom of individual congressmen to vote for or against issues would decline. Finding these consequences unattractive, members of Congress have been reluctant to establish a centralized party committee to shape legislative policy.

Amid the repeated calls for greater party responsibility in Congress and numerous suggestions for its reform, the Legislative Reorganization Act of 1946 was introduced. It called for the creation of policy committees for both parties in both houses that would formulate comprehensive legislative policy. The measure was passed by the Senate but rejected by the House. Nevertheless, the Senate created its own policy committees in 1947; 2 years later, the House Republicans followed suit, converting their steering committee into a policy committee. The House Democrats delayed creating a policy committee until 1973.

The two policy committees in the Senate differ significantly in both organization and function. The Republican committee is more institutionalized than its Democratic counterpart; it operates under formal rules with specified terms of service for committee members and a membership selected independently of the floor leadership. The members of the Republican Policy Committee are elected by the party conference;

although other party leaders—including the floor leader, whip, and the chairman of the Committee on Committees—sit on the committee, they have no vote. The elected members are limited to a 2-year term, and the committee's responsibilities are set forth by the Republican conference.

In contrast, the Democratic Policy Committee is not institutionalized; it functions as a tool of the party floor leader; its ten members are chosen by the floor leader and appointed for indefinite terms. The committee makes no pretense of functioning as an independent center of power. Before 1959, the Republican committee had been generally dormant, meeting irregularly, and characterized as "a debating society." Then, in 1958, junior and senior members of the House sought to strengthen the image of their party. With a new chairman, John W. Byrnes of Wisconsin, the Policy Committee became revitalized. The committee held regular weekly meetings to discuss pending legislation, issued policy statements, and hired a staff to conduct research on current policy issues. With these changes the Republicans began to formulate alternatives to policies offered by the Democrats.

Following this effort to remake the Republican Policy Committee into an instrument for building party consensus on policy issues, the committee established a Subcommittee on Special Projects to try to develop long-range policies; these policies were supplemented with research into specific policy areas. This was the beginning of the House Republicans' attempts to develop alternative sources of research so that they would not have to rely on the expertise of the standing committees' staffs. The Policy Committee has also tried to improve its image and to take a more active role in policy decision-making; it has done this by increasing the number of younger members on the committee, forming an independent Committee on Planning and Research to supplant the Subcommittee on Special Projects, trying to get press coverage of its activities.

The potential for dominating the Democratic Policy Committee was evident during Lyndon Johnson's term as Majority Leader. Lyndon Johnson, who believed that policy was the sole responsibility of the standing committees and not the Policy Committee, held a tight rein over this committee and used it only as a bargaining table, a meeting place for exchange and compromise among the party influentials. Instead of seeking a geographically balanced committee membership with varying amounts of seniority, Johnson installed a committee that was described as a "board of elders"—it was composed of those Senators who were closest to Johnson and nearly all of them came from the West and South.

Attempting to free the Policy Committee from the grips of the floor leaders, the Democratic conference, since the time of Johnson, has required a geographical balance and has asked that the floor leader's appointments to the Policy Committee be subject to party conference approval. Despite these admonitions, the Policy Committee still functions at the floor leader's discretion, and there has been no indication that the committee will emerge as an independent body.

Lawmakers have been unwilling to relinquish their independence from party control, and have cautiously guarded their freedom to relate to their constituencies without party interference. This is understandable, since the party's policy might be in conflict with the perceived needs of the congressman's constituency. Another reason why the parties have been unable to maintain stricter loyalty among their members is that they cannot provide essential campaign services. Each party has a campaign committee in each house that was created in order to assist party members either in their election or reelection; the committees provide campaign funds, information about the voting behavior of the state or congressional district and its pertinent issues, roll-call voting records of the members' opponents, a speakers bureau together with ghostwritten speeches, and a staff to help the candidates with public relations. The campaign committees are staffed by members of each chamber. Each state party delegation in the House selects one of its members to serve on the committee, while party leaders in the Senate appoint their colleagues to serve. The House committee usually has 35 to 40 members, while its Senate committee usually has fewer than 10 members.

Although the committees' resources have been limited, the Republican House Campaign Committee has tried to provide the type of assistance required in this era of "new politics." Sometimes the campaign committees' activities have caused dissension, especially in the matter of distributing campaign funds. Some Republican Senators complained bitterly over the way in which campaign funds were distributed in 1970; it was alleged that the Republican Senatorial Campaign Committee had favored George Bush, a senatorial candidate from Texas. The committee allocated $73,000 to Bush and $37,000 to Ralph Smith of Illinois; both of these candidates lost. On the other hand, Glenn Beall, a senatorial candidate from Maryland, received no financial support from the committee, and yet he won his bid for election.[4]

Party Leadership

The Speaker. The Speaker has several roles which together give him decisive power over the course of legislation and over his colleagues; thus, he is the principal leader of the majority party. The Speaker, selected by the party conference, does the following: (1) he serves as party spokesman to the president—communicating to him the pulse of the Congress, and in turn relaying the president's priorities to Congress; (2) as a strategist, he decides how best to maneuver the majority party's proposals through the legislative maze; and (3) as presiding officer of the House, he decides which committee will receive which bill—a discretion that eases the passage of the majority party's program through the legislative process. Together with these roles, the Speaker has resources that enhance his power of persuasion in the politics of the House. He is influential in deciding committee assignments and is valuable in disseminating information on policy issues. Finally, he dispenses invaluable, intangible rewards (what Ripley calls "the resources of psychological preferment"): recognition of a colleague, acknowledgment of a job well done, displays of trust or respect for fellow party members—rewards that cause other party members to look to him for recognition and approval.

Although the power of the Speaker is decisive, it is now a matter of personal influence. He can urge members to uphold party positions, but he cannot enforce party discipline. Up until the early part of this century, the Speaker used to exercise much greater power. At that time, the Speaker was essentially a despotic ruler. Among other things, the Speaker had exclusive authority to appoint committee members; he had absolute power of recognition on the floor; he was chairman of the House Rules Committee, and thus could interpret and create House rules to suit himself; he entertained floor motions as he chose; and he appointed committee chairmen.

As a result of various reforms, today's Speaker must secure through persuasion and bargaining that which former Speakers could obtain by autocratic rule. The Speaker can no longer appoint members or chairmen of standing committees, and he is no longer chairman of the Rules Committee. The role of the House of Representatives in the federal government, however, is said to be growing because the numerous programs that require federal funding must originate in the House; concomitant with this rise in the House's power will be an increase in the Speaker's influence. Although the Speaker must now share the power that was once exclusively his, he still controls the parliamentary machinery of the House.[5]

Floor Leaders. With the exception of the majority party in the House of Representatives, the floor leader is generally regarded as the principal spokesman for party positions and interests. In the House, the Speaker is the spokesman. The floor leader, chosen by the party caucus, acts as a mediator in both intraparty and interparty negotiations, and serves as a channel of communication between the President and his congressional parties. With no formal sanctions that he can use to shape the legislative programs, the principal tool of the floor leader is the art of persuasion.

In carrying out his job, the floor leader must decide on party strategy; this includes determining how to steer party-supported legislation through the legislative obstacle course and how to marshal votes to secure passage of the legislation. The party floor leader must work closely with chairmen and senior members of the standing congressional committees and develop a working rapport with the other party members. His role is chiefly conciliatory; in attempting to persuade most of his party's members to support certain legislation, he must usually avoid extreme ideological positions. To aid him in this role, the floor leader, like the Speaker, has several "rewards" he can confer upon party faithful, including committee assignment recommendations, support for desired legislation, campaign assistance, and consideration in the scheduling of legislation.

The Whips. The whips are selected to help the floor leaders in marshaling party members. They bear the chief responsibility for seeing that members are present for critical roll-call votes and for keeping party members informed about the legislative schedule. Before the vote, the whips must assess their fellow members' positions on the pending legislation and inform them of the party's position. Since "reliable information is a precious commodity in both houses,"[6] the whips must also determine the Speaker's or Senate President's legislative priorities and sympathies, as well as those of the other legislators. Party leaders, therefore, use the whips to relay information and to bargain with other members.

Informal Party Groups

In addition to the formal organization of the party in Congress, several informal party groups meet to discuss legislative issues and alternative strategies, including the Democratic Study Group and the liberal Republican organization, the Wednesday Club.

The House Democratic Study Group (DSG), the best-known of these groups, was begun by a group of liberal Democrats in 1957 to counter the Southern conservative wing of the party. The DSG has several functions, including conducting research on policy questions, preparing fact sheets on forthcoming legislation, and informing its members of the weekly schedule of floor action. Since its inception, the group has developed into a significant "whip" organization, making sure that its members are on the floor when votes are needed. The unity of the DSG members on party-supported programs and policies is notable; about 90 percent of members vote together on these legislative issues. Since 1964 the DSG has also been providing financial campaign assistance to liberal Democratic candidates.

The Wednesday Club represents only a small proportion of Republican House members. Established in 1963, the club has neither the detailed organization nor the budget of the Democratic group. However, it does research for its members; the members meet to exchange information on pending legislation; and the group shows a high degree of voting unity.

INFLUENCING THE VOTE

Aside from serving as an organizational base in Congress, do political parties influence legislative decisions? Can the parties influence policy by controlling the behavior of individual congressmen? To measure party influence, scholars have examined the behavior of party members on roll-call votes. For this purpose, they have defined "party vote" as simply a roll-call vote in which at least a majority of one party opposed at least a majority of the other party.[7] The relatively high number of party votes—one-third to one-half of the total roll-call votes—indicates that party identification is the most important factor in congressional voting behavior. The rise and fall of partisan voting has generally been attributed to two factors: (1) when the president is of a different party than the majority party in Congress, there is a larger proportion of party votes; and (2) as an election campaign draws near, there is less party unity in roll-call votes. "While party seems to influence the votes of individual congressmen to a greater extent than other factors, it is by no means always decisive."[8]

Another method of determining party influence in congressional decision-making is by examining the support given to president-supported legislation, for congressmen tend to support the president or unite against him according to their party affiliation. With but a few exceptions, party members in both houses can usually be counted upon to support their president's legislation.

Differences in Policy

Do the policy orientations of the two major parties differ? The answer is a qualified yes. There is often a partisan division on legislation pertaining to the government's role in regulating domestic and foreign affairs. Democrats have generally supported a broader, more inclusive role for the government, while Republicans have traditionally opposed such expansion. Keefe identifies five major policy areas in which the two major parties differ:

1. The tariff: Republicans have generally favored a high tariff, and Democrats a low tariff.
2. Agriculture: Republicans have traditionally opposed federal programs that give the government a larger, more regulative role in farming. Democrats have held that the government should help protect the farmer from the economic hazards of the marketing system.
3. Labor: Republicans have consistently opposed federal interference in labor-management negotiations; they have supported open-shop working conditions and opposed increased federal expenditures for either unemployment insurance benefits or health and welfare programs. Democrats, on the other hand, have wanted the government to develop more programs for improving education and health care and for combating poverty.
4. Business: While Democrats have favored the interests of labor, Republicans have been more concerned about the interests of businessmen, private enterprise, and the market system.
5. Foreign policy: The differences in party policy orientations are not always clear. Studies of congressional voting before World War II indicated that Democrats generally favored international organizations and increased defense spending, while Republicans leaned toward isolationism and a commitment to neutrality, with a concomitant limitation on foreign aid.[9] Studies of later voting behavior, however, indicate that there are no longer distinct partisan differences on issues of foreign policy; one can only say that "Democrats are more inclined than Republicans to internationalist and pro-foreign aid positions."[10] The region that the congressman represents, as well as the demographic and social characteristics of his constituents, affect his voting on foreign policy issues to a greater extent than party identification.[11] This was particularly evident in the 1960s; coastal lawmakers of both parties supported federal aid programs for foreign countries, while congressmen from the interior opposed not only the financing, but the principle of granting foreign aid.

Counter Pressures

While legislators of the same party tend to vote together "more often than not" (about 60 percent of the time), four other factors also influence the legislators' decisions. These include the legislator's background, constituency characteristics, committee membership, and decisions made by the standing committee. The exact weight of each factor is unknown, but it varies according to the issue under consideration.

There is a distinct relationship between a legislator's personal background and his voting behavior. "What a man once was before he became a politician, thus, may influence how he acts once in elective office."[12] Of these background factors, the legislator's religion, occupation, and the size of his home community are especially important. For example, congressmen from small towns in rural areas tend to be conservatives, while those from large metropolitan areas tend to be liberals. Legislators from the fields of law, teaching, or journalism, and those whose religious affiliation is Catholic, Episcopalian, or Presbyterian are more likely to support a civil rights program than those of other occupations or religious persuasions.

The characteristics of the legislator's constituency also are strongly related to his legislative decisions, including the degree of interparty competition, the geographical location of the constituency, and the demographic makeup of the district (particularly the urban-rural split). Although political scientists agree that constituency factors influence congressional actions, it is not clear precisely how. One group of researchers concluded that where interparty competition is high in a district where the margin of the legislator's electoral victory was less than 55 percent, the legislator is more likely to follow the lead of his party. This legislator feels compelled to weigh carefully his constituents' preferences. On the other hand, legislators from safe districts, where the winner receives more than 60 percent of the vote, generally feel freer to support or oppose the party's programs. The representative from a safe district may feel more at liberty to consider his own personal preferences instead of his party's or his constituents' positions. After examining the relationship between the size of the electoral victory margin and legislative voting behavior, MacRae concluded that Republicans from safe districts were more likely to ignore constituency preferences than their colleagues from districts where the victory margin was less than 55 percent. He did not, however, find such a relationship between the size of a Democratic legislator's winning margin and his voting behavior.[13]

Other party analysts, however, claim that increased interparty competition promotes individualism, since candidates seek to establish an identity that is distinct from their opponents; hence, Democrats in highly competitive districts will lean toward liberal positions, while Republicans will adopt a more conservative posture.[14] Although the precise effects of interparty competition on voting behavior are unclear, it appears that this variable either encourages support for the party's position on issues, or creates an environment in which the legislator feels greater freedom to follow his own preferences.

The geographical location of a legislator's constituency also seems to affect his vote. Congressmen from the same or similar areas have discernible similarities in their voting records. Among Democrats, there are significant differences between policies supported by Northern and Southern congressmen. Southern Democrats usually take more conservative positions, opposing increased governmental spending and advocating less federal involvement with civil rights, social welfare, and agricultural and foreign policy. Northern Democrats, on the other hand, tend to adopt a more liberal position, supporting increases in government spending and an expanding role for government in domestic affairs. While Republicans exhibit a similar split in policy preferences (between those representing coastal constituencies and those from interior states), this division is not so decisive; Eastern Republicans, however, do tend to take a more liberal stance on civil rights than their Midwestern colleagues.

Regional splits within a party are particularly obvious in the alliance of conservative Republicans with Southern Democrats in forming the "conservative coalition." Southern Democrats have found that they share many policy positions with their Republican opponents, particularly on civil rights, military and defense issues, foreign policy, and social welfare. When Southern Democrats have teamed up with Republicans on a roll-call vote, they have been remarkably successful in opposing the liberal faction of their own party; the frequency with which this coalition appears reflects the comparative frailty of party unity (see Table 9.2).

The alliance of Southern Democrats and Republicans has been remarkably successful in influencing public policy. Although the coalition acts to *support* major pieces of legislation, its most important victories have been in *blocking* bills and amendments favored by liberal Democrats. It was this coalition that gave President Nixon the necessary support for creating the antiballistic missile system and, in 1972, succeeded in blocking legislation that would have raised the minimum wage. The coalition was instrumental in defeating a number of amendments that called for an end to, or significant restrictions on, American military involvement in southeast Asia. In 1973, it

Table 9.2 Conservative Coalition Appearances and Victories: 1970-1976

Congress	Coalition Appearance[a]	Pecentage of Victories
1970	22	66
1971	30	83
1972	27	69
1973	23	61
1974	24	59
1975	28	50
1976	24	58
1977	26	68

[a]The percentage of the recorded votes for both houses of Congress in which the coalition appeared.

Source: *Congressional Quarterly Almanac*, 1976, p. 1008. *Congressional Quarterly Almanac*, 1997, p. B-6.

defeated amendments intended to reduce U.S. troop strength overseas, passed a bill expanding American trade with foreign nations, and blocked an amendment to halt American bombing of Cambodia. In 1976 the coalition successfully blocked attempts to cut funding for the controversial B-1 bomber and sustained presidential vetoes of legislation for increased milk price support. The coalition, however, has not always been successful. It was unable, for example, to steer the Haynsworth or Carswell nominations for the U.S. Supreme Court past the temporary alliance of Eastern Republicans and Northern Democrats.

The standing committee to which a congressman belongs also affects his voting behavior. There is a tendency for members of the same standing committee to vote together on many roll-call issues. For example, members of the House Foreign Affairs Committee are more likely to support foreign aid programs than are those who do not serve on that committee. Similarly, those serving on the Senate Foreign Relations Committee are more inclined to support "internationalist" foreign policy proposals than are those who are not on that committee. It would appear that the legislator either chooses his committee because he shares its values and preferences, or they shape his thinking after he becomes a member.

A fourth influence upon a legislator's voting behavior is his tendency to support the actions of the standing committees: "Congressional decisions are often committee decisions."[15] Believing that the relevant committee has conducted a thorough investigation of the legislation, and lacking time to investigate the issues himself, the congressman generally accepts the committee's recommendation as appropriate.

Other variables also affect legislative voting behavior, including public opinion and the lobbying of interest groups. Despite the many different factors that affect the congressman's vote, his party affiliation is still the most reliable single predictor of how he will vote on any particular issue.

PARTY IN THE STATE LEGISLATURES

As in Congress, party influence is evident in both the organizational and decision-making processes of state legislatures. In all states except Nebraska, the elections of legislators are partisan. Following the election, the majority party in each house selects the Speaker of the House and the President of the Senate. Appointing the standing committees and choosing the committee chairmen is generally done by the Speaker or President; in most instances, these choices are based upon party affiliation. Partisan influence is also apparent in roll-call voting in at least one-third of the states. Table 9.3 shows this influence on the roll-call votes in 26 states. A comparative analysis of party influence would be difficult to make since it varies from state to state. It would also be difficult to assess the precise importance of political party influence, requiring a voluminous body of information about each state; however, five major variables have been identified: the degree of party competition, district characteristics, the formal and informal rules of the legislative body, the particular issue under consideration, and the strength of state and local party organizations.

Table 9.3   Party Voting in State Senates

State	Party Votes: Percentage of Nonunanimous Roll Calls with Party Majorities in Opposition[a]
California	17
Connecticut	50
Delaware	62
Idaho	30
Illinois	27
Indiana	51
Iowa	39
Kansas	35
Kentucky	39
Massachusetts	74
Michigan	58
Missouri	35
Montana	37
Nevada	28
New Hampshire	62
New Jersey	46
New York	70
Ohio	69
Oregon	29
Pennsylvania	82
Rhode Island	100
South Dakota	44
Utah	26
Vermont	40
Washington	50
West Virginia	54

[a]All roll calls in which at least 10 percent of those voting dissented from the majority position.

Source: Derived from Hugh L. LeBlanc, "Voting in State Senates: Party and Constituency Influences," *Midwest Journal of Political Science 13* (February 1969), p. 36.

Degree of Party Competition. Partisan voting in the state legislatures depends upon the level of interparty competition, which varies widely from state to state. There are, for example, one-party states in the South where "Republican politicians come in contact with the state legislature only by visiting the capital;" here, the parties have little influence on the legislatures. As one Tennessee legislator said, "You never thought about the Democratic party unless the Republicans were trying something—for example, reapportionment." In the one-party states, the party is usually heavily factionalized. In the highly competitive, two-party states, political parties have much more visible influence on legislative voting; however, the levels of party cohesion vary. Party cohesion—the tendency of party members to vote as a bloc against a similar bloc of the opposite party—varies widely both among the states and the legislative chambers within one state.

District Characteristics. The degree of industrialization and urbanization within the legislator's district, as well as the socioeconomic characteristics of the constituent population, have been found to affect the legislator's voting behavior. Although there may be a relationship between party unity in the legislature and the urbanization or industrialization of the state, this relationship is not necessarily causal. In the states where partisan unity in roll-call votes is high, the party members are likely to represent similar constituencies. In the highly urbanized and industrialized states, the Democratic state legislators usually represent the urban areas which are populated by blue collar and ethnic groups; the Republican legislators represent the higher income, suburban areas. This homogeneity of a constituency increases the likelihood that the representatives will agree on certain issues and their legislative solutions. Thus, party voting may be due to similarities among constituencies rather than feelings of party loyalty. As with the other variables that affect party influence on state legislative decisions, accurate interstate measurements would be difficult because of state differences in demographic and other sociological characteristics.

The Formal and Informal Rules. The legal-constitutional framework, methods of leadership selection, party agencies (such as the caucus), and the formal system within which a party operates within a legislature all vary from state to state, as do the informal rules or norms that legislators obey. The formal and informal rules guide the legislators in relating to one another, to their political parties, and to the governor. One party may use the formal rules to reduce the representation of another party, thereby decreasing its influence in the state legislature. One of the most obvious examples of this is gerrymandering—the process of redrawing legislative districts so that powerful blocs of the opposition party's voters are split into different districts and mixed with enough of one's own party supporters to ensure the opposition's defeat. The aim, of course, is to gain as many legislative seats as possible for one's own party. Although it has been discouraged by court decisions, gerrymandering still occurs: "District lines in some cities are drawn so carefully that they wiggle around individual apartment houses or residential blocks as a way of avoiding or including certain social classes or ethnic groups."[16]

The party is also a significant factor in selecting legislative leaders. The Speaker of the House in most bicameral legislatures is chosen by the entire state house, but actually, the Speaker is first chosen by the majority party caucus. The floor leaders in the state legislatures are generally chosen by the party caucuses; these leaders play a significant role in the day-to-day operations of the legislature by managing the legislative calendar and marshaling party members to vote for or against particular measures.

Party leaders such as the governor of the state may also significantly influence legislative decisions. Many state legislatures do not have the resources to do adequate research on legislation. "Because of their weaknesses as innovative bodies, leadership often comes not from within the body, but from the governor's office."[17]

The Particular Issue. Party cohesion appears to depend upon what legislative issue is being discussed. Legislation on elections, labor-management relations, land management, financing, taxation, and social welfare tends to produce a split along party lines. However, such issues as liquor regulation, constitutional revision, agriculture, civil rights, business regulation, and gambling are more likely to produce schisms within the parties.[18] With these latter issues, the geographical area represented by the legislator seems to be more important in determining his vote than party affiliation; this is especially true for constitutional revision and legislative reapportionment.

Strength of State and Local Party Organizations. Those states that exhibit high levels of party voting on roll calls often have strong state and local party organizations. This is attributable to the fact that such organizations keep in close touch with the state legislators. This is true in Connecticut, but it is more usual for the party organization to have a loose, low-keyed relationship with the legislators.

Four generalizations can be made about the variables that affect the party influence on state legislatures. First, party cohesion is more likely to be found in the industrialized, urbanized Northeastern states, illustrating the correlation between the levels of urbanization and industrialization and the levels of legislative party voting. Thus, party influence appears to be higher in the legislatures of New York, Pennsylvania, Ohio, Delaware, Rhode Island, Massachusetts, and Michigan than in the U.S. Congress. Party alignments in these states are significantly stronger than in the West, South, and border states.

Second, party voting is higher in states that have substantial party competition. In the noncompetitive states the party is simply one of many political organizations that attempt to influence the state legislatures. Where the party competition is vigorous, the legislatures have greater incentive to seek intraparty cohesion. Those states that have the highest party voting scores are also those that have significant levels of party competition. Third, party cohesion is high on those bills that deal with social welfare, economic issues, or legislative organization, or that have been introduced or supported by the governor. This partisan voting is only sporadic, however, in most states. Fourth, while party unity is very flexible, a prototype of what has been called the "conservative coalition" in Congress is not discernible in state legislatures.

With certain exceptions, there is clear evidence of party influence in the state legislatures. As the minority parties gain strength in the traditionally one-party states, thus creating interparty competition (particularly in the South), there will undoubtedly be more partisan influence. Since the 1950s, there has been a marked increase in partisan voting in California, and this may well represent a national trend.[19] This increased party voting may not be due to greater party organizational strength but to a stronger ideological stance on the part of individual legislators.

The Party and the Presidency

Once the president has been elected, he must establish an administration and decide on a legislative program. Securing congressional support for this program is often difficult; many presidents have found it easier to win an election than to establish their authority as president. President Kennedy lamented that "there are greater limitations upon our ability to bring about a favorable result than I had imagined."[20] An aide expressed this frustration more pointedly:

> *Everybody believes in democracy until he gets to the White House and then you begin to believe in dictatorship because it's so hard to get things done. Every time you turn around, people resist you and even resist their own job.* [21]

Electoral victory simply gives the president the right to occupy the office; it does not guarantee that his legislative program will be implemented. To build and maintain a strong, effective presidency, the chief executive has a formidable array of resources and tools of persuasion; one of these tools is, of course, the political party. Once the president is elected, he is not bound by the party policy directives— party platforms are not absolute commitments. Nor is the party the best means for obtaining the necessary congressional support for domestic programs. The expanding role of the president in domestic affairs and the increasing complexity of the issues that require decisions have made the presidency more nonpartisan. Despite these developments, the party and partisan concerns are still important. In choosing Cabinet officers, in marshaling support and maneuvering his programs through Congress, and in making appointments, the president is still guided by party considerations.

Symbol of the Party. A president simultaneously assumes a number of conflicting roles. For example, he is both a representative of the people and symbol of the party. The public envisions the party in the person of the president and presidential programs are often viewed as party programs. This association between the party and the president begins early in the campaign. Roberta Sigel's study of voter perceptions of presidential candidates disclosed that the voter's image of the candidate was almost identical to the voter's image of the candidate's party. These data suggest that voters have firmly embedded perceptions of the two political parties, and that these images are later projected onto the candidates. During the 1960 presidential campaign, for example, the voters claimed that Kennedy "represents common people" and was a "liberal spender," and these attributes are often ascribed to the Democratic Party. Likewise, the public's perceptions of Richard Nixon resembled those of the Republican Party; Nixon was viewed as being conservative on fiscal matters. Sigel concluded:

A Presidential candidate is the standard-bearer of his party, and the voter usually knows this. Even those who are not highly partisan have some image— no matter how vague and general—of the two parties. Undoubtedly, they must carry this image with them when evaluating the candidates. The candidate is thus hardly ever seen just as an individual to whom voters may respond or on whom they may project as they see fit. Further, he stands for both himself and for his party, and often the image is intensely interwoven.[22]

The president's performance in office greatly affects the party's future success in both presidential and congressional elections.

Wildavsky reminds us that we actually have two presidencies: a president of foreign affairs and a president of domestic affairs.[23] If the two presidents are not distinctly different persons, at least the authority bestowed by Congress and the American people on the president in these two areas does differ. The president's authority over matters of foreign policy is widely accepted by both Congress and the public; this is evidenced by the great latitude that Congress gives the president in negotiating treaties and regulating foreign trade. Major setbacks to presidential leadership in this area are rare; perhaps the most notable example was the Senate's refusal in 1920 to ratify the Treaty of Versailles, which would have terminated World War I for America and enrolled this country in the League of Nations. A review of congressional action on presidential legislative proposals demonstrates clearly the discrepancy between the two presidential roles: in foreign policy, the president's preferences prevail about 70 percent of the time; on domestic legislation, however, it is only 40 percent.

Presidential policy on domestic issues is viewed as a partisan matter. While the Gallup Polls usually show that a president's popularity increases after he acts to solve a foreign crisis, the public views domestic issues more critically. Franklin Roosevelt was able to command awesome public and congressional support for his programs to deal with the Great Depression during his first 3 months in office; however, he could not gain support for his proposal to expand the size of the Supreme Court. Even after his court-packing scheme was withdrawn, Roosevelt's public and congressional support declined. A president may appeal for support on a specific domestic issue. For example, President Johnson wanted public approval of civil rights legislation, and his appeal was apparently successful—by January 1964, public support had risen to 61 percent from 49 percent 3 months earlier. The public tends to be more skeptical about presidential programs on domestic issues; public support in this area tends to rise and fall with changes in its enthusiasm about the president.

Just as the public's identification of the president with his party may significantly hinder his programs, the identification may hinder other party candidates. The idea that candidates profit from the popularity of the one who heads the ticket has been substantiated, only occasionally, and the trend is not clear. This coattail effect seems to have benefited the Democrats much more than the Republicans since the 1960s. The 1964 Johnson landslide was marked by significant Democratic inroads into

Republican state legislative strength. For the first time since North Dakota achieved statehood, the Democrats gained control of one of its state houses. Democratic congressional candidates also seem to have benefited from Johnson's presence on the ticket—the congressional delegation from Iowa reversed itself from six Republicans and one Democrat to one Republican and six Democrats.

Presidential landslide victories do not necessarily affect state legislature and congressional elections. The 1972 Nixon victory was the third most lopsided in American history—the incumbent president secured 60 percent of the popular vote, yet there was a net loss of two Republican Senate seats and one governorship, and a gain of only 13 seats in the House of Representatives. Jimmy Carter's victory in 1976 did not especially help Democrats running for Congress or state legislatures. Several states supported the Democratic presidential candidate while electing a Republican governor or U.S. Senator. Carter carried Pennsylvania with a margin of more than 100,000 votes, but Republican H. John Heinz III was elected to the Senate. Delaware cast a majority vote for Carter, but reelected both a Republican governor and senator. In 13 states, the coattail effect appeared to be reversed, that is, the Democratic presidential candidate ran *behind* other party candidates. Although a Democrat was elected to the White House, the party ratio did not change in the Senate and changed only slightly in the House.

Presidential assistance to other candidates' campaigns appears to be most significant in very close elections. President Ford's appearance on behalf of Senator Robert Dole of Kansas in 1974 may have been the decisive factor in Dole's election. His Democratic opponent, Representative William R. Roy, had been predicted to win by the opinion polls just before Ford's last-minute appearance, but then Dole managed to win the election with 51 percent of the total votes cast.

Just as the president chooses what role he will play in the formulation and passage of congressional legislation, he also decides what role he will play in his party's organization and function. Presidents have had quite different relationships with their party organization. President Franklin Roosevelt's silence as party leader was quite noticeable; a Democratic representative from Iowa wondered if Roosevelt "has ever mentioned the Democratic Party or even used the word 'Democrat'...since he took office."[24] President Eisenhower was isolated from party politics—he did not even publicly announce his affiliation with the Republican Party until shortly before beginning his presidential campaign in 1952; he chose to leave "the operation of the political machinery to the professionals." Several of his successors have followed suit; as a general rule, Kennedy, Johnson, and Nixon ignored their national party committees after they were elected to office. President Kennedy was a strong party leader before his election victory, merging his own campaign organization with the party's national committee. After his election, however, he began to focus on his own personal White House staff. Kennedy brought the members of the national committee into his administration through appointments, and that ended the active role of the Democratic National Committee during his term. Lyndon Johnson became noted for his hostility toward the Democratic national party machinery. He viewed the national committee as a political liability rather than an asset, and consequently relied heavily on his own personal staff. Richard Nixon conducted his 1972 reelection campaign through his own Committee for the Re-election of the President instead of relying on the Republican Party. These presidents have treated the parties as "no deposit-no return" bottles—they are used to win election and then are discarded. As Democratic Chairperson Robert Strauss so bluntly put it: "If you're Democratic party chairman when a Democrat is President, you're a . . . clerk."[25]

Presidents have also taken steps to reduce the power of the national committees by delegating campaign responsibilities to their own personal staffs, hiring campaign professionals, raising campaign funds through independent means, and reducing the size of the national committee by appointing some members to administrative posts.

The Party and the Executive-Legislative Relationship

One of the president's roles is that of chief legislator. The Constitution specifies that he must advise the Congress yearly on the State of the Union and that he has authority to approve or veto a bill. In addition to these constitutionally sanctioned responsibilities, however, the president has a much larger role in Congress's decision-making processes. The president is now widely regarded as one of the prime initiators of legislation, even though there was no formal extension of his authority by statute or constitutional amendment. Faced with the tough task of maneuvering his programs through the congressional maze, the president faces many obstacles. For example, Congress feels that it should have the exclusive task of legislating. Although grateful for the executive's suggestions, Congress often resents his attempts to ramrod policies through the legislature. To mobilize support for his legislative proposals, then, the president often turns to his party members in Congress. Declaring his legislative programs to be party programs, the chief executive as titular head of the party appeals to his colleagues in Congress to support them; toward this end, he may use favors, patronage, and threats. However, in rallying the party behind his programs, the president must use his power to persuade rather than his power to command.

Even though the majority in Congress may be of the president's own party, there is no guarantee that his legislative programs will be favorably received. Indeed, a look at the presidential support scores—the percentage of party members who voted for a president's proposed legislation—bears this out. Marshaling partisan support for presidential programs has become increasingly difficult for two reasons: First, as the electorate's affiliation with political parties has diminished, the coattail effect of a presidential victory has been reduced. Since congressional party members do not attribute much campaign leverage to the president, they feel little responsibility to that chief executive.[26] Neither President Ford's efforts in the 1974 campaign nor President Carter's in 1976 yielded many blessings for congressional candidates. Second, congressmen are increasingly dependent upon their own personal campaign organizations, not the party organization; thus, they feel little responsibility toward the party. The party cannot provide them with the resources they need for electoral victory, and so they feel little sense of loyalty.

There seems to be a vicious circle. The president and his party cannot deliver electoral help to congressmen; therefore, congressmen feel little commitment to vote for presidential and party programs. Because the party in Congress will not support the president, the latter must seek support for his programs through other channels; this weakens the political party and makes it even less able to help congressional candidates. Partisan support of presidential policies is still sufficiently important, however, so that the president must court the party's congressional leaders and members.

The Party and Presidential Appointments

A president makes appointments in order that his policies may be carried out in the executive branch; this, of course, will have a bearing on his future reelection. He seeks experts who can run the executive departments and agencies in a proficient manner, and he also wants those who share his political persuasion and policy preferences. Since partisan support is still an important factor in the president's relationship with Congress, and since party support is required for reelection, the president usually considers party affiliation in making appointment decisions and uses his appointive power to reward the party faithful.

A review of the Cabinet appointments made by Presidents Nixon, Ford, and Carter underscores the continuing importance of partisanship. Of the 11 cabinet positions filled by President Nixon, 9 went to men who had been highly active in the Republican Party. President Ford also appointed men who had been active in the party. President Carter selected an extremely partisan cabinet, labeled by some as the "best and the brightest—recycled;" although the appointees were not active party members, they were predominantly Democrats:

1. Cyrus Vance (Secretary of State): served as Deputy Secretary of Defense during the Johnson Administration; past assistant to the president of the Mead Corporation; counsel of the Defense Department; Secretary of the Army; Democrat.
2. W. Michael Blumenthal (Secretary of the Treasury): former Deputy Assistant Secretary of State for Economic Affairs during the Kennedy Administration; past chairman of the board of the Bendix Corporation; Democrat.
3. Harold Brown (Secretary of Defense): one of Robert McNamara's "Whiz Kids;" former research director of the Defense Department and Secretary of the Air Force; worked in both the Kennedy and Johnson administrations.
4. Griffin B. Bell (Attorney General): former judge of the Fifth Circuit U.S. Court of Appeals; served as co-chairman of John Kennedy's 1960 Georgia campaign; Democrat.
5. Cecil D. Andrus (Secretary of the Interior): former state senator and Democratic governor of Idaho.
6. Bob Berglund (Secretary of Agriculture): former three-term member of the U.S. House of Representatives from Minnesota; Democrat.
7. Juanita Morris Kreps (Secretary of Commerce): former director of the New York Stock Exchange; former administrative vice president of Duke University; former

member of the boards of Western Electric, Eastman Kodak, and J. C. Penney; Democrat.

8. F. Ray Marshall (Secretary of Labor): former economics professor at the University of Texas at Austin, Harvard University, University of Mississippi, University of Kentucky, and Louisiana State University; Democrat.

9. Joseph A. Califano, Jr. (Secretary of Health, Education and Welfare): Special Assistant to President Johnson in charge of domestic programs (Model Cities and Office of Economic Opportunity); served as counsel to the Democratic National Committee 1970-1972; won court battles to provide equal broadcast time for Democratic congressional leaders following President Nixon's State of the Union messages.

10. Patricia Roberts Harris (Secretary of Housing and Urban Development): former dean of Howard University School of Law; seconded Lyndon Johnson's presidential nomination at the Democratic national convention in 1964; ambassador to Luxembourg during the Johnson Administration; former board member of IBM, Scott Paper, and Chase Manhattan; member of a Washington law firm with strong middle-of-the-road Democratic ties.

11. Brock Adams (Secretary of Transportation): former Democratic representative from Washington.

12. James R. Schlesinger (Secretary of Energy): former senior staff member of the Rand Corporation; consultant to Bureau of the Budget; Chairman of the Atomic Energy Commission; and Secretary of Defense; Republican.

Although the vast majority of government jobs are filled through the competitive civil service system, some 2200 positions remain to be filled by incoming presidents. Listed in a government-issued paperback called the "plum book," the jobs range from stenographer to Secretary of State, and the president uses them to reward deserving congressmen and party loyalists. Despite presidential appointments to the federal bureaucracy, partisan influence in the executive departments and agencies is limited. The president's power over the bureaucracy is difficult to establish and to maintain. John Kennedy found it almost impossible to mobilize the vast machinery of the executive branch to carry out his programs; while discussing one of his low-priority objectives—the renovation of Lafayette Square—he quipped, "Let's stay with it. Hell, this may be the only thing I'll ever really get done."[27]

In part, a president's failure to goad the bureaucracy into action is due to its sheer size. The 2000 positions filled by the president is but a tiny fraction of the total number of positions in the federal bureaucracy. Also, the political appointees are generally only at the highest levels of the hierarchy, and their impact on the lower levels diminishes with succeedingly lower levels. Since most bureaucratic positions are filled through the merit system, these persons resent political pressures imposed upon them from above by new, often inexperienced, political heads.

Because of the cumbersome, reluctant bureaucracy, presidents have turned increasingly to their personal White House staffs to help manage this branch of government. President Johnson vested authority for departmental coordination in his White House domestic policy aides and in his Budget Bureau director; he believed that many of his Great Society programs had been undermined by lethargic federal officials. Claiming that a "sweeping reorganization of the executive branch is needed," President Nixon replaced Johnson's 60-button telephone console with only three direct lines to each of his top aides—Haldeman, Ehrlichman, and Kissinger. While each president has sought to make the burgeoning bureaucracy accountable to political authority, his use of the political party (aside from appointments) has been insignificant.

The Party and the Courts

Despite the traditional belief that judges are "above politics," judicial appointments and decisions reflect partisanship.

Federal Courts. Party affiliation is one of the criteria used by presidents to make appointments to the Supreme Court. Other criteria include the length of distinguished legal service that the nominee has rendered to the nation, as well as personal friendship or service to the president.

Approximately 90 percent of all Supreme Court justices have been members of the appointing president's own political party. For example, President Johnson nominated a Democrat and Washington, D.C., attorney, Abe Fortas, to the bench; Fortas had been both a distinguished attorney and a personal friend of the president. Arthur Goldberg had been a Secretary of Labor in the Kennedy Administration. Thurgood Marshall had been a noted representative of the National Association for the Advancement of Colored People during its arduous efforts to win civil rights for blacks; he later served as Solicitor General of the United States in the Kennedy Administration. President Nixon, seeking a more right-wing orientation, appointed Assistant Attorney General William Rehnquist and a Richmond lawyer, Lewis F. Powell, Jr., men who were thought to conform to the president's standards of "judicial conservatism." Rehnquist had been an active Republican precinct committeeman and later became the "president's lawyer's lawyer." Explaining why no women had been appointed to fill the two vacant Supreme Court seats, Attorney General Richard Kleindienst asserted that "All the qualified women were either Democrats or liberals."

The importance of partisanship in selecting judges is reflected in the remarks of one lawyer: "The most important thing, if you want to become a judge is to have good political contacts. You don't get to be a judge by practicing law. You've got to sit in the clubhouse and build your contacts."[28] Whether appointments to the bench are made for ideological compatibility, political rewards, personal friendships, party service, or prior judicial experience, Table 9.4 shows that presidents have found active party members to be the most qualified.

Party influence is even more apparent in appointments to the lower federal courts. The Supreme Court appointments are legitimately viewed as the president's personal choices; however, other federal court appointments are supposed to be made after consultation with congressmen and prominent party officials.

Table 9.4   Percentage of Federal Judges Appointed by Presidents of the Same Political Party 1888-1977

President	Party	Percentage
Cleveland	Democrat	97.3
B. Harrison	Republican	87.9
McKinley	Republican	95.7
T. Roosevelt	Republican	95.8
Taft	Republican	82.2
Wilson	Democrat	98.6
Harding	Republican	97.7
Coolidge	Republican	94.1
Hoover	Republican	85.7
F. D. Roosevelt	Democrat	96.4
Truman	Democrat	90.1
Eisenhower	Republican	94.1
Kennedy	Democrat	90.9
L. B. Johnson	Democrat	93.2
Nixon	Republican	93.7
Ford	Republican	82.1
Carter	Democrat	100.00[a]

Source: Henry J. Abraham, *Justices and Presidents: A Political History of Appointments to the Supreme Court* (New York: Oxford University, Press, 1974), p. 60. Reprinted by permission.

Ford appointment information from *Congressional Quarterly Almanac*, 1975, p. 966.

[a]As of December 1, 1977, President Carter had named 10 circuit judges and 21 district judges. All were Democrats.

Thus, all presidents since 1888, with four exceptions, have appointed members of their own party to the bench with at least 90 percent regularity; there is substantial party pressure on the president in the matter of selecting federal judges.

State Courts. There are three types of judicial selection: selection by a "merit system;" partisan elections; and nonpartisan elections. Partisanship is important in both the merit system and partisan elections. In the merit system known as the "Missouri plan," the existence of partisan influence is ironic, since the system was designed to remove it; in fact, what happens is that "politicians . . . select judges . . . while voters only ratify their choices."[29] Now used in more than 12 states, the Missouri plan provides for a nonpartisan commission that draws up a list of nominees, one of whom is chosen by the governor to serve until the next regular election. At election time, the appointed judge then runs for election on his record. Occasionally, the nominees have no competition, since the party leaders have agreed not to run competing candidates; this paves the way for faithful party members to be elected.

    Examination of the most important products of the judicial process—the decisions that are handed down—also indicate partisan influence. While presidents have often been surprised by decisions rendered by those Supreme Court Justices who were believed to be of his own political ideology, an investigation of the decisions of Democratic and Republican judges indicates significant differences. Stuart Nagel[30] in seven areas found that Democratic judges were more inclined to favor:

Public Law
1. *Criminal law*
   the defense in criminal cases
2. *Administrative law*
   the administrative agency in business regularion cases
   the private party in regulation of nonbusiness entities
   the claimant in unemployment compensation cases
3. *Civil Liberties Law*
   broadening free speech
   a constitutional violation in criminal cases
4. *Tax law*
   the government in tax cases

Private Law
5. *Family law*
   the divorce-seeker in divorce cases
   the wife in divorce settlement cases
6. *Business Relations law*
   the tenant in landlord-tenant cases
   the labor union in labor-management cases
   the debtor in creditor-debtor cases
   the consumer in sales-of-goods cases
7. *Personal Injury law*
   the injured in motor vehicle accident cases
   the employee in employee injury cases

These differences between Democratic and Republican judges, however, may be due to the judges' personal values, which may also explain their party affiliation.

CONCLUSION

Parties retain a significant relationship to government at both the state and federal levels. Congress and most state legislatures are organized along partisan lines; party affiliation is the single most reliable predictor of the congressman's or state legislator's vote on various issues. Presidents continue to appoint their respective party members to executive and judicial positions. Despite the general disregard of their party machinery, presidents continue to view the party as a reservoir of capable White House personnel. Even President Carter, initially an "outsider" to the Democratic Party, selected many party faithful to serve in his Cabinet.

Granted, the parties cannot decisively discipline their members on roll-call votes and have not been able to demand strict party loyalty in supporting the president or the party programs in Congress. Despite the Democratic sweep of the 1974 off-year elections, by which they secured more than a two-thirds majority in the House and almost a two-thirds majority in the Senate, Congress was not veto-proof. President Ford's 2-year record of 56 vetoes with only 11 overrides (the highest yearly average of vetoes since Harry S Truman) demonstrates the unlikelihood of a straight party vote on any major issue. Conservative Southern Democrats continue to vote with the Republicans on a number of issues. The parties still remain visible actors in the executive, legislative, and judicial branches of government. This continuing visibility leads us to believe that parties will remain significant political institutions in the foreseeable future.

FOOTNOTES

1. For the classic view of the party in government, see E. E. Schattschneider, *Party Government* (New York: Holt, Rinehart, and Winston, 1942).

2. For a concise discussion of the Democratic caucus in the 94th Congress, see *Congressional Quarterly Weekly Report*, XXXIII, No. 31, pp. 1674-1679.

3. Hugh Bone, *American Politics and the Party System* (New York: McGraw-Hill, 1971), p. 289.

4. James Glen Beall, Jr. (R-Maryland) House 1969-1971; Senate 1971-present.

5. For a concise summary of the power of the speaker, see W. J. Keefe and M. S. Ogul, *The American Legislative Process: Congress and the States* (Englewood Cliffs, N.J.: Prentice-Hall, 1977.

6. Randall B. Ripley, *Congress: Process and Policy* (New York: Norton, 1975), p. 133.

7. For a summary of party unity in Congress that uses this definition, see *Congressional Quarterly Almanac*, 1976, p. 997.

8. For an excellent summary of the activities of the House Republican Policy Committee, see Leroy N. Riselbach, *Congressional Politics* (New York: McGraw-Hill, 1973), pp. 271-275.

9. William Keefe, *Parties, Politics and the Public Policy in America* (Hinsdale, Illinois: Dryden Press, 1976), pp. 301-305.

10. Ibid.

11. Riselbach, op. cit.

12. Ibid., p. 272.

13. Duncan MacRae, Jr., *Dimensions of Congressional Voting* (Berkeley and Los Angeles: University of California Press, 1958), pp. 178-192.

14. For an investigation of these authors' work, see: Samuel P. Huntington, "A Revised Theory of American Party Politics," *American Political Science Review 44* (September 1950), pp. 669-677; "Congressional Responses to the Twentieth Century." In *The Congress and America's Future*, edited by David B. Truman (Englewood Cliffs, N.J.: Prentice-Hall, 1965), pp. 5-31; Warren E. Miller, "Presidential Coattails: A Study in Political Myth and Methodology," *Public Opinion Quarterly 19* (1955-1956), pp. 353-368; and Warren E. Miller and Donald E. Stokes, "Constituency Influence in Congress," *American Political Science Review 57* (March 1963), pp. 45-56.

15. Riselbach, op. cit., p. 280.

16. Raymond E. Wolfinger, Martin Shapiro, and Fred Greenstein, *Dynamics of American Politics* (Englewood Cliffs, N.J.: Prentice-Hall, 1976), p. 301.

17. Charles R. Adrian, *State and Local Governments* (New York: McGraw-Hill, 1972), p. 375.

18. Thomas R. Dye, *Politics in States and Communities* (Englewood Cliffs, N.J.: Prentice-Hall, 1973).

19. Sammuel C. Patterson, "American State Legislatures and Public Policy." In *Politics in the American States*, edited by Herbert Jacob and Kenneth N. Vine (Boston: Little, Brown, 1976). Patterson finds that "[A] most marked change in party voting over time occurred in California, where the House became significantly more partisan . . ." (p. 181).

20. As quoted in Thomas E. Cronin, "Everybody Believes in Democracy Until He Gets to the White House: An Examination of White House-Departmental Relations." In *Perspective on the Presidency*, edited by Aaron Wildavsky (Boston: Little, Brown, 1975), p. 362.

21. Ibid.

22. Roberta S. Sigel, "Image of the American Presidency: Part II of an Exploration into Popular Views of Presidential Power," *Midwest Journal of Political Science 10* (February 1966), pp. 123-137. Data are reported in Roberta S. Sigel, "Presidential Leadership Images." Paper read before the 1962 Annual Meeting of the American Political Science Association.

23. Aaron Wildavsky, "The Two Presidencies." In *Readings in American Government 76/77* (Guilford, Conn.: Dushkin, 1976).

24. Arthur Schlesinger, Jr., *The Coming of the New Deal: The Age of Roosevelt.* 3 Vols. (Boston: Houghton Mifflin, 1957, 1958, 1960).

25. Joseph A. Califano, Jr., *A Presidential Nation* (New York: Norton, 1975), p. 153.

26. President Johnson represents a unique case; in 1964 he won by a landslide, apparently sweeping many Congressmen into office with him. Consequently Johnson enjoyed the support of several freshman legislators who had benefited from the landslide.

27. For a review of President John Kennedy's presidential administration, see Arthur M. Schlesinger, Jr., *A Thousand Days: John F. Kennedy in the White House* (Boston: Houghton Mifflin, 1965).

28. Howard James, *Crisis in the Courts* (New York: David Mellay, 1974), p. 6.;

29. Herbert Jacob and Kenneth Vines, "The Role of the Judiciary in American State Politics." In *Judicial Decision-Making*, edited by Glendon Shubert (New York: Free Press, 1963), p. 246.

30. Stuart S. Nagel, "Political Party Affiliation and Judges' Decisions," *American Political Science Review 55* (December 1961), p. 845.

10
Can the Parties Successfully Adapt to a Changing Political Environment?

The obituary has been set in type, waiting. The epitaph is written. Here lie America's political parties—born of necessity, died of irrelevancy. Rest in peace. [1]

Stephen Hess

The above quotation by a Senior Fellow at the Brookings Institution and author of several books on the American presidency and political parties epitomizes one end of the spectrum of party watchers in America. It has become clear to even the staunchest party supporters that our parties have experienced a continuing, significant erosion in their vital political functions. These declines in essential functions have collectively formed the central theme of this book. The last remaining question that remains to be answered is: Can the parties successfully adopt to an increasingly hostile political environment? Unfortunately, although the problems that beset our parties are quite clear, the ability of the parties ultimately to cope with them is not at all certain.

What Could Be done to Help the Parties?
An association of political scientists and practitioners committed to strengthening political parties was formed in 1976. Its director, Professor James McGregor Burns, made in the following declaration:

We meet today ... to deplore the disintegration of a basic American institution. Our political party system, first inspired by Thomas Jefferson, is in serious danger of destruction. Without parties, there could be no organized and coherent politics. When politics lacks coherence, there can be no accountable democracy. Parties are indispensable to the realization of democracy. The stakes are no less than that. ... Local rebuilding is struggling against powerful counterforces that are undermining party structures everywhere. ... What would take the place of parties? A politics of celebrities, of

*excessive media influence, of political fad-of-the-month clubs, and massive
private financing by various "fat cats" of state and congressional campaigns,
of gun-for-hire campaign managers, of heightened interest in "personalities"
and lowered concern for policy, of manipulation and maneuver and management by self-chosen political élites. To reverse the decline of party and reinvigorate these great instruments of democracy, we urge the following
steps:*

1. *Public financing of campaigns through parties. Instead of giving money
   to individual candidates, the federal and state governments should provide funds to the parties which would use them both to strengthen their
   organizational and educational programs and to help candidates with
   their campaign costs.*
2. *Midterm conventions for both major parties where issues may be debated
   and voted upon, and the party's platform renewed. Delegates should include both elected officeholders and party rank and file.*
3. *A reversal of the trend toward more and more primaries. . . . Collectively
   these primaries are expensive, exhausting, confusing and unrepresentative.*[2]

Of these three suggestions, the only one that seems to have a reasonable chance of
being institutionalized is the adoption of midterm conventions. The Democrats held
their first midterm convention in 1974 and have one scheduled for 1978. There appears to be almost no possibility of the federal government funding the party organizations beyond the present 2 million subsidy to each party's national convention.
A reduction in the number of presidential primaries is the least likely of these suggestions to be adopted in the foreseeable future because states seem to be switching
from conventions to presidential primaries.

Of all the threats to the political parties mentioned earlier, the parties have responded most adequately to the challenge of the new politics. However, their response
has been mixed. Robert Agranoff, foremost student of American campaigns, observes that contemporary party partitipcation in the new campaigning is at best evolu-
tionary and peripheral:

> *In most cases central organizations are involved only in fragments of man-
> agement, information and the media. . . . Basically, parties have reacted to
> specific service requests made by candidates rather than assessing their role
> as an organization in a new era. In only a few cases has a central party or-
> ganization undertaken a full-scale campaign service organization.*[3]

There is some evidence to indicate that the national committees of the two major
parties could provide significant campaign services to their candidates. Both parties
have developed computers, media services, consulting services, and manuals to assist
candidates in organizing a contemporary campaign. The Republicans on the federal
level have made the greatest effort to adapt to the new style of media campaigning.

Both the Republican National Committee and the National Republican Congressional
Committee under their chairmen, Bill Brock and Guy Vander Jagt, respectively, have
revitalized their oganizations in preparation for the 1978 congressional elections.
Vander Jagt experimented with new approaches to media campaigning. The congressional committee has test-marketed 5-minute television commercials emphasizing constituent services and downplaying ideology. The plan is to televise these commercials in 16 key cities during 1978. In addition the Republicans will spend $1 million
on network television and other media to promote the party, not individual candidates.[4] The Republican National Committee raised more than $10.5 million during
1977 and has set aside $2 million for the 1978 congressional and state elections. Mean-
while, as of November 1977, the Democratic National Committee's debt was about
$2 million.[5] In 1977 the Republican congressional leaders had already begun to re-
cruit and groom candidates for the 1978 congressional elections. An interesting change
is that these candidates are being encouraged from the national, not the local, levels
to seek the nominations. It remains to be seen if local Republicans will support these
efforts. The Republicans have also established a national "S.W.A.T. team" to identify
"vulnerable" House Democrats and to determine what type of Republican candidates
could mostly easily defeat them, and then to seek out such candidates and encourage
them to run.[6] Unfortunately, these efforts have not been duplicated at the state and
local levels where they are most needed to build a base for the party. Consequently,
those party candidates with the greatest need have the least access to the parties'
modern campaign services.

In a very few cases such party services are being offered to state level candidates.
Agranoff recounts the successful adaptation of both political parties in Minnesota
to the demands of the new politics. The Minnesota Republican State Central
Committee:

> *regularly employs the services of political consultants to study its opera-*
> *tions, test the effectiveness of campaign techniques and train its staff in the*
> *modes of modern campaigning. All GOP candidates are given access to these*
> *management consultants. In addition, the party centrally contracts with a*
> *national polling firm, which conducts a series of polls for all Congressional*
> *candidates. The state party has a research operation, which supplies issue,*
> *roll-call and voting data for candidates at all levels. The organizations retains*
> *an advertising agency, which handles the media section of the campaigns for*
> *all major candidates. Finally, the party is involved in central fundraising and*
> *allocation—direct grants of funds to candidates from U.S. Senator to the state*
> *legislators.*[7]

A few other state party organizations appear to be following the examples of Minnesota. In Virginia, the only Southern state Ford carried in 1976, the Republican Party
is in the process of building an organization for the first time in the state's history.
During the first half of 1976, the party's headquarters received 7600 individual contri-

butions, as compared with only 1217 during all of 1975. The party leadership is establishing a centralized year-around program to collect money; register voters; coordinate local party organizations; recruit candidates for local, state, and federal offices; and offer these candidates a full range of campaign services. "We intend to provide services to candidates that will free them from reliance on professionals who are costly, but really can give you nothing but advice," said State Republican Chairman George McMath. In July 1976 the party distributed to its candidates a seven-page catalog of campaign services it can now offer;[8] these efforts proved to be successful since the Republicans won the governorship in 1977.

American political parties may decide to follow the British example of party adaptation to the demands of the new politics. In Great Britain, research, advertising, and consultants are part of the party bureaucracy. Thus, American parties could follow any of three possible routes: First, they could follow Minnesota's example of hiring specialists to provide services to the candidates through the party structure. Second, they could follow the British example of employing these technicians permanently as part of the party bureaucracy. Or finally, they could surrender the campaign function to non-party organizations.

Another area in which the parties have actively tried to recapture their declining role is political finance. Parties are struggling to reassert their influence as a fund-raiser, yet once again their most effective actions appear to be on the national level. The federal election campaign laws regulating political donations seem to have compelled private contributors to channel their contributions through the parties rather than directly to candidates. *The Washington Post* reported that a record $5 million was given to Republican House and Senate candidates by four national Republican organizations during 1976. This amount was more than twice the previous contributions from these organizations to Republican congressional candidates. S. I. Hayakawa, the Republican Senator from California who defeated the Democratic incumbent, Senator John V. Tunney, was given $5000 by the Republican Congressional Boosters, $15,000 by the National Republican Senatorial Committee, and $5000 by the Republican National Committee, which also picked up $100,000 of Hayakawa's media expenses. The potential for increased party contributions to senatorial candidates is enormous. For example, the law allows national committees to spend up to $320,000 on a candidate's behalf in California, and the state party is also allowed to spend an equal amount. The Democrats have relied more on non-party sources for campaign funding but have still managed to contribute approximately $1 million to their congressional candidates in 1976.[9]

The parties have responded less well to the decline of partisan identification. The task of regaining the loyalty of so many cynical voters appears to be beyond the ability of the parties at present. Two things that the parties have done are to establish voter registration and voter turnout drives. In 1976 the national committee of each party supported Gerald Ford and Jimmy Carter by making a significant effort to register and encourage the voting of large numbers of new voters. Right after the election, DNC Chairman Robert Strauss claimed that the committee had helped to add 500,000 voters to the roles in Texas and 600,000 in Pennsylvania—two states that were crucial to the Carter vitory.[10] However, voter registration and voter turnout are not the same as the reestablishment of traditional allegiance to the party organizations.

For all practical purposes the parties cannot hope to regain the loyalties of the voter until they confront the prevailing attitudes of anti-partyism. Historically, Americans have disliked and been suspicious of party organizations, and this seems to be even truer today; this antipathy is found on all levels of politics. To cope with this issue, parties must first rehabilitate themselves and then try to modify the public's image of them as essentially a negative force in politics. Then, perhaps, the public will be more supportive. The parties also have to deal with the essentially negative image that was projected by the ideological or issue activists who generated internal conflict during the 1972 Democratic and 1976 Republican conventions. The parties' leadership must cope with the growing number of activists who want to lead the parties toward the left or the right. The relative harmony of the 1976 Democratic convention suggests that the Democrats have survived the threat posed by the extremists, which apparently reached its height during the McGovern convention. On the other hand, the Republican Party continues to be plagued with ideological divisions that threaten its existence.

The parties recognize that they are no longer the exclusive or even the primary channel of communication between citizens and government. They have learned to co-exist with other political organizations and have accepted a much smaller role in the matter of communication. Government communicates directly with the public, and interest groups articulate the public's demands. Such groups as the medical profession, environmentalists, business organizations, and labor unions maintain lobby organizations in order to link their constituents directly with the appropriate persons in government. Interest groups have developed sophisticated techniques of lobbying to facilitate the exchange of information between citizens and their government without utilizing the once significant party channels of communication. Some have argued that the proliferation of interest groups and the expansion of their lobbying operations have also contributed to the further decline of party influence in Congress. "Its not the Republican party or the Democratic party that has a policy" [in Congress], said Representative Thomas S. Foley of Washington, chairman of the Democratic Caucus. "Its the environmental groups or the trade groups or the labor groups. We have all those parties out there now."[11]

The functions performed by political parties should not be viewed as a measure of the parties' value to society. Party functions, like everyone else, must adapt to changing conditions in our society. Some of the former party roles are now performed by other institutions, and these have proved to be more capable of providing certain services. For example, political socialization is now performed by the schools, family, and the media. The parties are now being challenged in their traditional monopoly fields of campaigning, recruitment, public opinion leadership, and articulating the public's demands; whether the parties will continue to function in these areas will depend upon whether the party leadership takes positive steps to reestablish the party's influence there.

THE FUTURE OF THE PARTIES

Parties will probably continue to be significant actors in the American political system. First of all, the parties still act as gatekeepers of the ballot; party nomination is the guarantee of access to the ballot. The Republican and Democratic nominations will continue to narrow the electorate's choice to two candidates; thus, these party nominations will continue to be highly valued and sought after. It is not likely in the foreseeable future that politicians can achieve high office without nomination by one of the major parties. Of the 174 presidential candidates officially certified by the Federal Election Commission in 1976, only the nominees of the two major parties were viewed as serious candidates for that office.

Second, the parties will continue to perform a brokerage role, bringing together within the party various and diverse groups from our heterogeneous society. The Democratic Party is a diverse coalition of women, blacks, Latins, youth, liberals, conservatives, labor, business, and various regional blocs. Despite the differences that exist among these constituent groups, they can come together occasionally and agree on basic programs and strategies for political action within the framework of the party.

Third, parties continue to be a significant factor for organizing government; both Congress and the state legislatures are organized along partisan lines. In Congress the best predictor of voting behavior continues to be party affiliation. Recently, California has experienced an increase in partisan division on roll-call votes. Executive branch appointments in the national government continue to be made almost entirely on the basis of party affiliation. Despite recent setbacks to the tradition of patronage appointments on the state and local levels, probably there will still be many thousands of political jobs into the foreseeable future. The judiciary will undoubtedly continue to be a special stronghold of party patronage.

Fourth, party identification (despite its recent decline) is still the best predictor of voting behavior. Many of the so-called independents, when faced with unfamiliar candidates or less significant offices, frequently vote according to the candidate's party. Although the electorate has indicated that it would support a third-party movement, especially for the presidency, voting patterns in recent years have shown firm ties to the two major parties.

Political parties will probably not regain the dominant position they once enjoyed. As Stephen Hess has concluded:

> There is no possibility, however, that the parties can recreate the friendly environment of the past. The changed social composition of the country works against them. . . . [Can the parties survive?] The answer can be yes—

if they again become responsive, but it will have to be in new ways that reflect the needs of a different kind of electorate. [12]

With imaginative leadership and a willingness to adapt to a rapidly changing society, American political parties can remain a vital force in politics. It would be difficult to predict whether the parties will acquire new political functions in the future, but it is safe to say that the parties will still be an important factor in American politics.

FOOTNOTES

1. Stephen Hess, "Political Parties: Dwindling Role," *Deseret News*, August 27, 1977.

2. *P.S. X*, No. 4 (Fall 1976), pp. 494-495.

3. Robert Agranoff, *The New Style in Election Campaigns* (Boston: Holbrook, 1976), p. 125.

4. Stephen Hess, "Can the GOP Get Its Act Together," *Deseret News*, November 26, 1977.

5. *The New York Times*, November 20, 1977.

6. *The New York Times*, February 23, 1977.

7. Agranoff, op. cit., p. 126.

8. *The Washington Post*, July 17, 1976.

9. *The Washington Post*, October 28, 1976.

10. *The New York Times*, March 26, 1978.

11. *The New York Times*, October 20, 1976.

12. Hess, "Political Parties," op. cit.

11
Tools for Analyzing Parties

INTRODUCTION

American political parties, unlike the "checks and balances" and "federalism" that characterize our nation's style of democracy, were not created as the result of centuries of political thought. Parties were not designed by a theory or blueprint; nor were they always considered necessary to a democracy. Previously they were viewed as infamous bodies of rabble-rousers and were dismissed by political thinkers as enemies of the democratic process and the orderly pursuit of society. Although some political philosophers eventually perceived them as beneficial, or even essential, to the democratic scheme, the parties had few friends until well into the 19th century.

Now we are awaiting the development of a comprehensive theory to explain the parties' development and behavior. Political scientists, who have different definitions of party, perceive different goals or purposes of the party, and see different effects of the parties on the democratic process, have various explanations or theories of some aspects of party development or behavior. Further, much of the writing on party theory pertains to particular countries; it is, therefore, culture-bound and not comprehensive. We have theories for classifying parties by their structure, for explaining the motives of party membership, and for explaining leadership, but, we have no *comprehensive* explanation of party. David Apter's assertion that "what is lacking is a theory of political parties"[1] is still applicable today.

It should be emphasized that theories are tools that can shed light on the behavior, development, and importance of party. Theorists have raised significant questions about the role and impact of party; as we review several theories, let us ask the following questions:

1. Are American political parties essential to democracy?
2. Are they ruled by an élite whose interests differ from those of the rank-and-file membership?
3. Do the American parties differ in structure from the parties elsewhere? If they are unique, what are some of the reasons for this?
4. What factors produce a two-party system? Our concern in this chapter is two-fold: first, to become familiar with the various theories or explanations of party

development and behavior; and second, to accumulate certain tools for evaluating American parties.

Party theorists have provided several tools for understanding parties; we will focus on three of them—analyzing their structure, analyzing their organization and membership, and comparing what they "ought to be" with their actual role.

Do Parties Promote Democracy?

The early development of party theory was hampered by a general fear of factions by both political philosophers and political leaders. Until the development of parties most political systems, with rare exceptions, had been monarchies. The monarch's interest in preserving his own power base had led him to suspect any opposing forces, which were viewed as divisive and therefore harmful. The party, as a newly developing social institution, was often considered to be a faction by government leaders, and thus was attacked.

Hostility toward parties was also evident in the newly emerging American nation. The definition of "faction" held by James Madison is, perhaps, indicative of the confusion between faction and party held by the Founding Fathers:

> By faction, I understand a number of citizens, whether amounting to a majority or minority of the whole, who are united and activated by some common impulse of passion, or of interest, adverse to the rights of other citizens, or to the permanent and aggregate interests of the community.[2]

In his Farewell Address, George Washington warned about the division of the electorate into factions and parties. He emphsized the common ties that bound citizens together, the benefits to be found in unity, and the inability of the party membership to prevent the rise of "cunning, ambitious, and unprincipled men" who will "subvert the power of the people" and "unsurp for themselves the reins of government":

> The alternative domination of one faction over another, sharpened by the spirit of revenge natural to party dissension, which in different ages and countries has perpetrated the most horrid enormities, is itself a frightful despotism. But this leads at length to a more formal and permanent despotism. The disorders and miseries which result gradually incline the minds of men to seek security and repose in the absolute power of an individual, and sooner or later the chief of some prevailing faction, more able or more fortunate than his competitors, turns this disposition to the purposes of his own elevation on the ruins of public liberty.[3]

Not all early political theorists and leaders perceived the party as a divisive, and hence a destructive, force in politics. For example, Edmund Burke in 1770 defined "party" as "a body of men united, for promoting by their joint endeavors the national interest, upon some particular principle in which they are all agreed."[4] He saw parties as respectable and at times a necessary component of a democratic system. And even as Washington warned against parties, members of his own cabinet were leading separate and hostile groups of government officials; with the growth of these groups and official acknowledgement of their leaders, the American party, for all intents and purposes, was born.

However, even after the parties had been formed and acknowledged, it was still not clear what role they would play in the democratic scheme. In the late 1800s and early 1900s two European theorists, Moisei Ostrogorski and Robert Michels,[5] actively opposed parties as inevitably anti-democratic. From his examination of the political structure of the United States during the late nineteenth century, Ostrogorski concluded that corruption was an inevitable outgrowth of the party system. Democracy, he said, was based upon an informed, active citizenry that was aware of the issues of local political life. Yet, changing social conditions—the mobility of the population, the heterogeneity of the cities, and the increasing complexity of urban life—had placed a great strain upon the public's ability to understand and deal with local political problems. Into this strained situation the party thrust itself. Ostrogorski believed that the party, primarily concerned with its own existence, would draw the attention of the public to national issues and the "rich" national patronage jobs while neglecting social political issues. Thus, political participation would be subordinated to party survival.

Ostrogorski's fear that the party would become an obstacle to voter representation was shared by Robert Michels. In his famous "iron law of oligarchy," Michels argued that party leadership would inevitably become an oligarchy—the few ruling the many. According to Michels, the party leaders would automatically have a vested interest in maintaining and increasing their power. In the quest for such power, the leaders would cultivate the friendship of other organizations and would broaden their base of voter support by avoiding more controversial positions. In this manner, Michels said, representative leadership within the party would be replaced by an élitist band of leaders, who would gradually have more in common with leaders of other organizations than with the members of their own party. The result would be a party dominated by an élite which did not represent the public. This anti-party attitude of Ostrogorski and Michels is apparent today in much contemporary American thought: "To the extent that we are all believers in the myths of the bosses, the smoke-filled rooms, and the deals between oligarchs, we are all children of Michels."[6]

However, as parties have become an integral part of the political system, the trend to view them as inherently anti-democratic has largely disappeared. Indeed, some American political scholars have argued that modern democracy would be impossible except in terms of party democracy. Schattschneider, for example, postulated that organization was necessary to the foundation and maintenance of a democracy. The most important question in politics, he said, was power; and the mark of a democratic regime was its ability to give the masses power; however, in order for the masses to receive power, some type of organization was necessary. The organization, representing the masses, would exercise power in their name.

Schattschneider claimed that the best organization to represent the masses and dis-tribute power was the party, and that the two major American parties were well suited to represent majorities for the purpose of controlling government. "Pressure groups" are incapable of taking "general control of the whole government" and are unable to "carry out a comprehensive over-all policy."[7] According to Schattschneider, not only were political parties necessary for a democratic government, but they helped to create it; His influential classic *Party Government* opened with these words:

> *The rise of political parties is indubitably one of the principal distinguishing marks of modern government. The parties, in fact, have played a major role as makers of governments, more especially they have been the makers of dem-ocratic government. It should be stated flatly at the outset that this volume is devoted to the thesis that the political parties created democracy and that modern democracy is unthinkable save in terms of parties.*[8]

A more moderate assessment of the role of parties in American democracy—yet one that still ascribes to the party a vital role—has been suggested by several party theorists; they hold that parties are just one of many democratic institutions which *together* perform the essential role of managing the leadership-selection process and the transference of power. S. J. Eldersveld describes the opportunity for parties to assist democratic government: "Despite reservations, there is clear evidence that if the party organizations choose to act, and when they act, they do produce outcomes which will maximize, and even make more rational, the participation of the ordinary citizen in the political process."[9]

Fortunately, the party is no longer viewed as the archvillain, the perverter of dem-ocratic principles, the spawning bed for the ruling classes. But neither is the party regarded as the shining Sir Galahad on the white horse—the sole savior of democracy. Although political parties have played an important role in the development of Ameri-can democracy, one must ask just how necessary they are to the survival of American democracy.

ANALYZING PARTIES BY MEANS OF THEIR STRUCTURE

Political parties, lacking a theoretical blueprint, developed in each nation to fill a void unique to its political system. Thus, parties have quite different strctures. The structural theorist attempts to classify parties and party systems (the environment in which a party functions and particularly the number of parties in that environment) according to certain physical factors, much as a biologist might classify animals by their physical similarities and differences. The factors that might be chosen by the structural theorist include the size of the party membership, the number and relative strength of party subgroups, the roles and relationships of these subgroups, and the effects of the electoral laws upon the party and its subgroups. Two structural factors that may lend themselves to understanding and classifying parties are their internal organization and the number of parties within a nation's political system. Let us consider each of these factors.

Classifying Parties by Internal Organization

In his classic 1951 book, *Political Parties: Their Organization and Activity in the Modern State*, Maurice Duverger discerned two general types of parties: the *cadre* party, and the *mass* party.[10] These were distinguished on the basis of: the units into which the parties were organized, the socioeconomic classes of the membership, the degree of party centralization, the number of members and the degree of their involvement, the importance of ideology to the party, and the strength of the bonds between party units.

The *cadre* party in Europe is generally composed of a small group of notable individuals, recruited by other party members because of their prestige or wealth. The group's small size means few lines of authority, and so the local leaders and members enjoy a great deal of autonomy with respect to their political positions and ideologies. The party leaders are, usually parliamentary leaders as well, and so deviance by party members from accepted policies within parliament leads to strict discipline and censure.

The major American parties, Duverger says, are also cadre, but with some important differences. The American parties actively seek out members, who do not need to be of the upper or middle socioeconomic classes. Typically, however, those who are active in the organization come from the upper strata. The fact that America elects both national and state political leaders also affects the American cadre party. The rigorous demands of electing so many officials, plus the fact that most states have primary elections as well as general elections, has brought about a much tighter organization than the European cadre parties require. Hence, American parties are predominantly local committees and practically nonexistent at the national level. Doctrine is not important in either American or European cadre parties.

Mass parties, the other general type of political party, are of three types: socialist, communist, and fascist. The mass parties differ significantly both from the American and European cadre parties.

While the cadre parties appealed mainly to the upper and middle socioeconomic classes, the mass parties have generally attracted persons from the lower and working classes. The socialist party was the first of the three mass parties to emerge, and this coincided for the most part with the development of the working class in the nineteenth century. The socialist party had two major functions. The most important of these was to finance the candidacies of working class persons, since they could not gain the support of the élites. The second purpose was to democratize the selection of party candidates and the regulation of party policy. The resulting party meetings, attended by a large number of relatively illiterate members, became educational in nature, providing civic instruction to help the electorate exercise its voting rights. Because of the large number of members and the variety of functions the party performed, socialist parties developed two sets of leaders—the elected, parliamentary leaders and the internal party leaders, which led to internal conflicts.

The remaining mass party types are much more tightly organized. The communist party differs from the socialist and cadre parties because of its organizational unit— the cell—which is formed of individuals according to their place of work, rather than according to their place of residence. Thus, there is daily contact among the members, leading to a feeling of unity in personal terms, in terms of common work problems, and in ideological terms. The cell is also the smallest of all party local groups, enhancing homogeneity and solidarity. The structure of the communist party is authoritarian. The party leaders and policies are developed at the top, and the lines of communication between cells and leaders are vertical. Ideology plays a dominant role.

The third type of mass party, the fascist party, has a militia as its basic unit of organization. The fascist organization is modeled after the military; its militias and assault platoons are small and quickly assembled. Its members undergo quasi-military training, wear uniforms, and utilize military (rough-house) political techniques; the chain of command is also militarily structured.

Another theorist, claiming that parties can be understood by analyzing the various component groups, holds that parties are more than simply membership and leadership. According to Sartori, "it is the interaction among a party's subunits or *fractions* that determines the characteristics and behavior of the party as a whole. These fractions may be compared along six dimensions:

1. Organization. Does the fraction have a more cohesive organization than the party itself—does it have its own networks of loyalty, seek its own funds, and hold its own congresses independently of the party?
2. Motivation. Are fractions motivated to secure power within the party because of the quest of power for its own sake or for the accompanying rewards?
3. Ideology. Fractions can range from the ideologically fanatic and future-oriented, to the purely pragmatic and realistic.
4. Left-right. Are the fractions oriented toward a leftist or rightist political philosophy?
5. Personalism of leaders. At one end of the continuum is the fraction that is dependent upon one undisputed boss; at the other end is the coalitional fraction, noted for a multitude of leaders.
6. The role played by the fraction. Some fractions are veto groups whose chief goal is to obstruct policy; some are support groups or bandwagon groups who are eager to join a winner; some are policy groups, or groups seeking to govern and impose policy. These distinctions are fluid, and the group goals will vary as the party environment changes.

Sartori found that by examining party fractions, using the dimensions listed above, he could understand why parties lose their cohesion. Sartori suggests that party unity depends upon party competition. When a party finds itself safe from serious election challenge, divisions occur within the party. One can ask whether this has been the reason for recent splits within both the Democratic and Republican parties. Sartori raises the interesting point that party dominance may actually produce greater problems than facing a competitive second party.

Classifying Parties by Number of Parties Within A Political System

Those who analyze parties according to their internal organization believe that the structural characteristics of the political system—especially the number of parties and the electoral laws—largely determine the parties' development and role in governing. Duverger identifies three different types of political systems: one-party, two-party, and multiparty. He holds that parties in one-party systems are typically mass parties because they have a monopoly over the political involvement of the citizens. In many one-party systems, the party is intimately related to the governmental function so that the party's hierarchy holds more power than the state's official hierarchy. In effect, the party is the government. Why only one party? Often, it is established because those in power want to limit conflict. In the Soviet Union, the party is viewed as an arm of the social class; and, since only one social class is acknowledged, only one party is needed—to protect the class from any future uprising of other classes.

However, according to Duverger, the two-party system is the most "natural" system, since "every policy implies a choice between two kinds of solution...."[12] There is almost a complete correlation between a simple plurality, single-ballot electoral system and a two-party system. Third parties are controlled, either by assimilation into an already existing party or by elimination. Elimination is not particularly difficult, since the third party must attract substantial electoral support in order to win votes and thus secure a voice in the legislature.

There is also a relationship between the ballot type and the multiparty system. In those countries with proportional representation (legislators of various parties elected according to the proportion of support that each party receives nationwide), the multiparty system is actively encouraged. Since almost every minority is assured of a voice in the legislature, there is nothing to prevent party division and the formation of new parties. According to Duverger, a given electoral system is seen as an "accelerator" or "brake" to the development of new parties. The American two-party system can be explained as a product of our simple-plurality, single-ballot electoral system.

Sartori also found that classifying parties by counting the number within each political system was a useful tool; he felt, however, that Duverger's classification could not reflect differences among party systems. Sartori believed that, to really understand a party system, one must also know the power of each party—the possibilities of a one-party system becoming a two-party system, and the degree of dissent permitted within a party. Therefore, he proposed a more elaborate classification scheme with eight categories: one-party totalitarian, one-party authoritarian, one-party pragmatic, hegemonic, predominant party, two-party, moderate pluralist, and polarized pluralist party systems.

The one-party system is not difficult to discern: "Only one party exists or is allowed to exist."[13] However, because one-party systems vary in oppressiveness, pervasiveness, and tolerance, Sartori differentiated three types. At one extreme is the one-party totalitarian structure, which is both a strong and strongly ideological party. At the other extreme is the one-party pragmatic structure; this type of party is less powerful and lacks the ideological cohesiveness of the totalitarian party. Because of its relative weakness, the pragmatic party must continually seek support; it can do this by assimilating potential rivals into its structure. There is also the authoritarian one-party structure; it lacks the all-embracing ideological framework of the totalitarian one-party group, and its control generally does not extend beyond the normal instruments of governmental power.

By hegemonic party, Sartori means one that is changing into a two-party or multiparty system. In the hegemonic party, one party is predominant, but it allows others to exist as "satellites," subordinante to the main party but unable to usurp its power. There is no evidence that other political parties can successfully challenge the main party for electoral offices.

In the predominant party system, there is also a major party, but little possibility that other parties can assume power. However, there are ample opportunities for open and effective dissent to the governing party. Sartori uses this category for those political systems in which the difference in strength between one party and the total of the other parties is about 10 percent or more of the electorate. This disparity in party strength must be present over a long period of time.

Our concern with Sartori's classification scheme is primarily with the two-party system and its implications. While it sometimes seems that our two-party system borders on the hegemonic or multiparty system with occasional rattlings from a third-party movement, our two major parties continue to prevail. Sartori's analysis of the electorate's ideological perspective helps explain the reasons for the continuation of our two-party system.

Sartori says that in the two-party system the electoral distance between the competing parties is quite small. The two-party system has four characteristics: (1) two parties are in actual electoral competition; (2) one of the parties will capture a majority of the parliamentary seats; (3) the winning party expects and is willing to govern alone; and (4) there will undoubtedly be an alternation between the parties for the purpose of governing. Sartori finds that the two parties tend to reach toward the political center; this, he says, is rewarding to the parties since these voters are moderates and lean toward the middle of the ideological spectrum. One can readily see that both the American electorate and the parties have a moderate ideological position; this is quite clear in the party platforms. The opinion polls also point to the pragmatic mood of voters who are more interested in practical solutions than politicial doctrines.

The next most fragmented political party system is that of moderate pluralism. The major distinguishing feature of this system, at least when compared to the two-party system, is coalition government. This means that there are at least three major or relevant parties, that no party usually obtains an absolute majority of the legislative seats, and that the parties must therefore bargain with each other to form a ruling coalition. Because the parties must bargain, the moderate pluralist system is typically *bipolar*; the government against the opposition coalition. Moderate pluralist systems usually have from three to five parties.

In contrast to the moderate pluralist system is polarized pluralism, which embraces six or more parties within the political structure. The polarized systems are not bipolar; instead, they have one party or a group of parties in the center. This center position must face opposition from both the left and right sides of the political spectrum. Under most circumstances, the center coalition will govern; however, continued dissatisfaction with the government will typically produce a loss of votes to either or both extremes. The resulting political system, says Sartori, is a morass of extreme and ideological politics, "conducive either to sheer paralysis or to a disorderly sequence of ill-calculated reforms that end in failure."[14] Finally, there is the "atomized" system, in which political parties are so numerous that governing tendencies and the groupings of party coalitions cannot even be clearly determined.

Despite the criticisms of Duvenger's and Sartori's classificatory theories, scholars agree that the classification of parties and party systems may provide a wealth of information on the party and its relationships to the political environment. We will now turn to other party theorists who, although offering different means for examining parties, do not provide comprehensive theories.

ANALYZING PARTIES BY MEANS OF THEIR MEMBERSHIP AND ORGANIZATIONAL BEHAVIOR

A number of political theorists have sought to explain parties in terms of the benefits they provide for the social system. They have attempted to answer such questions as: Who joins? Who rules? To what extent does the party communicate the demands of the general population to the nation's leadership and transmit information from the leadership to the public? We will discuss the views of only a few of these theorists.

Party Leadership: Is an Élite Inevitable?

Are all parties led by an élite? In his "iron law of oligarchy," Michels claimed that this development was inevitable.[15] He said that the mere formation of a political party meant the creation of an élite—the leaders of the party. With organizational growth comes organizational complexity, resulting in less influence for the mass party membership and more influence for the party leadership over party decisions and programs. The purpose of the party, according to Michels, is to provide a medium through which the masses can make their demands known, and to enable these demands to be converted into appropriate governmental policy. To serve a valid democratic purpose, a party organization must reflect the needs and interests of the mass membership and this membership must have access to leadership positions. Over time, however, a party's leaders tend to remain in office and to deviate from the preferences of the mass membership; this is so for several reasons:

First, there is a general sense of apathy among party members; only a small number take part in any decision-making functions even when everyone has the opportunity. Since, in order to express the demands of the membership and gain electoral power, the party must remain in existence, its survival is one of the goals of the organization, and those who have made decisions for the party before tend to continue in office— leadership by default. Furthermore, those who are appointed to head a party are usually leaders in other areas before they become party leaders; thus, they normally possess certain important skills that are above and beyond those of the masses.

Second, once leaders have been appointed to their positions in the party, they acquire a vested interest in the preservation of the party. The party organization itself holds a number of rewards, and when the party holds governmental control, there are even bigger rewards. As a consequence, party leaders seek to remain in power. Because of the leaders' superior knowledge of party affairs and because of their control over the channels of communication with the membership, the leaders are quite secure against any attempt to replace them.

Third, party leaders also seek to maintain their power by discouraging factionalism within the party and challenges to the legitimacy and appropriateness of party policy. Because of their ruling ability, leaders can specify to a large extent whom their successors will be by establishing guidelines for the succession to leadership, or by utilizing the party machinery to groom the "chosen" new leaders.

Finally, in an attempt to anchor their power, party leaders use the party's communication lines to manipulate the views of the members. This step completes the circle, and presents a paradox: The party, originally established to check the power of monarchical or economic élites by communicating the masses' demands to the governmental leadership, has instead become a tool of coercion, utilized by a new élite to convey its own commands to the masses. According to Michels, the possibility for democracy is quite hopeless since it "is inconceivable without organization."[16] Yet, an inevitable product of the political party organization is an élite leadership. The only logical conclusion, then, is that *democracy is an unattainable goal*: "The mass will never rule except *in abstracto*."[17]

Michels has been criticized for his rather simplistic view of leadership and its role in political organizations. His view that the interests of leadership are necessarily opposed to the best interests of the masses is an assumption with which many other party scholars disagree. It has been difficult to apply the iron law of oligarchy in the United States, where political parties are extremely broad-based, and represent many groups of people. With such diverse groups within each party, it is hard to conceive of a party mass with a collective will or interest that would differ significantly from that of the party leadership. Past studies of party leaders have found that they are more committed to democratic practices than is the general electorate.[18] Michel's law is more applicable to the class parties of Europe whose interests are much more homogeneous than those of the major American parties.

Membership Recruitment: Open or Closed?

Do American parties recruit from all groups, or are they selective? Believing that parties are not necessarily controlled by an élite, some party scholars have tried to understand parties better by analyzing their recruitment process. After studying local party politics in Detroit, Eldersveld concluded that American parties are somewhat selective in their membership recruitment but essentially open to most groups. Examining the recruitment process, Eldersveld did not find that the local party structure was ruled by a rigid élite, as envisioned by Michels.[19] Instead, Eldersveld postulated four characteristics that American political parties hold in common.

First, the party is a *clientele-oriented* structure. It must always be open to receive new party workers as well as voter support if it is going to be successful in winning elective offices. Therefore, the party must continually seek to broaden its base of support in terms of the sheer number of voters and workers. Unfortunately, the more open the system, the more heterogeneous the party becomes; this makes internal management difficult and ideological consensus unlikely. To preserve their efficiency, unity, and ideological consistency, parties may be somewhat selective in choosing new workers and supporters.

The limitations they may impose upon the recruitment process depend upon a number of factors. If the two parties are fairly well matched in strength, or if an aggressive minority party is rapidly gaining support, the party's principal goal—electing government officials—takes precedence over other goals, and the party will actively seek new supporters and new *classes* of supporters. If, however, the party has a sufficiently large plurality of voters to feel secure, recruitment may be more selective. A political party must maintain good interpersonal relationships among its workers in order to elect its candidates to office; this consideration, therefore, will affect the recruitment process. Finally, the social and demographic characteristics of the people in a given area will significantly affect recruitment. If most party members in a certain area are from lower-income groups, for example, a greater effort may be made to recruit workers from the middle and upper classes.

According to Eldersveld, the recruitment of new groups into American parties is virtually unlimited. He compares the broad range of ethnic and socioeconomic group support to an accordion: the American system, he says, is an *open* accordion. However, the accordion is not wide open; although most social groups are represented in the parties, their representation is not proportional to the general pupulation. "One cannot be sure whether this says anything significant about party recruitment, or about the capacity of such categories to be mobilized ... however, both parties seemed to recruit with abandon from the most remote sectors of population."[20]

Second, the party is composed of small groups representing a variety of social and economic interests in their quest to gain and maintain control of government. Because of its middle-man position between these small groups and governmental power, and because of the diversity of groups within it, the party is inevitably the scene of conflict among its constituent groups for party control. These conflicts are mediated to a great extent by the party itself whose one goal is self-preservation.

Third, the presence of subgroups within the party and the varied interests of these subgroups tend to reduce the possibilities of power being concentrated in the hands of a single leadership group. Eldersveld found that the party was not controlled by an identifiable and unified command structure; instead, power was distributed throughout the entire party structure.

> We suggest that, although authority to speak for the organization may remain in the hands of the top élite nucleus, there is great autonomy in operations at the lower "strata" or echelons of the hierarchy, and that control from the top is minimal and formal.[21]

Eldersveld called this form of organization a *stratarchy*; it describes the pyramidal design of American parties, with the local parties at the base, the state parties above, and the national headquarters at the apex. Each of these strata exists as a relatively autonomous unit. The national and state party organizations do not control the grassroots organizations, but a pattern of mutual interests, deference, and personal relationships occasionally results in the appearance of a coordinated and hierarchically directed organization. Communications among all party levels are both frequent and meaningful.

Fourth, Eldersveld attacked Michels's conception of a unified party command structure. Instead, he reasoned, party leaders in the United States were not sure enough of their positions in the party so that there could be any security of tenure. He claimed that the party leaders were a divergent group who entered the party and sought leadership for different reasons.

From Eldersveld's investigation of party leadership in the Detroit area, the extent to which leadership was self-generating—leaders selecting like-minded, lower-level leaders who were committed to maintaining the oligarchy in power—was haphazard. Precinct workers who had been chosen by upper-level leaders often had just as much difficulty in maintaining and expanding their power as other workers did. Many of the party leaders did not enter the party at the instigation of other leaders; often they decided to participate in party politics because of a sense of community duty; because of the urging of friends; or because of a desire for personal recognition, personal excitement, or social contacts. Once an individual entered the political party, however, the party changed his attitudes toward it, although often in insignificant ways. For example, the reasons given for remaining in the party typically differ from those given for joining the party in the first place. The party seems to impress the importance of winning elections more heavily on the leaders and workers than on the voters or supporters. The closer one's contact is with the party group, the greater one's loyalty is to that group. However, Eldersveld said that these changes in leadership perceptions were not sufficient to create a bureaucratic or oligarchical condition.

If the parties are not oligarchic (controlled by the few), and if the party leaders are not a united ruling élite, then what role does the political party play in the structure of democracy? Eldersveld sees the party as an important channel of citizen partici-

pation. He holds that parties are helping to ensure citizen representation and are therefore an important aid to democratic government.

Motivating Party Membership: Incentives and Joiners

Party workers are essential to party survival. Each party must continually find ways to
encourage people to contribute their time, effort, and money to the organization.
Analyzing the incentives that parties offer provides insight into the functions and
power of parties.

Exploring the question of "Who joins what, and why?" James Q. Wilson, concluded
that the motivation for joining political parties is related to the opportunities and the
incentives offered to those who join the fold.[22] Wilson claims that organizations take
steps to assure their own survival; party survival is threatened by strains, including the
loss of valuable members and available incentives, serious conflict over purposes, challenges from rivals, and the loss of morale or unity. Since leaders seek to maintain
unity, they try to reduce the strains stemming from conflicts both within and without the party structure. The range of rewards a party can offer vitally affect its ability
to minimize strains. Rewards include benefits or opportunities that attract workers.
The types and amounts of incentives offered by a political party and the opportunities
for potential workers to obtain such rewards lead to varying degrees and types of participation in the party. There are four general types of incentives, and parties may be
classified according to which types of incentives they require and distribute. Wilson
claims that most parties apply a combination of incentives.

Material incentives include items that have a monetary value, such as "wages and
salaries, fringe benefits, reductions in taxes, changes in tariff levels, improvement
in property values, discounts on various commodities and services, and personal
services and gifts."[23] A political organization that wants to acquire material incentives
will have as its chief goal the placement of its members in public office; how the office is attained, however, is not considered important. The greatest internal strain within a party of this type is the distribution of those material incentives.

Specific and *collective solidary incentives* are intangible, vague rewards that stem
simply from the association of party members with each other. Clearly, the distribution of these rewards cannot be as precise as the distribution of material incentives.
The fact that such rewards are intangible, however, makes them more readily available.
It should be noted that many groups using this type of incentive are civic- or public-
purpose-oriented. *Specific solidary incentives* stem from association with the party
and can be given to or withheld from specific individuals; these incentives include
party offices and honors. The number of these rewards that the party can distribute is
limited; among the groups that employ this type of incentive, the chief source of internal conflict will be threats to the status of those who are denied specific rewards.
Collective solidary incentives also arise from group association; however, they are distributed to all members. These incentives include the social and psychological benefits as well as just the fun of being a part of the group.

The final category of incentives are *purposive*. Those who receive these rewards gain satisfaction from contributing to a worthy cause. Parties that utilize these incentives will seek to implement laws or change social policies for the benefit of a large portion of the public. Purposive rewards are the primary incentives for those who support minor parties. Because the members hope to advance a certain cause, they don't mind making sacrifices. Thus, supporters of the Libertarian Party hope to spread their philosophy and reap benefits accordingly.

Once the incentives utilized by an organization have been defined, Wilson suggests three characteristics by which members may be grouped. Many organizations require expenditures of time, money, and other resources that lower-class individuals usually cannot afford. These *economic* restrictions literally force lower-class individuals into groups that offer economic and purposive incentives. Finally, certain *psychological* factors lead a person to join an organization. Here, also, the upperclass individual has the advantage, since he usually possesses more ego-strength, cooperative attitudes, and personality traits that enable him to fit in well with an organization. Thus, the upper-class person can perceive long-range benefits for himself and his community; he trusts those with whom he would be associating; and his sense of duty would lead him to be attracted to purposive incentives. Wilson suggests that these factors explain the greater tendency of upper- and middle-class individuals to join political organizations.

In studying the participation of individuals in political organizations, Wilson compared the American and British political systems to try to determine why there was greater participation by Americans than by the British. He found that institutional factors may affect the membership and growth of political organizations. First, the greater the division of power in the social and governmental structure, the greater the number of political organizations. When there are more divisions of government, there will be more opportunities for political groups to influence decision-making within those divisions. There are more than 80,000 units of government in the United States.

Having delineated the components of organization—organizational incentives, desire for those incentives by specific groups, and political-structural limitations—we need to place them into the context of a specific group, specifically, the political party. The types of incentives offered by various parties enable us to categorize them. Wilson identifies three general types of parties:

The *machine* relies on material rewards, including patronage jobs, preferments on contracts and receipt of government goods and services, increased business and economic opportunities resulting from political contacts, and exemptions from governmental taxation or regulation. Party members who are motivated by material rewards tend to be indifferent to the policies of the party except, of course, for the policy of taking care of one's supporters if elected. Although machines were once an important factor in American politics, today the material incentives are fewer and parties can no longer offer enough of them to motivate large numbers of people.

The *purposive party*. While the determination of public policy and the establishment of social goals are seldom the only motivating factors in deciding whether or not to organize a party, they have played an important part in American politics. The purposive component is most apparent in the ideological parties that have appeared periodically throughout our history. The purposive party has problems with survival. Few of the members of the party will find the benefits of belonging to the group (election to party office or bestowal of party honors) large enough to remain actively involved in the group. Purposive parties, therefore, suffer from a high turnover. In addition, since the goal of such parties is ideological and therefore inflexible, the leaders have only limited authority. The purposive party is sometimes so inflexible that it cannot negotiate a coalition with other political groups. Its candidate for public office is usually selected more for his ideological conformity than for his potential appeal to the voters, and so he often loses.

At the local level, Eldersveld found that most party activists participated in politics because of their enjoyment of group political activity; these individuals, according to Wilson, constitute the *solidary* party. These people do not seek material benefits or important social goals. Analyzing organizational incentives in order to understand political parties presupposes that individuals make rational decisions to join a party; people "join associations for a variety of reasons and . . . they are more or less rational about action taken on behalf of these reasons."[24]

ANALYZING PARTIES BY MEANS OF THEIR GOALS

Some researchers attempt to understand parties by examining the strategies of parties in seeking to control government. This is called the *positive* approach, and is unique in that it stresses the *goals* of the party rather than its *functions*.[25]

Positive political theory assumes that political participants are goal-oriented and that they will take rational steps to further their goals. Once this assumption has been made, the means individuals and groups use to further their goals become the focus of analysis. The political party is then defined as "a team of men seeking to control the governing apparatus by gaining office in a duly constituted election," and the party's goal is winning elections. Because the party is composed of rational men, it will make rational decisions in trying to expand its basis of support to ensure electoral success.

Besides parties, other elements in the conflict for power include the voter and the government. The voter, a rational being, selects the party that will give him the greatest benefit; he will then vote for this party. To determine which party will be the most beneficial, the voter examines the benefits he has gained from the government (in the United States, this is the ruling party) and compares these to his expectations of benefits from the competing party if it should replace the ruling party. If, however, there is a multiparty system, the voter considers the following three alternatives:

1. *If his favorite party seems to have a reasonable chance of winning, he votes for it.*
2. *If his favorite party seems to have almost no chance of winning, he votes for some other party that has a reasonable chance in order to keep the party he least favors from winning.*

3. *If he is a future-oriented voter, he may vote for his favorite party even if it seems to have almost no chance of winning in order to improve the alternatives open to him in future elections.*[26]

If he cannot decide among the competing parties, the voter may choose not to vote, or, if the present majority party's and the competitor's platforms are the same, he may vote to maintain the status quo. The voter tends to remain with a party once he has decided to vote for it. The voter typically has a number of sources from which he can obtain political information. Gaining such information about party policies, however, usually requires time and money, which most voters are unwilling to spend. The rational voter, balancing the costs of obtaining detailed political information against the loss of time and money for other things, often opts for a more generalized view of politics. The political party therefore can often make specific policy changes that may lead to a wider support base for the party, since the specific changes will have little effect on the voters who presently support it.

The political party seeks to gain and maintain power—it seeks to become the government. To gain power the party must attract voters. The strategy that the party adopts in order to secure voter support, however, is a matter of some contention among positive theorists. Downs, for example, believes that the political party will attempt to maximize its vote: "each party seeks to receive more votes than any other."[27] In order for the political party to do this, it must make its public positions more general, flexible, and ambiguous. On the other hand, Riker believes that political parties opt for a "minimum winning coalition", that is, a sufficient number of votes to guarantee the acquisition of power. This "size principle," Riker said, would make the stated program of a political party less amgibuous, since it would not seek to influence the entire electorate, but only enough voters to control the government. Attempting a compromise between Downs and Riker, Joseph Schlesinger, proposed that whether the party adopted the "maximization of votes" principle or the "minimum winning coalition" principle depended upon the types of benefits sought by the party members. Some of the members, for example, are office-seekers; their goals will be satisfied only if they are elected. Thus, the officeseeker will try to maximize the number of votes he receives in the election. The strategy of maximization has an added benefit; if the officeseeker is elected, he will feel less bound to any specific individual or group of individuals for their campaign assistance if his plurality of votes is high. As a consequence, the office-seeker-turned-officeholder will have more freedom to exercise the power vested in his office. There are also party members who are benefit-seekers, including anyone who hopes to affect government activity."[28]

Schlesinger proposes that the winning of elections is important to both types of party members; the means by which the elections are won, however, reflects the goals of the two groups. The benefit-seeker wants to keep the officeholder as accountable as possible in order to assure himself a maximum of benefits; hence, he wants the party to adopt the minimum winning coalition strategy of Riker, with its small voter turnout (to minimize the dilution of the spoils) and marginal plurality (to ensure the requisite gratitude of the officeholder for "swinging" the election). Opposing this strategy is the office-seeker, for whom a large victory means independence in office and a greater chance of continuing in office. The party, may therefore, adopt any of four electoral strategies—two of them are compromises between the extreme positions:

1. *The party may favor the office-seeker, trying to maximize both his plurality and number of votes.*

2. *It can minimize the vote and maximize the plurality; this, Schlesinger claims, would be the best compromise strategy for the office-seeker, since "narrow pluralities not only reduce the maneuverability of the winner; they pose a threat to winning the office itself."*[29]

3. *The other compromise is to maximize the vote and minimize the plurality. This is the best compromise for those who want the benefit of higher electorate participation.*

4. *Finally, there is the benefit-seekers' ideal solution—the minimum winning coalition—which minimizes both plurality and vote.*

Positive theories of political parties have certain advantages over structural or organizational-behavioral analyses. Because the positivist views the party as goal-oriented, and because the number of goals that a party seeks (notably, the goal of winning elections) is more easily determined and smaller than the number of functions a party performs, positive theory is much simpler. It is also easier to test. Organizational theory, because it is so complete, often mixes the important and unimportant functions that a party performs so badly that separation is impossible. Simplicity, however, may have certain disadvantages; positive theory loses much of its relevance to real world phenomena because it is so simplistic. The assumption of rationality made by the positive theorists has also been criticized. The rational voter is, of course, an ideal model of voting behavior that apparently is not common among the American electorate.

REFORMERS AND RESPONSIBLE PARTIES

Several party critics lament the decentralization of authority and the absence of a reasonably clear policy program within the parties. David Broder noted a declining voter faith in the government and then indicted the two parties for their failure to provide a sense of direction and program since the 1950s:

> *Millions of Americans now feel that they have lost control of the government and that government has lost its capacity to act, to respond, to move on the challenges that confront our nation.*[30]
> *The reason we have suffered governmental stalemate is that we have not used the one instrument available to use for disciplining government . . . that instrument is the political party.*[31]

Criticisms such as Broder's are neither few nor new; there have been many demands for party reform. Arguing that party government (strong party organizations) is indispensable if the will of the voters is to be realized, Schattschneider, writing in the early 1940s, criticized the Democratic and Republican parties for their lack of party discipline and cohesive policy.[32] Another call for party reform was made in 1950 by a committee of party scholars who were troubled by the absence of decisive party policy; they held that the main focus of the party is not to win elective office, but "the party struggle is concerned with the direction of public affairs."[33] Voters, journalists, and political scientists have frequently lamented the parties' failure to develop programs for dealing with major domestic problems—crime, inflation, unemployment, energy shortages, environmental problems. The politics of the 1970s testifies to the parties' failure to provide specific policy alternatives: witness the lack of party-created or party-directed guidelines for conducting the conflict in Southeast Asia, for controlling inflation, or for dealing with spiraling unemployment.

Underlying the arguments for and against more responsible parties are basic differences of opinion as to what the role of parties should be in a democratic government. Those who call for a more responsible two-party system perceive parties as a necessary and integral part of democracy. They believe that a healthy democracy requires two national parties to make clear policy positions and to discipline those members who "stray" from the party's position. A responsible party is one that is accountable to the public; it develops programs that address the issues of the day, as well as the future; and finally, it possesses enough cohesion to implement these programs. A responsible party is "able to organize electoral or popular majorities and officials behind party programs and thus be responsible for the conduct of office."[34]

On the other hand, some observers question the practicability, or reasonableness, of patterning organizations such as the Democratic and Republican parties after the responsible party model. American parties are not disciplined, these observers claim, because the electorate is generally non-ideological and the need for compromise and flexibility in seeking solutions to contemporary political issues makes rigid parties impractical.

Supporters and opponents of the responsible party model differ not only as to the purpose of party in a democracy, but also as to the relationship they feel the party should have with the electorate. Are parties essential to democratic government? Should parties formulate specific policy alternatives and require their members to abide by these decisions? Are voters able to discriminate among viable policy alternatives? To all of these questions, those supporting the responsible party model would reply "yes."

The case for responsible parties is based on the premise that political parties are essential to democratic government. Parties are believed to be the only instruments that can effectively mediate between citizen demands and the government to accomplish the following:

1. Provide the electorate with a choice between alternatives of action.
2. Develop policy programs and work toward carrying them out.

3. Maintain enough internal cohesion to implement their programs.
4. Criticize one another in presenting policy alternatives to the electorate.
5. Be accountable to the voters.
6. Hold party leaders accountable to the party membership.

The goal of responsible parties is to develop public policy; hence, parties must create legislation and articulate various policies. Elections are held primarily so that the citizen can choose among policy alternatives presented by the different parties. Parties are to provide explicit alternatives, explain their policies to the electorate, and then see to it that the elected officials remain committed to the chosen alternative. Parties are to be responsible for governing and educating the public; they must then be held accountable for the results of these policy decisions. Responsibility for governing the nation, thus, is shifted from individual officeholders to the political party. Proponents believe that by making this shift, many benefits would result:

First, with a responsible party system, voters would understand the party positions before the election and be assured that the winning party's policies would be implemented. Supporters of this "political truth-in-packaging argument" contend that at present the candidates' policy positions are often vague and that electoral victory is no guarantee that campaign promises will be kept. For example, voters might elect a Democratic Congress, but there is no working majority; instead, party members cross party lines, respond to the demands of a particularly vocal interest group within the constituency, or do not vote on party-supported measures.

Second, responsible parties could protect both congressional and executive leadership from undue interest group pressure, while ensuring that legislation would better reflect constituent needs and interests. Strong party discipline would make the party organization a buffer between interest groups and governmental leaders. Candidates would depend upon the party for campaign support—particularly financial support— and not upon interest groups. The party organization would emerge as a broker, a mediator between competing interest groups; since these groups would be forced to support both parties to guarantee some measure of cooperation, their impact would be lessened. Parties would thus be free to represent their total constituency.

Third, parties could formulate and implement policies that represented the needs of a *total* constituency, rather than the interests of powerful groups. Proponents of responsible parties contend that the present party system fosters disjointed policy implementation, which often leads to unnecessary financial waste and delay; this difficulty is compounded by the failure of American political parties to provide broad policy programs for voter review. If political parties do not step forward with new, well-thought-out programs, governmental policy tends to be reactive, responding only to immediate political needs.

Opponents of the responsible party model accuse the reformers of misreading political reality and overlooking the consequences of cohesive and disciplined parties. Defenders of the present system believe that implementing a responsible party system would be inappropriate for and harmful to American politics. They perceive the role of the party and the purposes of elections quite differently. They argue that:

1. The importance of parties to democracy has been exaggerated; parties are some-times dependent rather than independent variables in the political arena. The form and character of parties are determined by the form and character of the political system.[35]

2. It is by no means clear that political parties are competent, efficient, or appro-priate institutions for formulating public policy that will be binding upon legislators and executive leaders. Mapping out policy alternatives and solutions to major issues requires technical expertise, precise and up-to-date information, an immense knowl-edge of all possible solutions, and many resources for dealing with these issues. The parties do not have the necessary specialists and information. Even if the parties had these things, how could they bring together different public preferences into coherent programs and present distinct partisan programs to the voter? Or, how would the parties arrive at distinctly different policy positions while representing an electorate that is generally noted for its idological unity? Most political observers agree that Americans generally have a consensus as to the goals of the society, but that they differ on priorities and the means of achieving these goals.

3. Political behavior, as human behavior, is rooted in the whole person, and voters often make non-rational decisions. Voting studies have shown that the American electorate is nonideological; very few voters evaluate the parties or candidates from an ideological point of view. Only 3 percent of the total population has a closely woven set of attitudes that determines their stands on particular issues.[36] For most Americans, political ideologies are vague, superficial labels that they apply rather in-differently according to circumstances.

4. The parties agree on both basic democratic values and major directions of Ameri-can policy; thus, their programs are not, nor could they be, so different that the voter could make a rational choice between them, even if the voter were rational. Political parties strive first to win elections. Toward this end, they try to attract a broad range of support. Experience has taught both political parties that a strong ideological stance does not win elections. The Republicans tested the political waters in 1964 and found that the "hidden conservatives" within the electorate were so well hidden that they failed to appear. The Democrats learned a similar lesson in 1972, when they over-estimated the size of the American "liberal" vote, particularly among the young, newly enfranchised voters. The magnitude of defeat of both Goldwater and McGovern demonstrates the error of assuming that political parties either succeed or fail to represent an ideological electorate. The strategy for winning remains the same: the party and the candidate must avoid ideological positions and direct their campaigns toward those in the middle.[37]

5. The American electorate is so heterogeneous that it could not be accommodated in a strictly disciplined cohesive party organization. Enforcement of the party dis-cipline model would destroy flexibility in policy-making, discourage compromise, and produce a multiparty system.

6. Elections rarely give public officials clear mandates; often the voters elect con-gressional candidates of one party and the presidential candidate of the other party.

Thus, the argument runs, mandates are both impossible to identify and impossible to carry out. Parties are not purist because the voters are not purist.

7. There is already a large degree of party accountability to the public.

Those opposed to responsible parties generally feel that to force parties to become policy advocates would have a serious—and detrimental—impact upon democratic government. They find it preferable to have incremental decision-making. A slower, more deliberate process may permit more voices to be heard, avoid major miscalculations, and allow changes to be made in midstream to correct unwise decisions. The creation of highly disciplined parties would spell the end of intraparty democracy; policy made within the party might reflect the preferences of the élite rather than the electorate. As the opponents of responsible parties review the recent changes in party rules, particularly the establishment of many primaries, they conclude that the parties are being made more susceptible to take over by extremists. Those who are active in in the party are also the most idologically committed; they begin to participate in electoral campaigns earlier than the noncommitted party members, and are therefore in a position to influence the nomination process long before the conventions. Thus, a candidate with clear policy programs is likely to reflect the preferences of the ideological few rather than those of most party workers or the public. Goldwater and McGovern are oft-cited examples of candidates who secured their party nominations with the help of a minority of the party support. Opponents of the responsible party movement see policy government as leading inevitably to the conversion of the ideological few's concerns into policy binding upon the non-ideological majority; they are troubled about the possibility of an election that might pit a right-wing Republican against a left wing Democrat. The threat, then, is that a large number of people will discover that their policy preferences have been disregarded and that they have no place to turn. Opponents of the responsible party movement fear a tyranny of the intensive minority.

It would be wrong to assume that the opponents of a responsible party system are opposed to any and all reform; both sides of the responsible party issue agree that some party reform is needed. For reformers and opponents alike, the question is how much and what type of reform.

THE CONTINUING SEARCH FOR EXPLANATIONS

These partial theories of parties are attempts to explain *some* aspects of party structure and behavior. They are particularly helpful in recommending to students of parties where to look for explanations of party development and behavior. They stimulate us to ask further questions. We began this chapter with a series of questions; further questions might include: Why do third-party movements tend to disappear in American politics? Is it because, as Wilson suggests, the two parties are so favored by government that third parties see little opportunity for attracting enough voters? Why are American parties not subject to the iron law of oligarchy? Is this because, as Sartori and Eldersveld suggest, the parties must be oriented to their clientele in order to survive? Their description of the need for broad voter appeal may well explain why the parties do not take clear ideological policy positions. Theories of incentives also raise questions: As American parties increasingly lose their material incentives, will the party workers continue to give time simply because of their enjoyment of group political activity, or will these workers tend to be more ideologically motivated?

Analysis of political parties has varied during the past two centuries. Early analyses were largely confined to a description of the organizational components, legal status, and the value of parties to the government and the public. Later studies have combined innovative thought with empirical analysis, utilizing various data-gathering techniques: survey research, election statistics, and analyses of speeches and voting to determine the leadership's policy preferences and the intensity of party identification. Focusing less on what parties ought to be, these later studies have tried to measure the campaign activities of the parties, analyze why individuals join parties, and assess party influence on legislators. Mid-twentieth century investigations have examined the activities of the party, the party's relationship to the voter, and how these activities and relationships have changed since the 1960s. The party is being scrutinized both as a product and as a creator of its political environment.

Unfortunately, investigations of parties have not often been buttressed with a consistent party theory from which deductions could be drawn. Upon finishing his manuscript, Sartori concluded that there was still no general theory of parties: "I have . . . discovered that this lack has not been remedied—indeed, it has steadily grown."[38] A review of theories of parties indicates that what has actually developed is not a general theory but rather a multitude of approaches to studying parties that focus on specific aspects, such as their organizational structure, the leadership—mass relationship, their functions, or perscriptive suggestions as to how parties could become more effective instruments of voter representation.

The result of these diverse approaches has been the acceptance of several explanations of party development and behavior and a belief that most have some value. Although these theories cannot be integrated into a general, inclusive explanation of parties, they are valuable as a framework for guiding systematic thinking and investigation of parties. Without this framework one can only accumulate unrelated pieces of information. The approaches to the study of parties—be they structural, functional, organizational, or otherwise—provide a framework.

FOOTNOTES

1. David E. Apter, *The Politics of Modernization* (Chicago: University of Chicago Press, 1965), pp. 179-222.

2. James Madison, *The Federalist*, No. 10 (1787).

3. Washington's Farewell Address of September, 17, 1796. Reprinted in *Washington's Farewell Address: The View from the 20th Century*, edited by (Burton Ira Kaufman, Chicago: Quadrangle Books, 1969), p. 158.

4. Edmund Burke, "Thoughts on the Cause of the Present Discontents." In *The Works of Edmund Burke* (Boston: Little, Brown, 1939), pp. 425-426. For an excellent analysis of the

changing perceptions of political philosophers of the late eighteenth and early nineteen centuries, see Giovanni Sartori, *Parties and Party Systems: A Framework for Analysis*, Vol 1
Cambridge, Eng.: Cambridge University Press, 1976), especially pp. 5-18.

5. An edited edition of Ostrogorski's work is available; the page references to Ostrogorski's
    work are from Mosisei Ostrogorski, *Democracy and the Organization of Political Parties*,
    edited and abridged by S. M. Lipset (New York: Anchor, 1964). References to Michels are
    from the 1962 edition: Robert Michels, *Political Parties*, trans. by Eden and Cedar Paul
    (New York: Free Press, 1962); excellent critiques of the political thinking of these two
    writers are given as introductions to the respective editions cited here, and written by Sey-
    mour Martin Lipset.

6. Frank J. Sorauf, *Party Politics in America*, 3rd ed. (Boston: Little, Brown, 1976), p. 111.

7. E. E. Schattschneider, *The Struggle for Party Government* (College Park, Md.: University of
    Maryland Press, 1948), p. 11.;

8. E.E. Schattschneider, *Party Government* (New York: Rinehart, 1942), p. 1.;

9. S. J. Eldersveld, *Political Parties : A Behavioral Analysis* (Chicago: Rand McNally, 1964),
    p. 543.

10. Maurice Duverger, *Political Parties : Their Organization and Activity in the Modern State*
    (London: Methuen, 1954). This was the first English translation. Citations in this chapter
    are to the 3rd edition, published in 1969 (trans. by Barbara and Robert North). Duverger
    clarified many of the relationships discussed in his earlier book in *Party Politics and Pressure
    Groups*, trans. by David Wagoner (New York: Crowell, 1972).

11. Sartori, op. cit., Chaps. 1 and 2.

12. Duverger, *Party Politics and Pressure Groups*, op. cit., p. 9.

13. Sartori, op. cit., p. 72.

14. Ibid., pp. 85-86.

15. Michels, op. cit., p. 61.

16. Ibid., p., 365.

17. Ibid., p. 366.

18. Herbert McClosky, "Consensus and Ideology in American Politics," *American Political
    Science Review LVIII*, No. 2 (June 1964)), pp. 361-382.

19. Eldersveld, op. cit., p. 59.

20. Ibid., p. 60.

21. Ibid., pp. 99-100.

22. James Q. Wilson, *Political Organizations* (New York: Basic Books, 1973).

23. Ibid., p. 26.

24. Ibid., p. 33.

25. Anthony Downs, *An Economic Theory of Democracy* (New York: Harper and Row, 1958),
    p. 5. Following the lead of William H. Riker and Peter C. Ordeshook, the term "positive"
    is used here to describe those economic-oriented theories promulgated in works such as
    Downs; William H. Riker, *The Theory of Political Coalitions* (New Haven: Yale University

Press, 1963); William H. Riker and Peter C. Ordeshook, *An Introduction to Positive Political Theory* (Englewood Cliffs, N.J.: Prentice-Hall, 1973); Joseph A. Schlesinger, "The Primary goals of Political Parties: A Clarification of Positive Theory," *American Political Science Review LXIX* (September 1975), pp. 840-849; and David Robertson, *A Theory of Party Competition* (London: Wiley, 1976).

26. Downs, op. cit., pp. 49-50.

27. Ibid., p. 14.

28. Ibid., p. 843.

29. Ibid., p. 845.

30. David S. Broder, *The Party's Over* (New York: Harper & Row, 1971), p. 1. Ibid., p. xx.

31. Ibid.

32. E. E. Schattschneider, "The Idea of Party Government." In *Politics and People, edited* by Leon Stein (New York: Arno Press, 1974), pp. 31-32.

33. American Political Science Association Committee on Political Parties, "Toward a More Responsible Two-Party System," *American Political Science Review XLIV* (Supplement 1950), p. 15.

34. Schattschneider, *Party Government,* op. cit., p. 1.

35. Evron M. Kirkpatrick, "Toward a More Responsible Two-Party System: Political Science, Policy Science, or Pseudo Science?" *American Political Science* 65 (December 1971), p. 976. (1971), p. 976.

36. William H. Flannigan, *The Political Behavior of the American Electorate* (Boston: Allyn and Bacon, 1968), p. 87.

37. Thomas R. Dye and L. Harmon Zeiger, *The Irony of Democracy* (North Scituate, Mass.: Duxbury Press, 1975), p. 235.

38. Sartori, op. cit., p. ix.

Index